HEART SHOTS

HEART SHOTS

Women Write about Hunting

MARY ZEISS STANGE, EDITOR

STACKPOLE BOOKS

Published by
STACKPOLE BOOKS
5067 Ritter Road
Mechanicsburg, PA 17055
www.stackpolebooks.com

Printed in the United States

First edition

10 9 8 7 6 5 4 3 2 1

Library of Congress Cataloging-in-Publication Data

Stange, Mary Zeiss.
  Heart shots : women write about hunting / Mary Zeiss
Stange.—1st ed.
    p. cm.
  Includes bibliographical references (p.   ).
  ISBN 0-8117-0044-5 (hardcover)
  1. Hunting. 2. Women hunters. I. Title.
SK33.S6488 2003
799.2'082—dc21
                                        2002156352

To my sister outdoorswomen, past, present, and to come . . .

"For us nature has spelled new lessons in the art of woodcraft; new meanings in the beauty of sunsets; new aims and desires along the highroad of life. Perhaps the magic influence of the forest does not enter alike into every human soul. Some require a different geography from others. We have feasted and are content."

—Paul [Paulina] Brandreth, *Trails of Enchantment* (1930)

Contents

Acknowledgments

BEHIND AN ANTHOLOGY OF GREAT WOMEN'S WRITING ABOUT HUNTING, there are bound to be a few good men: My thanks, particularly, to Stephen Bodio, who originally suggested I take on this project; to Doug Stange, without whose bibliographic zeal and savvy this book would have been impossible; and to Ken Barrett, for inadvertently suggesting its title. Thanks, as well, to those writers and others who over the years have in one way or another enlightened, enlivened, shaped, and deepened my own thinking and writing about hunting: Jan Dizard, Jody Enck, Ted Kerasote, Richard Nelson, Dave Petersen, Jim Swan, Jim Tantillo, and Rob Wegner. And to those sister-hunters who are a consistent source of insight, enthusiasm, and encouragement: Maggie Engler, Susan Ewing, Anne Hocker, Gayle Joslin, Diane Lueck, Virginia Mallon, Carol Oyster, Marilyn Stone, and the gals from Realtree.

Skidmore College provided crucial financial and clerical support for this project, in the form of a Faculty Research Initiative Grant and funding for my indispensable student research assistant, Gina Calcagno. My thanks also to Rebecca Burnham, our departmental office administrator, for her assistance regarding technical matters large and small. And to my colleagues in Women's Studies, particularly Wilma Hall and Mary C. Lynn, for their intellectual support and suggestions.

Several individuals provided invaluable help when it came to weathering the choppy waters of British and American copyright law. With regard to the former, I am particularly grateful to Judy Watkins of the British Library and Ruth Traynor of the Copyright Licensing Agency. Thanks as well to Carl Van Ness of the University of Florida's Special Collections Library for his help regarding Marjorie Kinnan Rawlings; to Richard A. Goodwin, executor of Mary Jobe Akeley's estate; and to Jorge A. Aja Espil, for assistance regarding Courtney Borden. Special appreciation goes as well to Kenneth Czech and Derrydale Press, for sharing with me the galley proofs of his *With Rifle and Petticoat: Women as Big Game Hunters, 1880–1940.*

Sandra Dal Poggetto did me the terrific favor of researching the photo collection at the Montana Historical Library and turned up the two wonderful photographs from that collection that appear in this volume. And Bess Edwards, President of the Annie Oakley Foundation, graciously agreed to allow me to print here a never before published photo of her great aunt upland bird shooting.

Judith Schnell of Stackpole Books is an anthologist's dream editor: Captured from the start by the idea of *Heart Shots,* she has been frank and forthcoming and in every respect a joy to work with. Her assistant Amy Dimeler also deserves high praise, for the care and efficiency with which she has handled various aspects of the production of this book.

Finally, always and in all ways, I thank my hunting and life partner Doug Stange, for his passion for women's hunting, as well as for their best writing about it.

Introduction

A HEART SHOT IS WHAT EVERY BIG-GAME HUNTER HOPES FOR: THAT PER-
fect shot placement, whether of bullet or arrow, which ensures a
quick, humane kill. A heart shot is also what the best hunting writing has
always aimed for—that certain image, or theme, or turn of phrase that
strikes to the core of our flesh-and-blood humanity, piercing the tissue-
thin membrane between life and death. Neither the shooting, nor the
writing about it, have commonly been regarded as women's work. Yet not
only do we live in a time when women are hunting and writing about it
in apparently unprecedented numbers, it is a fact that some women have
always hunted, and some of them have written dazzling accounts of their
experiences. Too many of these foresisters in the field have been forgotten.
Their words have drifted out of print, into literary oblivion. And too few
of the outdoorswomen writing today are getting the audience their work
deserves.

This book seeks to begin to set the historical and literary records
straight, by bringing to light some of the best women's writing about hunting in English over the past century. As the reader will discover, the more
some things have changed, the more others have remained the same. Now,
as a hundred years ago, women hunt for the same reasons men generally
do and derive the same sorts of satisfaction from hunting. And regardless
of the sex of the hunter, every hunt begins with a stalk and ends with a
story. The essential appeal of the hunt, the drive to get back to nature and
to basics and to express in narrative, image, and metaphor the complex
meanings of one's experience of oneself as a predator: Such impulses are
not only ageless, they are surely also genderless.

And yet, when women are hunting—if only because of long-standing
social prohibitions against their engaging in "manly" pursuits—there are
differences, many of them subtle, both in the ways they go about doing it
and telling its story. The reader familiar with the literary tradition of outdoor writing by men is, therefore, in for some surprises in what follows:
in some instances, shocks of narrative recognition; in others, startlingly

different ways of perceiving and framing what it is about hunting that makes us more fully human.

The differences and the similarities span time and space. Every hunter is in her own fashion a wayfarer into uncharted territory. English adventuress Isabel Savory, one of the earliest writers in this volume, reflected upon the subjective value of her far-flung travels, of which hunting formed an integral part:

> *I have felt* stands for more than *I can imagine what others have felt.* Experience teaches a variety of things: it includes the development of perceptive powers, dependence upon self, and a wider knowledge of self; it inculcates generous views; it causes, in short, a great mental expansion . . . To see more is to feel more; and to feel more is to think more.
>
> Travel teaches us to see over our boundary fences, to think less intolerantly, less contemptuously of each other. It teaches us to overlook the limitations of religions and morality, and to recognize that they are relative terms, fluctuating quantities, husks around the kernel of truth. Travel dismisses the notion that we are each of us the biggest dog in the garden.[1]

One hundred years later, Wyoming writer Geneen Haugen would write, in kindred spirit:

> There is a difference between fantasies beyond ability, and fantasies within, or at the boundary of, ability—but over the edge of fear . . . Yet anyone who hikes could walk alone. Anyone who hikes in daylight could walk at night . . . It is culturally taboo . . . for a woman to travel solo in country inhabited almost exclusively by men.
>
> This is the terrain to which I am drawn over and over. It's a kind of reclaiming, I suppose, for myself, for girls and other women. Reclaiming the ability to navigate beyond known safety, to be at ease as our ancestors were in the dark and unfamiliar world. Reclaiming survival instinct. To survive not by retreat, but to approach—and sometimes cross—the boundary of witless fear.[2]

Regardless of their sex or the time in which they live, hunters must learn to take risks, one of which is to think feelingly. It may be that women, who in our culture have traditionally been allowed, indeed encouraged, to keep their emotions closer to the surface of awareness, are therefore especially well-equipped to express the "feel" of the hunt on many levels, including its emotions—the fear as well as the elation.

Numerous selections in this volume would seem to bear this out. Yet what makes these women's writing work so marvelously well is that they express the complex of thought and emotion that constitutes hunting, in every case, with such intelligence and insight. And although more recent writers who have benefited from the women's liberation movement and other changes in Euro-American culture over the past few decades may express themselves in somewhat different terms, there is in these selections a certain consistency of orientation, which seems to be grounded in the authors' awareness of themselves as hunters who happen to be female. This is by no means to say that they all think or write alike: There are hard-edged realists as well as more contemplative naturalists in this, as in any, group of hunters. But, regardless of their individual perspectives, almost to a woman, these writers are alive to the fact that, in their hunting and their writing about it, they are doing something distinctly out of the ordinary.

There is no small irony here, in that most of the contemporary women writers who make up roughly half of this collection have, with perhaps such notable exceptions as Marjorie Kinnan Rawlings or Beryl Markham, probably never heard of, let alone read, the work of the other half. Not only are many of the best writers in this book long out of print, they were fashionable—some of them very much so—in American and British literary circles well before any female authors had gained more than token inclusion in the literary canon. One of the contemporary writers included herein commented to me, when I was describing this project to her as something of a labor of love on my part, "You're giving women back their history!" I wouldn't make such a grandiose claim for it, myself. But I do believe it is important to see the works included in this book in light of their historical context: specifically, the appearance and disappearance of women in the shifting contours of popular literature about hunting over the past hundred years or so.

WOMEN'S HUNTING, THEN
Back in the early 1970s, whenever we were confronted with yet another anthology chronicling the deep thoughts and bracing adventures of (mostly dead) men, my college classmates and I would joke somewhat ruefully that "Anonymous" must have been a woman. It required the concerted efforts of a generation of scholars in the evolving field of women's studies to correct the skewed picture of literature and history with which we, like previous generations, had grown up: the picture, as feminist historian Gerda Lerner has remarked, in which history is a drama written, directed by, and starring men.[3]

One might expect this to have been nowhere truer than in the field of outdoor writing, and more specifically writing about hunting. After all, it was common knowledge, by the time feminism's "Second Wave" was beginning to lap our cultural shores, that hunting was an overwhelmingly masculine activity. Men hunted, women gathered; they quested, we nested. Or some variation on that theme. Anthropologists who framed the so-called hunting hypothesis of human origins had cheerily argued that, in order for us to evolve into *homo sapiens* in the first place, it had been necessary for women to, as Desmond Morris phrased it, "stay put and mind the babies."[4] They put forth the image of prehistoric hunters bringing home the bacon—or, more accurately, a nice hunk of wooly mammoth—for the women to cook, complemented with greens and tubers gathered close to the home site. The world of the Pleistoscene, in their rendering, looked in its social organization little different from the modern asphalt jungle. It was such a comfortable picture, from the point of view of conventional gender expectations, that one outdoor writer could muse, as late as 1991 in an article on "Instinct and Reality" for *Field & Stream* magazine, that he could not imagine why any girl or woman would really want to venture out into the "cold, wet realm in which ducks, dogs and certain males seem to thrive—unless, by sharing a blind, a girl might make her father proud, or a young lady might find a husband like her own duck-hunting dad."[5]

Yet by the time that writer, obviously enamored of an older order, penned those words, the order itself had changed. Sisters had long since commenced "doing it for themselves" in a variety of fields once assumed to be exclusively male territory. By century's end, the number of women entering the ranks of American hunters had trended dramatically upward, from about three to roughly ten percent of the total. Many of these women were overcoming considerable odds just to get out into the field: Not only were they violating what in the minds of many, hunters and non-hunters alike, was a sort of gender taboo, they were doing it—as social psychologist Robert Jackson observed in his 1987 study of female Wisconsin deer hunters—without the guidance of any immediate female role models. "Their development as hunters," Jackson remarked, was "almost revolutionary."[6]

But only "almost," because these outdoorswomen were hardly doing anything new. While the hunting community has always been predominantly male, the "No Girls Allowed" sign only went up outside the average American hunting camp in the latter half of the twentieth century. Prior to the Second World War, American women appear not only to have hunted in significant numbers, but like their sisters in the United Kingdom they seem to have been fairly welcome among the ranks of the hunting "fraternity." Hunting publications—in their editorial copy as well as their advertising—bear this out. A survey of major American outdoor periodicals like *Forest and Stream* (*Field & Stream*'s precursor, which began publishing in 1873) or *Outdoor Life* (begun in 1898) would show that from the last quarter of the nineteenth century through at least the 1920s,

women figured regularly, often prominently, in their pages, and sometimes even on their covers. Over those same years, and into the 1940s,
huntresses here and abroad were publishing books about their adventures—works which, as the reader will discover below, compare more
than favorably with the best male writing on the subject of hunting.

Indeed, in one sense their work bears out the fact that, at least for
those who cannot seem to live without it, the experience of hunting is in
many ways gender-neutral. As Paulina Brandreth remarked over seventy
years ago, there are simply some individuals for whom the forest—with *its*
sunsets, *its* deer, *its* trails of enchantment—is the sine qua non for life
itself. Yet in her own life and writing Brandreth illustrates that any woman
venturing into hunting camp was crossing a sometimes subtle, yet
nonetheless clearly drawn, boundary. This may have been especially the
case, if her hunting gear included pens and notebooks in addition to rifles
and shotguns. Brandreth generally dressed as a man and wrote about
hunting for numerous publications under Paul, rather than Paulina. It is
unclear whether she did this because it was easier for her to publish as a
male, or because of a tendency toward transexuality; most likely, both factors were at work. In any event, according to family members, her publisher apparently never suspected that Paul was a woman.[7]

The majority of women hunters, while aware of the gender line they
were crossing, were not concerned about "passing" in the men's world of
hunting. Ironically, therefore, Brandreth is unusual among the writers

"On the way to camp." From Paul [Paulina] Brandreth, Trails of Enchantment. *Brandreth is standing in the center of the photograph.*

included in this volume, in that she did not devote attention to what it meant that she was a *woman* hunter. Her contemporary Courtney Borden, by contrast, described an experience of (to use her word) "initiation" into hunting that was—and indeed, remains today—far more typical of women hunters: She married into it. Borden recalled her introduction to upland shooting as a newlywed years afterward:

> It was going to be entirely different from anything I had ever tried before. It would be an experience, an insight into a man's world and why many husbands spend autumn weekends away from home.

When in 1927 her husband subsequently suggested she accompany him on the cruise of his ship, the *Northern Light*, to Alaska, she eagerly went along: Otherwise "the summer would be spent alone, taking care of home and children." (The children, one of them an infant, were no doubt left in good hands: Captain John Borden ran the condensed milk company bearing his name.) Borden came to find hunting far more congenial than more genteel women's work. In her 1933 *Adventures in a Man's World* she wrote, "'Mother has gone hunting,' my children now smile and say to any casual visitor who might be calling, and to them it seems little different than as though they had said, 'Mother is planting tulips.'"[8]

A generation earlier, Grace Gallatin Seton-Thompson had been introduced to hunting in the American West by her husband, the noted naturalist Ernest Thompson Seton, whom she dubbed "Nimrod" in her 1900 narrative of their first hunting trip, *A Woman Tenderfoot*.[9] In a brief prefatory remark, she proclaimed the book a "tribute to the West," containing true stories of adventure which "being a woman" she "wanted to tell . . . in the hope that some going-to-Europe-in-the-summer-woman may be tempted to go West instead." In order to help other potential outdoorswomen outfit themselves, she included in her book detailed descriptions of the necessities for a female-friendly camp, and of such accoutrements as the ingenious split-skirt she had designed, which allowed one to ride a very un-ladylike cross-saddle, and to mount and dismount quickly, all the while remaining fetchingly turned out.

Her British contemporary Agnes Herbert cared little about such sartorial niceties, but she cared passionately about hunting. In the first decade of the twentieth century, Agnes and her cousin Cecily hunted big game on three continents (on one of which hunts, Cecily managed to bag a husband among sundry other trophies). On their first safari, to Somaliland, Agnes and Cecily—outfitted for the bush in men's trousers and no-nonsense attitudes—made a wager with another, all-male, safari that they would outhunt them. The women won. When a female reader of her account of that hunt, Herbert's first book *Two Dianas in Somaliland* (1908), objected that she "didn't like so much killing," Herbert retorted: "She may be right, and books on sport and adventure are only for men and boys, the sterner sex. If, therefore, you, reader o' mine, should regard all forms of taking life as unwomanly, read no more."[10] Herbert, with good reason, regarded herself as no man's inferior in either the hunting or the literary field.

In this, she had something of a kindred spirit in the American journalist and novelist, Mary Hastings Bradley. Bradley hunted Africa and later India during the 1920s; on the first of her African safaris in 1922, she was accompanied by her husband, their nanny, and five-year-old daughter Alice. She reassured friends who were shocked at her exposing a young child to such an adventure that "Alice was as safe in Africa as in Chicago. Safety means ceaseless vigilance in either case."[11] A photograph from Bradley's *On the Gorilla Trail* (1922) shows little Alice, beaming, in a boat with several native porters.

Bradley had been drawn to Africa, in part, by the installations she had seen at New York's Natural History Museum, the work of renowned taxidermist Carl Akeley, who served as a sometime guide on her first safari. Prior to the advent of television and widespread tourism, specimen collection for museums, and subsequently nature photography, were primary reasons why many men and women ventured to Africa and other regions after game large and small. Among the authors in this book, several went on such expeditions: Courtney Borden's husband John was collecting walrus and polar bears (one of which Courtney took) for the Field Museum in Chicago. Mary Jobe Akeley not only assisted her husband Carl, she also completed his work for the Natural History Museum after his death. Vivienne de Watteville accompanied her father Bernard to collect specimens for the natural history museum in Berne, Switzerland, and—like Mary Akeley—completed the work after her father was mauled to death by a lion.

Meanwhile Osa Johnson and her husband, Martin, a protégé of both Akeley and Jack London, were pioneers in the art and science of wildlife photography: Osa hunted with a gun, freeing Martin to stalk with his camera. Helen Fischer ultimately traded her gun for a camera, using the stalking and calling techniques she had perfected as a hunter to draw animals into the range of her lens. De Watteville made a similar move.

It is important to note that while women like these "accompanied" men who were their mentors, or friends, or lovers, they not only stood their own ground (with gun, or pen, or camera), they also frequently struck out on their own adventures and forged their own careers.[12] But few women of the period had the wherewithal or the desire to strike out entirely on their own.[13] In part, this owed to the gender dynamics of the times in which they lived, and the generally limited horizons for adventure these times afforded even affluent women. Yet, in the light of those same dynamics, the expanded horizon not only of experience, but also of equality, that hunting could provide for women is strikingly evident. Martin Johnson said of his wife Osa:

> For bravery and steadfastness and endurance, Osa is the equal of any man I ever saw. She is a woman through and through. There is nothing "mannish" about her. Yet as a comrade in the wilderness she is better than any man I ever saw.[14]

In similar spirit, as a friend rather than a lover, Ernest Hemingway wrote of Beryl Markham's *West with the Night:*

> . . . she has written so well, and marvelously well, that I was completely ashamed of myself as a writer. I felt that I was simply a carpenter with words, picking up whatever was furnished on the job and nailing them together and sometimes making an okay pigpen. But [she] can write rings around all of us who consider ourselves as writers. The only parts of it that I know about personally, on account of having been there at the time and heard the other people's stories, are absolutely true. . . . I wish you would get it and read it because it is really a bloody, wonderful book.[15]

Of course, not all men were so welcoming of women who wanted to hunt, let alone to publish their adventures. Indeed, more often than not, the attitude on the part of male editors of hunting publications reflected a good deal of ambivalence. They might gingerly encourage a woman to join her husband afield, as did a writer for *Outdoor Life* in 1915, responding to a letter from "An-Aspiring-Woman-Hunter" in Ohio:

> You are a good shot (for a woman), you are a "good fellow" in the outdoors, you are not afraid to wear sane clothing, you have hunted bears and killed one, and best of all, you have the inherent love for the woods and streams that is the most necessary essential to a successful and enjoyable hunting trip. Therefore we hope that on his next hunting trip your husband will find you by his side.[16]

Such less-than-resounding endorsements of women's hunting no doubt owed to the fact that for many men, the connections between women's hunting and other traditionally "unfeminine" activities were all too apparent. It is surely no coincidence that women's initial emergence, in the popular literature about hunting, occurred when they were asserting their rights in other spheres as well. The First Wave of American feminism appears to have produced hunters as well as suffragists. Consider these remarks, by "A Michigan Sportswoman" identified only as "J.M.," in the February 1880 issue of *Forest and Stream:*

> It behooves us women to improve every opportunity that is presented for us to come to the front and show that we are competent to write, speak or vote, just as the case demands. We as a class are not thought to be quite so inferior to the opposite sex as we were in days gone by, yet there is still existing a feeling of superiority over us. To prove this a fact, take a remark I heard a gentleman make concerning the first article that appeared in the Woman's Column in *Forest and Stream.* It was this: "No one need try to make me believe that a woman wrote that, for it is too well written." Now I believe a woman wrote it, and that said gentleman will see ere twenty years have elapsed that a woman can not only write a spicy article for a sportsman's journal, but is capable of doing any work that requires brain power equally as well as a man.[17]

Two other early champions of women's equal capacities to "write, speak or vote," the pseudonymous "Marjorie" and the "Wyoming Girl" Alberta Claire, are represented in this collection.

Our "Michigan Sportswoman" had gone on in her essay to say that she refrained from writing "a suffrage article" because she did not know whether her editor was "a woman's-rights man." He probably wasn't. Indeed, a year earlier, in an unsigned editorial about "Women in Arcadia," a *Forest and Stream* writer took pains to remark that "Although opposed to 'women's rights' in the Anthonian or Walkerian sense, we are willing champions for her rights to health and happiness."[18] Indeed, many writers of the day seemed to regard women's increased involvement in outdoor activities as healthier outlets for female energy than political enfranchisement would be. In 1912 *Forest and Stream* editorialized that one seldom encountered a sportswoman "in the ranks of suffrage," elaborating that "Man never yet objected to woman taking part in his outdoor recreation, and in some outdoor sports women excel . . . and yet among this class of women, how many are suffragettes? None."[19]

Not surprisingly, women's hunting, and their writing about it, would therefore yield two models as far as feminism was concerned. On the one hand, there was a figure like Grace Seton-Thompson. In addition to co-founding the Campfire Girls with her then-husband Ernest, she was after their divorce one of the first women to explore remote areas of China, Africa, South America, and India, and to write about all of these explorations. She was also a prominent suffragist and became an internationally celebrated campaigner for women's and human rights, winning several major awards both for her writing and for her humanitarian serv-

Unknown huntress, fully armed, and her dog on the Lolo Fork. Myrta Wright Stevens, photographer. Maloney Collection, Montana Historical Society, Helena, Montana.

ice during World War I. Seton-Thompson clearly saw a direct link between women's equal ability to wield gun, pen, and ballot.

Yet her contemporary Annie Oakley took pains to stress what she called her "ladyhood," and to distance herself from the suffragist movement. This did not prevent her from arguing for equal pay for equal work, for women's right to armed self-defense, and for the possibility of female sharpshooters in combat, long before such concepts had gained much currency in feminist circles. Oakley perhaps had reason to be circumspect when it came to politics. As the highest-profile female shooter of her day, she was arguably the first genuine American superstar, and she had achieved that status by, quite literally, beating men at their own game. Oakley may simply have thought it prudent, for the sake of public relations, to demur on the subject of the vote. Or she may have genuinely agreed with those male writers and editors who supported women's involvement in activities like hunting and fishing as healthy surrogates for political engagement. In any event, she clearly shared with her sister-outdoorswomen the conviction that when it came to shooting, "Sex makes no difference."[20] As for hunting, Oakley wrote that "Any woman who does not thoroughly enjoy tramping across the country on a clear frosty morning with a good gun and a pair of dogs does not know how to enjoy life . . . God intended women to be outside as well as men, and they do not know what they are missing when they stay cooped up in the house enjoying themselves with a novel."[21]

While the question is undoubtedly of interest to women's historians, it may ultimately be beside the point whether a woman like Annie Oakley chose to call herself a feminist. She was arguably living many of the freedoms for which her suffragist sisters lobbied. So, to a greater or lesser extent, were untold numbers of her sister outdoorswomen. This was liable to be threatening to men concerned with upholding the values of the status quo. Editors were happy to encourage these women in their outdoor pursuits, so long as they kept their social and familial priorities in order.

In fact, whatever individual women's motivations may have been, one of the strongest arguments for women's hunting one customarily finds in the hunting periodicals of the late nineteenth and early twentieth centuries was that women should take up hunting to make their outdoorsman-husbands happy. In an 1880 issue of *Forest and Stream*, for example, a female writer, obviously herself a shooting enthusiast, identified only by her initials N.B. asked:

> Why do not more women accompany their husbands or brothers on hunting expeditions? Is it because they don't know how to do it, or because they are not encouraged in the idea by their respective lords, or because they don't know how delightful it is? I am quite sure that there are many women who now sit at home and in the secret depths of their hearts cherish a little hard bitter feeling of being neglected when their husbands go off on shooting trips. Now, to these women I would like to become a sort of feminine guide-post, pointing out to them an easy and pleasant path. I know that a woman can go with her husband on his shooting trips, and not only not be a hindrance to him, but greatly increase his pleasure.[22]

This author, writing with the ladies' interests squarely in mind, offered practical instructions about clothing and equipment. She went on to enjoin the men in her female readers' lives to do their part to make their wives' field experiences as positive as possible ("And my dear sir, the first time she sees the dogs point and asks what is the matter with them, don't laugh"). With a few easy lessons, and "the courtesy that you would naturally show any woman under such circumstances," N.B. assured her male readers that they would soon find themselves blessed with willing and able shooting partners. She knew, because she herself was living proof.

Her editors may not have been *quite* so sanguine about women's potential outdoor prowess, yet they nonetheless saw some clear advantages to having women in hunting camp. A few months before N.B.'s women's column, they had observed that "It would seem that the aim of the schools and drawing-rooms of to-day [sic] was to perfect woman in artificial accomplishments, and so crowd out her natural longings and tastes." The remedy was to bring women to hunting camp, where they could clearly benefit from a bit of fly-casting or light recreational shooting. There were other benefits, too:

And what an added charm to camp life does woman's presence lend? After a hard day's work at those heroic sports in which she cannot participate, how pleasant to return and find that brightest ornament of the home, whether wife, sister or mother, waiting to receive you? Ah! The ministrations of the hands man loves are better than the studied attention of trained lackeys, and never so appreciated as in the far-off camp. But don't let our lady readers imagine that this article is written with selfish motives in view. It is their companionship man wants, not their skill at compounding from the "Sportsman's Cook Book" tempting dishes, nor the deft display of their orderly natures in brightening up the camp. Far from it, although a willing exercise of their culinary or aesthetic taste is no detriment to their womanhood, and, if possible, lends an additional grace to their presence. Be that as it may, there is a place in the true sporting field for women.[23]

It is tempting to ponder whether women read such articles as these in the same ways as their menfolk did. But whether the ladies' initial motivations for venturing afield had to do with pleasing their husbands or, as is far more likely, themselves, it is clear that by the early twentieth century, sportswomen were a prominent part of the outdoor community. In a telling 1911 editorial on "The Modern Sportswoman," we find *Forest and Stream*'s editors trying to move with the times:

The active participation in field sports by women marks a modern development. Fifty years ago no woman would have handled a gun, much less a rifle, or would have dared to beard a lion or a tiger in the field, or have dreamed of a day on the moors all to herself or taken a hunting box with a string of hunters for the winter. Yet women do all these things now. Sport for women is catered for as amply as sport for men. . . .

They even grudgingly acknowledge that feminism might have had something to do with this trend:

It would appear as though the masculine development of women, the sense of rebellion and revolt had driven them to enter the same sports as men, a tendency strongly developed in modern girl schools, where hockey, golf and cricket are more highly appreciated that [*sic*] the ladylike accomplishments and quiet study of our mothers. Needlework is at a discount, but the eye, the ear, the hand and the body are all trained in field sports, and the modern Diana, with her zest, her joie de vivre and her independence has apparently come to stay.[24]

What a difference a generation could make!

There was, however, another factor at work during this period, which led outdoor writers and editors to celebrate women hunters, however vexingly out of men's control some of these "Dianas" appeared to be becoming. The late nineteenth and early twentieth centuries witnessed what might legitimately be called the "first wave" of American environmentalism. And hunting—specifically, market hunting, which had brought about the extinction of such species as the passenger pigeon, and the near-extinction of the American bison—was the target of intense criticism. Against this backdrop, sportsmen like Theodore Roosevelt and Gifford Pinchot argued for the principle of "fair chase," and sought to replace the market hunter in the American mind with the figure of the hunter-conservationist, a figure rooted simultaneously in America's frontier heritage and in the tradition of hunting as a productive leisure pursuit of the middle and upper classes. The sporting press was a primary arena in which to effect the transformation of hunting in the American mind.

In addition to drawing the distinction between market and sport hunting, outdoor editors also had to combat the stereotype of the boorish, rapacious hunter, who goes off to camp with his companions for the primary purpose of engaging in generally loutish behavior. This stereotype—still, alas, familiar today—was itself something of a carry-over from the United Kingdom. And, like all effective stereotypes, it derived its power from the fact that there was, at least in certain individuals and settings, some truth to it. Hence, there was a deliberate effort, on the part of sportsmen of the period, to enlist the fairer sex in the service of fair chase. One the one hand, it was argued, women might well have a softening and civilizing effect on hunting camps. At the same time, their visible participation in "blood sports" would gain for those activities a higher level of public approbation.

There had been a recent historical model for precisely this sort of "public relations" initiative in the outdoor press: In the 1870s and 1880s (as, again, much more recently), British fox hunting had come under attack, although then less on grounds of cruelty to animals than of licentious behavior on the part of hunters. British outdoor publications like *The Field* countered by featuring women's widespread participation in riding to hounds. This in turn not only encouraged more women to take up the sport (with the desired moderating effect on male hunters' comportment, especially when those hunters were their spouses), it also had the hoped-for effect of raising public levels of approval for fox hunting. Precisely the same logic and dynamic seem to have been at work on American shores, roughly a generation later. And it was in this atmosphere—self-serving as it may have been, from the vantage point of sustaining a male-dominated hunting establishment—that women like the earlier writers in this volume flourished.

That atmosphere would change dramatically after the Second World War.

WOMEN'S HUNTING, NOW

The change may have had something to do with getting Rosie the Riveter off the assembly line and back into the kitchen. Having survived the Great Depression, and sacrificed "the best years of their lives" to one of the most brutal wars in recorded history, American men returned to the home front expecting more than to simply get their old jobs back. In a post-war world that had seen the collapse of old empires and the rise of a new Cold War between superpowers, Americans of both sexes seemed to crave the ostensible security of "traditional" family values, and the fairly rigidly defined gender roles that went with them.

Around this time, female images and voices disappeared from the outdoor press, and the assumption took hold in the public imagination that hunting was a males-only thing. During the fifties and sixties, girls and women were for the most part actively discouraged from such outdoor pursuits. Fathers took their sons out, as part of a male rite of initiation, and the men-only hunting camp was ironically depicted as a safe haven, a refuge from the females back home. Hunting came to be so identified with manliness that by 1968, *Outdoor Life* editor William Rae, reviewing issues of the magazine from the turn of the century and noting the presence of a perplexing number of women, wrote, with tongue not entirely in cheek: "One wonders whether men really were men in those days, as we have been led to believe."[25]

Five years later in 1973, however, *Field & Stream* magazine took the novel, if not really unprecedented, step of inaugurating a women's department. Observing parenthetically that, "Actually, this men-only image never was all that real, but that's a different story," contributing editor Margaret Nichols offered the rationale for the new department:

> [W]e are initiating this new department, designed to present ideas and information of particular interest to women, and to encourage them to stretch out, forgetting "men-only" ideas that may be keeping them from the fullest enjoyment of the outdoors. . . . Most of us know for certain that there are some things we will never be able to do—ski jumping, for example, or sky diving, to name two of my own absolutes—but we also have a list of things we simply *think* we can't do, and so we never try them, and never find out what fun we are (or aren't) missing.[26]

This is hardly the "I am Woman, hear me roar" brand of feminist assertion then current. But considering that Nichols, who joined the *Field & Stream* editorial staff in 1963, had spent her first several years on the masthead as the gender-neutral "M.G. Nichols," her tentativeness in evoking images of Second Wave feminism was probably well-placed. Like the "Michigan Sportswoman" who had written a women's column nearly a hundred years before her, she most likely was uncertain as to whether her editor was "a woman's rights man."

And, as a century earlier, he probably wasn't. Apart from the occasional (quickly dropped) women's column, and rare, usually male-authored articles about women taking the remarkable step of becoming hunters, the outdoor press remained generally cool to the notion of women's increased participation in hunting from the 1970s through most of the 1980s.[27] The outdoor gear industry continued to pitch its wares almost exclusively to men. One would search virtually in vain for quality hunting books written by women (the only writer appearing in this collection from that period is Astrid Bergman Sucksdorff, a Swede). One editor of a prominent outdoor publication ventured, privately, that it would be "death" to his magazine's sales, were a woman to be featured on its cover.[28] Whereas American men at midcentury had suffered from what historian of science Donna Haraway has termed the "crisis of white manhood," toward the century's end they seemed to feel in Susan Faludi's phrasing "stiffed" by the social and cultural advances women were making, whether or not these were actually at male expense.[29] In this context, hunting—with its traditions rooted in masculine rites of passage—looked to many like the last bastion of true manhood.

For their part, feminists of this same time were less inclined than had been their First Wave forebears to draw a ready association between social and economic liberation on one hand, and hunting and shooting on the other. This owed in part to the fact that the women's liberation movement developed alongside and in interaction with the anti–Vietnam War and civil rights movements, from both of which it tended to derive an essentially pacifist outlook which rendered firearms use and the idea of "killing for sport" problematic. This period also saw the rise of the gun control movement in America. The commonly held assumption that to be feminist was to be anti-gun, coupled with the perception fostered by the outdoor press that hunting was and had always been a "guy thing," provided powerful disincentives to many women's considering taking up rifle or bow and venturing afield.

Still, some did. Indeed, by the close of the 1980s, the complexion of hunting was changing, and its face becoming decidedly more feminine.[30] The reasons were complex. By the last decade of the last century, American women had made significant inroads into virtually every arena of male activity and privilege. American society was becoming, on the whole, more egalitarian, and gender equity was far less a fiction than a fact of life in most families. Women had more disposable income than ever before, they were less daunted by the prospect of vigorous or challenging physical exertion, and they were statistically more likely to find themselves the heads of single-parent households. Many began wondering whether there was something happening in those woods and cornfields and duck blinds that they might want to know about.[31] And so they ventured where many of them believed none, or few, had dared tread before . . . although they were in fact retracing the steps of women very like themselves, a few generations older, some of them still living.

One such woman, whose hunting life spanned the twentieth century, appears in this volume. Frances Hamerstrom, a pupil of Aldo Leopold and one of the first American women to become a wildlife biologist, began hunting in the early 1930s and continued hunting well into her eighties, until shortly before her death in 1998. (One of her last adventures, recounted below, involved floating the Amazon with native fishermen.) Hamerstrom achieved a certain amount of celebrity, appearing on the *David Letterman Show*. No doubt far more people know her today as that plucky old woman who told outrageous stories to Dave, than as a pioneer in wildlife management and the author of two memoirs of her life as a hunter.

Still, her appearance on late-night television is itself symptomatic of changes that were occurring in the hunting world. By 1990 it was undeniably the case that the numbers of male hunters were declining, even as the numbers of female hunters were rising. A few of these hunters had (like Diana Rupp in this volume) been taught to hunt as children, by their fathers; fewer still (see Jill Carroll's story), by their mothers. The vast majority came to hunting, as had most of the huntresses of a century before, as adults, through men in their lives—friends, husbands, lovers. They also had in common with earlier female hunters the fact that they frequently had barriers to overcome, if they wanted to hunt. Some of these barriers were social or psychological, for example, negative peer pressure, or the idea that a good woman doesn't want to kill things. Often, the most daunting obstacles were, however, practical or logistical, having to do with finding hunting partners, or the right gear and clothing . . . a theme that likewise figured prominently for women hunters in earlier times.

The outdoor press had to pay attention to these women's interests, and to the evidently growing women's market. Indeed, the 1990s may well be termed the "decade of the woman," in publications like the "Big Three" (*Outdoor Life, Field & Stream,* and *Sports Afield*), as well as virtually every other nationally distributed hunting magazine. Far more frequently than since perhaps the 1920s, articles by, as well as about, women appeared. As had earlier been the case, articles authored by men and women (including three by the editor of this volume) provided instructions and encouragement for fledgling female hunters.[32] Of course, then, as a century earlier, outdoor editors were celebrating women's hunting with an agenda, not

Elk hunters, Lewis and Clark National Forest, November 2001. © ANNE PEARSE HOCKER.

altogether hidden, in mind. As had earlier been the case, the fact of women's hunting looked to be a potential remedy for some of the hunting "fraternity's" problems, and good publicity for hunting in general.

To put it bluntly, hunting was not nearly so popular as it used to be. Over the past century, the United States had shifted demographically from having a predominantly rural to an overwhelmingly urban and suburban population. Hunters, of either sex, were no longer a familiar part of the landscape for the vast majority of Americans. Nor, increasingly, did a general public better acquainted with Disney and nature programs on PBS than with the complex world of nature itself, comprehend how or why hunting could be normal, or necessary, for those who still engaged in what was coming, more and more, to look like a remnant of the past. The threat of hunting's becoming culturally irrelevant was, from the sportsman's point of view, perhaps bad enough. But in addition, the 1980s had seen the rise of the animal rights movement, with numerous advocacy groups and publications specifically dedicated to the abolition of hunting. Partly because (as the writings in this volume surely demonstrate) discourse about hunting does not lend itself to sound-bites as readily as does animal rights philosophy, spokespersons for animal rights effectively commandeered media attention, and with it public sympathy. Surveys began to show that while the majority of Americans said they approved of hunting, at least in the abstract, they also disapproved of hunters.

Now, it was and, for that matter, continues to be the case that on the grass-roots level, the animal rights movement is generally reckoned to be 80 to 85 percent female in its constituency. And so it was clearly advantageous to shed the spotlight on the fact that women were hunters, too. The anti-hunting arguments animal rights activists tended to use (ironically, especially if these activists were self-proclaimed feminists) depended on age-old stereotypes of female weakness and nonviolence on the one hand, and male rapaciousness (the "slob hunter") on the other. The sheer fact of women's hunting flew in the face of these arguments. Whether or not women's presence altered the atmosphere of hunting camp (many hunters, male as well as female, have argued that it did), whether or not women as a group present a more ethically mature image of hunting than the old male-rite-of-passage model (and while the jury is still out on this question, evidence suggests they might), for the second time in roughly a hundred years, the fair sex was called upon to justify fair chase. Women writers were certainly up to the task: Nine of the selections in this volume were originally published in one form or another in a national hunting magazine during the 1990s.

I would love to report, at this juncture, that there has been a resurgence of women's writing about hunting. Alas, the vagaries of publishing and of popular culture being what they are, hunting, and good writing about it—whether by women or by men—continues to be more marginal, as far as the general public is concerned, than any of the writers in this volume would wish it to be. One editor remarked to me quite recently, "Hunting books by women don't sell." Another, more generically, told me, "Hunting books don't sell." But then, as the writers in this volume would also affirm, really good writing is never, ultimately, about what sells. It is about what keeps us, writers and readers, alive.

And so, to the writers themselves. While this book incorporates historical as well as contemporary works, it is arranged thematically, rather than chronologically. As the reader will discover, much of the delight in reading these selections comes from the "conversation" they create among women writing today and authors long departed. They represent, to my mind, the best of what all good writing, but perhaps more especially good writing about hunting, has to offer: an experience in words that brings us home to ourselves. In her only book, *The Roaring Veldt,* Gretchen Cron reflected:

> For hours I have clung to the branches of some great tree, peering anxiously along a faint trail below me, straining my eyes for the smallest stir in the foliage, or listening for the snapping of a twig. And finally at evening, with the lights of the distant villages twinkling like fireflies, I have watched till the last of the afterglow died in the west—and then have gone home without a

glimpse of my quarry, but happy to have been able to hunt him in this enchanted wood.[33]

I suspect that none of the writers included in this volume would dispute that the hunter's quarry—at least if that hunter is also a writer—is, ultimately, her self. And her gift to the reader is, more than anything else, a profoundly shared sense of their mutual humanity.

Welcome, reader, to an enchanted forest. And welcome home.

PART ONE

Initiation

C ALL IT BLOOD-KNOWLEDGE: WHAT HUNTERS SEE, AND KNOW, THAT makes them markedly, if subtly, different from those around them. In most times and places where hunting has been a meaningful part of collective and individual life, the various aspects of the hunt have been ritualized, the transmission of hunters' lore from one generation to the next recognized as constituting an important rite of passage. The skills-training and knowledge come first, the blood and the wisdom follow. The hunter is initiated into a new way of perceiving and experiencing the world.

But ours is a culture largely lacking in ceremony. And even where hunting rites of passage have survived in vestigial form—in family traditions, in local customs, in the attempts of Native groups to preserve the Old Ways—girls and women have mostly been on the outside looking in. The perspective of the outsider turns out, in the selections that follow in this section, to be a blessing in disguise, to the extent that they help us to see hunting itself in new, and deeply refreshing, ways. All of these writers began as non-hunters. Some of them remained so, others resolved to hunt, and one, having hunted, exchanged her rifle for a camera. But, in every case, their initiation into the hunter's world view fundamentally altered their relationship to the world around them, in powerful ways: learning how to read the mystery in a track, how to call in game, how to confront and see through one's fears, how to tell and hear a story . . . even how to fall in love, for the first and last time.

TERRY TEMPEST WILLIAMS

Deerskin

(1984)

IREMEMBER, AS A SMALL GIRL, WAKING UP ONE MORNING TO THE WILD enthusiasm of my father and brothers. They were outside my bedroom window, and I could vaguely hear them talking about some sort of tracks they had found. Their voices conveyed a sense of awe as well as excitement. Not wanting to miss anything, I ran out to see.

The front door had been left open, and through it I could see all four of them crouching in the snow.

"Deer tracks . . . ," my father said, touching them gently.

"Deer tracks," I said. "So?"

"Deer tracks," my brother restated emphatically.

"Deer tracks," I said again under my breath. No, something was missing when I said it. Feeling out of place and out of touch, I went back inside and shut the door. Through the glass I watched the passion that flowed between my father and brothers as they spoke of deer. Their words went beyond the occasion.

Many years have passed since that morning, but I often reflect on the relationship my brothers and father share with deer. Looking back and looking forward into the Navajo Way, I have come to realize the power of oral traditions, of stories, even in our own culture, and how they color our perceptions of the world around us.

Nowhere is this relationship of earth and story more poignant than in the Navajo perception of living things, *nanise*. The Diné have been told in their origin histories that they will receive knowledge from the Holy People, from plants and animals. As with other Indian peoples, the Navajo do not "rank-order" animals. Barry Lopez writes:

> Each creature, from deer mouse to meadowlark, is respected for the qualities it best seems to epitomize; when those particular qualities are desired by someone, then that animal is approached as one who knows much about the subject. . . .

And elsewhere:

23

In the native view, each creature carried information about the order of the universe—both at a practical level (ravens might reveal the presence of caribou to hunters), and at the level of augury. Moreover, each creature had its own special kind of power, and a person who wished knowledge in those areas—of patience, of endurance, of humor—would be attentive to those animals who possessed these skills.

Gregory Bateson points out in *Mind and Nature* that ". . . the very word, 'animal,' means endowed with mind and spirit."

This idea of animal mentors is illustrated in the Navajo Deerhunting Way. The Deerhunting Way is a blessing rite, a formula for corresponding with deer in the appropriate manner. Traditionally, hunters would participate in this ritual as a means to a successful hunt and their own personal safety.

Claus Chee Sonny, a Navajo medicine man who lives in the Tunitcha mountains near the Arizona–New Mexico border, tells the following story, which is part of the Deerhunting Way. He learned the Deerhunting Way from his father, who had obtained it from his father, who was instructed by his father—Claus Chee's grandfather—and the many teachers who preceded him. The First People who taught the Deerhunting Way were the Deer Gods themselves. The Deer supplied the first divine hunters with the knowledge that was necessary to hunt them. And so the story begins:

There was a hunter who waited in ambush. Wind had told him "This is where the tracks are. The deer will come marching through in single file." The hunter had four arrows: one was made from sheet lightning, one of zigzag lightning, one of sunlight roots, and one of rainbow.

Then the first deer, a large buck with many antlers, came. The hunter got ready to shoot the buck. His arrow was already in place. But just as he was ready to shoot, the deer transformed himself into a mountain mahogany bush, *tsé ésdaazii*. After a while, a mature man stood up from behind the bush. He stood up and said, "Do not shoot! We are your neighbors. These are the things that will be in the future when human beings will have come into existence. This is the way you will eat us." And he told the hunter how to kill and eat the deer. So the hunter let the mature Deerman go for the price of his information. And the Deerman left.

Then the large doe, a shy doe, appeared behind the one who had left. The hunter was ready again to shoot the doe in the heart. But the doe turned into a cliffrose bush, *awééts'áál*. A while later a young woman stood up from the bush. The woman said, "Do not shoot! We are your neighbors. In the future, when man has been created, men will live because of us. Men will use us to live on." So then, for the price of her information, the hunter let the Doe-woman go. And she left.

Then a young buck, a two-pointer, came along. And the hunter got ready to shoot. But the deer transformed himself into a dead tree, *tsin bisgá*. After a while, a young man stood up from behind the dead tree and said, "In the future, after man has been created, if you talk about us the wrong way we will cause trouble for you when you urinate, and we will trouble your eyes. We will also trouble your ears if we do not approve of what you say about us." And at the price of his information, the hunter let the young Deer-man go.

Then the little fawn appeared. The hunter was ready to shoot the fawn, but she turned into a lichen-spotted rock, *tsé dláád*. After a while, a young girl stood up from the rock and spoke: "In the future all this will happen if we approve, and whatever we shall disapprove shall all be up to me. I am in charge of all the other Deer People. If you talk badly about us, and if we disapprove of what you say, I am the one who will respond with killing you. I will kill you with what I am. If you hear the cry of my voice, you will know what trouble is in store for you. If you do not make use of us properly, even in times when we are numerous, you will not see us anymore. We are the four deer who have transformed themselves into different kinds of things. Into these four kinds of things can we transform ourselves. Moreover, we can assume the form of all the different kinds of plants. Then when you look, you will not see us. In the future, only those of whom we approve shall eat the mighty deer. If, when you hunt, you come across four deer, you will not kill all of them. You may kill three and leave one. But if you kill all of us, it is not good.

"These are the things which will bring you happiness. When you kill a deer, you will lay him with the head toward your house. You will cover the earth with plants or with branches of trees lengthwise, with the growing tips of the plants pointing the direction of the deer's head, toward your house. So it shall be made into a thick padding, and the deer shall be laid on that. Then you will take us home to your house and eat of us. You will place our bones under any of the things whose form we can assume— mountain, mahogany, cliffrose, dead tree, lichen-spotted rock, spruce, pine, or under any of the other good plants. At these places you may put our bones. You will sprinkle the place with yellow pollen. Once. Twice. Then you lay the bones. And then you sprinkle yellow pollen on top of the bones. This is for the protection of the game animals. In this manner they will live on; their bones can live again and live a lasting life."

This is what the little fawn told the hunter. "You will be able to use the entire body of the deer, even the skin. And we belong to Talking-god. We belong to Black-god. We are in his hands. And he is able to make us deaf and blind. Those among you, of whom he approves, are the good people. They will hunt with success and will be able to kill us. According to his own decisions he will surrender us to the people. The Black-god is Crow. But when you hunt do not refer to him as Crow but as Black-god."

Then, referring to what the fawn had said, the other three deer said, "This is what will be. And this is what will be. And this is how it is."

So these are the four who gave the information; the large buck, the doe, the two-pointer, and the fawn. Man was created after. All these events happened among the Gods, prior to the creation of man. All animals were like human beings then; they were able to speak. Thus, this story was not made up by old Navajo men. These events were brought about by Black-god. Then, after having obtained all this information, the hunter let the four deer go.

As final hunting instructions, Claus Chee Sonny shares the Deer People's knowledge:

You will not throw the bones away just anywhere. Everything of which we are made, such as our skin, meat, bones, is to be used. . . . Anything that we hold onto, such as the earth from the four sacred mountains, the rainbow, the jewels, the corn, all the plants we eat, will be in us. Our bodies contain all these. And because of this we are very useful. . . . Needles can be made from the bones of the front and hind legs. This is what we use to stitch buckskin together. . . . A deer not killed by a weapon shall be used in the sacred ceremonies. All the meat is very useful. You can put deer meat as medicine on sheep, on horses, and on other domestic animals. All livestock lives because of deer.

The usefulness of the deer is the foundation which has been laid. It serves as an example for other things. This is what is meant when we say that the deer are first in all things.

Through the Deerhunting Way one can see many connections, many circles. It becomes a model for ecological thought expressed through mythological language. The cyclic nature of the four deers' advice to the hunter is, in fact, good ecological sense. Out of the earth spring forth plants on which the animals feed. The animal, in time, surrenders its life so that another may live, and as its body parts are returned to earth, new life will emerge and be strengthened once again. Do not be greedy. Do not be wasteful. Remember gratitude and humility for all forms of life. Because they are here, we are here. They are the posterity of Earth.

It is this kind of oral tradition that gives the Navajo a balanced structure to live in. It provides continuity between the past and the future. They know how to behave. Stories channel energy into a form that can heal as well as instruct. This kind of cosmology enables a person to do what is appropriate and respect the rights of others. N. Scott Momaday tells the following story:

> There was a man living in a remote place on the Navajo reservation who had lost his job and was having a difficult time making ends meet. He had a wife and several children. As a matter of fact, his wife was expecting another child. One day a friend came to visit him and perceived that his situation was bad. The friend said to him, "Look I see you are in tight straits. I see you have many mouths to feed, and that you have no wood and that there is very little food in your larder. But one thing puzzles me. I know you are a hunter, and I know, too, there are deer in the mountains very close at hand. Tell me, why don't you kill a deer so that you and your family might have fresh meat to eat?" And after a time the man replied, "No, it is inappropriate that I should take life just now when I am expecting the gift of life."

True freedom is having *no* choice. In this case, the man knew exactly what he had to do with respect to the land. Behavior became gesture. "It isn't a matter of intellection. It is respect for the understanding of one's heritage. It is a kind of racial memory, and it has its origin beyond any sort of historical experience. It reaches back to the dawn of time."

My thoughts return to that winter morning—to the deer tracks—and then to a crisp day in October when finally, at the age of sixteen, my father invited me to go deer hunting with him in the Dolores Triangle of Colorado. We participated in the rituals associated with the season, clothing ourselves in yellow sweatshirts, fluorescent orange vests, and red caps. We polished our boots with mink oil and rubbed Cutter's insect repellent all over our bodies, so as not to be bothered by remaining insects. We rose before the sun, and stalked west ridges to catch the last of day's light. Finally, around the campfire, I listened to the stories my father told until the stars had changed positions many times.

It was only then that I realized a small fraction of what my father knew, of what my brothers knew about deer. My brothers had been nurtured on such tales, and for the first time I saw the context they had been told in. My education was limited because I had missed years, layers of stories.

> *Walk lightly, walk slowly,*
> *look straight ahead*
> *with the corners of your eyes open.*
> *Stay alert, be swift.*
> *Hunt wisely*
> *in the manner of deer.*

I walked with reverence behind my father, trying to see what he saw. All at once he stopped, put his index finger to his mouth, and motioned me to come ahead. Kneeling down among the scrub oak, he carefully brushed aside some fallen leaves. "Deer tracks," he said.

"Deer tracks," I whispered.

DOROTHY DOOLITTLE

A Girl's Version of a Turkey Hunt

from Outdoor Life *(16 November 1905)*

OUR HOME IS SITUATED IN THE NOTED OZARK MOUNTAIN REGION OF south Missouri. We surely live in the backwoods, as it is twenty-five miles to the nearest railroad, but it would surprise many to learn that, nevertheless, in certain favored localities, there are many families of as thrifty, well-educated and refined people as can be found in any section of our land. Yet, a few miles back from the settlements, the virgin forests extend in one unbroken stretch for miles and miles. Wild game such as deer, turkey and pheasant, is still quite plentiful, and many fur-bearing animals such as the fox, raccoon, wildcat, mink, opossum and weasel, are much too plentiful for the safety of the farmer's poultry. Nearly every resident has one or more well-trained dogs with which to hunt such animals, and the sale of furs brings in many a welcome dollar at a time of year when there is hardly any other opportunity to turn an honest penny. The swift-flowing mountain streams teem with bass and many other species of fish that delight the heart of the angler. Bold and beautiful scenery spreads out before the eye in every direction to those who can find beauty in noble forest trees, moss-covered rocks, and tall, cedar-crowned bluffs, and sweet and tall, cedar-crowned bluffs, and sweet music in murmuring waters or winds sighing through the tops of the yellow pines.

An incident that lately occurred is only similar to many others that occur in the course of a year and may perhaps prove to many that our isolation is not without many compensations in the way of amusement and excitement for young people, even if so much different from that of the more thickly settled section.

During the holidays the weather was unusually warm and favorable even for this sheltered nook, and my father had directed my two brothers, John and Billy, to finish husking out some shock corn in one of the back fields on our farm. They were working quite late one evening and just as they were starting home they were attracted to the fluttering made by wild turkeys when flying up to roost, in the woods just back of the field. They crept cautiously in that direction and discovered the treetops in a little branch bottom literally black with these noble birds. Having no gun they could do nothing but creep cautiously back again, with a promise that later they would call again, better prepared to secure a roast.

After supper John hastened over to a near neighbor to get his friend, Philip Shone, while Billy went to another neighbor to get Dan Jones, his chum, to go with them. As the boys were going to have such a good time, I thought I might too, so I sent by them a request to bring Nettie Shone and Susie Jones, my two most intimate friends, to spend the evening with me. Within an hour all were on hand, but a new phase appeared on the program. Nettie was coaxing her brother to let us girls go along and see them get the turkeys. Philip said he would like to have us go first rate, but he just knew we couldn't keep still and would scare the turkeys before we could get within a half mile of them. But we solemnly promised we would be "good" and quiet, if they would let us go. Billy put in a good word for us. He said "Oh, pshaw! Of course let 'em go. What if they do scare the turkeys? We can take old Mingo along and have him tree a coon and have lots of fun anyhow." So thanks to brother, it was agreed, but we had mamma's consent to win yet, which we soon accomplished, by promising to wrap up warm and to be home by ten o'clock. When we finally got started we were certainly a crowd fit to scare tame turkeys, even, not to mention wild ones. John and Philip each had double barreled breech loaders that were excellent guns, while Billy had a single barrel that was fully their equal. Dan cut a most comical figure with his gun, an old muzzle-loading army musket, about six feet long, which his father carried in the Civil War and who sets great store by it on that account. But, from what the boys say, it is more dangerous to the one behind it than to the object shot at.

Dan was chosen to carry the cow bell, a great deep-toned bell we use on one of our work oxen when they are turned out on the range, so we can find them readily. I will explain that when hunting turkey after night if you jingle a cowbell you can get close up to them, as they merely think it some animal they are accustomed to.

Now, there wasn't a bit of use jingling the old bell until we got reasonably near to where the turkeys were roosting, but that didn't suit Dan's idea. He had fastened the strap of the bell under the iron ram-rod at the end of his musket, and away we went, ling-a-ling-ding-dong-clink-clink—as if that were not enough to give all an attack of the giggles, every once in a while he would give a bawl in very poor imitation of an old cow. It was at such a time that Nettie chose to make some of her wittiest comments, which finally ended in all screaming with laughter. Philip gave Nettie a good scolding and threatened to take her straight home, but Philip's bark is always worse than his bite, and we girls got off by just renewing our promises. Brother John told Dan to please not bawl any more. He said the turkeys might hear him and all drop dead, and said he wouldn't blame them much if they did, as he wouldn't want to live long himself, in a world where cows bawled like that.

In due time we arrived near to the roost, and John and Philip went carefully forward to look over the situation and plan the attack. In a few minutes they were back, and had agreed on a signal which was to be given by Billy, who would go to the farthest point, when he was ready to shoot. Susie was given charge of the bell and told to ring it about as she usually heard them ringing in the woods. I held Mingo, our hunting hound, by a strap, as we couldn't risk having him loose for fear of scaring the game, but he was alert and watching as though he knew there was "something doing." It is surprising how still boys can be when they want to. They crept off into the underbrush as silently as Indians and we girls were apparently left alone in the dark woods where the only sound, the who-hoo-hoo of the owls, made it seem more dismal still. We were beginning to wish we had stayed with mamma, when the mournful notes of a dove rang out clear and musical on the night air, followed an instant later, by bang, boom, bang, bang, until it seemed the very hills were tearing asunder, such was the fearful noise. Then we heard the flapping of many wings, and heard heavy bodies strike the ground. The very air overhead seemed filled with dark bodies flying swiftly away. We heard John and Philip give a cheer; then Billy called excitedly for Mingo. Knowing he needed the help of the dog I unsnapped the strap from his collar and he was off like an arrow. We soon heard his yelp, and later, Billy's cry of triumph:

"I got him all right, all right, and he is a smasher, too." Nettie turned up the light of the lantern, which had been left with her, and we went forward through the thicket as fast as we could, guided by the shouts of the successful hunters. We came to them, standing under a giant burr oak which had been the roosting place of the two fine turkeys John and Philip were proud to exhibit. But it was Billy who had laid low the patriarch of the flock, a monster gobbler weighing as much as both the others. He had broken a wing and would have lost him had not the dog with his unerring scent soon run the gobbler down.

Poor Dan! his turkey flew away. He was so angry at the old musket that he threatened to smash it over a log. "Better not," said Susie. "Papa would never forgive you. You know the old gun was never intended to shoot small shot." "Never mind," said Billy, "you can come over and fill up on my gobbler. I'll go halvers with you." John suggested having more light on the subject, and, suiting the action to the word, they soon had a roaring fire from the dry brush that was lying plentiful and convenient around them. The bright firelight shining on the trees and the dark shadows made a scene most unusual to young girls and one not soon forgotten. The boys were full of praise for our behavior at the critical time and promised that we should go hunting with them again at any time we wished. We reached home even before the appointed time. Mamma laughingly told Dan that he and his bell were a great institution to send along with young people, as a person could always tell just where they were.

HELEN FISCHER

Introduction

from Peril Is My Companion *(1957)*

WHEN I THINK BACK ON HOW I CAME TO BE AN ANIMAL PHOTOGRAPHER, I realize that my path lay by way of being a hunter. This is how it came about:

In the autumn of 1939, I left Switzerland, my homeland, for America, and arrived on a fine September evening in Santa Fé. And what a scene greeted me there! Wherever I turned I saw groups of excited noisy people, wearing red trousers, red jackets or anyhow red caps, when they were not clad in brilliant scarlet from head to foot. At first I thought I had happened upon some sort of carnival, but then I observed, with, I must confess, some misgivings, that all these good people were armed. At that moment I would have preferred above all else to have got in the train again and left the place, for the only conclusion I could reach was that the town was up in some sort of armed rising or rebellion. However, when I had sufficiently mastered my fears to take another look around I noticed with astonishment that the horses and even the cars were decorated with red ribbons. The situation was becoming rather uncanny, and not wishing to appear conspicuous among this excited throng, I slipped unnoticed into the nearest draper's shop, which happened to be just behind me, and bought myself a large red headscarf and a red handkerchief. I quickly tied the headscarf round my neck, and left the shop suitably disguised. Feeling now much more secure, I attached myself to the nearest group of red-clad people and was able to discover what it was all about.

It was, in fact, the beginning of the great hunting season. When later I penetrated a little further into the town, I saw notices everywhere bearing in large letters the legend: "Gone hunting. Back next week." I also discovered that practically every shop was shut and displayed a notice saying: "Hunting. Shop closed." It was fortunate for me that my little draper's shop had belonged to one of the few non-hunters. Now I understood why everyone was wearing red. This was an important precautionary measure, so that the thousands of eager huntsmen streaming through the woods should not mistake one of their own kind for one of the animals they were hunting. The horses had their red ribbons and their

32

red covers too, so that from a distance they would not be mistaken for deer.

In America there are no private hunting preserves, and anyone, man or woman, provided they have reached their sixteenth year, can get a hunting licence. For a native of the country this licence usually costs five dollars. I discovered that the main object of the hunt was a very realistic and practical one, namely to bag as much meat as possible. The fathers of large families did very well by it, as they bought for each member of the family present at the hunt a hunting licence at five dollars a head. Now and again you could even see an intrepid grandmother taking her place as a member of the party. Such family enterprises often ended with the whole clan nearly breaking down under the weight of the meat they had to carry back home, but at any rate their food worries were at an end for quite a spell as their bag would last them comfortably for the whole of the following winter, assuming of course that they were good shots.

It was now quite clear to me that I simply must share in this unique occasion, so I bought myself a licence, a pair of field-glasses and a 300 magnum gun. I got the addresses of some guides and ranches whose sole function was to help hunters during the season, engaged a guide and started off. Unfortunately my guide was not a particularly good one and my success was correspondingly small. But it was all great fun and a pleasant introduction to the hunting regions of New Mexico and Colorado. In the course of the day you could hear hundreds of shots resounding through the woods, emphasizing the great importance of the red attire, in spite of which seven or eight people in each State were killed on the opening day. That meant eight hundred in the course of the season. Thus the public hunt, while perhaps a very pleasant affair, was by no means without its dangers. However, I was now seized with hunting fever and from that time onwards chose a fresh scene for my activities every autumn, one year going after bears, another hunting wapitees.

I had made up my mind to get to know a new animal every year, to study its habits, its language and its reactions, and I thought this could be done only on the hunt. Therefore, on all these expeditions I took my Leica with me. It was light and did not take up much room.

I began to get a great deal of pleasure from recording the hunt photographically in every detail: how the people lived in tents; how the tracks of a moose were distinguished from those of an elk; the environment in which the various animals lived; what they ate and all their peculiarities great and small, which were often so lovable and which at that time I was unable fully to appreciate. In short I photographed everything that looked interesting to me, and when all was said and done, there was always the inevitable final picture of the trophy.

Every year in late autumn, when the season was over, I visited New York, and in 1943 I took the opportunity to call on the editors of some of the sport and hunting journals. I showed them my series of photographs and was somewhat surprised when all my pictures were immediately snapped up and I was sent back to my two-fold hunt with a flood of new commissions.

When I saw that business was booming and realized that as a woman I had no competition, I began to specialize in series of this kind and eagerly set about improving and extending my skill as an animal photographer.

Then there came a turning point in my life which was to be decisive for my photographic career. I was once more hunting in Utah and had taken my guide with me. We had been following for hours a trail that was both exciting and perilous. It was the trail of a mountain lion.

These beasts are especially feared by the shepherds as they manage to devour something between a hundred and a hundred and fifty sheep every year. The puma (to give him his more formal name) is one of the few animals who in the course of one night, will kill twenty to thirty sheep out of sheer lust for killing, without touching the flesh. It is found mostly in the vicinity of deer as the latter are the puma's main source of food. It is said that a mountain lion will exterminate one hundred deer a year in addition to the sheep it kills.

As the mountain lion causes such great depredations, some States pay a reward of fifty to a hundred dollars for every one killed.

We had been on the trail a long time and had utterly failed to uncover the puma. I was tempted to call the whole thing off when suddenly I heard a sound in my immediate neighbourhood. I swung round but saw only the tail and hind-quarters of a mountain lion disappearing into the greenery. This was the signal for the start of a mad chase in which we were led by eight blood-hounds trained exclusively for mountain lions. Quite often they were close on the scent as we could hear from their shrill, excited barking, but the puma was crafty and sly and outwitted them again and again, leaving them howling miserably. After eight hours, however, the dogs, excited almost to the pitch of frenzy, had at last succeeded in surrounding the prey.

Suddenly I found myself face to face with the mountain lion. The beautiful noble beast was standing under a tree, and with its great animal eyes, gave me a desperate look. It was obvious to me that I would have to shoot at once, if I were not to become the prey of my own prize, but before I could do anything the beast had leapt on to the tree with one lightning bound and instead of going over to the attack was now clinging anxiously to a branch directly above me.

The animal had evidently seen the hopelessness of its situation and realized that after the long chase it was beaten. Exhausted, with trembling flanks, the great beast was clinging tightly to the branch and a gaze met my eyes so full of fear and torment and at the same time so hypnotic that my arms fell limply to my sides. No one could have imagined and easier target, but under the spell of those eyes I was incapable of moving a muscle. The barking of the dogs meanwhile had mounted to a shrill, persistent, deafening roar.

What happened within the space of the next second can hardly be retold. As if dispatched by some invisible weapon the beast collapsed. Suddenly shorn of all strength the heavy body released its encircling hold on the branch and fell with a heavy thud at my feet. Before the terrified animal eyes became glazed with death, it threw me one last beseeching look in which was mingled so much reproach that I shall never forget it as long as I live.

Had he collapsed from exhaustion, or had he, with all the indomitable pride of the beast of prey, finally brought about his own end? I do not know. I can hardly describe my own feelings; it was one of the most moving moments of my life, but it was also the moment in which, for the first time, I became really conscious of my own affinity with animals. I knew that from that moment I would never again be able to bring myself to kill an animal just for the sake of killing.

Later on I told Hemingway of this incident and this great animal lover just took my hand without saying a word. We understood each other. Just as one must observe the laws of the society in which one lives so must the animal lover hold fast to the basic laws of the land, and of these the most important principle is: Live and let live.

Is it, for instance, to be wondered at that a wild elephant will if it gets the chance trample a man underfoot when one considers that elephants particularly, because of their ivory tusks, have become the target of every eager tourist hunter, so that a living elephant often has ten to twenty bullets in its body? An elephant never forgets and regards every white man as its enemy. It has been known for an elephant, by means of its sense of smell, to recognize a man who once shot it after an interval of fifteen years, and to attack and kill him.

My decision to kill no more animals was also received with understanding by the editors of the papers for which I worked. But all the same I was suddenly confronted with an entirely new set of problems. When formerly I had been photographing animals, I had always been ready to shoot if they should become dangerous, and as I was a relatively good shot there was no great risk to me. But now I should first have to win the sympathy of the wild animals, sharing their private life as one of humankind and a friend, and through the eye of a camera gain an insight into all the joys and sorrows, great and small, of their daily life as well as of their intimate moments.

The mastery of this method of work was much more difficult than I had imagined. The first and fundamental requirement is a fabulous knowledge of the animals and enormous patience. Accordingly my first experiments in this direction were more or less catastrophic. My pictures were shockingly boring as I photographed all the animals from the front only and in rigid pose. This made them look wooden and lifeless and they ogled anyone who looked at them like stuffed specimens in a museum. The editors were horrified and I was in despair. But as has so often happened in my life a piece of luck came my way in the shape of Hans Richter, whom I met on one of my photo-hunts. He was one of the greatest animal experts in Invermere, B.C., Canada and also of course a good hunter. This guide was a German by birth, but for fifteen years had lived deep in the forest, away from civilization, where he and his family subsisted on preserves, the natural fruits of the woods and the prizes of his gun. Throughout his long life in the woods he had become so closely linked with the animals there that he knew their every habit. I was delighted to make his acquaintance for I knew that this man could be of enormous help to me. I engaged him as my guide and we decided to go into a "primitive area" that lies near Banff. Two days on horseback from Invermere, it is known as a great hunting region.

We arrived on the second of September, which date marked the climax of the rutting season. There could have been no better opportunity for studying and photographing elk and moose. We were out of luck for the first few days, for absolutely nothing happened. Not a single animal showed itself far and wide although we waited for hours on end. On the third evening it rained and we went once again to the pool which was our observation post.

We sat there for close on two hours. The rain poured in torrents, and apart from us there was no sign of life anywhere. I was absolutely frozen and wet through and my whole joyous anticipation had evaporated into nothingness.

Richter tried to keep my spirits up and told me that there should be a chance of seeing something towards evening that day as the moose would come to that spot to drink. And he was quite right. At a quarter past six we saw a moose five hundred yards away trotting leisurely along. I could hardly believe my eyes. The time had now come for Richter to demonstrate his art, and by imitating the mating call of the moose, he began to attract the animal's attention. Upon Richter's first roar the moose raised its great horned head and walked slowly and cautiously in our direction. It was now up to us to seek cover as quickly as possible behind a tree, for the moose was still far enough away not to be able to recognize us. Hardly had we concealed ourselves than the moose approached to within three hundred yards.

Richter introduced another tactic and changed his call. He imitated the mating call of the love-lorn moose cow. The success of the manœuvre was altogether striking. The moose, who until then had been coming along so thoughtfully, was suddenly as if bewitched by these cherished notes.

Tripping along with the air of an eager and confident suitor he now took our direction. I photographed his every movement from between two branches. We were still concealed from him but Mr. Moose was not going to give in. His desire for the still invisible loved-one became almost unmanageable. Evidently Richter had hit upon the love-call of a particularly seductive lady-moose.

Richter now gave off another irresistible love-call whereupon our courtier, unable to restrain himself any longer, tore off in a wild gallop towards the tree behind which he imagined lay the object of all his yearnings. Once again I photographed him, although I was beginning to feel very uncomfortable. After all I had as yet no idea of how to conduct myself in the face of a love-lorn moose. Apart from that I was quite unarmed and there were only ten yards between us.

"The bull is in a passion," Richter whispered to me. "There's nothing for it now but to climb the tree." But this was easier said than done for the trunk was thick and it was a long time since I had climbed a tree. However, in my desperation I landed on the tree as nimbly as a squirrel, right into the arms of Richter, who was already awaiting me above. In less unusual circumstances this would have seemed quite romantic. However, hardly had I hoisted myself up, than there was the bull, snorting beneath the tree.

There was now nothing left of the love-lorn gallant. A snorting, fuming lover, suffering from injured pride and a feeling that he had been made a fool of, stood below us with ruffled coat, looking at us with hatred. Clearly he had but one wish, and that was to get us on his horns. But we sat on in safety. However the vengeance of the moose was sweet, for he made us sit up in the tree for an hour, two hours, three hours, because he simply refused to move from that spot. It was a game of patience, and the question was who could hold out the longer.

Night meanwhile had fallen and I had become acutely conscious of all my limbs. A certain part of my body was completely numb. Richter produced his latest jokes to try to keep my spirits up but at that moment I was unable to raise any interest in them whatsoever.

As daylight dawned the siege was raised at last. Shamed and embittered the moose moved off. It can be imagined what a state we were in. Those were the longest hours in my life and, in the most literal sense of the word, the hardest. But at least I had recorded everything on my camera and they were certainly no petrified portraits.

This series was the first pronounced success of my new career, and it appeared all over the world. I suddenly discovered too that my newfound way of establishing contact with animals, that is calling to them in their own language, was far more fascinating than anything I had done before. My one desire now was to master this language and bring it to perfection as Richter had. For indeed in him I had found the best master.

So now we sat together night after night while he taught me everything he had learned in his long years of experience. When I thought I knew enough, I decided on my own accord, that is to say alone, to try out the mating call which I had learned so well. It was getting towards the end of the rutting season and there was no time to be lost.

Accordingly I drove off into the Banff National Park. My way took me along by a swampy pool, from which a narrow thorny path led me into an impenetrable thicket. The time—it was half past five—was ideal. My work could now begin.

I began with lesson number one, and gave the long-call. With breathless excitement I awaited the things which should then happen. Ten, twenty, thirty seconds and a long drawn-out call came to me through the trees. An elk was answering me. Growing bolder, I started up again, making my call rather longer this time, and was able to observe with eye and camera how the elk came into view, bounding along in my direction.

Now I came to lesson number two. I fluted on a high note, imitating the seductive moan of the elk-cow. Again the same situation as with Richter. The elk became a dancing, impatient male, driven on by passion. There he was, already at the pool, looking round him wildly as he searched for the beloved. Two yards away from me I saw a cave which would have to serve as shelter, for the thicket alone did not provide cover enough.

When the elk was only seven yards away from me I quickly made to duck into the cave, but either it was much smaller than I had imagined, or I was much fatter than I could have wished, so that it was only with the greatest difficulty that I could squeeze myself inside. My hands and face got so scratched in the process that they were bleeding freely, but at least I was safe. I put some brambles on my head as camouflage.

This elk showed a little more consideration and made me sit alone in that beastly cave for only two hours. Once again I had escaped a great danger and was richer for the experience, for I knew that my animal language had been well learned. This time too I recorded everything with my camera.

Richter, to whom on the following day I recounted my experience, was well pleased with me. For the last few days of the rutting season we went into the elk country again and we took up position in a raised clearing from which we could observe and photograph for hours on end.

On the second day we saw an elk herd, twenty strong. There were nineteen cows and only one bull, whose sole duty was to pair with the ladies. It is well known that in the rutting season the bulls are particularly jealous and rather hostile to any outside disturbance. They will not even take time off to eat as they are constantly on the watch for younger or stronger bulls who might break into their harem. Once more our calls found an echo but this time we could not be seen. This adventure too yielded up some magnificent pictures.

Then in 1946 I went to Alaska to photograph and by 1949 I had photographed practically everything that Canada, America, Mexico, and Alaska could offer in the way of big game. Now there was only one unexplored region for me—Africa!

GENEEN HAUGEN

Stalking Fear

(2000)

THE SKY WAS LIT ONLY BY CLOUD-SCUDDED STARS WHEN I DROVE TO BUF-
falo Valley; dawn wouldn't come for more than an hour. It was below
zero. I parked and let the engine run, the heater blast. It had taken a half
hour—half the drive—to warm up the interior; I was finally comfortable
and loathe to walk into the cold. Except for the shroud of snow, it was
dark as death outside and I was in unfamiliar terrain.

I made myself turn off the engine, open the door. Arctic air stung my
eyes. I layered on a hat, mittens, blaze orange vest. Shrugged into my pack,
uncased the rifle, slung it over one shoulder. The loaded magazine and a
single cartridge went into a jacket pocket. Locking the doors, I stepped
away, startled by the sudden quiet. When I moved, snow crunched underfoot. A trail led uphill, away from the road. *You're not really doing this,*
I thought. The warm car beckoned like a feather bed. *I am doing this,* I
answered myself as I sought the shadowed depression that marked the
snow-covered trail.

A thin wail stopped me. Coyote. Then a pack, howling and barking
from willows near the river. An answering pack upstream. Shivering, I
turned back to look at my car, below me. All I had to do was walk down,
get in, turn the key and drive home. It seemed foolish not to.

Over the first ridge, car out of sight, I lost track of anything familiar
beyond my own body. Like a babe cut loose from the umbilical. Like a
space voyager. Disoriented, I stepped carefully in the seam that looked
like a trail.

Straining to distinguish shapes of stumps or animals against the
snow, I felt for the bear spray on my hip. Anything could happen here.
Anything. This was grizzly habitat. There had been sightings of south-
bound Yellowstone wolves. In addition to bears and wolves, night fills
with creatures who detach from imagination and take form. Apparitions
appear and vanish like dreams: Headless horsemen. Monstrous rodents.
Winged predators. Is it worse to walk with a headlamp, seeing only what
falls in the flickering circle of light? Or worse to stare into the black, hoping for the acute vision of wild creatures?

Fear wrapped me like a tarry veil. I could not run from it. But sometimes terror unravels slightly, loosens its choking hold. I hoped for such an unbinding, when I would not fight fear, but accept that I felt afraid.

My heart fluttered wildly. Irregular gasps of breath froze on my hair and lashes. I blinked away slivers of ice, though adrenaline combined with the aerobic ascent generated plenty of body heat.

I was still alive and warm enough in the dark new country.

I'm not sure what makes me do it, turn away from the familiar world and stagger forth as if I knew where I was headed, what would happen. For as long as I can remember, I've been going off alone.

I grew up by a lake in the Northwest, in remnants of ancient forest. In an early memory, my mother escorts my brother and me down to the lake, where she chases away the crawdads in the shallow water. She leaves us there. I am probably three years old. My brother, almost five.

No one taught us to swim. We did not even teach each other.

Paddling farther out, or deeper under the surface, we went on solo explorations. I don't remember feeling afraid, don't remember being aware that the lake held danger.

But then we discovered the octopus, the nasty, many-limbed beast who inhabited the deep, murky water between our dock and the neighbor's. The octopus grabbed with its terrible tentacles whenever a swimmer neared. Though the creature was far too sly to show itself, stories of close encounters and escapes filled our ears and mouths. But the neighbor had a springy diving board and a twenty-foot-high dive platform—who could keep away? Naturally, we didn't consider walking the beach path, and so had to contend with the octopus every summer day.

We evolved.

We adapted, floating on our backs like otters, kicking and paddling in shallow strokes, shrieking if there was anyone listening, or gasping alone.

My mother taught me to attempt dangerous things on my own. I doubt this was her intention.

The octopus first taught me to swim across fear.

I flicked on my headlamp for the iced-over stream crossing, for the deepest shadows. Each time I turned it off, I had to pause while night fogged my vision until I blinked and blinked, and the trail came back into focus.

I had done it many times already, traveled a trail by starlight. But every other time, it had been country I knew. Even then, darkness rendered the terrain grotesquely unfamiliar. In the Buffalo Valley, I didn't know the cloven land, the forks and draws, the standing-dead and uprooted trees. As if in a dream, I stepped in excruciating slow motion, alert to the faintest shifts of shadow and light.

Streaking by without a sound, two low-flying stealth craft caused me to duck and cover, until they alighted in the dead limbs of a lodgepole and I could identify them: a pair of great gray owls. Following my progress like spies, the owls flew ahead and landed, lifted off, coasted away, clutched another branch and waited. How did they know where I was headed?

I got used to the owls' sudden fly-bys; I got used to seeing bears that resolved into stumps; I got used to unidentifiable cracks and thuds in the brush. I got used to adrenaline electrifying my body. Fear had begun to fray, had begun to feel familiar and about as comfortable as a balding hairshirt.

By dawn, I'd hiked a couple of miles. I loaded the rifle. I wasn't sorry for the pale gray light, though I almost wanted to start over—like when I'd made my first climbing rappel, so alien, terrifying and exhilarating that I'd felt compelled to step backwards off a hundred-foot cliff again, right away.

Hoof beats in the timber behind made me stop and turn, confused to think elk had sneaked up on me. But two horsemen came into view, their startled expressions synchronous with my own.

"Are you lost?" one of them asked.

"Are you *okay?*" the other said simultaneously, in the same tone with which one might inquire, "Are you *out of your mind?*"

Was I? From their disbelieving faces, I could tell they had not expected to encounter an armed woman walking solo, so early, so far from the road.

Who has not foreseen a lifetime of regret for an aspiration never attempted?

"I'll die if I don't at least try," some people might say. It is not always an exaggeration. The psychic numbing, the entropy, that results from abandoning longed-for dreams is a kind of perishing, a slow diminishment.

There is a difference between fantasies beyond ability, and fantasies within, or at the boundary of, ability—but over the edge of fear. Certainly, some things are only marginally safe alone: skiing avalanche terrain, many climbing routes and river descents. Yet anyone who hikes could walk alone. Anyone who hikes in daylight could walk at night.

But to be outside alone in the dark verges on the culturally taboo, particularly, and with good reason, for women.

It is culturally taboo, as well, for a woman to travel solo in country inhabited almost exclusively by men.

This is the terrain to which I am drawn over and over. It's a kind of reclaiming, I suppose, for myself, for girls and other women. Reclaiming the ability to navigate beyond known safety, to be at ease as our ancestors were in the dark and unfamiliar world. Reclaiming survival instinct. To survive not by retreat, but to approach—and sometimes cross—the boundary of witless fear.

Twenty years earlier, I had loved sleeping outside beyond almost anything, but had recently split with a camping boyfriend and was mad as a rattler to think I would have to give up something I loved until I hooked up with another guy in a plaid shirt. What if I never did? I didn't want the old boyfriend; I wanted the pine-scented wind, the blanket of stars, bird calls against the still morning.

I'd slept often in the backyard, or alone in national park campgrounds, but never out of sound and sight of others. Never where no one knew or particularly cared where I was. It made me coil with outrage to think I could not go solo in the dark. But diamondback anger has its uses: Strike or be annihilated.

Of course, there is always the possibility of striking and being annihilated anyway. But I was a determined young woman, shedding skins as fast as I dared, leaving boyfriend, home and allegedly-promising career in the dust. Leaving behind everything that I'd wrapped around me like armor, like a safe husk. The husk was not me. It needed to be shed in a dramatic way. A solo camp seemed the perfect thing.

I had a sagging, second-hand pup tent that required careful positioning to prevent unexpected flop-overs. To keep it upright, I stretched the guylines, pounded the stakes deep into the dirt. The crack of a rock against the metal stakes sounded like a loud announcement: *Here I am.* I stopped pounding often to listen for crashing in the brush, for the sneaky approach of large mammals.

In those days, I felt reasonably—or perhaps naively—confident I would not encounter rapists or homicidal lunatics in the backcountry: Why would they go to the trouble, when there were such easy pickings elsewhere? Hairier predators clawed hold of my fearful imagination.

When night came, I huddled in my sleeping bag, certain that every bear within a hundred square miles could smell my terror. It seemed entirely possible I would be dragged screaming from the tent. But if I couldn't camp alone, survive ten hours of fear and darkness, it wouldn't be much of a life, not one I'd consider worthwhile. I laid myself out like a sacrifice, behind a door that didn't zip closed, behind the thin ripstop of the worn walls. Every creaking branch arrested my breath; every scurrying small rodent made my heart drum loud and arrhythmic as an adolescent punk band.

I didn't expect to sleep. I barely expected to survive. So when I woke to sunlight and birdsong I was elated, as if I'd passed through a well-guarded gateway into a new country, expansive and beckoning with possibility.

The horsemen passed by, the hoof beats faded into the quiet dawn. I walked on the softest snow, pausing often to listen and sniff the air. Chickadees sounded their friendly calls. When the trail forked, I took the route the horses had not. Fresh elk tracks led toward timber stands; I followed them. Icy, hair-speckled nests marked where elk had bedded, but they were always ahead. Ghost elk.

The trail became an animal track. Deep drifts were postholed by elk legs, criss-crossed by coyotes. Stepping carefully, mostly staying atop the snow, I traversed uphill toward a ridge. One foot slipped and I shot the other ahead quickly, trying to regain balance. The snow gave way to my thigh and I lurched forward, leg caught like a pencil in a vise with weight and momentum pushing at an angle. I fell on my belly, rolled to the side and extricated my boot from the branch-trap bottom of the hole, thinking how easily legs snap, thinking of people who have died from the twin mortifications of a broken bone and hypothermia. I *could* break a leg, and it was possible that no one would find me until too late. I could fall on my face with a loaded rifle in my hands. What was I doing here?

But the snow was deep in every direction and the elk were not behind me. I climbed on.

I didn't know exactly where I was going. I had a vague notion of making a loop. At the ridgetop I glassed for elk in the timber, on the exposed south faces. I glassed in every direction for landmarks. But clouds draped the mountains and rose from the valley. I pulled on another layer and drank a cup of tea.

I had only the faintest idea where I was.

One summer I wandered away from a canoe camp in Northern Saskatchewan. Like many who live in the arid Rocky Mountains, I've relied on shorelines and distant peaks to guide me; it's hard to get truly lost on a river, or in a range a strong person could traverse in a day. But the flat, heavily treed island in Saskatchewan scrambled the internal compass I'd always relied on, which became specifically apparent when I came to the beach and didn't recognize the view at all. Naturally, I felt more than a fleeting panic.

But on an island, especially a small one, it's always possible to follow the shore. And in the mountains there are drainages to follow: If I were unreasonably lost, I'd go in the direction of water.

When sunlight broke through the ragged clouds, I stopped hoping I'd encounter elk and started thinking about going home. I considered the options: Continue in what seemed a loop, or return the way I'd come. Backtracking too closely resembled retreat, and I was not yet finished exploring.

I took the downslope of the ridge, then contoured toward a shallow draw. A pair of hunters slogged out of the pine. "Hello," I said quietly.

"See anything?" one of them asked, looking me up and down.

"Tracks," I said.

The other hunter averted his eyes, barely glanced at me. The first hunter looked uphill, studying the track I'd made. "Are you alone?" he asked.

"I'm just out for an armed hike," I said.

"Good idea," he said, and laughed.

The tangle of fear over real and imagined predators is accumulated over a lifetime and is a complicated unsnarling. Though primarily I'd learned to trust these armed men who walk the cold mountains, you never know.

For a woman, there are worse threats than getting lost or breaking bones. But to shy away from seemingly hostile terrain is itself a kind of captivity.

The sun coasted higher by the time I intersected the route I'd taken in the dark. At the top of the last ridge before the drop to the road, fresh canid tracks crossed the trail.

I bent to examine them, to study their articulations with my bare hands. A single impression equaled the size of my full palm. Wolf. In either direction, the track of one animal, no apparent overlap of multiple wolves stepping precisely in each other's trail. The fine hair on my neck lifted, though I knew the wolf was gone. A lone hunter, like I was, migrating into country unknown to this individual, but familiar to long-vanished kin.

As I examined the trail the wolf had broken, I wondered what scared wolves, what raised hackles and hesitation. I imagined wolves stalking by starlight, slipping past places they feared, traveling beyond known safety, reclaiming this ancestral home.

FLORENCE KRALL SHEPARD

The Shape of Things

from Ecotone: Wayfaring on the Margins *(1994)*

WHEN THE LETTER FROM WALTER PROTHERO, PROFESSIONAL HUNTER and free-lance writer, arrived inviting me to accompany him on an Arctic expedition, I accepted without hesitation. Alaska beckoned in complex and obscure ways.

Amidst preparations for departure, two fears gave me pause to reconsider: doubts of my ability to withstand the demands of the harsh Arctic wilderness and a dreadful fear of *Ursus arctos horibilis,* the grizzly bear. But longing for repose and escape from the stress of academic life, I was drawn toward the pristine ambience of the National Arctic Wildlife Refuge, some three hundred miles north of the Arctic Circle.

With summer school and administrative duties behind me, I was packed and standing self-consciously in line at the airline baggage check-in counter with my well-worn walking stick in hand. The ticket agent and people in line stared at me with curiosity and amusement as I checked my baggage, a 30-gallon steel drum, purchased according to Walt's instructions and filled with warm clothing, camping equipment, and 180 dehydrated meals that I had prepared for the journey.

DAY 1, CIRCLE, ALASKA

"This is the End," the sign reads as you enter Circle, Alaska. Walt met my plane last night in Fairbanks, and we drove the 150 miles over the graveled Steese Highway to this Kutchin Indian village where he has built a cabin and makes his home. The sign refers to the most northern point of the U.S. highway system on the banks of the Yukon River, but with my unrelenting fear of bears, I take the message literally. I am prepared for any eventuality. Before leaving home, I updated my will and in my pack I carry a white bear fetish with shell, turquoise, and sinew given me by Terry for protection.

We have been busy all day preparing to fly out tomorrow with Roger Dowding, a bush pilot. I have been writing letters and trying unsuccessfully to eliminate and lighten the contents of my backpack. I cannot leave behind the books that I carefully selected for this journey: Simone de Beauvoir's *The Ethics of Ambiguity,* which speaks to my present state of mind; the words of Henry Moore in *Henry Moore: The Reclining Figure,* whose sculptures have fascinated me of late; Maurice Merleau-Ponty's *Sense and Nonsense,* which I hope will help me make sense of the nonsense of the past few months; and *The Sacred Paw,* written by Paul Shepard and Barry Sanders on the "bear in nature, myth, and literature" and given to me by Paul whom I recently met and whose books have been primary resources for students and myself.

The neighboring families of this village are drying salmon. The men mend nets while the women fillet the red-meated fish. Down the road the trapper in a vest fashioned of caribou and grizzly pelts is feeding the dogs that pull his sled to trap lines in the winter. They rise out of their kennels snarling viciously each time I pass by. The Yukon River flows past the cabin. Sandhill cranes that nest on its banks fly over in twos and fours, sounding as they pass.

DAY 5, THE SHEEP CAMP, BROOKS RANGE
We are camped at forty-five hundred feet on a soft bed of lichen that absorbs the rain and provides a cushion for our tents. The campsite allows a panoramic view to the southeast of tundra slopes, mostly above timberline, tumbling to the Sheenjek River far to the east. Above to the northwest the steep faces of the mountains in the Brooks Range rise majestically to eight thousand feet. We are within a valley where glacier and water have sliced through the soft sediments of a great anticline. Traces of bedrock are visible in cliff faces above where the severe climate has worn the mountains to pearly-gray, rounded contours. Nestled at the center, our tents sit within a huge reclining Mother Goddess with knees, breasts and long, ridge-limbs separated by green tundra space.

An eternity has passed since that morning only four days ago when I stood shivering at the edge of a gravel runway waiting for Roger to ready his blue and white Cessna 185 for take-off. He was unable to get a weather report—usually obtained by calling various spotters on the telephone for visual observations—but that day they couldn't see the sky. Three raging muskeg fires had reduced visibility at Fort Yukon and the surrounding area to zero. We took off nonetheless. Parts of the Yukon Flats were obliterated and at one point we had to climb out of smoke that engulfed the cabin. Beyond the fires, Roger put the plane on automatic, took a copy of *Playboy* from the pocket behind his seat, and began reading. With some concern, I watched him out of the corner of my eye as at times he leaned against the instrument panel and dozed as we bumped along over rough air currents above a jigsaw of lakes, dwarfed spruce, and caribou trails. Soon muskeg gave way to an expansive valley flanked by mountains with a stream meandering in huge sweeps across its width. Peering over the instrument panel, Roger pointed to Lobo Lake where, he said, he would meet me in 24 days if all went well. We flew up the valley toward the Brooks Range whose north face drains into the Arctic Ocean. From time to time Roger executed unannounced dives (that left my heart in my throat and my stomach in disarray) to check on wolves and moose. Then as we approached the south face of the mountains, he swooped low, circled a steel-gray sandbar along the Sheenjek River, touched down on the near edge, and stopped a "heartbeat" (to use a trite but very true expression) from the water on the opposite end.

Walt and Roger hopped from the plane and began unloading our gear quickly as I for a moment stood on wobbly legs trying to gain control of my stomach and bearing. Roger took off immediately tipping his wing as he headed south. Walt inflated rubber rafts into which we loaded the gear, and we floated to the confluence of the Sheenjek and the unnamed stream we were to follow into the Brooks Range. We cached our supplies in two thirty-gallon steel drums and hid them in the willows. Then Walt sprayed them with oven-cleaner to deter bears, which, he said, had once ripped his drums apart. On the beach were tracks of caribou, moose, wolf, fox, and grizzly. I looked at the huge footprints of the bear and then placed my hands within them as I tried to visualize the animal that left such an impression.

It took us two days to hike to this campsite, through a treacherous mountain stream with smooth tumbled boulders and across muskeg thick with cushions of buoyant lichen and moss that have overgrown rock and fallen trees that form hidden pitfalls into which we occasionally broke. I hiked with extreme caution knowing the difficulty a broken leg or sprained ankle would present. Huge fresh scats of bears, tinted red and blue with berries, dotted the landscape. Walt walked ahead with his rifle and proceeded cautiously whenever we did not have an open view. When the mountains were clearly in sight, he began scanning them for Dall sheep that grazed high on their tops and, from the distance, appeared as small white dots.

We chose this campsite because it sits high on the mountainside with a view on all sides and is near a stream—and because, at the time, I could hike no farther. As we set up our tents, caribou from the Porcupine Herd streamed along a trail above the camp oblivious of us. A grizzly roamed a near-by ridge eating berries. High above on the edge of a cliff was a lone Dall sheep.

Shortly after we made camp, it began to rain. I watched incredulous as Walt took his rifle, said he was going hunting, and headed up the mountain. Exhausted and fearful, I crept into my tent and fell asleep trembling. Somewhere in my dreams, I heard the shot and later I was awakened by the sound of heaving and puffing and something heavy falling to earth with a thud outside my tent. I peered out at an enormous head of a ram, with a cape of white fur flowing from its neck. I reluctantly emerged from the tent, lit the gas stove, and prepared food for Walter as he changed into dry clothes. He drank warm liquids and ate until his body had regained warmth and energy. Then he spread the cape of fur about the huge ram skull and faced it into the night sky with glassy-eyes peering into the rain and circular horns framing its ghostly face. Before turning in, he announced that we would hike up to get the sheep meat the next day and carry it back down to the Sheenjek. My firm reply as I crawled into my tent was that there was no way I would go anywhere the next day.

Exhausted from the flight and hike, and Walt additionally depleted by the hunt, we slept deeply and almost continually for two days. Arctic days and twilight nights merged as the rain continued to fall. Except for an hour or two in the middle of the night, there was enough light to read by. I nibbled trail mix, and at times, when I heard him stir, prepared a meal with Walt. Today, on the third day, we arose from our death-like torpor to hike to the high slope to retrieve the sheep meat. Walt removed the ribs and sliced meat from the bone, leaving the carcass for ravens and bear. Back at camp, we hung the meat in a willow near the stream away from camp. This evening we braised ribs over a fire of willow and birch. The taste of tallow reminded me of my childhood on the sheep ranch in Wyoming. I felt at home. There was no more talk of returning to the Sheenjek.

DAY 6, SHEEP CAMP

Today we went "hunting" with binoculars and cameras. We climbed the steep tundra slopes laced with scree, leaned into gale-force winds, and crossed the divide into the headwaters of Old Woman's Creek. I nestled down in a protected spot among boulders as Walt, with next year's hunt in mind, stalked and photographed six Dall sheep grazing under cliffs nearby. The sun played across the slopes. Buoyant cumulus clouds driven by high winds created a kaleidoscope of shadow and light and changing hues. I waited expectantly in this sea of color for brief moments of sunshine and warmth. During the days we have been here, the slopes have changed from pea green to burnt umber. Berry bushes are scarlet, magenta, and burnt orange. Giant saxiphrage leaves are yellow, edged with brown, and the willows are golden.

We hiked the creek bed back down to camp. Signs of *Ursus* were everywhere. In a huge mound hollowed at the center, a day bed for the mother bear and cubs, Walt found golden clumps of her under-hair which he gave to me. It was soft as down and had a sweet, spicy fragrance.

Bordered by a mossy carpet, the stream grew as we descended, and, in places, it coursed under limestone into dark caverns that echoed its subterranean sounds. Near camp we found a fresh caribou kill, probably by wolves, Walt said. The skull and vertebrae were entirely stripped of flesh; only the skin ripped in many pieces remained, and the legs were missing.

Back at camp we saw a grizzly crossing the skyline high on the ridge where we had gone to retrieve the ram. Silhouetted against the twilight sky, it lifted its nose to the heavens and then turned and ambled over the hill unaware of two respectful humans, dwarfed, far below staring in awe at its massive, shaggy form.

DAY 9, SHEEP CAMP

For two days storms have repeatedly moved through this valley. Each morning the snowline descends, and the mountains are shrouded in clouds. Last night the splatter of raindrops on my tent turned to the rustle of granular snow. At midnight, all was quiet. This morning I awoke to a thick, white blanket of snow that covered landscape and tent. As I made a quick trip to empty my bladder, I saw the grey form of a wolf trailing a lone caribou across the stream.

During these stormy days, we have again returned to the privacy of our tents/nests/caves. Rested, I now spend my time reading, writing and thinking. I roll over my thoughts as I find a new position of repose. The raindrops and stream below provide background for meditation. I have been reading Paul's description in the *Sacred Paw* of how from the time she gives birth to her young in the den during hibernation until they leave her side, the mother bear "licks them into shape" and educates them as they grow. She cuffs them if necessary, and "when they are old enough, she deliberately sets them on their own." My thoughts dwell on relationships, duties to others, and my perceived role to form, lick, and "shape up" my children and as a teacher, as Madeleine Grumet pointed out in her *Bitter Milk*, "other people's children" as well. Bear mother. Have I licked these children well? I sniff bear hair, anticipate fleeting possibilities out of the corner of my eye. I have been too busy licking others. Now I must lick my own wounds.

DAY 11, SHEEP CAMP

Early yesterday, Walt left camp for an all-day hike into the high mountains. He did not invite me along; in fact, he strongly suggested I do a "solo" to overcome my "irrational fear of bears." After cleaning up around camp and gathering wood, I decided to take his advice, although the prospect of hiking without Walt and his gun terrified me.

I climbed straight up from camp toward a ridgeline. The tundra was pock-marked with bear diggings for roots and ground squirrels. As I walked toward the ridgetop, I kept imagining meeting a bear head on as it came over the top from the other side. My heart raced with exertion and fear until I crested the ridge and could see in all directions. Another drainage basin fell away on the other side joining the creek that ran through camp and on down to the Sheenjek. In the distance were the Davidson Mountains, snow-covered at high elevations. I lay in the sun, listening to the wind howl around a matterhorn to the east, an uncommon feature in this land where everything is weathered smooth. After years of reclining figures, Henry Moore, the famous British sculptor, had returned to this primal landscape, where knees, breasts and hips are separated. Here the form of space becomes more understandable and more palpable.

Walking back to camp, I kept alert, scanning the tundra for signs of movement. Having faced the bear alone, I was beginning to understand my fears. I respect the bear all the more, and should I meet her, I will undoubtedly quake, or perhaps faint dead away. But now I am beginning to deal with the bear herself and not some spectral creature hidden behind each knoll and shrub upon which I have heaped my unnamed anxieties.

Today I joined Walt for a hike up the canyon where yesterday he saw a sow and her two cubs. At one point, I left him and crossed a saddle to look down the long slopes toward the north. Rocky pools held tobacco-colored sphagnum. Mounds of cushion plants, grizzly gold, were swollen plump from recent precipitation, and nutmeg-brown saxiphrage smelled like incense. Frosted bear berries and blueberries that had lost their juicy turgidity, left a bittersweet taste in my mouth, and cranberries growing flat on the ground were crisp and tart.

My legs grow short as I walk across the vast tundra. It dwarfs me; I become squat and stocky. As I lean over to sip water from a placid pool, I expect to see reflected the face of a crone, wrinkled, leathered with a toothless smile and squinting eyes shining with secrets of what has been, of things yet to come.

Walt has made no mention of leaving this camp, I suspect he has enjoyed the stay. But time for leaving draws near. Our food is running low. He believes we are the only humans to have walked on this land since time began. The Indigenous People did not come this way, he says, and modern hunters do not come here. I accept his declaration although it is difficult to comprehend. Nonetheless it makes me tread lightly and respectfully.

DAY 13, SHEENJEK RIVER

Yesterday morning we awoke to sunshine and, with only one day's supply of food left, decided to leave the "sheep camp," hike down to our cache and begin our float down the Sheenjek. The temporal dimension of the mountain experience will remain eternal and deep. Time had substance, quality and persistence.

Walt walked ahead with the ram's horns on his pack like some Paleolithic hunter. We hiked hard all day, across muskeg rather than down along the creek. When finally we crossed its confluence with the Sheenjek, I felt a deep affinity for this little stream that sang to us in the mountains. It was like a child whose beginnings I had witnessed. It had grown and now joined another stream on its path to the Pacific. We set up our camp on a sandbar near it and near our cache of food.

Walt went fishing for grayling this afternoon. It was a sunny, warm day. I gathered wood and then decided to bathe. Unable to withstand the icy cold waters of the stream, I filled every canteen and pan, built a fire, and heated the water. I stood on a plastic bag and lathered my entire body with Dr. Bronner's Eucalyptus Soap, shampooed my hair, and rinsed down all at once. I saved the last pan of hot water and poured it over me slowly. Although I used only about two gallons of water, it felt luxurious, my first "shower" in two weeks.

Just as I finished dressing, Roger flew over, circled twice, tipped his wings and headed up the Sheenjek. Walt returned, propped up his duffle bag as a backrest, asked if I'd cook dinner, lay back in the sun, and fell asleep. Using his cast iron fry pan (now that we're floating rather than backpacking, we have more equipment), I prepared a good-looking fried quiche. I broiled the last of the sheep meat and called him to dinner. As we finished eating, Rick, a friend of Walt's, appeared on the river in his raft. He had flown in with Roger—two weeks earlier than expected. He and Walt will hunt moose together after I leave them at Lobo Lake.

DAY 15, SHEENJEK RIVER

We started floating down the Sheenjek early this morning. Time on the river was peaceful and restful. Huge clouds formed and dissipated in place just above us. High above, cirrus clouds rippled in windrows across the sky and alto-cumulus encircled the horizon. Here clouds are proximate and at times form around us as they do in the stratosphere.

A mew gull began circling, diving and crying in order to distract us from her offspring, a gawky brown juvenile barely remaining airborne below her. I lay back on my backpack to witness her aerobatics against the backdrop of streaming cirrus clouds, her show staged and choreographed precisely. She dove, crying out loudly. At raft level, her cry changed to a chatter that sounded like talk. As I talked back to her, she would rise, dive, cry and chatter again. She repeated the sequence over and over, and each time she turned sharply at eye level and soared up into her airy world, I was carried aloft.

The fall colors have deepened. Golden willows are luminous and cotton grass and opening pods of fireweed, back-lighted, stand like candles along the shore. The long, red pods of fireweed have always fascinated me since the day I gathered a huge bouquet and placed it on my dining room table. The next morning when I came down stairs, I thought I had died and gone to heaven. The pods had opened during the night releasing seeds with feathery plumes that floated throughout the first floor of my home.

After most of the day on the river, we chose this sandbar for our new camp. It is about a half-mile long. Brushman Mountain rises to the west. The terrain has changed; there are more trees and willows. We will stay here several days before floating to my final camp at Lobo Lake.

DAY 16, SHEENJEK RIVER

The loon's call reaches me each morning on the mists of cold, gray dawns, the sound rising like a baby's wail. Penetrating and sad, yet somehow familiar, it takes me back to times that match the tones.

Rick, Walt, and I hiked up Brushman Mountain day before yesterday to view the Sheenjek Valley; yesterday they headed out alone in opposite directions. Walt wanted Rick to do a "solo" to prepare for the hunt. They took their rifles in case of unexpected encounters with bear or moose.

I was writing in my journal when I heard the shot echo down the mountain. I had stayed in camp to do chores, clean up, write, and read. It occurred to me that perhaps one of them had come across a caribou, which had all but vanished from the valley since that storm. Later Rick returned from his hike downstream and asked if I had heard the shot. It was getting late so we prepared dinner, placed some aside for Walt, and ate.

Later I stroll along the river. The sandbar was criss-crossed with tracks of the "big four": moose, caribou, grizzly, and wolf. At one point wolf and grizzly tracks ran perfectly parallel as if the two had been out together for an afternoon jaunt. When I returned to camp, I could hear Walt talking to Rick.

"Well, did you bring home the bacon?" I asked Walt as I approached.

He walked up to me, held out something in his hand and said, "Here give *this* to your friend."

In my hand he placed the bloody penis of a grizzly bear.

DAY 18, SHEENJEK RIVER

I have spent the best part of two days helping Walt "flesh" the grizzly skin. I now appreciate the labor that goes into the preparation of animal hides. After removing all of the fat we rubbed it well with salt. It has been hard, tedious work and made my head ache.

We hiked up above camp yesterday to retrieve the skin and bring back some grizzly meat. Last night we had grizzly steaks and spinach soufflé. Walt and I had great difficulty swallowing. Rick ate with gusto. Later in my tent, I heard Rick comment that the night before, after the grizzly kill, Walt looked and acted differently.

I too had noticed the change. He had a strange look in his eye and was trance-like and euphoric. Usually a quiet man, his voice was louder and more animated. Along the way I have been questioning him about his drive to hunt. When he encounters an animal, he says, adrenalin flows, breathing and heartbeat increase. He is primed for action. He has to consciously disengage from the experience in order to aim and shoot accurately. Hunting, he says, is a primal instinct and as natural as eating and sex, an experience that cannot be rationalized, is tremendously challenging, and reinforces what he values: independence, power, skill, and self-sufficiency. It is a statement of what he is.

Today I questioned him further about his response to killing the bear. This time, he said, there was something more than excitement and reinforcement in the hunt. He had encountered the bear unexpectedly at close range as he came up over a ridge. He immediately engaged a shell and the noise startled the bear who stood up and then lunged toward him on all fours. Walt shot him in the neck at twenty feet. As the bullet hit, the bear looked Walt in the eye before falling over backward, dead. At first Walt would not say what meaning the look carried. Finally he explained: "I saw the look of death in his eyes and knew that it could have been me just as easily. If the shot had been one inch more to the right, he wouldn't have fallen. That look made me realize all the more that we all count the same. I am no more privileged than he. It was his time, but mine is coming." It was very hard to eat the bear, he added, because he realized it was just a matter of chance that the bear was the one being eaten for dinner.

The hunt seemed indeed to be a primal activity that challenged Walt to the utmost and took him to death's door in humility and thanksgiving. It called up an ancestral image that still ran through his veins. He preserved and prized the heads and skins and admired the beauty of the animals he killed. He ate the meat and shared it with others. His aim was straight as an arrow. He was fearless and independent, and he challenged the physical limits of his body. His dedication to hunting did not seem based on violence and domination but rather appeared congruent with Tribal People's respect and thankfulness to the animal for the life taken—and given.

DAY 20, SHEENJEK RIVER
Today I boiled the bear penis and removed the tissue from the small delicate *os bacculum*. Penis bones, called *usiks*, here in Alaska are collectors' items. I will have this one fashioned as a pendant for Paul when I get to Fairbanks.

My "irrational" fear of bears has been replaced by caution and respect. I am sorry Walt killed the bear; I eat him nonetheless and am joined to him in that sacred act. One cannot fear her own flesh and blood. He has taken part in the ritual of my transformation in celebration of *prima materia* the "flesh of the earth" that joins creatures, rock, and vapors rising from dark caverns with resounding melodies.

DAY 22, SHEENJEK RIVER
This morning on a brisk walk across the tundra, I began weeping unexpectedly. Until that moment I had not acknowledged my reluctance to leave this pristine wildness and return to civilization with all of its

turmoil. In the subdued morning light, a cone-shaped pingo, an upthrust of permafrost, was perfectly mirrored in a glass-smooth pond as were the clouds and surrounding mountains. The animals were tame at that hour. A gray jay followed me, almost landing on my head as I sat to rest. An arctic ground squirrel froze and observed me as I passed. The silence of the morning was broken intermittently by piercing cries of ptarmigan and raucous quarreling of ravens flying by with heavy wing beats.

Animals here are in place. Their utilitarian ethic is apparent in all they do. Their actions as well as their curiosity are purposeful, efficient, and aimed at harmonious exploitation of their environs. They have no questions to ask, no dilemmas to face. They do what they do without the conflict of choice. They are healers and teachers and vehicles to other realms.

Last night in my dreams I lay in a coffin. Yesterday afternoon, lying in soft lichen on the top of an esker facing the sky, I watched ravens circle me in anticipation. Images of death are all around as is the intense surge of life. Here the integration of death and regeneration is complete. Like a reclining figure frozen in eternal repose, a part of me wants to remain here in a dark, musky den sheltered by the bear's warmth and held in the embrace of roots. But it is time to move on. I begin the separation.

DAY 24, LOBO LAKE

I am sitting on a blue, white, and orange Chevron gasoline can nursing a small fire with my back to a chilling wind. The can is testimony to the use of this sandbar near Lobo Lake as a rendezvous point and of the insensitivity of humans to wilderness designation. If all goes well, Roger will pick me up here tomorrow morning. The snow-line that keeps descending and is only a few hundred feet above me gives me cause for worry. A tiny speck in this vast landscape, I am gripped with fear momentarily. Why in the world am I here? Will I ever get out?

The tundra has lost its glow. The drainage basins are only faintly yellow and willow leaves along the river are changing to brown. Poplars, berry bushes, and birch are bare and equisetum is the color of porcupine quills. The season has progressed to early winter in the four short weeks since I arrived. It is frigid. I have to wear my heavy down jacket in addition to four layers of clothes in order to stay warm.

Until three days ago, I had not seen the moon. Then it rose full and orange. And last night after midnight, Walt called me out of my tent to witness another spectacle. A shaft of light streamed from Little Brushman Mountain to the north and extended across the sky toward the moon. Wavelike it dispersed to reform in an undulating pale yellow and green curtain in the northwest sky. The aurora borealis was breathtaking but familiar. I had seen it before in a dream that entered my sleep a year before:

Carrying a child in my arms, I was walking with a man at my side. Vast expanses of tundra fell away in all directions around us. The man walked slightly ahead of me, and as I followed him, I kept a wary eye on two young bears following behind. Noticing, he assured me I had nothing to fear. We stopped on the crest of a ridge; the sky was beginning to lighten. Anticipating a sunrise, I was surprised by shafts of light flaring up and undulating like curtains in a breeze across the entire horizon. I turned to speak to the man, but in his stead was a magnificent bear with a head so large it filled my entire field of vision. I was unafraid, assured by some primordial faith that we should be there together. We stood side by side, he on his hind legs, swaying back and forth, witnessing the spectacle of the sky.

DAY 28, WESTERN 708

My spirits rose and fell with the clouds that brought more snow the night before. Without forewarning, Roger's plane suddenly appeared and skimmed the sandbar as he tested it for landing. He disappeared from view but in a moment returned, barely clearing the ridgeline and, with his magical touch, dropped out of the sky onto the sandbar. He made plans with Walt and Rick to pick them up after their moose hunt downstream in two weeks. I said good-bye, and we took off with the usual foot to spare at the end of the sand bar, and just missing the spruce trees on the other side of the river.

We flew down the west side of the Sheenjek along the edge of the mountains, skirting storms, and, when that was impossible, flying through curtains of snow and rain. As we flew south, fall returned. Red-leaved berry bushes surrounded gray stone outcrops on ridge-tops. Flaming yellow drainage basins spilled like lava to the Sheenjek; the tundra had turned brown. Spruce trees cast long shadows northward.

We landed at Fort Yukon, where I caught a flight to Fairbanks. There I visited the Federal Building to buy maps, the University Museum to submerge myself in the natural history of the region, and a jeweler down on Second Avenue who knew all about *usiks*. He polished it to a pearly sheen and then attached a gold loop. As I looked at it, the tiny, ivory-colored bone grew in dimension and accentuated the explanation of scale and size Henry Moore gave in his book, *The Reclining Figure:*

A small thing only a few inches big might seem as if it has a monumental scale. . . . I can't explain what it is that gives monumental scale to something . . . I think it's an innate vision, a mental thing rather than a physical thing. It is in the mind rather than the material.

Bear Paw. Ink drawing from September 2001. DURGA BERNHARD.

POSTSCRIPT

Looking back at this Arctic adventure, I am deeply grateful to Walter Prothero who invited me on his hunt. Although a non-hunter, but, raised among hunters, I gained added appreciation of the sacredness of this life-taking and life-giving experience that has been integral to our condition since we became human. Like images on placid Arctic water, themes of death and transformation in my journals do not reflect a nihilism that turns back on itself in hopelessness and self-destruction, but a human struggle, that although spawned in failure and disappointment and the feminine psyche, emerges hopeful.

The natural world is a good teacher. Animal behavior is never deceitful. Appearances, rather than falsifying and mystifying, are thick with deeper meaning: cone-like pingos rise in response to the pressure of permafrost wherein "form pushes out" as it does in Moore's sculptures. The bear voraciously laps berries in preparation for winter sleep. The northern shrike hovers over me because I move and may be prey. The aurora borealis glows in response to solar flares. The gull becomes an exhibitionist in defense of her young. In these forms, we find clarity, integrity, and hope as well as delight—a soothing balm for embodied pain. But Nature carries metaphorical meaning as well and gives us answers to questions we have not yet asked. I am especially grateful to the bear that Walt killed for its part in this integrating experience.

Autumn in Love

(2000)

TODAY, IT RAINS. DRIZZLES. THERE WILL BE SNOW IN THE MOUNTAINS. A harbinger of winter—when this land will be covered white and the most mundane task becomes a chore. I spend the day at home for the first time in weeks, it seems. The last I can recall it was summer. I devoted most of it to the high country: backcountry patrol, surveying, fighting wildfires. But now I awake and another season is sneaking its foot in the door. Aspen trees with one small clump of south-facing leaves turn yellow overnight, poking out, hanging like a tail or an afterthought. It creeps in slowly like this, then one day I can't help but notice patches in the landscape burning brighter than the sun—yellows, oranges, pinks and reds.

Autumn is a time of fast-paced business: bears are getting fat, ungulates are crazed with love and regeneration, migratory folk head south. In the human community we work, getting winter's wood up, hunting, fishing, berry picking, making last-minute trips to the backcountry—trying to squeeze a year's activities into one season before the rhythm of winter sets in.

I live in a remote cabin in the foothills outside of Bondurant—a small ranching community caught between the prosperity of Jackson and the simplicity of Pinedale. Hunters, ranchers, outfitters, carpenters—and lovers of the wild—inhabit this small valley with their log houses and cabins quietly dotting the rolling hills. I've lived in this humble dwelling for only a few years, but long enough to have the winged, planted and four-legged creatures of this place capture me, weaving me into their lives and deaths.

The hypnotic constancy of rain on my rooftop with dark gray clouds engulfing open space and my body can't help but fall into a slower pace. I think of the quilt I will work on this winter, during the long dark evenings, pieced of the seasons and colors of this land—the pink and rusty-red hues of the Hoback Range, remnants of an ancient sea; the lavender of milk vetch; the pale green of sagebrush in late autumn; the brown and tan coats of elk; the bright yellows of evening grosbeaks in early spring; the velvet greens of spruce and fir; the oranges and reds of leaves fading to fall; the white of snow with a breath of blue and gray; the sparkling, deep-blue sky on a morning of forty-below-zero. It's a patchwork of colors engendered in scraps of fabric taken from memories of times now past. Reincarnating dresses, old lover's shirts, pillowcases, pieces from the workplace and handed-down skirts. I'll use new fabric as well, promises to the future—of memories not yet made.

Perhaps because I am originally a native of western Oregon, the rain always makes me reminiscent, flying me in circles and bringing me back. It is as though rain is the symbol of the circle of life and of seasons, always on the return—however late or desperately needed. And today I'm taken back twelve months: to last year's autumn.

I remember how I did something that fall. I, a vegetarian of nine years, ate steak. Elk steak. I was at the house of a man with whom I'd been carrying on a flirtation. He was young, a ranch-hand and a hunter. He didn't know I was a vegetarian and he offered me a steak. I declined in that polite way people refuse something they really want. I wanted to eat of that elk. He insisted and so, I accepted.

As I cut into the lean steak and worked my teeth into the tough, chewy meat—my jaw moving in circles like an ungulate chewing its cud—I saw a bull elk grazing in a mountain meadow. So clearly did I see his parched, sun-bleached antlers and the drying grasses on which he fed and the sun and the soil and the surrounding pines and the autumn colors of cool heat. And as I ate of that elk and that sun and that grass, I felt for the first time since I moved here that I was sinking my bare feet into the soil and getting dirt under my toenails and bit by ants and cut by small, sharp rocks, and I could feel my blood dripping into the land and the land embedding itself inside me. I ate slowly. I did not feel guilty.

Later, he and I made love and I felt as though I was making love to a young bull elk and to the colors of fall: blood, sex, death, decay and the coming renewal. In the whirl of it all, I could not tell the difference between eating and making love—between the hunter and the hunted.

Not long afterwards—when the earth was white but the sagebrush still stood tall—he disappeared. He was lost to me in the folds and valleys of this place. This man was not a lover, per se. He was more of an encounter—like with a moose—where your paths cross for a few moments, silent words are exchanged, and both parties continue on. Does he remember me? Do the moose remember me? I remember them.

Sometimes I realize how a city attitude has followed me here. In that anxious, desperate, hurried way, I grasp at the bird flying south, trying to hold it in my hands as though time were linear and the bird would not come back of its own accord—sometime, next spring. I live in a world where nothing, it seems, lasts forever. Entire species enter extinction, wild lands

are destroyed, wildlife corridors are severed by mining and logging operations. It is no wonder I'm always in a hurry to fall in and out of love, to
grasp it, hold it—like trying to hold water. But what if love did last forever? Could I flow with the river, instead of trying to hold it still?

Since then, another twelve moons have passed and the pine grosbeaks
returned to my feeder this winter, the sandhill cranes back to the wetlands
this spring and once again, the aspen leaves are turning the colors of the
setting sun. Perhaps living in this place has brought me closer to another
logic. The logic of beauty and of seasons. The logic of wildness.

Now, I've met another man—Adam. He is the First Man and yet for
me, the last. I found his heart swimming, up stream, in the Upper Green
River. He is a fisherman. And a hunter. He has a bony lump on the back of
his head and says it's because he is a Neanderthal. While hunting, he gets
aroused—he says it's the chill in the air, being in the woods. But I think
he's taken enough elk into his body that he's become one. Adam is not
entirely human, which—in my humble opinion—is to be fully human.
And like the deer and elk and moose rubbing their antlers on aspen
trunks, on each other—it is that time of year when my wild lover and his
prey stumble around the woods, driven by hormones and the desire to
love. Hunting season. Mating season. Autumn, in love.

Today, as I listen to the rain patter on the rooftop, I daydream of the
kind of time and space I'll be in this winter, hand-quilting a patchwork of
stories—the fabric of place. Every stitch made in mindful meditation, in a
slower time. Wintertime. Earth time. My lover is beautiful and he is wild.
I think beauty and wildness rest in the kind of space where quilts are
stitched by hand, the kind of place where love is born and nurtured. I
hope he and I will wallow there this winter—our hot breath meeting cool
air, our bodies engulfed in the warmth of a patchwork quilt. And I hope
our love is lived not in modern time, but rather in the rhythm of seasons.
Earth time—eternally slow. I think I've realized now that love can last forever; that as long as there is wild nature there will be lovers in—and of—
wildness.

Early evening and the sun burns through the slowly lifting rain clouds. As
I sit on the grassy knoll above the cabin, looking toward the horizon
stretched pink with hues of the Hoback Range, I can feel the warmth of the
sun kiss the side of my neck with a lover's gentle touch and a loner's timid
smile. They say wolves are moving down from Yellowstone, into the Upper
Green River basin. They say grizzlies are more plentiful. And the ravens,
they're getting fatter. There are obstacles, no doubt, and there will be more.
Yet now, at this moment, I can't help but think we have everything to look
forward to.

PART TWO

First Kill

ONE DOES NOT HUNT IN ORDER TO KILL, ONE "KILLS IN ORDER TO HAVE hunted." This remark by the Spanish philosopher José Ortega y Gasset is surely one of the most frequently quoted—and almost as frequently misunderstood—sentiments about hunting. Invoked as an apology for hunting, and generally by way of responding to arguments against hunting, it makes the kill seem almost beside the point, as if it were at best a necessary evil. And yet, while it is certainly true that hunting is a complex process that involves so much more than taking an animal's life, there is no getting around the fact that, ultimately, the purpose of hunting is to kill. If this were not the case, there would be no meaningful difference between hunting with a gun or bow, and hunting with a camera.

At no point in any hunter's career is she or he more alive to this fact than at the very beginning. All of the preparation and practice, the study and training, the mental and physical conditioning the fledgling hunter undertakes are concentrated on that one event which has yet to happen, which—with a profound sense of responsibility—the hunter herself must make happen. She will know when the moment is right, to take that first life. And she knows that when she does, she will be forever changed.

Perhaps because the first kill plays such a transformative role in hunters' self-understanding, crafting a story about it is itself something of a rite of passage for hunting writers. Yet it is deceptively easy to lapse into cliché in such stories, to cover or evade the emotional complexity of the central moment of the narrative. It's easy to fudge the details about what exactly happened, how it felt and what it meant. The four writers in this section resist such temptations.

Realization

(1997)

A LL THE HUNTERS I KNEW WERE COMFORTABLY INSIDE THAT DAY, SMUG with the season's success. That rankled as I trudged up the ridge on this last day of what had seemed a very long doe season. How many times had I made similar climbs?

The wind was freezing. My heavy boots made my feet sweat when I walked and froze my toes when I stopped. I was 14, had never killed a deer, and was beginning to think I never would.

"I'll make a swing around," Dad whispered, indicating the hemlock-covered slope on the right side of the hollow. "See if I can move some to you."

I nodded and tightened my grip on the .30/06, but 14 year olds aren't very good at hiding their frustrations. Dad took only a couple of steps in the squeaky, thin snow and turned around.

"Hunting isn't a contest," he said quietly.

As he moved off I stomped my feet to warm them, feeling bad that he'd seen how I really felt. But he couldn't possibly under-stand—he *always* got his deer. I sighed and leaned back against the broad tree trunk, the rough bark biting into my shoulder blades through the down of my hunting coat. I began scanning the hillside, moving my eyes and not my head, as Dad had shown me.

They came about 20 minutes later, crossing the hollow above me, moving toward the hemlocks. They were strolling along in a

"Stacey, Laramie Range, Wyoming."
© BARBARA BOSWORTH, 1993.

63

line, three of them, all does. I peered through the scope and saw only the safe, tree-covered side hill behind them. I took a shaky breath, put the crosshairs on the chest of one of the deer, and pulled the trigger.

I didn't hear the shot go off, and I was astonished as I recovered from the recoil to see the deer on the ground, unmoving. I cranked another shell into the chamber, put the safety on, and ran up the hill as fast as I could.

I fell to my knees, gasping, beside the dead deer, seeing the wind ruffle its coat, the bright blood on the snow. It seemed a gift I didn't deserve. Then I saw Dad bounding across the hollow, grinning so crazily I hardly recognized him. That's when I realized that the greatest hunter I knew hadn't killed a deer for the last three years.

He'd been too busy hunting with me.

The Imps and My Elk

from A Woman Tenderfoot *(1900)*

IF YOU WANT TO SEE ELK, YOU JUST FOLLOW UP THE ROAD TILL YOU STRIKE a trail on the left, up over that hog's back, and that will bring you in a mile or so on to a grassy flat, and in two or three miles more you come to a lake back in the mountains."

Mrs. Cummings, the speaker, was no ordinary woman of Western make. She had been imported from the East by her husband three years before. She had been "forelady in a corset factory," when matrimony had enticed her away, and the thought that walked beside her as she baked, and washed, and fed the calves, was that some day she would go "back East." And this in spite of the fact that for those parts she was very comfortable.

Her log house was the largest in the country, barring Captain Jones's, her nearest neighbour, ten miles up at Jackson's Lake, and his was a hotel. Hers could boast of six rooms and two clothes' closets. The ceilings were white muslin to shut off the rafters, the sitting room had wallpaper and a rag carpet, and in one corner was the postoffice.

The United States Government Postoffice of Deer, Wyoming, took up two compartments of Mrs. Cummings's writing desk, and she was called upon to be postmistress fifteen minutes twice a week, when the small boy, mounted on a tough little pony, happened around with the leather bag which carried the mail to and from Jackson, thirty miles below.

Drawings by S. N. Abbott from Grace Gallatin Seton-Thompson, A Woman Tenderfoot.

"I'd like some elk meat mighty well for dinner," Mrs. Cummings continued, as she leaned against the kitchen door and watched us mount our newly acquired horses, "but you won't find game around here without a guide—Easterners never do."

Nimrod and I started off in joyous mood. The secret of it, the fascination of the wild life, was revealed to me. At last I understood why the birds sing. The glorious exhilaration of the mountains, the feeling that life is a rosy dream, and that all the worry and the fever and the fret of man's making is a mere illusion that has faded away into the past, and is not worth while; that the real life is to be free, to fly over the grassy mountain meadow with never a limitation of fence or house, with the eternal peaks towering around you, terrible in their grandeur and vastness, yet inviting.

We struck the trail all right, we thought, but it soon disappeared and we had to govern our course by imagination, an uncertain guide at best. We got into dreadful tangles of timber; the country was all strange, and the trees spread over the mountain for miles, so that it was like trying to find the way under a blanket; but we kept on riding our horses over fallen logs and squeezing them between trees, all the time keeping a sharp watch over them, for they were fresh and scary.

Finally, after three hours' hard climbing, we emerged from the forest on to a great bare shoulder of the mountain, from which the whole country around, vast and beautiful, could be seen. We took bearings and tried to locate that lake, and we finally decided that a wooded basin three miles away looked likely to contain it.

In order to get to it, we had to cross a wooded ravine, very steep and torn out by a recent cloudburst. We rode the horses down places that I shudder in remembering, and I had great trouble in keeping away from the front feet of my horse as I led him, especially when there were little gullies that had to be jumped.

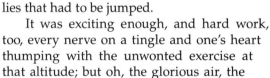

It was exciting enough, and hard work, too, every nerve on a tingle and one's heart thumping with the unwonted exercise at that altitude; but oh, the glorious air, the joy of life and motion that was quite unknown to my reception- and theatre-going self in the dim far away East!

We searched for that lake all day, and at night-fall went home confident that we could find it on the morrow.

Mrs. Cummings's smile clearly expressed 'I told you so,' and she remarked as she served supper: "When my husband comes home next week, he will take you where you can find game."

The next morning we again took some lunch in the saddle bag and started for that elusive spot we had christened Cummings's Lake. About three o'clock we found it—a beautiful patch of water in the heart of the forest, nestling like a jewel, back in the mountains.

We picketed the horses at a safe distance, so that they could not be seen or heard from the lake. At one end the shore sloped gradually into the water, and here Nimrod discovered many tracks of elk, a few deer, and one set of black bear. He said the lake was evidently a favourite drinking place, that a band of elk had been coming daily to water, and that, according to their habits, they ought to come again before dusk.

So we concealed ourselves on a little bluff to the right and waited. The sun had begun to cast long lines on the earth, and the little circle of water was already in shadow when Nimrod held up his finger as a warning for silence. We listened. We were so still that the whole world seemed to be holding its breath.

I heard a faint noise as of a snapping branch, then some light thuds along the ground, and to the left of us out of the dark forest, a dainty creature flitted along the trail and playfully splashed into the water. Six others of her sisters followed her, with two little ones, and they were all splashing about in the water like so many sportive mermaids when their lordly master appeared—a fine bull elk who seemed to me, as he sedately approached the edge of the lake, to be nothing but horns.

I shall never forget the picture of this family at home—the quiet lake encircled by forest and towered over by mountains; the gentle graceful creatures full of life playing about in the water, now drinking, now splashing it in cooling showers upon one another; the solicitude of a mother that her young one should come to no harm; and then the head of them all proceeding with dignity to bathe with his harem.

Had I to do again what followed, I hope I should act differently. Nimrod was watching them with a rapt expression, quite forgetful of the rifle

in his hands, when I, who had never seen anything killed, touched his arm and whispered: "Shoot, shoot now, if you are going to."

The report of the rifle rang out like a cannon. The does fled away as if by magic. The stag tried also to get to shore, but the ball had inflicted a wound which partially paralysed his hindquarters. At the sight of the blood and the big fellow's struggles to get away, the horror of the thing swept over me.

"Oh, kill him, kill him!" I wailed. "Don't let him suffer!"

But here the hunter in Nimrod answered: "If I kill him now, I shall never be able to get him. Wait until he gets out of the water."

The next few seconds, with that struggling thing in the water, seemed an eternity of agony to me. Then another loud bang caused the proud head with its weight of antlers to sink to the wet bank never to rise again.

Later, as I dried my tears, I asked Nimrod:

"Where is the place to aim if you want to kill an animal instantly, so that he will not suffer, and never know what hit him?"

"The best place is the shoulder." He showed me the spot on his elk.

"But wouldn't he suffer at all?"

"Well, of course, if you hit him in the brain, he will never know; but that is a very fine shot. Your target is only an inch or two, here between the eye and the ear, and the head moves more than the body. But," he said, "you would not kill an elk after the way you have wept over this one?"

"If—if I were sure he would not suffer, I might kill just one," I said, conscious of my inconsistencies. My woman's soul revolted, and yet I was out West for all the experiences that the life could give me, and I knew, if the chance came just right, that one elk would be sacrificed to that end.

The next day, much to Mrs. Cummings's surprise, we had elk steak, the most delicious of meat when properly cooked. The next few days slipped by. We were always in the open air, riding about in those glorious mountains, and it was the end of the week when a turn of the wheel brought my day.

First, it becomes necessary to confide in you. Fear is a very wicked companion who, since nursery days, had troubled me very little; but when

I arrived out West, he was waiting for me, and, so that I need never be without him, he divided himself into a band of little imps.

Each imp had a special duty, and never left me until he had been crushed in silent but terrible combat. There was the imp who did not like to be alone in the mountains, and the imp who was sure he was going to be lost in those wildernesses, and the imp who quaked at the sight of a gun, and the imp who danced a mad fierce dance when on a horse. All these had been conquered, or at least partially reduced to subjection, but the imp who sat on the saddle pommel when there was a ditch or stream to be jumped had hitherto obliged me to dismount and get over the space on foot.

This morning, where we came to a nasty boggy place, with several small water cuts running through it, I obeyed the imp with reluctance. Well, we got over it—Blondey, the imp, and I—with nothing worse than wet feet and shattered nerves.

I attempted to mount, and had one foot in the stirrup and one hand on the pommel, when Blondey started. Like the girl in the song, I could not get up, I could not get down, and although I had hold of the reins, I had no free hand to pull them in tighter, and you may be sure the imp did not help me. Blondey, realizing there was something wrong, broke into a wild gallop across country, but I clung on, expecting every moment the saddle would turn, until I got my foot clear from the stirrup. Then I let go just as Blondey was gathering himself together for another ditch.

I was stunned, but escaped any serious hurt. Nimrod was a great deal more undone than I. He had not dared to go fast for fear of making Blondey go faster, and he now came rushing up, with the fear of death upon his face and the most terrible swears on his lips.

Although a good deal shaken, I began to laugh, the combination was too incongruous. Nimrod rarely swears, and was not quite unconscious what his tongue was doing. Upon being assured that all was well, he started after Blondey and soon brought him back to me; but while he was gone the imp and I had a mortal combat.

I did up my hair, rearranged my habit, and, rejecting Nimrod's offer of his quieter horse, remounted Blondey. We all jumped the next ditch, but the shock was too much for the imp in his weakened condition; he tumbled off the pommel, and I have never seen him since.

Our course lay along the hills on the east bank of Snake River that day. We discovered another beautiful sapphire lake in a setting of green hills. Several ducks were gliding over its surface. We watched them, in concealment of course, and we saw a fish hawk capture his dinner. Then we quietly continued along the ridge of a high bluff until we came to an outstretched point, where beneath us lay the Snake Valley with its fickle-minded river winding through.

The sun was just dropping behind the great Tetons, massed in front of us across the valley. We sat on our horses motionless, looking at the peaceful and majestic scene, when out from the shadows on the sandy flats far below us came a dark shadow, and then leisurely another and another. They were elk, two bulls and a doe, grazing placidly in a little meadow surrounded by trees.

We kept as still as statues.

Nimrod said. "There is your chance."

"Yes." I echoed, "here is my chance."

We waited until they passed into the trees again. Then we dismounted. Nimrod handed me the rifle, saying:

"There are seven shots in it. I will stay behind with the horses."

I took the gun without a word and crept down the mountain side, keeping under cover as much as possible. The sunset quiet surrounded me; the deadly quiet of but one idea—to creep upon that elk and kill him—possessed me. That gradual painful drawing nearer to my prey seemed a lifetime. I was conscious of nothing to the right, or to the left of me, only of what I was going to do. There were pine woods and scrub brush and more woods. Then, suddenly, I saw him standing by the river about to drink. I crawled nearer until I was within one hundred and

fifty yards of him, when at the snapping of a twig he raised his head with its crown of branching horn. He saw nothing, so turned again to drink.

Now was the time. I crawled a few feet nearer and raised the deadly weapon. The stag turned partly away from me. In another moment he would be gone. I sighted along the metal barrel and a terrible bang went booming through the dim secluded spot. The elk raised his proud, antlered head and looked in my direction. Another shot tore through the air. Without another move the animal dropped where he stood. He lay as still as the stones beside him, and all was quiet again in the twilight.

I sat on the ground where I was and made no attempt to go near him. So that was all. One instant a magnificent breathing thing, the next—nothing.

Death had been so sudden. I had no regret, I had no triumph—just a sort of wonder at what I had done—a surprise that the breath of life could be taken away so easily.

Meanwhile, Nimrod had become alarmed at the long silence, and, tying the horses, had followed me down the mountain. He was nearly down when he heard the shots, and now came rushing up.

"I have done it," I said in a dull tone, pointing at the dark, quiet object on the bank.

"You surely have."

Nimrod paced the distance—it was one hundred and thirty-five yards—as we went up to the elk. How beautiful his coat was, glossy and shaded in browns, and those great horns—eleven points—that did not seem so big now to my eyes.

Nimrod examined the carcass. "You are an apt pupil," he said. "You put a bullet through his heart and another through his brain."

"Yes," I said; "he never knew what killed him." But I felt no glory in the achievement.

SUSAN EWING

To Each Her Own

(1993)

WALKING BEHIND A MAN WITH A RIFLE USED TO MAKE ME FEEL LIKE the original natural woman. Male and female, single file: the hunter and the helpmate. Sometimes I would hear movie soundtracks playing through my head, since I wasn't using it for much else. Then I got born again. This nearly religious rebirth came not in a vision in the night but in a yellowed figurine, probably plastic, that almost certainly came from a garage sale; I never asked the man upon whose windowsill she sat. Artemis, Greek moon goddess and huntress. Flowing up from the bare back of a fluid steed, she surged forward with her pack of hounds, wild, elusive, needful of nothing, open-eyed knower of nature. Helpmate of her own damned self. *This*, I suddenly knew, was a *real* woman.

Female hunters are anomalies, like women saxophonists and CEOs. You know they exist, but you rarely meet one in the flesh. Perhaps more fathers and husbands don't encourage the females in their lives to hunt because the girl-woman who carries her own rifle, sleeps in the woods, and brings home her own meat will never be fully tractable. But with or without familial encouragement, some girls find they can't sleep through a full moon night and go forth to prowl the path in search of their she-animal selves. They take role models and inspiration in any form, including statuettes of questionable origin.

When a woman decides to hunt, it's a steep step up a scree slope. If I want sexy underwear—the culturally declared basic female building block—I can simply place an order from one of the five hundred *Victoria's Secret* catalogs that arrive in my mailbox each month. But woman-sized camo coveralls and decent field boots? Unfortunately, Victoria must not hunt.

Besides finding properly scaled clothing and equipment, the other trick is finding a mentor who doesn't care how emotionally independent becoming a successful huntress will cause you to become. The ideal mentor is married to someone else and has hunted well for many years. Like Ron. Ron and I are neighbors in the Gallatin Valley of south-central Montana. A retired Army colonel, Ron grew up in this state but spent his career

72

with Uncle Sam two-stepping around such testing grounds as Vietnam, Nepal, and Salt Lake City. He helped me choose the right rifle (7mm .08 Remington Youth Model 7) and explained the terms cartridge, bullet, and shell so I could speak intelligently in sporting goods stores. Ron is calm, beneficent, and can walk the legs of younger people to stumps.

The first time he took me deer hunting I wounded a small forked-horn mule deer. I had been afraid, pulling the trigger, afraid of exactly what happened. I tried to take a second shot but jammed the rifle as the buck limped away.

"Oh Jesus," I whimpered. "Jesus," I moaned. We tracked the deer for three hours before losing the trail. Neither of us said much, just followed small, scattered dots of blood, vivid red against the snow. In the beginning, the tracks took us over, then back over, a fence. Maybe he would be okay.

In addition to the knifing hurt for the deer, I was disgusted with myself. Instead of the strong, respectful, transcendence I had imagined would be born of this act, I had been fainthearted and irresolute.

My grandmother always said if a person showed gumption, most other failings were forgivable. So, instead of wallowing in woe-is-me and withdrawing from the whole affair, as I might have predicted before this happened, I thought of Artemis and the moon and hitched up my psyche. I would keep going out until I had atoned for my equivocation; until I had paid for my ticket to ride this earth with money out of my own pocket.

I still needed Ron. I've cleaned countless fish and skinned a couple of beavers, but my feminine education had thus far not included field dressing a deer. We went back out that same afternoon and the next morning with no luck. The next afternoon we went out again, in the hills behind home.

Parking at the gate just past the last neighbor's house, we pitched up the bank toward the forest. We were crossing the first high meadow when a slobbery blur shot past, grinning wildly at our guns. You would think a good bird dog should know the difference between a shotgun and a rifle. Cody, who belonged to that last neighbor, Larry, was a goofy-headed English setter with a knack for getting loose and ending up at the wrong place at the wrong time. Except in this case, his timing shifted the turn of events in a fortuitous way. He ripped a few circles around us, then theatrically pointed a bush, checking our reaction from the corner of his eye. He failed to make the sell.

"*Shit.*" I had never heard Ron swear before. We tied Cody to the bush but as we walked away he began to shriek. Leaping, twisting contortions accompanied his high-pitched, pitiful cries. Every coyote and mountain lion in the county was surely cocking its head thinking, "Mmm. Dying wounded animal. My lucky day." Ron volunteered to take Cody home and we agreed to meet back at the truck at dark. He would find me if he heard a shot, I would do likewise. I hurried off into the trees pleased at the unexpected opportunity of being ushered to the door of experience then left to venture on alone. Once in the shadows I slowed to take stock. Loaded rifle—my own—hanging comfortably on my shoulder, torso warm under a too-big brown field coat. Gray sky, light breeze from the southwest, lots of sign. In my head were sounds and tracks, no cinematic scores.

I walked for about an hour up and down gullies, across snowed-over, hollow-sounding creeks, around clearings, and through thick stands of Douglas fir. Single, female file, I scrambled over blow-down and side-stepped crisp patches of winterkill arrowleaf balsamroot, mentally mapping the game trails. Snow tucked itself around sagebrush and juniper in the clearings and drifted where it could into the forest.

Having walked long enough to satisfy that pleasure and having explored the area to some point of understanding, I figured to pick a place to sit and wait for a deer to add itself to the scene. I wandered from possibility to possibility like Goldilocks looking for the perfect porridge.

I finally selected a consonant clearing on a harmonic knoll and sat down by a tall bush. Presently, a stump with ears materialized 125 yards downslope, a whitetail doe, legal on my "A" license. She fit well enough in my scope, even sharing space with a limping deer. Her young of that year wandered out of the woods, and through the scope, I watched them browse until they meandered back into the trees out of sight. I could probably have hit the doe, but my shot at atonement disallowed even the mere shade of maybe. Thinking there might be more deer following the route, I skirted down nearer where they had been. As I was wondering what to do next, the *crush,* pause, *crush,* pause of footsteps through dry balsamroot carried up over the side of the knoll. Ron? I was standing there, rifle down, safety on, when a four-by-four whitetail buck stepped into the open 35 yards away.

You can be a tracker, a guide, or an observer of nature without killing an animal, but you can't be a huntress. I thought about wolves. The wolf has been my special animal advisor since before wolves and totem animals were the stuff of calendars and wrapping paper. Would wolf ever speak freely to me in dreams if I never stepped inside her bloody, joyful, essential inner circle? Realizing I might really kill a deer, I began to shake so much I thought I might fall down. But I wasn't afraid. I sank slowly to one knee, but tall clumps of dried grasses blocked the view so I stood back up. The buck was watching.

There is a lovely, romantic notion that in some instances animals give themselves to hunters. In my mind, the conversation began:

"I'm looking for a deer to shoot in atonement and declaration of can-do womanhood. If you don't want to be it, please go away." The doe barked from the woods, the buck held. I raised my rifle, found him alone in the scope and clicked off the safety. He stepped toward me, ears forward.

"I'm shaking too much to feel good about shooting you from this unbalanced position, so I'm going to move my left foot forward to get a better stance. If you run, so be it."

I plopped my left foot forward into a pile of brittle leaves. The deer took two more steps toward me and wheeze-barked. He either really wanted me to have him or my hunting methods were so unconventional they irritated him beyond his better sense.

"I still don't feel steady enough, so I'm going to back up three steps and lean against the tree."

Crunch, crunch, crunch, lean. A sharp branch poked the back of my neck, but at least now I wouldn't keel over. Taking a better wrap of the sling, I breathed deeply and willed calmness.

"I'm ready."

Elegantly focused, the buck faced me for another quarter minute before turning broadside. From him: "If you have the gumption, do it now, because in three seconds I'm gone."

BOOM!

He dropped without so much as a forward lurch. I reached him in time to feel his last heartbeats die away. Sadness and elation, pride and humility draped a cloudy gray comforter around huntress and deer. In the quiet few minutes of death, spirits met, shifted, passed.

Ron heard the shot and came running. "Hallelujah!" he howled.

The buck's clean, white belly hair glowed in the falling dark. We opened him up and slid out the innards, bloodying our hands and knives in this completing ritual. Steam and a delicate freshness rose from the body, the ear that had been so warm when I first touched it turned cold. With a pull-rope around his head and front hooves, we began the trip back to the truck. Down the knoll, across the creek, and up the next draw we dragged him. Across a side hill and down again.

At the last rest stop I leaned back on my elbows and rested the deer's head on my feet, his face pointed toward the stars. Past his profile Orion crouched low on the western horizon. A coyote yipped in the vicinity of the gut pile and a mouse scuttled near my elbow as an owl flew overhead. In ecological equilibrium we trust.

On the way to my house we stopped by Larry's, then Ron's. Daughters, sons, and wives came out coatless in the cold dark to appreciate my first deer. Around here, a dead game animal draws people like a campfire around which they talk and warm themselves. I thought I detected a subtle shift in their tones of voice when they spoke to my newly anomalous and now slightly more elusive self.

It was dark at home; the man in my life was out of town. He would make room for the bigger me. I didn't wash my supper dishes and went to bed with blood under my fingernails. Visiting the buck in the morning where he hung stiffly in the yard, I picked a burr off his nose.

His death—at least for me—is far from final. I will talk with his skull as I bleach it, eat his Host, and dream of wolves. Venison stews will sustain my little family through a Montana winter and deer spirits will sustain a huntress's heart.

Victoria's secrets are fine, but in the moonlight Artemis whispers this: It takes more than underwear to make a woman a woman.

JENNIFER BOVÉ

A Place Among Elk

(2002)

Wᴇ'ʀᴇ ᴏɴʟʏ ᴡᴇᴀʀɪɴɢ ʟᴏɴɢ ᴊᴏʜɴꜱ ᴀɴᴅ ᴘᴀᴄ ʙᴏᴏᴛꜱ ᴡʜᴇɴ ᴡᴇ ᴀʀʀɪᴠᴇ at the turnout on Fisher Hill Road, just outside of Glenwood, Washington. Our motley assortment of fleece, flannel, and camouflage is reserved in a bag with cedar bark so as not to absorb the scent of anything remotely human. Tonight is the night. I am sure of this because it is Sunday, and Ben has an early meeting at the Natural Resource Conservation Service tomorrow morning. I, however, will not be getting up for work with him anymore. Two days ago, I celebrated the first day of my eighth month of pregnancy and the last day of my foreseeable career as a field biologist for the U.S. Fish and Wildlife Service.

Ben parks the truck beneath the heavy boughs of the Doug fir we've come to recognize like a friend and opens the door to the cold. As he begins to unload our gear, I shuffle behind the truck. Ours is the only set of tire tracks in the new dusting of snow, but a girl likes her privacy just in case.

"Announcing our arrival?" he whispers as I crouch awkwardly beside the tire.

I can't look at him or I will start giggling, so I stare at a scattering of raven tracks on the ground.

"At least I won't need to go in the woods."

Ben bundles up in underclothes and camouflage as fast as he can stuff his shivering limbs into them, and he secures his pants with an old skull and crossbones belt buckle. It's a tradition. He reaches out a hand to help me up, and he smiles.

"Missed your boots this time, I hope?"

I give him a shove. "Yeah, thanks. Now will you shut up? You're gonna scare my elk away."

He passes me my flannel pants, sweater, jacket, and the camouflage coveralls that are just barely big enough to accommodate me. This suit is the closest thing I've got to maternity camo, and I wriggle into it like a snake trying to get back into its skin. With my gloves tucked perfectly into my sleeves, I can't get a grip on the zipper, so Ben closes the coveralls

77

over my bulging middle, stretching the material tight. We look at each other and grin. He leans down with his hands cupped on either side of my belly and whispers something I can't quite hear.

Each of us dons a wool hat, and Ben stuffs the ends of my scarf into my collar. I take a pinch of baking soda to swish around in my mouth if for no other reason than it makes us *believe* we are scentless. He grabs his compound, and I sling my recurve and quiver over my shoulder. We double-check our pockets for flashlights, lighters, compass, trail flagging, and the cell phone.

Daylight is fading.

We cross the road and find the broken wire in the fence. Our foot-prints from last weekend have been erased by snowfall, and now there are large cloven tracks on either side of the fence that suggest the herd's passage earlier today. I point to a tuft of sand-colored hair wedged into a barb, and Ben nods. If instinct serves us, they are not far.

Ben drops and slides beneath the bottom wire. As he holds it up a few more inches for me, I do a clumsy knees-and-elbows scoot underneath, careful not to snag my bow on the barbs. He helps me stand and brushes snow from my coveralls.

"You're beautiful," he whispers.

I give him a quick kiss, and crystalline droplets of breath that have already begun to condense on his mustache wet my upper lip.

We march onward, deeper into a grove of stark and skeletal scrub oaks. Our steps are as light and swift as is possible in pac boots, and the new snow is mercifully soft. When we reach the edge of the old-growth conifer stand, we survey the snow for tracks. Scant turkey and a lone blacktail. Just a few paces inside the treeline, though, we discover a gener-ous pile of marble-sized droppings. Definitely elk. Ben picks up a piece and it crumbles between his fingers. Definitely not fresh. We rub our boot soles in the pile anyway, and then we move on.

Within the big woods, we wind along our own familiar path because evidence of the herd's presence is sketchy and tough to follow. The dense forest canopy has filtered the morning's snow into a mosaic of white islands that cautious animals seem to carefully avoid. Fresh track upon fallen sticks and frozen ground are difficult even for a couple of biologists to discern.

Fortunately, the terrain rolls gently from ridge to draw, as I'm not up for much hill-humping anymore. I wrap my hand under my belly for sup-port and comfort. It is weighing heavy tonight, aching near my pelvis like it does frequently these days, and as I walk, I send soothing thoughts to the mysterious little one within.

Rest easy, I tell her, *it's not time for you to stir just yet.*

Finally, after a good mile or two, I spy the clearing ahead. At its far eastern rim, a bright semicircle of sunshine still rings the open meadow and washes the surrounding trees in gold. We are just in time. Ben taps my shoulder, and I stop to look at him. He points to his ear. I am breathing hard, so I take a gulp of air and hold it so I can listen.

The distant snap of a twig splinters the icy quiet.

Ben's blue eyes are locked on mine, and we stand as still as the air.

There is a brushing sound from the trees and then the beating of broad wings—no doubt a turkey roused from its roost.

I continue to lead the way to our secret niche. Now that it is so close to my due date, Ben refuses to let me out of his sight, so we had to find a place where we could hide together. Of course I protested, insisting we'd never see an animal—much less get a shot at one—unless we separated. He wouldn't hear of it, though, and he can be as stubborn as stone.

Ben takes his place among a tight trio of cedars, and I lower myself onto a mound of exposed dirt beside an upturned root wad that serves as a crude blind. On the other side of the downed tree is an elk trail that, although recently used, bears no blemish of prints tonight. It is simply a curving ribbon of dusted snow along which we anticipate the elk will travel.

I pull the glove off my right hand with my teeth so that I can wet my index finger with saliva, and I see Ben doing the same thing. We hold our fingers up in synchrony to the air for some indication of motion. My finger feels almost uniformly chilled, but if there is even the slightest breeze, it is from the east and shouldn't betray us.

I watch Ben for a moment. How many times have I observed him like this in the woods? He scuffs the ground with his boots to move leaves and debris aside. He places another pinch of baking soda on his tongue. He readies his release and pulls his facemask down. Then, he gives me a wink and nestles against the ragged cedar trunks, broad shoulders becoming burls and bow blending into brush.

I move a rock out from under me and settle as comfortably as I can beside the underbelly of the fallen tree. I am still warm from the hike, but I keep my left glove on and slide my scarf up over my face because it will get nothing but colder while I pose motionless, as if asleep. My leather finger tab is stiff in my bare hand so I clench my fist a couple of times to break it in and check my draw length to make sure I have room to pull back my string. Ben pats my head, and I give him a wink back.

I think I'm ready.

The woods are hushed. They, too, seem to hold their breath and listen, waiting for movement. But we do not move. I feel tendrils of patience unfurling as I relax, twining to bark and soil. I study my surroundings— linear edges of tree trunks, the subtle dappling of light on a rust brown rock, and the arch of a bulbous root against a jagged pattern of frost-tinged grass. It is this lovely minutia I think I miss most as an adult. When I was closer to the ground, I knew the secrets of nature's detail.

Gripping my bow, an arrow knocked, it is still a little surprising to find myself in the role of hunter. I was a self-proclaimed animal activist and devout vegetarian throughout college, and I thought that researching wildlife thereafter made me some sort of an expert on wilderness and hunters and cruelty. It was not until I accompanied Ben on our first white-tail hunt that I understood the extent to which my love for nature had been that of an outsider. I began shadowing Ben more often, as a curious observer and student of his skill, and I came to immerse myself in the ways of the animals. As I witnessed the beauty of the ritual, I stepped down from a soapbox built by people who long ago buried their roots beneath concrete, and I began to understand that true hunting has far more to do with patience and awe than bloodlust, and that death in the absence of fear or suffering is not cruel. So I guess it was only a matter of time before I assumed a bow and my own identity on our expeditions. I wanted to join the circle. Now, in my debut season as a huntress, I also carry our first baby, and her presence fills me with purpose. I am an animal mother, wild with child.

As the forest releases its breath, I begin to hear twittering juncos and the *pik* of a downy woodpecker. It seems Ben and I are no longer cause for suspicion—the predators have vanished. I raise my gaze from the ground to see that the halo of sun has faded from the clearing, and with it has fled the fickle warmth of the afternoon. Shapes and lines have smudged into nuances of shadow, transforming my field of vision into a confusing chiaroscuro until my eyes adjust. The air smells like frozen evergreen and sleeping earth through the thick weave of my scarf. It won't be long now.

Dusk will spur the herd. I picture them rising from their beds and mulling around the darkening woods, chirping in low tones of familiarity. One member, an aging cow perhaps, will grow restless. Experience has taught her the signs of safety, and I pray she will sense no danger tonight. The matriarch will strike out along a well-trodden path, leading the others toward this open feeding ground. The herd bull will lumber behind them, slower and more apprehensive now that the rut has ended. I remember his chocolate mane and widely branched antlers perfectly from my glimpse of him in September, and the fevered clarity of his bugle still rings in my ears. I am sure, if he eluded the onslaught of rifle season, that the bull is now more keenly attuned to the threat of hunters. With any luck he, too, will remain at ease, and the dark caravan will draw close to where we hide.

Time passes slowly as we wait, the minutes more viscous in the deepening cold. I am all too aware that the slightest influence may cause the herd's routine to shift, that they may not come at all. Countless hours in the woods have taught me that while humans operate on graceless schedules, elk dance to the rhythm of intuition.

An audible sigh escapes my lips, muffling the sound of a branch breaking somewhere west of us—I can't begin to guess how far. Another moment oozes by, long enough for my conscience to start cussing at me for being careless and potentially blowing our cover, and then I hear it again. It must be the footfall of an animal.

I steal a peek at Ben from the corner of my eye. His gaze is intent on the direction of the sound and his elbow is cocked, ready to draw. I constrict my grip around the bow's riser.

Am I ready?

My heart flutters like a trapped moth even though I know the sound does not necessarily indicate elk. It could be anything from a hefty porcupine to a black bear with a case of early winter insomnia. Images flash through my mind of a 350-pound boar ambling toward us, his pliant nose tugging scents from the air. Would he smell us beneath the baking soda? And if he did, would he approach? An unfamiliar sensation of vulnerability surges hot to my chest. I have never been scared of bears, but pregnancy has changed my perspective on a lot of things. I am acutely conscious of how difficult it would be to shield my belly in the rare event of an attack, and running isn't even a consideration.

I wonder how quickly an arrow would stop a bear.

But whatever kind of creature I might have heard seems to slip away without even a rustle to indicate its retreat, and I am left to wait again in the lingering gray of dusk. I'm getting colder by the minute; the chill of the ground is seeping through my boots and multiple socks to my toes and up into my calves. I wrinkle my nose and the creases are reluctant to smooth. My stomach is growling, quietly for the time being, and on top of the rest I am fighting the urge to yawn. However tightly I cling to my newfound hunter's resolve, I recognize these symptoms as the onset of doubt.

I lean forward slowly, one centimeter at a time, to regain some semblance of a vigilant posture and to rest my belly between my legs. In this position, one of my thighs ends up high-centered on a knobby root or rock that will inevitably begin to deaden my sciatic nerve if I don't shift my legs, but I bite the inside of my cheek and resist the urge to move it. There can be no allowance for the indiscretions of my impatience now that elk season is nearing its end and we have no meat.

Focus, I tell myself, *focus.*

"So, are you ready to go?" Ben whispers.

I turn to him, aghast. "What?"

"I'm hungry, aren't you? Anyway, I don't feel like it's gonna happen tonight." He takes a step away from the tree where he'd been leaning.

He knows how easy I am to sway (as pathetic as that may be) when it's freezing and the prospect of food is involved, so even though we'll both feel guilty about it later, I just shrug and lurch to my knees. So much for focus and resolve. Pausing with my bow planted in preparation to pull myself up, my eyes are enticed around the fallen tree by the outline of a tear-shaped silhouette. Ben is replacing his arrow in its quiver, which he rarely does before we're out of the woods, as I trace the dark shape downward into the curve of a long neck and realize I'm staring at an elk cow not even a hundred yards away.

"Okay," I whisper. "But I have a different feeling."

Incredibly, the cow seems completely unaware of our commotion because she is heading right for us at an easy gait, and there are others following her. I don't know how I didn't hear them before, tromping along like a bunch of cattle. Despite their amazing agility, they are heavy on the hoof and crush deadfall noisily as they move through the woods.

Ben stiffens, knowing he can't risk pulling out an arrow—the cow is too close. I just keep kneeling there, clutching my bow with such intensity that I begin to tremble. My scarf has slipped from my face, which is surely glaring like a beacon through the veil of dusk, and I am jutting from the forest floor in plain sight, an incongruous figure in a realm the elk know intimately. I need to raise the bow several inches in order to draw, and there is no real reason I should not try it. I tell myself to pull back the string, sight in on the cow's lungs, and let the arrow fly with the same confidence I possess when I shoot targets. I am a good shot, consistent and accurate. But the cow is now less than thirty clear yards from me with a calf, a second cow, and possibly more of the herd behind her. There is no question one of them would see me move. If the cow were to stop or sidestep or bolt, I could wound her.

And so I can't. I can't do it.

Blood is throbbing in my ears so loudly that I fear the elk will feel the resonant beat like thunder through the ground. The cow, glorious in her tawny winter coat and every bit as big as a mare, traipses past me on the narrow trail. She is within twenty feet, so close I see the auburn tips of her mane and a healed scar across her foreleg, so close I can smell her heady musk. I am certain she will notice me and startle at any second, but she is fixed on the clearing ahead. She doesn't bat an eye.

The second cow strays from the trail and moves alongside of the first, and I think I might be able to get a shot at her from this angle, but something tickles the calf's curiosity and he steps toward me with his head lowered, attentive to secrets the ground might tell. Each careful placement of his chiseled hooves brings him boldly closer to the strange new tree stump that must bear the smell, if ever so faint, of a different animal. The calf's wide amber eyes roll from side to side, and I could nearly reach out and touch the wetness gleaming in the bowl of his flared nostril. I keep painstakingly steady, though, breathing no more deeply than leaves. I have to remind myself that I am not, nor have I ever been, one of his herd. However burdened I might be by the persistence of empathy, however desperately I might long to run with him, just once, I am the predator.

The youngster turns casually, clambers over a tree limb, and then stops to sniff it. Any seasoned hunter would take advantage of this situation somehow, and I know Ben is so crazy watching all of this that he's considering taking my arrow and plunging it into any one of these elk by hand, but I am new at the game—I am still soft.

One of the cows, who has paused at the edge of the clearing, mews sharply. The calf raises his head and begins to plod away reluctantly, barely missing the toe of Ben's boot. That's when I glimpse the other cow standing fifteen or twenty yards beyond the three cedars. She is mostly hidden behind the trees so that all I can see are pieces of her—the hump of her shoulder and a stout hind flank fringed in creamy light fur. This time, maybe because my chances are better or more than likely because I know she is the one without a calf, I dare to twist my body and thrust the bow out in front of me, brushing Ben's pant leg. My best bet is to aim through the trees so that when she moves I am guaranteed a lung shot. With my left eye squeezed shut, I stretch the string back to the corner of my mouth, steady my broadhead in the open V between the cedars, and I hold.

One of the other elk snorts, and I hear the uneasy shuffle of hooves. They must have seen me draw. My shoulder is burning, and the muscles in my belly are strained. The cow moves forward just enough for me to sight in on the broad barrel of her ribcage, and in that chaotic instant before I decide to release my arrow, I hear the other two bolt. The cow wheels and lunges furiously into the woods, and even if I could have wrenched my torso another inch, I never would have been able to take a shot.

It's over.

I let the bow fall from my frigid fingers and slide the arrow into my quiver. Ben remains silent as I grab his jacket to pull myself up.

All I can think to say is: "I missed my chance before."

He still doesn't speak, and maybe for the first time ever, I'm not sure exactly what he's thinking. Then he hugs me and starts to laugh.

"What's so damn funny?"

"Nothin'," he chuckles. "I'm just proud of you, my tough, crazy, pregnant wife."

My face breaks into an uncontainable grin. "I was good, then, huh? I was invisible."

"Yeah, you were." He looks at me and frowns. "But I don't understand why you wanted to give up so early . . . "

"Oh, no—you're not pinning that one on me," I try to tell him seriously, but I can't keep a straight face. We may be leaving empty-handed, but my spirits are high.

Reaching down to pick up my bow, I feel the baby awaken and start to squirm, so I rub the curve of her back where it protrudes from my stomach and shiver just a little. On some level deep beneath civility or compassion, I am exhilarated by my pursuit of wild and wary prey. I found a place within the circle tonight. Here among the elk, I realize, guilt is of no consequence and there is no such thing as sin.

"You okay?" Ben asks.

"Yes," I assure him, "I am."

"Well, then what do you say we go get something to eat?" He takes my bow and quiver and tosses them onto his shoulder.

"I say it's about time. I'm starving."

Hand-in-hand, we hike back to the road by the light of a luminous moon, feeling our way gingerly along the path. When we get to the truck, we will peel off our layers, crank the heater, and ease into the pleasure of thawing. Ben will slide a Townes Van Zandt cassette into the tape deck, and once we are revived on the warm ride to town, we will begin to reflect on the hunt. Descriptions will flow fast and full like a river in flood, coursing through bottomless bowls of chowder beside the woodstove at the Shade Tree Inn. Our shared images will grow over time into a living, breathing entity with bones of truth and the blood of reminiscence. Such, I imagine, is the birth of any good story.

PART THREE

Adventure

"A WOMAN THAT'S TOO SOFT AND SWEET IS LIKE TAPIOCA PUDDING — FINE for them as likes it." So said Osa Johnson, who appears elsewhere in this volume. The writers in this section, to a woman, would heartily agree with her. The stereotype that men need to "quest" while women prefer to "nest" has probably never accorded very well with reality. The call to adventure—to explore, to test one's limits, to experience the new and the strange—is surely less tied to gender than to individual temperament. Just as there have always been some men who, given a choice, would rather sit at home by a nice warm fire, there have always been women who yearned for something more and different and were willing to put up with considerable inconvenience to break out of the bounds of conventional femininity. Throughout most of Western history, their ability to do so has been largely a matter of class and privilege. The writings in this section bear this out. With the exception of Elinore Pruitt Stewart, whose outlook on women's proper place is the most conventional among this group, these are all women of means, who either came from affluent backgrounds or married into wealth.

Yet they neither wanted nor expected to be pampered. Quite the contrary, in fact. Isabel Savory tolerated scorching heat and Courtney Borden bone-numbing cold, on their respective expeditions. The pseudonymous Marjorie and Agnes Herbert insisted on cutting their own swath as outdoorswomen, rejecting the kindly interventions of well-meaning men. Frances Hamerstrom embarked, at the age of eighty-three, on hunting excursions more rigorous than she had ever undertaken with her late husband. What made these women embark on adventures many men twice their size would shy away from? In part, it was the simple fact that they could. But, surely, a larger part was the fact that they needed to: that for them, a life could not be fully lived in drawing-room or nursery.

MARJORIE

A Breach of Convention

from Outdoor Life *(March 1900)*

PART I. THE HEN CAMP

When I first proposed it, the girls were shocked, then amused, and finally morbidly interested. All the world over, woman is the slave of conventionality, and cringes obediently to its most capricious and illogical dictates as humbly and servilely as a spaniel beaten for chicken-killing fawns at the feet of its chastiser and licks the hand that agonizes it. And there is much that is spaniel-like in every good woman.

Natural instinct is as directly opposed to the overstrained conventionality of these foolish days as can well be imagined—only in women it has been so long habitually subordinated that the instinct has become a latent quantity; while in the dog it breaks occasionally into irrepressible potentiality. So he kills chickens from hereditary intuition in his natural exuberance, while woman, schooled in the bitter lesson of experiences, sins only by enforced omission and makes no commissional bad breaks. With the Nemesis of merciless conventionality ever holding the sword in one hand and her hair in the other she can't afford to!

That was why, on first blush, the girls were shocked.

"Why, Marjorie dear, what can you be thinking of!" said Tess, just fresh from the Bostonian hot-bed of over-cultured propriety. "What would the world say about such an escapade?"

F——— looked up with twinkle in his gray eye. "With no ulterior motive and an apology for presumptuous intrusion into the discussion—I am tempted to remark that it would depend on what world you mean. Your Eastern sphere would doubtless stop aghast in its diurnal revolutions; our Western world at least the man part of it would think it an infer—beg pardon!—an immensely plucky and admirable thing. But you don't dare! You are afraid of Mother Grundy, to say nothing of owls and horn toads and the terrors of unchaperoned solitude. And you couldn't exist two days without the more or less necessary companionship of our despised sex!"

"The very idea!" scornfully exclaimed all three of my girl friends. "Your presumption certainly demands an apology." But I, being older and

87

wiser, only smiled indulgently at the conceited old fellow, and gave him the mental acquiescence which the conditions did not audibly justify. Men ARE almost indispensable nuisances, come to think of it.

Of course his taunt settled it! Passing from the amusing to the interesting stage, our visitors soon began discussing ways and means, and at 10 o'clock they had practically decided on the venture. When F——— generously proffered his assistance in getting us located he was met with an encouraging rebuff of proposed independence which set him to laughing quite unaccountably, and insistently went on poking fun at our project, professing a contemptuous incredulity which had exactly the result he contemplated. When we retired, late that night, it was with the avowed determination of an exclusive "hen camp," as he disrespectfully termed it, on the banks of a creek in the Upper Yampah country as soon as the moon was full enough to make "al fresco" nights a luminous glory.

Five days later found us enroute to a certain excellent camping place where F——— and I had put in many a beatific hour. Our light "democrat" wagon and the four gentlest horses on the ranche—combination team and saddlers, all of them—had been impressed into service and loaded with all the necessary impedimenta to a good outing, we made quite an imposing display.

I, of course, drove the team, and my Boston friends, whom I call Tess, Clarice and Ruth, lolled at ease upon the mountains of bedding, tent, etc., which were placed on top of the load. In addition to comestibles enough to last a full month, we had a full complement of cameras, fishing tackle, extra clothing, etc., and just before leaving F——— stowed away under my feet a case containing his beloved 30/30 Marlin, a Stevens .22 Favorite and ammunition enough to kill all the game in the hills. Then, with much mock solemnity, he strapped about the waist of each of the Bostonese the most gigantic six-shooters that our neighborhood afforded, with the solemn injunction to kill every "he objector" that should presume to question our operations.

At the end he even relented enough to beg to be allowed to go along and see that we were properly encamped, but Bunker Hill was aroused and he was scornfully discouraged.

As we drove over the Thornburg bridge we were somewhat disconcerted to find every ranchman and cowboy for miles around assembled "en cavalcade" to do us honor. It was rather enervating for the pretty "soft soles" behind me to hear the serio-comic observations on the makeup of our outfit, and the grave admonitions on the proper method of killing predatory bears and cougars, but the girls rose to the occasion and Tess rather turned the tables on our delighted tormentors by flourishing her gigantic ".45" and naively inquiring, "And where shall I shoot impudent cowboys?"

That parting shot brought us a yell of approbation and an inspiring "ki-yi-yi!" of farewell cheer as we topped the Sand Creek ridge and dipped into complimentary solitude.

"You'll do!" was the terse cowboy verdict as they rode back, and the girls' faces were a study in crimson as one stalwart young fellow partingly emphasized it with a "Do to eat, bless 'em!"

The trip to camp was uneventful, we stopping overnight at the hotel in Craig, where several of F———'s friends, forewarned, proffered many kindly offices for us. Conventionality here was all on our side and the girls' spirits rose with the sincere frontier plaudits of our pluck and independence. At daybreak we breakfasted and went out to find our team harnessed and ready and everybody embarrassing us with well-meant and timely offers of assistance, all of which were firmly declined as a matter of principle. At 4 that afternoon we were at our camping place. To a ranchman's wife the care of horses presents no difficulty, and ours were soon unhitched, hobbled, and turned loose to their own devices in the rich, sweet, knee-deep mountain grasses which surrounded us. They could be depended on to come back morning and evening to camp after their propitiatory oats and gave me no further concern, water being easily accessible to them.

Then we found a delightfully situated level tent-site contiguous to good wood and water, and after an hour's laughing persistence we managed to get a passable "stand" of our canvas house and all our imperatively requisite and perishable dunnage under cover. Tess and Ruth fossicked for firewood while Clarice and I made down the beds and "tidied" our boudoir. By 6 o'clock we had a good wholesome meal prepared, and four hungry "hens" sat down to a well-earned picking.

In the novelty of it the girls were enthusiastic and lavish in their encomiums of the excellence of the coffee, the tender succulence of the beefsteak, the rich sweetness of the corn-cakes and the general superiority to any house cooked food they had ever eaten. They meant it, too, for hunger is an admirable sauce and our appetites were of the keenest from our long ride and unaccustomed exercise.

Supper over, the fire was replenished generously with large sticks of fat pine, the easy accumulation of which had been a matter of some surprise to me until an investigation, the next morning, revealed a profusion of good dry timber lying about in easy proximity to our camp, each tree and log ending a telltale familiar streak in the soft ground, strewn with broken twigs. Following up on these I found fresh horse tracks, and F———'s kindly consideration was apparent. The reason why "Reddy" had been sent up to Steamboat two days before our departure from the ranche was now clear to me. I smiled at F———'s astute guess as to our unknown destination, and blessed him for his forethought. Half our labor was hereby eliminated. As the girls were totally unsuspicious of his agency in the matter, I did not enlighten them—it would have detracted from the essence of their independence.

It was 10 o'clock when we cuddled up to each other in the two really sumptuous beds of soft blankets, with a foot of live springy hay underneath, and looked out of our open tent door at the brilliant splendor of the moonlit night. Our trusty old ranche dog Colin, a fine specimen of "The Squire" progeny, lay collie-wise curled in comfort at our feet, with eyes half shut, yet wholly alert and vigilant in his sentryship. Brave old dog! The test of his mettle lay thick in evidence along his rugged head and neck where the scars were almost as plentiful as the hairs, and I dozed in assured confidence until a sudden nervous pull from my bedfellow roused me into instant consciousness.

"What is it?" I demanded, with an assumed nonchalance for their benefit, for the girl beside me was trembling in every fibre and her teeth were a-chatter. Nevertheless, my hand cautiously closed on the loaded Marlin at my side. F——— has had to use it more than once on very similar occasions.

"Oh, Marjorie, listen! T-h-e-r-e!" with a gasp that was almost a sob as the hoot of a big horned owl on a dead tree rods from the tent door dismally jarred the silence.

"Pshaw! Only an owl. He won't hurt you. That is our first caller and likely to grow into a familiar, welcome friend before we leave. See him on that branch yonder—against the moon?" And possibly two hours later the dog snuggling closer to my feet awoke me and I heard their peaceful breathing.

The sun was an hour high and shining in our faces when we awoke next morning, and the horses clustering around the wagon were neighing for their oats.

PART II. IN THE BREACH

It is an exquisite pleasure, this coming back to life again from the chaotic land of nescience, whose fullest degree is only possible to the healthily young and happily free. My Bostonese yawned dreamily in blissful content and stretched out their fair white arms in sheer physical delight.

"Oh, Marjorie, what a heavenly morning and how good I feel! Is breakfast ready?" This was what I had hoped for. There are no heart pains in healthy hunger, and the other aches I was apprehensive of for the first night in camp is seldom passed on a bed of roses did not materialize. By the time they had resigned themselves to the necessity of arising, I had ascertained that our old bathing pool was still intact and for the next quarter hour the peeping wood elves regaled themselves with the unwonted sight of three splashing, screaming naiads hilariously disporting themselves in its crystal keep.

As for me, I went fishing. There was a tender gray light on the dark reaches which broke into a pearly iridescence on the ripples with a fore-promise of good sport. My first cast was rewarded with a strike and as I gave him the butt I forgot I was old and superannuated, and tingled to my toe-tips with rejuvenating response. By the time I had reached the bathing pool, I had eight pounds of fish and hooked an elegant fellow just in the ripples above. The girls, who had never seen a trout taken, came swarming in hysterical admiration about me as he broke the water for the last time, and simultaneously implored to "let me try . . . only just once!"

"All in good time, my dears," I assented, "but just now we have more than enough for breakfast, and F———'s first camp law is 'waste no game.'"

"Oh, darn F———!" said the vivacious Tess, and the others looked it, but I was obdurate and dismounted the rod. When they rejoined me at the tent I proposed a police arrangement in which they all acquiesced. Tess was to wash dishes and make the beds, Clarice was to be our drawer of water, while Ruth hewed the wood. I was to be "mule chief" and look after the stock, cook and exercise the function of general superintendent. I am in duty bound to confess that this arrangement was but nominal for they all helped each other out, and sang like larks and chattered like wrens while about it.

All but me—I am too old and set in my ways to indulge in any such emotional excesses. I gave the horses an occasional pat, loafed culinarily and let these superfluous-energied youngsters help me all they wished without returning the favor. My responsibility was enough to counter-balance their aid and I "let them lift the log and helped by grunting," as F——— says.

Breakfast over and the camp tidied neatly, we sat down to a council of ways and means. "In camps like these one always has venison to eat, I have heard," said Tess, insinuatingly. I smiled her an encouragement. "And trout every meal," added Clarice, with gustatory reminiscence. I nodded her another. "And they take pictures," said Ruth, patting her camera anticipatingly. "So we will," I assented, "but just at present—and for a large majority of the succeeding time—we are going to loaf. This evening we will try for a deer, and in the meantime I will give you lessons in fly-casting for it seems"—with a reproachful look at the empty creel—"that I greatly underestimated the piscatorial capacity of this crowd. We'll have to have fish for dinner and you'll have to help catch them!"

"For shame!" they chorused, indignantly. "You ate more than either of us, and you know it!"

"Just so," I complacently agreed, "but all the same we four and Colin here just cleaned up ten good pounds of trout, and the prospect is appalling. Lucky for us the river is full of them!"

There were still stretches of sunless water, and we were soon deep in mysteries of old Izaak's gentle art. After successive hookings of brush, tree-tops, clothing and Ruth's ear, they soon acquired a passable knack, and when we quit at noon we had trout enough for dinner and supper, Tess leading with six while Clarice and Ruth had four each. I superintended and caught nothing except impatient admonitions and a trio of kisses when my pupils landed a fish. They were apt scholars and I felt relieved to know that we were in the future reasonably assured against any fish famine.

Dinner over, by my suggestion the girls brought up a stock of firewood sufficient for the night and remade the tumbled beds.

"We may not be back before dark," I informed them, "and it will save a lot of belated bother. I always like to be beforehand in things while camping, and you'll know why when we get back."

Catching up the horses, I saddled up three of them, and my Bostonese began preparations for the hunt.

"Only two of you can go along," said I, shortly, remarking this. "Or, better still, only one. We need the extra horse to pack in our game."

They demurred somewhat at this, but dutifully agreed finally and drew straws for the choice. It fell to Tess, who looked very Diana-like in her rational costume on top of old Vic.

Promising that the others might subsequently go in their turns, we left them getting their cameras out for a snapping bout and expectantly took our way hillward to a little Mesa that F——— and I had killed many a deer on.

Most deer hunts are alike to the initiated, and I have hunted deer for many years. We rode slowly along the ridge tops, keeping a sharp lookout in the heads of the short ravines and carefully scanning every suspicious shape in the scrub oaks. Suddenly Tess reigned up her horse, and nervously pointing to an adjoining thicket of quaking asps gasped out, her voice tremulous with excitement.

"I am almost sure I saw something moving there. Oh, Marjorie, can it be possible that it is a real live deer?"

It was a likely enough looking place and I quickly dismounted, assuring her that it was more than possible that it was. As I threw a cartridge into the chamber the slight click worked a wonder in that clump! In an instant a dozen pairs of shapely legs glanced in the level sunlight, and Tess screamed aloud in her excitement. Out of the clump went six deer in a rush, but as they cleared the ridge and stopped for a final backward look I lowered the rifle. They were all does and fawns, and F——— was not going to ask me contemptuously after this trip "where are those horns?"

"Oh, the beautiful, beautiful darlings!" rapturously cried my Boston friend, almost beside herself with delight. But with the wisdom of long experience I glared around expectantly, asking impatiently, "Where is that buck?"

I saw him in a trice, some twenty yards from the crest of the ridge, his eyes dilating with mild curiosity, his fat sides gleaming against the green background like a bronze statue. He was only a short hundred yards away and so big that I almost missed him in my foolish confidence. As it was, the bullet intended for the center of his shoulder wabbled back and downward, and he went down the hill and out of sight in a dozen frantic jumps whose recklessness told me the tale that the bullet spat confirmed.

Tess saw him at the first leap and screamed again, while I, almost as excited as she, shrieked out to Colin, "Take him!" and the sound of a snarling snuffle as I hastily mounted my horse directed us to where he lay, still and limp, with the collie tearing at his throat.

Talk about emotional girls! I positively had to keep the crying creature at my side from kissing that dead deer, and it was with a gasp of horror that she saw me bleed and galloch him. It is a nasty job, this deer dressing, and the less said about it the better. But it had to be done, and when I finally had him in shape to handle then came the real difficulty of the whole exploit. How were we to get him up on that pack horse!

He was a big "five-point" and "ugly fat" as my uniquely-speeched husband would say. We couldn't lift one-half of him, and for a time I was in a quandary which I took religious good care to conceal from Tess. It would not do to acknowledge being at any loss now.

Providentially remembering one of F———'s recitals of a similar experience, I looked around for a handy tree and fortunately discovered the very thing some twenty feet below in the gulch bottom. It was an experiment entirely for heretofore I had always hunted in F———'s company and he attended to all such matters, but I "tackled" it with the assurance of a veteran.

Putting the rope around the buck's neck I snubbed the other end to the saddle horn and dragged him down nearly to the tree. After a dozen attempts, I managed to get the end of the rope over a projecting limb and resnubbing it to Vic's saddle horn, I dragged him clear of the ground sufficiently to have Tess lead our pack-horse directly beneath him. Vic was an old-timer and "eased up" as skillfully as a man could have done, and by a fortunate chance the deer dropped across the saddle in just the right position.

After that it was easy, for had I not spent days—yea, even weeks in the acquiring of the knowledge how to tie a "diamond hitch"? Just as the sun dropped over the ridge, we rode into camp among the shrill cheers of the whole hen brood and that night we feasted on liver and bacon with fried heart on the side.

Pass we the volley of questions and complimentary hugs that were showered upon us. Tess and I shared the glory equally, for had she not first seen those wonderful deer? But it would have sent F——— off into a fit had he been there to watch the four of us skin out and quarter up that deer prepatory to sacking it as a protection from possible flies! We managed to get it done by 9 o'clock, however, and it was midnight when I was awakened for the last time by the interrogative chatter of my pullets.

The next morning we had our first visit, humanely speaking. Some iterant home-seekers, afloat in prairie schooners, stopped to ask the way to Rawlins, and, smelling the aroma of our skillets, begged a little meat, saying they had no gun to kill any. Of course, they got a quarter and went on their way rejoicing, with much complimentary speech. And that afternoon, a deputy game warden snooping around in the hills, happened upon the offal of our deer, and tracking us down, came to see about it!

I was nearly scared to death, for it was close season and this particular warden was noted for his severity against offenders but finding that there was no man in this case he generously refrained from asking any embarrassing questions and praised unstintedly the "fresh mutton" we gave him for supper and was real nice generally. I always did like that young fellow and am glad to say that Tess has recently confessed a similar tender regard—but that is telling tales out of school.

He offered to cut wood etc., and hung around a considerable time, but at my innocent suggestion that "the roads were bad after dark" he promptly took the hint and his leave.

The next day one of our cow-punchers "accidentally" happened upon our camp and was solicitous about our welfare until I took him by the ear and leading him to our improvised larder briefly said:

"Venison, grouse (we killed four that morning) and here come the girls with a big string of trout for dinner. Wood, grass and water a-plenty. Do we look like we needed any pity or help? After dinner you pull your freight and don't come snooting around here and more. Sabe."

He "savveyed" and acknowledged it sheepishly while the pullets guyed him mercilessly.

He played even, however, on departing, by suddenly stooping from his saddle and kissing Ruth squarely on the lips.

(They have the ranche next to ours now, and Clarice was married to his brother last month.)

I was properly shocked, of course, and said so. "Why, Marjorie, didn't you know?" she queried, innocently. "It happened last week and I thought he had told you." The vile mendacity of that shameless creature!

And so the days wore along, each one a succeeding delight and the girls lived in the fullness thereof. Before we left each had new roses in her cheeks and a new light in her eyes. In "dolce far niente" we wiled away the happy hours in a blissful content, each enjoying herself in her own fashion and all now contemptuously oblivious of what the conventional world would say.

We were not eaten by anything, not even deer flies or mosquitoes. We had no mishaps, and we came back as we went, unaided by any of the all sufficient egotistical sex. My Bostonese went on that junket servile slaves to convention, they came back emancipated forever, and our example is one worthy the following of all women. In those few days of untrammeled liberty, thrown and dependent upon our own resources, we learned how little absolute necessity there is for the many artificial wants that perplex and annoy women. We learned that woman can hunt, fish, chop wood and most efficiently "rustle" for herself if she has to that the bread and meat earned literally by the sweat of her own brow is wondrously sweet and satisfying when partaken in the open air and congenial female society alone. That there are but few things man done which a good healthy woman cannot do—and generally do better than he with similar practice.

But we learned also of the tenderer dependence which all good women find themselves honored by placing in the dear men who, after all as Tess remarked, "are very handy to have around the house at times."

Our independence was not so exclusive and our self containt not so strong but what we were glad to have the men take the teams as we drove up to the ranche door, and the supper which followed was none the less enjoyed for that it was bachelor cooked. Nor when that night I saw the glow of manly devotion and honest love in the clear eyes of the young cowpuncher who fondly imagined that he was squeezing Ruth's hand under the table unobserved and heard the tittering confidences that floated out from Tess and Clarice's bed room in the wee small hours when my own hubby was felicitously asnore did I have any misgivings as to the result of our breach of convention—or the slightest anticipation that we would ever repeat it!

For there is a dependence that is better than any independence, a tender thrill that is sweeter than any liberty, and turning at the rugged face on the pillow by my cheek sealed my acknowledgement of life's long bondage as grateful bondswoman should.

AGNES HERBERT

We Set Out for Alaska

from Two Dianas in Alaska *(1909)*

M Y LAST BOOK, WHICH WAS THE RECORD OF A SHOOTING TRIP IN SOMALI-land, has just been returned to me by a lady to whom I gave a copy, as she said she "didn't like so much killing." Are we not all killing creatures every day? In savage and animal life it is done as a matter of course, and if no one wants to describe savage life the killing cannot be left out. My friend shudders at my slaying a rhinoceros, but manages to eat part of an unfortunate sheep immediately afterwards. I wonder if the good lady's words ring true. She may be right, and books on sport and adventure are only for men and boys, the sterner sex. If, therefore, you, reader o' mine, should regard all forms of taking life as unwomanly, read no more. An you do, it is on your own head. We went to Alaska to shoot, and—we shot. Perhaps I should like you to persevere, and if for no other reason, because the book is mine.

Our little expedition to Alaska consisted at its onset of the cousin who shot over Somaliland with me, none the less a sportsman for all that she is a woman, and myself. Our preparations consisted in sending on some of the heavy kit to Victoria, British Columbia, which place we meant to use as a base, and where we knew we could garner in all the stores to fit out the small sealing schooner which we meant to hire for the trip. On sport and adventure bent, the ways and means thereof were more or less as yet a matter for conjecture, since nothing could be really definitely decided until our arrival in Victoria.

Leaving England in early December we made New York in record time, and put up for a day or two at one of the largest caravanserais in the town. Our immediate intention was to proceed to Victoria by way of Butte City, Montana, as Cecily, my cousin, wanted to see a young brother of hers who is ranching "Out West." I know now that she had excellent reasons for this strenuous desire to include Butte in our route. It was not her brother who acted as magnet, but some one else's brother.

We were much interested with everything in our short two days in New York, and the hotel was "immense" in every way. So was our bill. When it was presented we thought we really must, inadvertently, have purchased the building. Baths at fifty cents each are not conducive to the state of cleanliness which is next to godliness, for the reason that it is too expensive to indulge in them very often. Our regret was that we hadn't known the charge at the time. We should certainly have run the taps all over again, and had a second dip, in the laudable desire to get our money's worth.

A trip across America is so familiar to most people that there really isn't much that is new to say about it. The gymnastic feat of undressing on one's berth, with the upper one pressing down upon one's head like the lid of a box; the persistency of the ticket collector, who acquires a sort of second wind of most unnecessary activity during the midnight hours; the delight of playing Horatius in the poky little dressing-room, holding it against a crowd of infuriated fellow-passengers, cease to interest at last from constant habit. But the astonishment one feels at the much-vaunted excellence of the sleeping arrangements is ever new. Could publicity farther go? Is a Pullman sleeping-car the place for domesticity run rampant? I only ask mildly. It seems to me that to portion out the car o' nights, half for the men folk, half for the women portion of the travelling community, would improve matters all round. Then, by dropping a curtain in the centre of the passage-way, the joyful consummation of somewhere to undress would be arrived at, and all the embarrassing waving of apparel, muddled up with curtains and cuss-words, would be avoided. But I hate carping, so I'll stop.

It is glorious lying on one's berth, with the blinds and the windows up, as the vast train sweeps up some snow-clad giant slope, and down again to a path-

"Agnes Herbert in Native Parka Dress." From Agnes Herbert, *Two Dianas in Alaska.*

less plain. A panorama which can banish sleep, and give a glimpse into a wonder-scene more perfect than a world of dreams.

I love the friendliness of Americans. Every one on the cars talks to every one else without a suspicion of being taken for a bandit or footpad as is the rule in England. We shared our "section" with a voluble little lady, whose business and hopes and aims were all spread out before us in the first quarter of an hour. Not to be ready to say whither you are bound, and wherefore, is a contemptibly close way of travelling about the States. If you don't want to tell the truth you must tell a fib, but you must tell something, since you will be asked a multitude of questions *instanter* on making a new acquaintance.

Our companion presented us with her visiting-card. It read—

> *Miss Mamie G. Carlson Potts, C.S.,*
> *Great Falls,*
> *Miss.* [*sic*]

I thought C.S. must stand for Civil Servant, but it signifies, Miss Mamie told us, Christian Scientist. She was a "healer," and I suppose that it carries a kind of accolade. It seems odd to have the sect you belong to printed on your visiting-card.

Miss Potts was in a fix. She had so many lovers she did not really know which to select. She told us all about them, and we did our best to help her to choose. Cecily was all for a man "in the drygoods way," but I strongly advocated the claims of a persistent "drummer." A musical husband is such an acquisition. I did not know until later that "drummer" is merely Americanese for a common or garden commercial traveller. Miss Mamie could not make up her mind. It did seem hard that one woman should have such a glut of would-be husbands, while we two were with not even one husband in sight.

"Husbands ain't come by easy," said Miss Mamie sententiously. "What you two gals need to do is to go out and scratch for 'em."

How energetically she must have scratched! Such a list came up every minute. And Miss Mamie was quite old, older than we were, quite thirty-two, I'm sure. But I notice that the older a woman gets the more proposals she can remember.

Cecily whispered to me what a joke it would be if we could only put all the myriad lovers into the same cage, and let them fight the matter out as bucks and tigers do. I said very likely they wouldn't do it, and it would end like a great scorpion and tarantula battle we once went to see. Instead of fighting they were tremendous pals, and took to one another like anything.

Miss Potts spent her entire day with her front hair wound in and out of a spiky fence of tin arrangements, and this *chevaux-de-frise* was only let out for a brief half-hour before bed-time, when it didn't matter, and in this resplendent condition our friend considered her "bang," as she termed the mass of short hair tangled to a fuzzy mass of on-endedness, "real cute."

The most interesting man aboard the cars was a splendid type of strenuous America, a man with a mind, a great personality. He had chosen a wife who made the whole scheme of things inexplicable. If, as I hope, she touched the spot somewhere, she could not have touched the machinations of his brain. They were travelling in great state, with their own car and servants, and were most hospitably anxious that we should join them, Miss Potts too, if she liked, but we thought it would be too much like a pasha travelling with a harem.

Our friend of the private car had made a vast fortune by coming in at the right moment. Any one who really studies human nature and discovers what it is human beings most stand in need of, and then supplies this want, is bound to lay up treasure on earth, and, moreover, the cheaper the article the more universal will be the demand. In Mr. Quilter's case it was quinine, and through quinine life had become to him as a gigantic game of draughts, opposing forces cleared from the board, and all his men in the king row. One evening we dined with him in splendour, and Miss Mamie would have gone to the party with prisoned hair had we not pointed out to her that no greater occasion was likely to come her way just then. We had a merry dinner, only darkened by the upsetting of a cup of scalding coffee all over Miss Mamie's foot. It was her last night on the cars, and she retired to her loft early, telling us that she had "a bad claim," which is, it seems, Christian Science talk for a scalded foot.

We reached Great Falls at breakfast-time, and the cold was so intense the windows of the heated car became steamed beyond a possibility of outlook, and when one wished to view the snow-covered landscape there was nothing for it but to brave the terrors of the chilly platform of a rear car. Everything in Great Falls was on runners, made into sleighs, and the last we saw of Miss Potts was her departure in a hired hack, its body set right on the snow, and all the portmanteaux and kit bumping along behind, tied on to an improvised platform.

It was a world of dazzling whiteness, the whole of the vast Missouri River, with a water-power second only to Niagara, frozen over.

So at last we came to Butte City, surely the ugliest town in all America. Like some Gargantuan barnacle it clings to the hillside, and over it, grey and sombre, looms a pall of smoke, tinged green with the fumes from the famous smelters. No flowers or grass grow in Butte. They cannot. And if some stray enterprising young shoot does peep out it soon alacks the day and withers away in horror at the vista it has been born to. Never was there such a rushing place as Butte. It just seems to take away one's breath. The drum of the energetic Salvationist fights for the mastery over the strident music of the myriad saloons, which with doors ever a-swing, radiate warmth and Nirvana. All the hurrying men—and no one ever walks slowly—look tense and anxious, everybody is in a furious hurry. They have all the time there is, but not nearly enough. In the hotel each man dips constantly into his pocket for bits of blue ore, and the words "seventy per cent.," "claims," "options," sing in the very air. Does all the ore smelt seventy per cent.? It would seem so. We were invited to take shares in at least six different mining ventures before we had seen as many hours in Butte, and all the prospective ore was bound to smelt seventy per cent. For its size no city produces more wealth than Butte, seething whirlpool of plots and plans, and groans and griefs.

Everything was a source of interest. Even to listen to the many mining men who lived at our hotel talking the jargon of the smelters fascinated us. The passing through guest is referred to as "a transient."

"You're a tranjan?" said our chambermaid, dashing in with my *chota hazari.*

"I suppose so," I answered doubtfully, wondering whatever on earth I had claimed to be.

One evening as we sat in the ante-room off the main hall we heard the bustle of a new arrival, and all inquisitive ears caught the sound of an English voice. "All right," it said. "All right," just that. Cecily and I looked at one another, for we should know that voice wherever we heard it in jungle, debate, or Babel of tongues. It could belong to one man only, and that one he whom we had christened the Leader of the opposition party that formerly shot over Somaliland at the same time as we did. My kinsman, Ralph Windus, would of a certainty be here also, for these two never part, if they can help it. They were at Sandhurst together, and afterwards joined the same regiment.

Then, in a flash, I guessed why Cecily had come by way of Butte!

"You are as good at scratching as Miss Mamie Potts," I said sternly.

Cecily looked guilty, and I hope she blushed. We peered round the door, and yes, there was Ralph, running his finger down the back numbers of the hotel register. He turned and spoke to his friend, standing alongside, and in another moment came in like a whirlwind, afire with pleasure at seeing Cecily—us, I mean. Ralph and his *fidus Achates* had been after big-horn and wapiti in Wyoming and Montana, and had come off with some fine heads, which we might see on the morrow. Don't you love to-morrow? To-morrows have but one drawback, they so soon become yesterdays, and I hate yesterday as much as old Omar did.

'Twas such a glorious evening, such a merry dinner, such retrospections, quips, and teasings. If Cecily found a seventh heaven in a corner seat with Ralph, I felt equally contented in my chat with the elder warrior. He caught my meanings so quickly, the playful, the joyous, the pitiful, the pathetic, the imaginative. We discussed the heads they had, and the heads they hadn't, for with the sportsman it is always that heads that are most worth having which are not there. We spoke of our prospective Alaskan trip, and showed them our route so far as we knew it ourselves by the map. And this time our friends threw no cold water on our schemes. They looked at one another. "A splendid trip, isn't it?" said Cecily meditatively.

Then like a bombshell came, "May we go too?" from Ralph.

The silence of intense surprise fell on Cecily and myself.

"May we go too?" repeated Ralph.

"We are going," said his *fidus Achates* firmly, and that seemed to settle it.

Next morning we arranged matters. We four would go together to Alaska, and yet not together. That is to say, in some ways the expeditions would be separate, in others amalgamated. Our camps should at times be one camp, at others, when it suited us, they should be distinct. There should never be any demanding the same hunter at the same time; no seeing too much of each other.

We bestowed the accolade of commander-in-chief of the trip on the one time Leader of the opposition shoot of Somaliland days, but reserved to ourselves the right of vetoing any command he might make. What Mrs. Grundy thought of the whole arrangement I do not venture to say. In the wild such a personage does not exist, and we only thought of the wild. How it called us, how it never ceases to call if once you have answered! Besides, women who have passed the rubicon of thirty—let it be "wropt" in mystery how long since—do not need chaperons anywhere, being by right of age and common-sense each one a full-blown chaperon in herself.

We mapped out the united trip, the route, the ways and means, as well as we could at the time, and collecting our mountains of kit, took train for Seattle, the Sound Port, and from there crossed to Victoria.

COURTNEY BORDEN

Wrangel Island and Polar Bears

from The Cruise of the Northern Light *(1928)*

AUGUST 11th.

There in the glistening morning sunshine lay the goal of our desire: the island. We were the first white women ever to reach it. Around its rock-strewn shores clung a narrow band of shimmering ice. The patches of snow on the steep shale cliffs were white and untouched.

Everyone was nearly beside himself with laughing and hilarious excitement. The Eskimos had already climbed on to the furled mainsail, and were straddling its broad width, with borrowed glasses glued to their eyes. The sea-scouts, too, were elated.

"May we hang our flags to the shrouds?" asked Ryan. In a few minutes the Jackson Park and Columbia Yacht Club pennants fluttered, one above the other, from the turnbuckles. These little flags waved into shreds before the boys took them down, preparing to bring back in triumph "flags that had flown at Wrangel Island."

Mr. Hine was equally excited. His thrill lay in the prospect of bringing the first birds from this Arctic island to the Field Museum. As for the rest of us we were prepared with both cameras and guns.

At ten o'clock we were close in shore between Pillar Point and Cape Hawaii. The menacing polar ice-pack lay solid on the north and west coasts, and we realized would encircle the bleak island again with any northerly wind, but our only chance of seeing a polar bear lay in remaining near the pack itself.

We continued to look over the drift ice near shore. Suddenly—"We see polar bear!" cried both Eskimos in the same breath.

Nothing can adequately describe our feelings. "Polar bears! Polar bears!" Rang over the ship. . . . Here were the wild beasts we had sailed thousands of miles to find. I believe I did not know whether to laugh or cry in our frantic excitement.

"Look at them!—They are just standing there," called Mrs. Slaughter. . . . Yes—there they were—two huge white bears on that gleaming streak of moving ice. We could even see them with our naked eye. Whether they saw the boat we didn't know, because bears are supposed to have poor eyesight. But their smelling powers are excellent. . . . Both animals were evidently startled. They began lumbering from ridge to ridge. A heavy swell, the remains of a storm, unfortunately blew on to shore. The whaleboat was being made ready.

Then followed the usual argument on who should go off first. "No— you go!—Please go!" was all I heard. In the meantime the game was moving faster. Consenting very reluctantly, Mr. Slaughter stepped into the boat which still hung on the davits, followed by the natives and Dahl. They were slowly lowered into the water. "Good-by" he waved. Off they went. The rest of us hung over the rail, as excited as though we were ourselves approaching the two beautiful white creatures we could still see.

The little wooden boat rose and fell on the large, swelling waves, nearly going out of sight in the valleys between. From where we watched, it looked as though every wave would sweep over the four men. Finally they neared the ice. In our suspense we were almost nailed to the deck.

The two bears approached the oncoming boat, one from the left, the other from the right and very close to the water's edge. We saw the Eskimos raise their arms. The bear on the right continued to amble toward them with a slow, steady gait, its head moving back and forth between the shoulders just like the polar bears in any zoo. We knew Mr. Slaughter was by this time within rifle range of this last animal. . . . A sickening moment of waiting. We thought we would see it fall.

But no—in another second the boat appeared to be turning away. It was heading toward us. We watched them row back to the yacht.

"Too much swell, I guess," exclaimed Captain Borden.

He was right. A heavy northeast swell pounded against the ice hummocks, making it out of the question ever to get the body off the ice, if he had shot. Besides, moving ice surrounded them. It became exceedingly precarious to remain longer and take the chance of being dashed to tinder in a second's time. Apparently the Eskimos and the mate were so excited at witnessing our expedition's first polar bear hunt that they had paid little attention to the imminent danger. Mr. Slaughter was not anxious to take any unnecessary chances.

After they came on board, and the boat was hoisted, we continued to steam along shore with everyone on deck searching for more excitement. It still seemed like a wonderful dream: Wrangel Island and polar bears! . . . There was no sign of human life on this east coast. Sheer granite cliffs rose high and forbidding toward a rolling brown, cold looking land. Two large river beds wound toward the sea, banked with snow and heavy drifts which lay in the gulches. There were no shrubs of any kind, it was the usual grim land such as we saw on the dreary ice-bound wastes of Siberia. It is not necessary to mention there were no trees: The last trees we had seen were in the Inside Passage in May, and the next ones would be in San Francisco.

After lunch we proceeded within the lee of Cape Hawaii. Here we spotted three more bears. These were also unapproachable since they were too far within heavy drift ice through which a small boat could not possibly penetrate.

Since no soundings had been previously recorded on the chart from Pillar Point to Cape Hawaii, Captain Borden ordered soundings taken. We were two miles off shore: The results showed between ten and thirteen fathoms with black sandy bottom.

At 2:15 we saw another bear not far from the yacht. Once again the whaleboat was lowered. This time Frances Ames, one sea-scout, and the Eskimos started off. We watched them stalk the animal unsuccessfully in the boat for over an hour; whether their wind was wrong or the beast was naturally restless we could not tell from the yacht, but their prey never stopped walking away from them. From the deck the hunt looked terribly mismanaged. The bear was moving when Miss Ames left us and we did not think the whaleboat allowed for this in striking for a position behind their quarry. Later we understood that the hunters had pulled toward the only open lead through the jagged hammocks. They were unable to reach the disappearing animal because of the large cakes which were pounding up and down and drifting steadily, changing the boat's position from one minute to the next. The second disappointed party turned back towards the yacht at four o'clock. From the stern where our view over the ice was better, we could still see the bear lying in a hollow between two large cakes. It was completely invisible from the small boat.

Mr. and Mrs. Slaughter and Mr. Hine, with the first mate and second engineer, started off in the launch to continue the pursuit. Captain Borden was busy in the chart-room and rather than have too many in the launch, I remained on board with him and watched Miss Ames and the natives climb from the whaleboat into the launch. On passing the yacht they called out that the Eskimos believed it quite useless and very dangerous to continue hunting among the enormous cakes that were jamming together on the swell.

The writer continued to stare longingly at the bear just stalked, while my husband took a sight and wrote up his log. Before long—hardly possible—but a second monster appeared far in the pack, asleep on the highest pinnacle of ice available. It seemed even more inaccessible than the first. I said nothing and looked further. Almost immediately two unusually white creatures suddenly loomed from behind a large round-topped cake of ice. This odd shaped cake we had been calling "igloo"; it was always necessary to name the fantastic ice-shapes by appropriate names. When one sighted game on such a long expanse of white drifting ice one was forced to mark the location by certain irregular cakes, since the ice traveled fast, and, with the yacht drifting at the same time, the exact position could not be retained by noting snow patches or formations on land.

While I watched, the two beasts wandered down to the very edge of open water which meant comparatively easy hunting. My husband, on hearing a yell, ran out of the chartroom. By this time there were four animals now visible in the same direction. At this intense moment Sparks came aft with a message from the children who, sorry to say, were just then far from my thoughts. But, pulling myself together, I read it to make sure all was well.

Sparks! . . . "Take my glasses!—Keep your eye on those four bears so you can tell just exactly where they are when we come back. We have to get our white *parkas* and rifles. . . ."

When we came on deck again, hardly three minutes later, the cow and cub were nowhere in sight.

By this time the entire crew was on deck. "I thought they were foolish not to stay over there," remarked Harry the first mate, referring to the party in the launch. When we hurried down the steps everyone shouted good luck.

What a moment as we started off in the dory with the second mate in the stern and two sea-scouts rowing! It did not take long to reach the fast moving "igloo" which was at the very edge of the ice. We circled round three sides in a lead of open water filled with mush ice. No signs of the two lovely creatures. They were gone, no telling where. But we did not lose hope. We steered out into open water. Again no traces anywhere!

"We'll find the others, then," hopefully from the mate.

Entering a lead, or opening, between formidable and restless ice-hummocks gave one a queer sensation; when looking back one saw no passage-way. Soon we were tightly wedged in between towering houses of ice that nearly rolled entirely over as they tossed on the swell. The scraping of mush ice crackled under us and every so often it was impossible to avoid crashing into a cake. Crunch—crunch was all we heard. A sharp brittle sound. By this time the space was too narrow for the men to row. The four men paddled while I looked ahead. As we wound in and out the drifting floes we again looked back to see the large bobbing ice entirely encircle us. There was no way out visible. Even my husband felt we were not particularly safe.

"Sure we're all right," optimistically answered the mate who had had more experience than Captain Borden with polar ice. Nevertheless, we were in the very probable danger of being rammed to pieces, in which case we were prepared to hang on to the overturned craft if possible until we could crawl on to an ice cake and signal to the yacht. Captain Borden had left instructions with Captain Joe to take charge in his absence and keep track of the two hunting parties from the crow's nest. Little did we know that we were out of sight after passing the igloo.

There was something so glorious about hunting bears within the lee of Wrangel Island that danger itself was glamorous. The men now paddled very carefully, piloting the bow ahead as the huge cakes separated. We struggled on, endeavoring to wind our tortuous way toward a monstrous brute we could now see lying on the high hummock. No other animals were in sight. Our former fears of accident were immediately forgotten as all eyes looked toward the enormous beast which we conjectured to be a she-bear and two cubs. The mate was excited enough to steer his boat through anything. The boys imagined they were living in *The Arabian Nights:* One wished hard and a polar bear appeared.

Finally the large cakes jammed together and we could penetrate no further but we were not more than two hundred yards from the great somnolent object. Most unexpectedly it lifted up a black nose and sniffed the air suspiciously. I was in the bow so that rather than attempting to scramble out on to the heaving ice, not only because of the danger but it would have lost time, my husband hurriedly changed places with me. As

"The author—'One must wear white in stalking Arctic game.'" From Mrs. John Borden, The Cruise of the Northern Light.

he kneeled in the bow and pulled the trigger, we watched the bear raise two large hairy pads which we had taken for cubs. Captain Borden had made a pretty shot that hit just below the back of the neck and broke the back. He used the 220 grain soft-point Western Cartridge.

"Gee, Capt'n, that's great!" shouted the mate and sea-scouts in a chorus. "That's what we came to the Arctic for," added one of the boys.

The ice was constantly changing. It was decided to take me back to the yacht before tackling the dead animal. Our trip out was as difficult and exciting as our entrance, since the former leads had closed up. When we emerged from the labyrinth of ice and reached open water, the boat seemed, amid the restless desolation of ice and sea, as solid as the rock of Gibraltar. After putting us aboard, the mate asked two other boys to accompany him, leaving us at about 6:30 P.M., to skin the bear. Meanwhile the launch returned with another successful hunter: Miss Ames had shot a walrus. This terminated our walrus hunt, as each person had one.

We went below for warmth and relaxation. Sometimes I was Caliban secretly fearing the elements, but on this night of many thrills, the dangers and the possible fate of seafarers were soon forgotten. The victrola played incessantly and we sang loudly to our favorite tunes. Strange as it may sound on reading this, while sitting snug and safe at home, we knew we were safer on the *Northern Light,* although riding out a storm, or piloting through dense fog among reefs and shoals, than we would have been crossing State and Madison Streets, Chicago. (While writing last night—a crash resounded outside my window—four people were killed in an automobile accident.) I even reasoned to myself that in a train wreck one would have little chance of coming out alive, but in a shipwreck on a well-equipped yacht one would generally have time to prepare for exposure and hardships. How different it all seemed before sailing from San Francisco last April! . . . Striking out in unknown waters seemed a hazardous undertaking. There were moments when I secretly longed to wake up some morning and find our plans a dream, but how foolish! Now we can truthfully admit that the five months' trip was an experience so marvelous that we could never duplicate it. None of us, I am sure, would give up one day of that wonderful voyage on the high seas; fresh air and health, serene peace, and glorious adventure. . . .

AUGUST 12th.
Abruptly and unexpectedly someone cried, "Look!" . . . I do not remember whether it was a member of the crew, or not, who first saw the sight that was to cause so many stirring thrills. "Look . . . Smoke!" The voice actually shouted. Then ensued a stampede toward the side of the boat nearest land. Most everyone had been staring out the opposite direction where the ice cakes were being thoroughly examined—there being very little ice between us and shore.

"A village . . . A village . . . A village!" hoarse cries echoed from one end of the vessel to the other. Everyone jumped up and down—pounded the nearest person on the back. The chef stumbled out of the officers' hatch. Someone loaned him a pair of glasses—pandemonium reigned.

Out there on that hillside were houses! . . . We could announce to the world that there is a Russian settlement on Wrangel Island! . . . A delirious, sensational, and intoxicating moment. The intoxication came from our burst of pride. We were the only people on earth, excepting those on the ship that had deposited these isolated souls on the bleak island, who had seen this recent historical event.

England herself made no further attempt to explore the land her Captain Kellet had been the first white man to discover. The United States Government made no effort of the actual occupation to follow up the explorations accomplished by the scientists on the *Rogers* and the *Corwin*. Canada, despite the energy and patriotic ambition of Stefansson, seemed apparently uninterested in making a third attempt to fly her ensign on the tragedy-ridden Arctic Island. Instead—Soviet Russia read Stefansson's agitation in books and the press. If Wrangel Island would ever be a base of supplies, a landing base, for trans-Arctic travel—Russia must hold it herself. Some may say, "What is the advantage of Wrangel Island to any country?" Perhaps none—just at present. But history records other isolated islands in other seas that seemed entirely inaccessible and useless at the time they were claimed. In the twentieth century these have come into their own since all the world has become so closely woven into a net of intricate complications.

We were steaming nearer and nearer to the tiny group of houses we were watching so intently. Smoke poured out of only one chimney, curling lazily through the crisp, cool air up into the mountains behind. The dwellings were clustered on a gravel beach fairly close to the water's edge, well protected from the fury of north winds (much better situated than the Eskimo village at Pt. Hope) by Berry Peak and other mountains. There was no flat ground visible except the narrow beach in the center of Rodgers Harbor. The ridge of land rose abruptly out of the sea and continued ascending toward the blue foothills and loftier peaks beyond.

Before we found ourselves directly opposite the village we spied what we deemed to be a possible look-out of some sort hanging over a high steep ridge two or three miles east with an excellent view of the harbor, and to the south, east, and west. Since it was too far away for us to see very distinctly at that height, one cannot state positively that it was a fortification. In the only two books, however, that we have found available containing observations of men who have reached Wrangel read nothing concerning a strange rock formation just below the tope of the highest ridge in Rodgers Harbor. The boys who lived there for one winter in 1922 are gone. So with the exception of a handful of *Karluk* survivors, and Mr. E. W. Nelson (former Chief of Biological Survey and author of many books on Alaskan and Arctic mammals and birds), a member of the *Corwin* expedition on August 12, 1881 (a strange coincidence that the date should have been August 12th—to the day forty-six years before our expedition reached there), when it formally took possession of the island in the name of the United States, there is no one with whom we can compare notes. In our minds, after we had stared at it until our eyes smarted, there was no doubt but that this ominous appearing spot on the land was made by man. It appeared to be a fairly solid affair with openings, supposedly to mount guns.

At any rate, it is to be expected that Russia would fortify this newest acquisition of her already sprawling possessions.

Therefore it was with obvious trepidations that we looked over that wild land in front of us, perilously near.

There were so few large ice-hummocks that we managed to stand in toward the village, about a half mile off shore. On deck lay cases of sugar, tobacco, tea, cartridges, canned goods, and other necessities of life. Also we hoped to send out for these wretched people, any radio news for the outside. The launch still hung on the davits, but the second engineer and mate were ready to lower it on a minute's notice. The engines were rung off, the Stars and Stripes were flung out from the stern. Three blasts of our whistle echoed shrilly against the brown mountains.

At first we saw no one. Except for the smoke it could have been an abandoned village. There were three small, well-built wooden houses (resembling those of Montgomery Ward). From the center house smoke continued to rise. Huddled near these larger houses were ten or twelve much smaller dwellings, either skin *yourts* or tents, we were not sure. Further to the right were three other houses, probably wood, but certainly not mere native hovels. While we watched, hoping for some sign of human activity, a woman came to the door of the house from where we had seen smoke. (Evidently this was the main headquarters for the little band of so-called exiles.) Her dress was light colored and flounced along the hem of the skirt, much in the style of the calico *parkas* worn in summer by the Pt. Hope Eskimos. Details of the dress we could not see, but on her feet were the usual *mukluks*. She stood there, it seemed to us, several minutes, but no other sign of life was noticeable. . . . We blew the whistle again, merely a friendly salute. (If only others could imagine how terribly exciting it was to stand there—not knowing what would happen next. My heart was in my throat most of the time.)

When still no other people were visible a red flag of the "Union of Soviet Socialist Republic" suddenly flung out from the flagpole behind this same house. Someone had at last admitted our arrival. . . . Afterwards we stopped to wonder what those people were thinking about, undoubtedly gathered together discussing the strange ship that had interrupted their splendid isolation.

A few minutes later quite a considerable number assembled on the beach, looking out toward the schooner. There was one woman, we knew, and many dogs. We thought that they would immediately find their *umi-aks* and set out toward the boat, in the way that we were visited by the Chukchees. But no—there was no boat of any description along the beach. They made not the slightest attempt to speak with us.

That was a strange turn in events! These human beings, perhaps thirty or thirty-five Cossacks and Siberian natives in all, were living on a desolate, ice-bound island, not far from the very edge of the Pole of Inaccessibility. The great polar ice-pack hemmed them in on the north and west coasts, leaving them only the exceedingly slim possibility of a navigable passage opening in the drift ice near the island again the following summer—perhaps not again for two or three years. Yet—they did not make a move to beg for any supplies we would undoubtedly be carrying. . . . Hard to understand!

What a scene! . . . A barren, rugged island spotted with snow drifts. A tiny little group of dark figures huddled together at the base of the highest mountain, staring curiously at a white yacht that lay calmly on a clear blue sea. Pillars of white ice glided by. On the deck of the boat stood other brown and white-clad figures—gazing toward land. Above all floated white clouds, and a glorious warm sun played down upon the tense, human drama.

Whether the Cossacks kept the natives from coming out, whether they had no boats, whether they one and all feared us, perhaps we may never know.

As anxious as we all were to climb on those shores—to be able to collect specimens of flora and fauna on that much-wrangled-over Wrangel Island—Captain Borden did not permit anyone to go ashore. We were glad enough to be safe on the yacht, in those uncertain ice-filled waters.

How we would have enjoyed giving food or help to those lonely, stranded inhabitants! . . . But we reluctantly and even sorrowfully left them to continue in their desperate struggle for food and existence in that ice-bound solitude of the Frozen North. . . .

AUGUST 13th.
"Come on girls—there's a bear!" called a voice.

Mrs. Slaughter hurriedly went for her rifle, and pulled on her white *parka*. This time the dory was lowered and Captain Borden decided to paddle the boat himself. The Eskimos were too excitable.

In my notes of the day: "While looking for Kodiak bear half the fun was lost in not having the pleasure of watching others. It is marvelous being an onlooker at polar bear hunting. Mrs. Slaughter shot her bear and how I did envy her. Supposing we do see another bear and I miss it again?"

While almost everyone was watching the hunt and the yacht was peacefully drifting, the steward yelled, "Madam, there's another bear!" Big John Eskimo had gone off in his *kayak* to help pack Mrs. Slaughter's bear to the boat but the remaining native ran up to me, crying: "Get your gun—get your gun!" . . .

Thank goodness—this time I was successful! If another miss—my disgrace would have been complete . . .

The two bears were hoisted on deck—both large males weighing probably around 1,500 pounds. Although the Eskimos and Dahl made a fine job of skinning and pickling the skins, they were in pretty poor shape when they reached the Museum. Apparently this could not have been helped since the oil secreted by a polar bear in summer acts like an acid and burns through the white fur.

All six bears were males and unusually large, measuring within a few inches of one another in length, from ten feet two inches to eleven feet. Dahl told us he had never seen six such uniform sized animals taken out of one place. In one summer near Franz Josef Land two or three hundred bears are taken during the season and brought to Norway. This means large numbers of animals are killed before they attain any great size, the average found there are seven or eight feet, and smaller. (Of course, some large polar bears are shot in the Greenland Arctic.) We saw eleven bears the first day, and nineteen the remaining three days. Of this number four were cubs. It seemed almost incredible! It is impossible to tell whether or not we counted some of the same animals twice, as the ice was always changing, but at the same time many more were undoubtedly lost to us as they lay asleep hidden behind ice hummocks. A gun-shot seldom disturbed bears that appeared nearby during the hunt: They have not been shot over often enough to know fear. Instead they often walked toward the men to satisfy their curiosity. Also—the shot probably sounded to them very much as though ice was breaking away, an ordinary event in their far northern haunts. There is no telling how many we could have shot; but we carefully restricted ourselves to one trophy apiece and a fine male for the museum. Our hunt was over. We then concentrated on birds. Mr. Hine went off in the launch toward evening. He was particularly interested in taking two species of both murres and guillemots distinct from those he found on Fairway Rock and the Diomedes: Pallas murres and Mandt's guillemots; also some glaucous-winged gulls. He found most of his specimens near the rookery on Waring Point.

We found all the game south of Pillar Point, although we steamed back and forth for four days between Cape Waring and a point a short distance beyond Rodgers Harbor. This is the weather side of the island and we believed the bear congregated there to feed on dead walrus, which had been killed along the Siberian shore from East Cape to Cape Serdzekamen, and had drifted with the current. We saw very few seals for the animals to feed on and surprisingly few live walrus, but a carcass was found not far from every bear shot. The polar bear, apparently, is willing to take his meat a little high if he can thereby avoid the discomfort of attacking a large bull walrus.

Before the night was over we saw a most perfect specimen not far in the ice. "Polar bear!—Fine polar bear!" cried both Eskimos in a chorus. They climbed down from the top of the pilot-house, and ran toward my husband.

"Capt'n—Natives like hunt polar bear—Natives eat fine polar bear meat—use 'em skin!" pleaded the two happy, excited little men. (They were strong and sturdy but their feet and hands were no larger than a small boy's.)

"All right, you two boys go after it," my husband answered. "Here is my gun—one of you can use it."

So off they went in a dory. We watched them scale a sheer, high, hummock. The bear was soon lost to us on the far side of the ridge. When they reached the top we heard, I think, six shots. Then they disappeared over the sharp edge. More shots. A few minutes afterwards both men reappeared, and standing on the very top of the large ice-cake, outlined against a cool grey sky they looked toward the yacht, raised their arms in the air—and clapped heartily . . .

Primitive man had conquered the beast. King Island would honor the returning heroes!

We hung over the railing—waiting to add the congratulations they so longed to hear.

"Me polar bear . . . Me first shot!" called Big John. Again he was the master-hunter. When they were hoisted on deck in the dory, and the precious beast was there also, we flocked to see it. The bear was indeed a beauty: the only female we had taken, with a thick winter coat and long white fur.

"I give him Captn's wife!" announced Big John very pleased. So, we now had a lovely female to add to the Museum case.

Having accomplished everything and even more than we dared hope for on leaving San Francisco, our thoughts turned toward home, and the flags were hoisted. From the main mast soon floated a lovely thin streamer over a hundred feet long with thirteen stars in a row, followed by the red and white stripes. It was our Homeward Bound Pennant, following the time-honored custom of whaling ships on the Arctic after they had boiled down their fill of whale oil. In those brave days the streamer had a foot in length for every man on board and was flown on entering each port on their return, whether the voyage terminated in San Francisco or continued around Cape Horn. The sea-scouts' small and important flags still waved from the shrouds. The ship was in holiday attire . . .

Herald Island was visible in the clear atmosphere forty miles away. It distinctly appeared to be two separate islands, one further away and considerably lower than the other. We had seen this optical illusion almost all afternoon and after many hours it still retained the same shape. Of course, we again had visions of exploring that land mentioned before as Bordenland which some people believed might possibly exist. The high granite headlands stood boldly above the horizon outlined against the evening sky, while a long low stretch in between was clearly visible. We steamed closer to make sure; and the two resolved themselves into nothing but Herald Island. Now and for all time any new land in that position has been refuted. We were a bit disappointed although we had sense enough to realize an undiscovered land in that location was in 1927 practically an impossibility.

Before reluctantly turning away from our hunters' paradise everyone came on deck to watch the lavender-tinted hills of the island, and the pink afterglow of a wonderful Arctic sunset. Over the bow hung a large round pink moon covering the white vessel in its silvery radiance. By ten o'clock we were under full sail. The sea-scouts beamed with delight and everyone forward and aft rejoiced in a splendid climax to a long successful voyage. We had cruised for four cloudless days along the shores of this thrilling Arctic island. We had been sailing for many weeks along the white upper crust at the "Top of the world." And we were the first white women ever to reach Wrangel Island. Our party was first to see the Russian village. Anyone with a spark of romance in his or her city-bred soul could not help but feel the enchantment of that pale but glowing night. A magical lure gripped our senses. A fresh breeze blew almost caressingly, the flapping of the sails filled one with passionate ecstasy. It was a moment when one could easily appreciate a sailor's love for his ship, far greater than his desire for home. A fair wind, a fine ship and we were homeward bound!

ISABEL SAVORY

Tiger-Shooting

from A Sportswoman in India *(1900)*

TIGER!—TIGER!
What of the hunting, hunter bold?
Brother, the watch was long and cold.
What of the quarry ye went to kill?
Brother, he crops in the jungle still.
Where is the power that made your pride?
Brother, it ebbs from my flank and side.
Where is the haste that ye hurry by?
Brother, I go to my lair to die.
—Rudyard Kipling

We left Bangalore one day in the middle of our last April, J. and myself, in answer to a wire from Captain F. at Secunderabad, *"Arrangements for shoot complete,"* which meant getting leave from the forest authorities, police authorities, and a thousand-and-one minor details.

From Secunderabad a night journey got us to Warungal station at two in the morning. We spent the rest of the night uncomfortably in the waiting room, and as soon as it grew light were only too glad to set off. I would impress upon every woman following our example the necessity of taking every precaution against the heat. Not only wear a large *solà topi*, but have a spine pad sewn inside the coat, which should be of thin green *shikar* material. I had a second pad hooked on outside. I often kept a wet rag on my head, inside my pith helmet; and I wore dogskin gloves, minus half the fingers, which enabled one to hold the burning barrels. The temperature was 104 degrees in the shade in our tents, and later on 115 degrees.

Our caravan really formed a most imposing train as we set off from Warungal station. Fifty-one pack-bullocks with panniers carried one hundred and sixty pounds each, which consisted of guns, ammunition, tents, beds, chairs, table, clothes, food and drink enough to last the three of us for eight weeks, corn for our ponies and the ponies of our two head *shikaris*, filters, cash-box, etc., etc. Our own luggage had gone straight through from Bangalore to Warungal with our boy. It was twenty-six maunds over weight—that is, two thousand and eighty pounds! It blocked up the platform and alarmed the guard considerably.

Our whole party consisted of our three selves, our own boy for each of us, a *syce* for every pony, a cook, a *mati* (or scullery-boy), a *peon* for supplies, letters, etc., ten *shikaris*, and four-bullock-men to look after the bullocks. So we formed quite a camp. When on the march, we started off our fifty-one pack-bullocks at three o'clock in the morning, following ourselves at six o'clock, marching from fifteen to twenty miles a day. According to this plan, bullocks and all of us reached the new camp much about the same time; the tents were all put up; and we avoided being out in the hottest time—from twelve to four o'clock.

Up to our third camp out of Warungal we did nothing at all; we were unlucky, for at all three places we were, through some mistake, preceded by a party of the Nineteenth Hussars, who had left Secuderabad a fortnight before. We sent on to them, and they arranged to branch off to the left, so that our next camp was on unbeaten ground.

It *was* hot on the march. I made my *syce* carry a large kettle of cold tea or coffee wherewith to refresh myself, and J. and Captain F. supplied themselves also with something cold. The *syces* carried our guns, too, after the first day, when we saw a lot of jungle-fowl and a splendid peacock, which we would fain have shot, for they are excellent eating! Since then we stalked several when we got into camp, but they were too cunning.

Every day, as soon as the bullocks were unloaded, they were driven down to water, and there they *wallowed*, covering themselves with mud, and often only showing just their noses above the mud and water. Whenever the camp was in a likely place the *shikaris* [trackers] tied up bullocks for the tigers to kill the same evening, and we went and saw what had happened the next morning. For the first two or three marches, as I said, we had no luck, and went on at once, instead of staying in one camp a week or so, as we did later on.

Our marches were all through jungle, sometimes really thick with fine trees, occasionally rough scrub and steep, rocky hills. The track was always rough and very stony, a mere path, and in many places would have been quite impossible for the roughest bullock-cart. We rode all of it at a walk, and the *syces* followed on foot.

At last we had *khubr* (news) of a tigress and two large cubs; full of elation, having reached the camp, six bullocks were tied up that same evening.

Next morning we started about half-past six and went out to see what had happened. We rode, two *shikaris* walking with us, till we were about half a mile from the tie-up; then, dismounting, we left the ponies with the syces, and crept with infinite caution up to the spot, for if the tiger has killed the bullock, he generally only drags the body a few hundred yards, and having hidden it, lies down somewhere within reach. Of course, it seems cruel to the unfortunate bullock; but, as a matter of fact, if you kill the tiger in this way, you save the lives of a number of other bullocks, for a cattle-killing tiger devours an enormous number in a year, and, in occasional cases, may take to killing men too.

Besides, how else is a tiger to be found at all? Roaming the countryside and hunting all night, they cover an enormous range of ground, and in a wild, rough scrub and jungle country, extending for hundreds of miles, without any clue to the tiger's sleeping-place during the day, one might beat perhaps for weeks and weeks, and see nothing at all.

Judged by the standard of the greatest good to the greatest number, the laws of humanity justify the working of a tiger shoot, to my mind.

Bullocks are tied up in the most likely places—always near water. The tiger, delighting in thick cover near streams, visiting the spot on his nightly beat, kills the bullock, drags the body away a few hundred yards, and hides it under a bush, or somewhere where the vultures will not see it. He makes a large meal at once, drinks at the stream, and then lies down for twelve hours or so in cool shade somewhere near at hand. If undisturbed he will sleep during the day, and returning to the carcase at night, continue his meal. One bullock will last him three or four nights.

Therefore, upon visiting cautiously in the early morning the tie-up, and finding that the bullock has been killed and dragged off, the odds are greatly in favour of the tiger's being somewhere close at hand. He is, so to speak, *located*.

And now it is worth while having a beat. And here a really good *shikari* is absolutely necessary—a first-rate man, who knows all the ground, understands exactly the right places to beat, and how to beat them, and where to post his guns.

The extraordinary, intuitive knowledge which a few *shikaris* possess, makes it almost a dead certainty as to which path a tiger will come along in a beat, and has made sportsmen complain that tiger-shooting is a well-planned, preconceived, cut-and-dried *battue*. And as for danger! I have heard it compared with shooting a mad dog from the top of an omnibus. Read the rest of the chapter.

On the morning of which I speak we crept up to the first bullock and found it still unharmed; but we could track plainly where one of the tiger cubs (they were nearly full-grown) had walked up to it, and right round it, but had not seen fit to kill. We sent the reprieved bullock to water and back to camp, and crept on about a mile and a half to the next.

It was gone! We stole up to the stake. The rope was broken off short, and in the dust, close to the stake, was an enormous scratch-mark, with all the marks of the nails imprinted sharply, exactly like a gigantic cat at home might make. There was a broad trail where the body had been dragged off.

As the tiger might be lying down close to the body, it is better never to follow this up. No one who values his life should walk up to a tiger. Every one has heard how tigers which have been mortally wounded have struck down men even in their dying agonies, and almost every year some fatal accident occurs to add to the warnings, but they are still unheeded. Other animals may be dodged and avoided; but if a tiger *does* charge home, death is nearly inevitable.

Leaving two *shikaris* to arrange the general idea of the beat, we went back to camp, four miles off. While we had breakfast, and coolies were collected for the beat, a concentrated excitement seemed in the very air.

It is best not to begin to beat till eleven or twelve o'clock; by that time the tiger is probably asleep, and is less likely to be disturbed too soon. Even should this happen, the sun and the rocks are by that time so scorchingly hot, that he is very reluctant to leave his cool sanctuary. From fifty to a hundred coolies are wanted for a beat; on this occasion we had eighty. Their pay was one rupee to eight coolies—that is barely twopence each; but it was double if a tiger was shot. As Furreed, the head *shikari*, remarked, "it takes very clever business" to arrange skillfully a good beat.

We beat a long nullah (a valley) on that first day, two miles long and half a mile wide. Most of the coolies and *shikaris* were sent to one end, the guns were posted at the other; but besides this, stops had to be placed all along the sides, at any point where the tiger is likely to break out. The coolies who act as stops all climb up into trees, and if they see the tiger coming their way with the idea of breaking out, they snap a twig or two, which invariably turns him back at once.

Besides this, we had brought with us about ten rolls of broad, white cloth stuff, each piece a yard wide and twenty yards long, and called "stopping cloth." This was fixed on to trees or bushes along the edge of the beat, at places where the tiger was known by the *shikaris* to be particularly likely to break out—all this with the same idea of keeping him in the desired direction of the guns, of course.

We three guns were posted in trees, seated each in a *machān*, which is, as a rule, a stout, hard, stuffed leather cushion, with straps and buckles, or else ropes, on the four corners, by means of which it is fastened up in the branches, about fifteen feet from the ground. The *machān* is reached by a little, rough ladder; and having climbed up into your perch, your gun-bearer with your second gun standing or sitting on some branch near you, your *chāgul* (leather water-bottle) slung below, you sit, still as death, perhaps for as long as two hours, while the beat goes on.

No. 1 place was the likeliest and best, and No. 2 second best. We changed numbers every day; and so astute are the *shikaris*, that out of seven tigers six came past No. 1.

The first morning, much to our disappointment, the tigress was never found at all. But, partly because it was the first time and all so new, it was *most* exciting; in fact, the excitement was so intense that in my heart of hearts I felt almost glad when it was all over. The *shikaris* did not think the tigress had gone far.

The next morning we had another beat, and though J. saw the tigress, he did not get a shot at her. She came back in the night and ate more of the dead body, and the *shikaris* said she was in some long, thick elephant-grass beyond either of the two preceding beats. We were up in *machāns* on one side, and by-and-by could hear her move. They set alight to one end. It did not burn very well; but after a bit, the fire and the yells of the coolies, and the blank cartridges which they kept letting off, made her move at last. She sprang up with a loud roar; but instead of coming out near any of the guns, as we hoped, she rushed off down through the grass right-handed, and I only saw her striped back for one second, only that and her trail, about sixty yards off in the grass, not enough to fire. She went right off. For more than ten miles the *shikaris* tracked her, still travel-ing on, and then they gave it up.

Leaving this camp, we reached that day a place called Tarwai, where we met with the first actual and sad signs of the famine, which was preva-lent. We had passed across waste after waste, which should have been rice, paddy, and other grain, but lay now all uncultivated, owing to the *non est* of water.

In all the villages so far they had had rice left from last year, sufficient for a miserable pittance for this year; but at Tarwai the wailing, walking skeletons crawled up to us—heart-stirring spectacles! They clamoured for rice—with their shrunken little ones in their arms—and of course we spared them all we could, and gave them a little money to send and buy more. But it was terribly little we could do for the starving, hollow-eyed, weary supplicants, who, after we had distributed the rice, clustered over the ground where it had lain, like ants by spilled honey, searching for another grain.

The heat throughout this time could not be pictured at all by any one at home. It cannot be realised by those who have not felt it, and it gives the ordinary Britisher no adequate idea whatever to read that it was 104 degrees in the shade. When there was any wind at all, it was generally a sort of burning, furnace-like blast. Of course, we streamed with perspira-tion all day and most of the night. The only cool moments were for an hour just before dawn. Captain F. and J. always slept outside, with nothing over them but their pyjama suits. The rocks would grow so hot in the sun that we could feel them all burning to our feet through boots. However, it was a healthy, dry heat, which was a blessing, and none of us were the least ill.

At last, after several days of inaction, we met with our first real excite-ment, and at the same time I shot my first tiger. He was well known, for three gunners who were in the same place last year had three beats after him—ineffectual beats. He was fond of killing bears—a very uncommon thing; and the villagers told us he had been seen to climb a tree after a bear which scrambled up it to get out of his clutches. He managed to reach the bear, and attacked him. Both fell out of the tree on to the ground, when the tiger promptly killed the bear.

This we did not at the time believe; it is most rare for a tiger to climb trees—in fact, almost unheard of. But it proved to be true. He was what they call a very *bobbery* (pugnacious) tiger, the first news we heard of him being that he had killed and eaten another bear six miles from our camp. We went out and had a beat, and found the remains of poor Bruin; the tiger was in the beat, but he broke out through the stops on one side without being fired at. However, the following night he killed one of our tie-ups, close to camp, and he made of it his last meal in this world.

The next morning found all three of us up in our respective *machāns.* Captain F. and myself were about eighty yards apart. The tree which he was in was not quite upright; it leaned slightly, and it had several branches at intervals up the trunk, the *machān* being fastened upon one of them. I sat on my little seat with feelings so intense and so mixed that they were absolutely painful; the strain and excitement great enough to suggest a blessed relief when all should be over. Occasionally Captain F. and I looked across at each other, as we sat, keenly alive to every leaf stirring in the dry scrub, while down upon the burning sands and rocks blazed the relentless sun.

Suddenly there was a sound—monkeys trooping through the jungle, high in the trees, grasping the pliant branches and shaking them with rage! A tiger *must* be in the neighbourhood. Another second—the jungle-grass waved and crackled, and out into the open emerged and advanced slowly—a picture of fearful beauty. A tiger seen in the Zoo gives no faint idea of what one of his species is, seen under its proper conditions. Beasts in captivity are under-fed, and have no muscle; but here before us was a specimen who had always "done himself well," was fit as a prizefighter, every square inch of him developed to perfection. On he came, his cruel eyes lazily blinking in the sun. His long, slouching walk, suggestive of such latent strength, betrayed the vast muscle working firmly through the loose, glossy skin, which was clear red and white, with its double stripes, and the W mark on the head.

The sight of such consummate power, as he swung majestically along, licking his lips and his moustache after his feed, was one of those things not soon to be forgotten, and while it had a bracing effect on the nerves, at the same time struck rather a chilling sensation.

The tiger moved on. I sat with my rifle at full cock, but he went straight up to Captain F.'s tree, looked up, saw him, gave a fierce growl, and then stood still about ten yards off. A loud detonation followed; but Captain F. must have made a poor shot—he hit him behind, much too far back, the bullet going down almost to his hock. The tiger looked magnificent still—he stood on a little knoll, lashing his tail and looking vindictively up into the tree.

At one and the same moment Captain F. and myself fired; somehow or other we both missed him. This was rather too much. In one moment, like a flash, the tiger darted round, deliberately galloped at the tree, sprang about half-way up into its lowest branches, and, assisted by the natural oblique inclination of the trunk, swarmed up to the *machān* as quickly and easily as a cat. It was a terrible moment, one of those of which we pray that they may be few and far between; most of us can lay a finger on two or three such moments in our lives.

Poor Captain F., both barrels fired, and helpless, had in desperation sprung to his feet, his hand on the side of the *machān*. Either the tiger's teeth or his claws tore his finger all down the back of it to the bone but the whole action took place with such lightning speed that it was hard to say which.

In my mind's eye, as the great body flew up the tree, I pictured a ghastly struggle, a heavy fall, and a sickening death; at the same instant a moment's intuition suggested a difficult but not impossible shot at the tiger's back as he clasped the tree. With my last barrel I fired. There was no time for a long and steady aim; but as the smoke cleared away—what a relief!—the tiger had dropped to the ground. With nine lives—cat-like— he was not dead; he walked off and disappeared.

We dared not look for him then and there, dying and savage in such rough and dangerous cover; but next morning we found him cold and stiff. He was a magnificent male, very large and heavy, enormous paws and moustache—a splendid "great cat."

FRANCES HAMERSTROM

And Now with the Pygmies and Indians

from My Double Life *(1994)*

Y CHILDHOOD DREAM, AS I HAVE SAID, WAS TO LIVE WITH WILD ANI-
mals all my life and to marry a tall, dark man. I did both. I was married to Frederick for fifty-nine years. After he died I realized that he had
skillfully avoided hot, wet places. He took me *north* on expeditions to
places like Siberia and Lapland. I had always wanted to hunt with the
Pygmies. My age was 83. I said to myself, "You'd better hop to it before
you get old."

At the time I was a Visiting Scientist at Welder Wildlife Foundation
in Texas, but I took time off every day for a month to walk, to run, to do
push-ups, and to climb trees. Then I went to Mombasa on the Indian
Ocean and went through the same routine in the heat—except I climbed
no trees, they all had spines.

My good friends in Africa ran a biological station. For a month I
stayed at the station and collected plants in the rain forest with Kenge,
a Pygmy. After that I was ready to go hunting. The next time I weighed
myself, I had lost twenty-seven pounds.

For me it is of the utmost importance to travel alone (rather than
with a white companion). I am with the native people and I don't want to
keep in mind what my companion may be thinking of my behavior. For
example: I had been very strictly brought up and knew that no lady
brushes her hair in public. She brushes it in her bedroom, in her boudoir,
or in the bathroom.

My little pup tent, pitched between two leaf-thatched Pygmy houses,
was very low. Crouched on my knees and one elbow I struggled to brush
my hair—living up to the standards I had been so carefully taught.

Finally I said, the Hell with it, crawled out of my tent with my hair-
brush, and sat on a sort of chair that Atoka, a Pygmy, had made for me.
The village seemed empty, so I gave my hair a good brushing. Then I put
my head down and brushed my hair toward the ground, as I had been
taught to do.

When I lifted my head, my hair was every which way, and at eye level was a sea of faces—those little men, some bearded, were watching me at close range.

Now, Fran Hamerstrom, is the time for poise. I pulled myself together and slowly finished brushing my hair, gave it a little pat, and laid down the brush.

Everybody clapped.

Nobody said, "Fran, why do you keep showing off?"

"Primitive" people test whites, just as we test them, and just as we test each other. My next test came before daybreak on my second day in the village. We went on a massive net hunt. The drivers drove the game into a 300-yard-long net, and the pouncers sat ready to pounce on whatever animal ran into the net before it had a chance to get away.

I sat on a little mound of earth (it is not nice to sit on the ground), I knew how far a Pygmy sat to my right, but I still needed to know how far away the Pygmy to my left was: How much net did I need to be prepared to pounce on?

Moving my head so slowly that the motion was essentially imperceptible—a trick that all hunters and many birdwatchers know—I peered slowly to the left. Then I saw a flash of white. It was the teeth of a Pygmy smiling. He was doing just what I was and in the same way: neither of us would frighten game.

Next I moved my head back to its normal position and sat still; ants bit me and insects buzzed, but I sat without moving for about an hour and forty minutes.

That Pygmy must have told everybody about it because thereafter I was treated differently—accepted as a hunter!

People keep asking me, "What were you hunting?"

Sports hunters are shocked at my answer: *anything we can get!*

Subsistence hunting and sport hunting have both been important parts of my life. Sport hunters limit the size of their weapons and virtuously set obstacles in the path of success. The families of subsistence hunters may die if the hunter is not successful.

Sometimes I am sorry that I'm not a cartoonist. I want a cartoon of a Pygmy, saying to his friend, "Sure is great that the monkey season opens next month!"

Never travel with two guides. All they do is talk with each other in some foreign language or a Spanish I do not understand, while I sit in the middle of a dugout canoe and watch birds along the Amazon.

At least that's all my two guides did last year until Secundo, a famous spear fisherman, said something I understood perfectly:

"Have you noticed her long white legs?"

(I continued to watch the birds.)

Alfredo answered, "Yes, and have you noticed that the flies prefer her long white legs to our long brown legs?"

I didn't move a muscle—just kept my binoculars handy. Secundo spoke once more, "Those flies have a lot of sense."

I know they stopped talking about me, because I couldn't understand a single word after that. Secundo traveled with us for two days and then I had Alfredo to myself. He showed me how to forage in the river-bottom woods of the rain forest, and how much easier it was to find food on the nearby uplands, and he took me to blowgun hunters. We traveled for a month in a dugout canoe. Sometimes we camped and sometimes we stayed at Paul Beaver's lodge. Of course Alfredo was testing me and I was testing him. I learned how brave he was when he killed a baby aquatic boa constrictor—seven feet long. It was dangerous.

Alfredo learned how indifferent to pain I was when a piranha bit my index finger. Fortunately it bit me while we were in camp, and fortunately it bit me in a place that bled a lot.

I watched birds, feeling the warm blood run down my hand. Finally Alfredo couldn't stand it any longer and called, "Fran! You are bleeding."

I looked at my hand. The piranha had taken out a nice little chunk of meat. "Yes." And then I watched the birds again.

Sometimes Alfredo told me stories about his life. He told me about the time that he and another Indian guide had tall, muscular young Germans as clients. These massive mighty-muscled men watched the two slender Indians struggle with the great loads of heavy luggage that had to be carried up an embankment.

Alfredo muttered, "I do not like Germans."

"But not all Germans are the same. I like Germans. I've lived in Germany. Not all Germans are nice, but most of them are."

This, I thought, closed the subject forever.

On our last day Alfredo said, "You paddle too. We are going upstream." I grabbed a paddle and put my muscles to work.

Alfredo kept changing the rhythm—with sudden rests. I think he was testing to make sure that I was really paddling.

Finally he said, "You *look* German."

I suddenly remembered what he said about those strong young Germans watching their guides struggle.

Alfredo shook his head in bewilderment. "You look German, but you aren't."

It is one of the strangest compliments I ever got.

I treasure my next compliment too, but it has a different ring to it. Alfredo loaded our gear into the dugout and took me to visit Ramón—a member of the Head-shrinkers' Tribe, and a famous blowgun hunter. Ramón had a rapidly growing family that was almost a village. My count was fifty-four people. They showed me utensils and artifacts, fed me, took me fishing. We laughed and we talked.

At last I said, "Ramón, when are we going hunting?"

Ramón's answer sounded as though he had a fishbone stuck in his throat. "Ungh."

I didn't add, "You have been *paid* to take me hunting." We both knew this.

Suddenly I felt white, female, and one of those pestiferous tourists.

Silence is a strong weapon.

At last Ramón loaded the dugout, and we paddled upriver. We tried one place after another. I asked Ramón, "Are birds always so scarce?"

"Ungh."

He beached the dugout by some river-bottoms. Sunlight poured into the rain forest, and the tall vegetation was thick, dry, and noisy. Ramón stepped out of the dugout and almost immediately brought down a small bird. "Bueno! Splendid!" I cheered. But we couldn't find the bird.

Next he started through the noisy vegetation. "Alfredo, let's stay here."

We heard Ramón trying to make his silent way through the vegetation. Three people would have scared *all* the game out of the country. Crash, crash. After what seemed a long time, we heard him crashing back.

Ramón had two birds about the size of robins impaled on darts. The darts looked rather like long knitting needles with a wad from the silktree at one end and a sharp point at the other. They ran through the birds from up near the neck, down through the chest and the belly, and came out near the tail.

Both birds were alive and fluttering.

I wasn't brought up that way.

"¿Los mataré? Shall I kill them?"

"Ungh."

I thought of what Frederick and I had learned from the old Scottish gamekeeper long ago. "If you down a grouse and it is not dead—bite it just back of the ears. It will die *very* quickly, and will be *very* easy to pluck."

Biting heads soon became my time-honored way of dispatching small birds quickly. Absent-mindedly I bit one bird and then the other. Their heads hung limp.

Alfredo exclaimed, "Fran, you are a tiger!"

Ramón laughed nervously—and then roared with laughter. I had taught him—on his own home ground—something about hunting that he did not know. In one quick instant he had learned that I really was a hunter.

That evening we sat on a log in his camp. Paulilla, his granddaughter, brought him a plate of soup. He slid the plate over so it rested on my thigh too. We ate with our fingers, pulling out bits of fish, vegetable, and monkey meat—just like an old married couple.

I am going back to the rain forests. Pygmies and Indians, among the oldest races of mankind, have lived in forests and jungles since time immemorial and have not destroyed their habitat. No white people can say the same.

Also, whenever I have gone in my far, wide travels in "civilized" countries, in each I have encountered overpopulation with its twin horrors: human misery and despoliation of the environment.

If we are to preserve this beautiful world of ours, with its creatures great and small and their wondrous homes, we must have fewer people on earth, we must have fewer children, or the beauty of the wild will be gone—and our security as well.

ELINORE PRUITT STEWART

The Hunt and *The Seventh Man*

from Letters on an Elk Hunt *(1915)*

VII. THE HUNT

Camp Cloudcrest,
October 6, 1914
DEAR MRS. CONEY,—

It seems so odd to be writing you and getting no answers. Mrs. O'Shaughnessy just now asked me what I have against you that I write you so much. I haven't one thing. I told her I owed you more love than I could ever pay in a lifetime, and she said writing such *long* letters is a mighty poor way to show it. I have been neglecting you shamefully, I think. One of the main reasons I came on this hunt was to take the trip for *you*, and to tell you things that you would most enjoy. So I will spend this snowy day in writing to you.

On the night of September 30, there was the most awful thunderstorm I ever witnessed, flash after flash of the most blinding lightning, followed by deafening peals of thunder; and as it echoed from mountain to mountain the uproar was terrifying. I have always loved a storm; the beat of hail and rain, and the roar of wind always appeal to me; but there was neither wind nor rain, just flash and roar. Before the echo died away among the hills another booming report would seem to shiver the atmosphere and set all our tinware jangling. We are camped so near the great pines that I will confess I was powerfully afraid. Had the lightning struck one of the big pines there would not have been one of us left. I could hear Mrs. O'Shaughnessy murmuring her prayers when there was a lull. We had gone to bed, but I couldn't remain there; so I sat on the wagonseat with Jerrine beside me. Something struck the guy ropes of the tent, and I was so frightened I was too weak to cry out. I thought the big tree must have fallen. In the lulls of the storm I could hear the men's voices, high and excited. They, too, were up. It seemed to me that the storm lasted for hours; but at last it moved off up the valley, the flashes grew to be a mere glimmer, and the thunder mere rumbling. The pines began to moan and soon a little breeze whistled by. So we lay down again. Next morning the horses could not be found; the storm had frightened them, and they had

126

tried to go home. The men had to find them, and as it took most of the day, we had to put off our hunt.

We were up and about next morning in the first faint gray light. While the men fed grain to the horses and saddled them, we prepared a hasty breakfast. We were off before it was more than light enough for us to see the trail.

Dawn in the mountains—how I wish I could describe it to you! If I could only make you feel the keen, bracing air, the exhilarating climb; if I could only paint its beauties, what a picture you should have! Here the colors are very different from those of the desert. I suppose the forest makes it so. The shadows are mellow, like the colors in an old picture— greenish amber light and a blue-gray sky. Far ahead of us we could see the red rim rock of a mountain above timber line. The first rays of the sun turned the jagged peaks into golden points of a crown. In Oklahoma, at that hour of the day, the woods would be alive with song-birds, even at this season; but here there are no song-birds, and only the snapping of twigs as our horses climbed the frosty trail, broke the silence. We had been cautioned not to talk, but neither Mrs. O'Shaughnessy nor I wanted to. Afterwards, when we compared notes, we found that we both had the same thought: we both felt ashamed to be out to deal death to one of the Maker's beautiful creatures, and we were planning how we might avoid it.

The sun was well up when we reached the little park where we pick-eted our horses. Then came a long, hard climb. It is hard climbing at the best, and when there is a big gun to carry, it is very hard. Then too, we had to keep up with the men, and we didn't find that easy to do. At last we reached the top and sat down on some boulders to rest a few minutes before we started down to the hunting ground, which lay in a cuplike val-ley far below us.

We could hear the roar of the Gros Ventre as it tumbled grumbingly over its rocky bed. To our right rose mile after mile of red cliffs. As the last of the quaking asp leaves have fallen, there were no golden groves. In their places stood silvery patches against the red background of the cliffs. High overhead a triangle of wild geese harrowed the blue sky.

I was plumb out of breath, but men who are most gallant elsewhere are absolutely heartless on a hunt. I was scarcely through panting before we began to descend. We received instruction as to how we should move so as to keep out of range of each other's guns; then Mr. Haynes and myself started one way, and Mr. Struble and Mrs. O'Shaughnessy the other. We were to meet where the valley terminated in a broad pass. We felt sure we could get a chance at what elk there might be in the valley. We were fol-lowing fresh tracks, and a little of the hunter's enthusiasm seized me.

We had not followed them far when three cows and a "spike" came running out of the pines a little ahead of us. Instantly Mr. Haynes's gun flew to his shoulder and a deafening report jarred our ears. He ran forward, but I stood still, fascinated by what I saw. Our side of the valley was bounded by a rim of rock. Over the rim was a sheer wall of rock for two hundred feet, to where the Gros Ventre was angrily roaring below; on the other side of the stream rose the red cliffs with their jagged crags. At the report of the gun two huge blocks of stone almost as large as a house detached themselves and fell. At the same instant one of the quaking asp groves began to move slowly. I couldn't believe my eyes. I shut them a moment, but when I looked the grove was moving faster. It slid swiftly, and I could plainly hear the rattle of stones falling against stones, until with a muffled roar the whole hillside fell into the stream.

Mr. Haynes came running back. "What is the matter? Are you hurt? Why didn't you shoot?" he asked.

I waved my hand weakly toward where the great mound of tangled trees and earth blocked the water. "Why," he said, "that is only a landslide, not an earthquake. You are as white as a ghost. Come on up here and see my fine elk."

I sat on a log watching him dress his elk. We have found it best not to remove the skin, but the elk have to be quartered so as to load them on to a horse. Mrs. O'Shaughnessy and Mr. Struble came out of the woods just then. They had seen a big bunch of elk headed by a splendid bull, but got no shot, and the elk went out of the pass. They had heard our shot, and came across to see what luck.

"What iver is the matter with ye?" asked Mrs. O'Shaughnessy. Mr. Haynes told her. They had heard the noise, but had thought it thunder. Mr. Haynes told me that if I would "chirk up" he would give me his elk teeth. Though I don't admire them, they are considered valuable; however, his elk was a cow, and they don't have as nice teeth as do bulls.

We had lunch, and the men covered the elk with pine boughs to keep the camp robbers from pecking it full of holes. Next day the men would come with the horses and pack it in to camp. We all felt refreshed; so we started on the trail of those that got away.

For a while walking was easy and we made pretty good time; then we had a rocky hill to get over. We had to use care when we got into the timber; there were marshy places which tried us sorely, and windfall so thick that we could hardly get through. We were obliged to pick our way carefully to avoid noise, and we were all together, not having come to a place where it seemed better to separate. We had about resolved to go to our horses when we heard a volley of shots.

"That is somebody bunch-shooting," said Mr. Struble. "They are in Brewster Lake Park, by the sound. That means that the elk will pass here in a short time and we may get a shot. The elk will be here long before the men, since the men have no horses, so let's hurry and get placed along the only place they can get out. We'll get our limit.

We hastily secreted ourselves along the narrow gorge through which the elk must pass. We were all on one side, and Mr. Haynes said to me, "Rest your gun on that rock and aim at the first rib back of the shoulder. If you shoot haphazard you may cripple an elk and let it get away to die in misery. So make sure when you fire."

It didn't seem a minute before we heard the beat of their hoofs and a queer panting noise that I can't describe. First came a beautiful thing with his head held high; his great antlers seemed to lie half his length on his back; his eyes were startled, and his shining black mane seemed to bristle. I heard the report of guns, and he tumbled in a confused heap. He tried to rise, but others coming leaped over him and knocked him down. Some more shots, and those behind turned and went back the way they had come.

Mr. Haynes shouted to me, "Shoot, shoot; why *don't* you shoot!"

So I fired my Krag, but next I found myself picking myself up and wondering who had struck me and for what. I was so dizzy I could scarcely move, but I got down to where the others were excitedly admiring the two dead elk that they said were the victims of Mrs. O'Shaughnessy's gun. She was as excited and delighted as if she had never declared she would not kill anything. "Sure it's many a meal they'll make for little hungry mouths," she said. She was rubbing her shoulder ruefully. "I don't want to fire any more big guns. I thought old Goliar had hit me a biff with a blackthorn shilaley," she remarked.

Mr. Haynes turned to me and said, "You are a dandy hunter! You didn't shoot at all until after the elk were gone, and the way you held your gun it is a wonder it didn't knock your head off, instead of just smashing your jaw."

The men worked as fast as they could at the elk, and we helped as much as we could, but it was dark before we reached camp. Supper was ready, but I went to bed at once. They all thought it was because I was so disappointed, but it was because I was so stiff and sore I could hardly move, and so tired I couldn't sleep. Next morning my jaw and neck were so swollen that I hated any one to see me, and my head ached for two days. It has been snowing for a long time, but Clyde says he will take me hunting when it stops. I don't want to go but reckon I will have to, because I don't want to come so far and buy a license to kill an elk and go back empty-handed, and partly to get a rest from Mr. Murry's everlasting accordion.

Mr. Murry is an old-time acquaintance of Mrs. O'Shaughnessy. He has a ranch down on the river somewhere. Mrs. O'Shaughnessy has not seen him for years, didn't know he lived up here. He had seen the game-warden from whom she had procured her license, and so hunted up our camp. He is an odd-looking individual, with sad eyes and a drooping mouth which gives his face a most hopeless reproachful expression. His nose, however seems to upset the original plan, for it is long and thin and bent slightly to one side. His neck is long and his Adam's apple seems uncertain as to where it belongs. At supper Jerrine watched it as if fascinated until I sent her from the table and went out to speak to her about gazing.

"Why, mamma," she said, "I had to look; he has swallowed something that won't go either up or down, and I'm 'fraid he'll choke."

Although I can't brag about Mr. Murry's appearance, I can about his taste, for he admires Mrs. O'Shaughnessy. It seems that in years gone by he has made attempts to marry her.

As he got up from supper the first night he was with us, he said, "Mary Ellen, I have a real treat and surprise for you. Just wait a few minutes, an' I'll bet you'll be happy."

We took our accustomed places around the fire, while Mr. Murry hobbled his cayuse and took an odd-looking bundle from his saddle. He seated himself and took from the bundle—an accordion! He set it upon his knee and began pulling and pushing on it. He did what Mr. Struble said was doling a doleful tune. Every one took it good-naturedly, but he kept doling the doleful until little by little the circle thinned.

Our tent is as comfortable as can be. Now that it is snowing, we sit around the stoves, and we should have fine times if Professor Glenholt could have a chance to talk; but we have to listen to "Run, Nigger, Run" and "The Old Gray Hoss Come A-tearin' Out the Wilderness." I'll sing them to you when I come to Denver.

> With much love to you,
> Elinore Rupert Stewart

VIII. THE SEVENTH MAN
Cloudcrest, October 10, 1914
DEAR MRS. CONEY,—

I wonder what you would do if you were here. But I reckon I had better not anticipate, and so I will begin at the beginning. On the morning of the eighth we held a council. The physician and the two students had gone. All had their limit of elk except Mr. Haynes and myself. Our licenses also entitled each of us to a deer, a mountain sheep, and a bear. We had plenty of food, but it had snowed about a foot and I was beginning to want to get out while the going was good. Two other outfits had gone out. The doctor and the students hired them to haul out their game. So we decided to stay on a week longer.

That morning Mrs. O'Shaughnessy and I melted snow and washed the clothes. It was delightful to have nice soft water, and we enjoyed our work; it was almost noon before we thought to begin dinner. I suppose you would say lunch, but with us it is dinner. None of the men had gone out that day.

Mr. Harkrudder was busy with his films and didn't come with the rest when dinner was ready. When he did come, he was excited; he laid a picture on the table and said, "Do any of you recognize this?"

It looked like a flash-light of our camping ground. It was a little blurry, but some of the objects were quite clear. Our tent was a white blotch except for the outlines; the wagons showed plainly. I didn't think much of it as a picture, so I paid scant attention. Mrs. O'Shaughnessy gave it close scrutiny; presently she said, "Oh, yis, I see what it is. It's a puzzle picture and ye find the man. Here he is, hidin' beyont the pine next the tent."

"Exactly," said Harkrudder, "but I had not expected just this. I am working out some ideas of my own in photography, and this picture is one of the experiments I tried the night of the storm. The result doesn't prove my experiment either way. Where were you, Stewart, during the storm?"

"Where should I be? I bided i' the bed," the Stewart said.

"Well," said Harkrudder, "I know where each of the other fellows was, and none of them was in this direction. Now who is the seventh man?"

I looked again, and, sure enough, there was a man in a crouching position outlined against the tent wall. We were all excited, for it was ten minutes past one when Harkrudder was out, and we couldn't think why any one would be prowling about our camp at that time of the night.

As Mr. Stewart and I had planned a long, beautiful ride, we set out after dinner, leaving the rest yet at the table eating and conjecturing about the "stranger within our picture." I had hoped we would come to ground level enough for a sharp, invigorating canter, but our way was too rough. It was a joy to be out in the great, silent forest. The snow made riding a little venturesome because the horses slipped a great deal, but Chub is dependable even though he *is* lazy. Clyde bestrode Mr. Haynes's Old Blue. We were headed for the cascades on Clear Creek, to see the wonderful ice-caverns that the flying spray is forming.

We had almost reached the cascades and were crossing a little bowl-like valley, when an elk calf leaped out of the snow and ran a few yards. It paused and finally came irresolutely back toward us. A few steps farther we saw great, red splotches on the snow and the body of a cow elk. Around it were the tracks of the faithful little calf. It would stay by its mother until starvation or wild animals put an end to its suffering. The cow was shot in half a dozen places, none of them in a fatal spot; it had bled to death. "That," said Mr. Stewart angrily, "comes o' bunch shooting. The authorities should revoke the license of a man found guilty of bunch shooting."

We rode on in silence, each a little saddened by what we had seen. But this was not all. We had begun to descend the mountain side to Clear

Creek when we came upon the beaten trail of a herd of elk. We followed it as offering perhaps the safest descent. It didn't take us far. Around the spur of the mountain the herd had stampeded; tracks were everywhere. Lying in the trail were a spike and an old bull with a broken antler. Chub shied, but Old Blue doesn't scare, so Mr. Stewart rode up quite close. Around the heads were tell-tale tracks. We didn't dismount, but we knew that the two upper teeth or tushes were missing and that the hated tooth-hunter was at work. The tracks in the snow showed there had been two men. An adult elk averages five hundred pounds of splendid meat; here before us, therefore, lay a thousand pounds of food thrown to waste just to enable a contemptible tooth-hunter to obtain four teeth. Tooth-hunting is against the law, but this is a case where you must catch before hanging.

Well, we saw the cascades, and after resting a little, we started homeward through the heavy woods, where we were compelled to go more slowly. We had dismounted, and were gathering some piñon cones from a fallen tree, when, almost without a sound, a band of elk came trailing down a little draw where a spring trickled. We watched them file along, evidently making for lower ground on which to bed. Chub snorted, and a large cow stopped and looked curiously in our direction. Those behind passed leisurely around her. We knew she had no calf, because she was light in color: cows suckling calves are of a darker shade. A loud report seemed to rend the forest, and the beauty dropped. The rest disappeared so suddenly that if the fine specimen that lay before me had not been proof, it would almost have seemed a dream. I had shot the cow elk my license called for.

We took off the head and removed the entrails, then covered our game with pine boughs, to which we tied a red bandanna so as to make it easy to find next day, when the men would come back with a saw to divide it down the back and pack it in. There is an imposing row of game hanging in the pines back of our tent. Supper was ready when we got in. Mr. Haynes had been out also and was very joyful; he got his elk this afternoon. We can start home day after to-morrow. It will take the men all to-morrow to get in the game.

I shall be glad to start. I am getting homesick, and I have not had a letter or even a card since I have been here. We are hungry for war news, and besides, it is snowing again. Our clothes didn't get dry either; they are frozen to the bush we hung them on. Perhaps they will be snowed under by morning. I can't complain, though, for it is warm and pleasant in our tent. The little campstove is glowing. Mrs. O'Shaughnessy is showing Jerrine how to make pigs of potatoes. Calvin and Robert are asleep. The men have all gone to the bachelors' tent to form their plans, all save Mr. Murry, who is "serenading" Mrs. O'Shaughnessy. He is playing "Nelly Gray," and somehow I don't want to laugh at him as I usually do; I can only feel sorry for him.

I can hardly write because my heart is yearning for my little Junior boy at home on the ranch with his grandmother. Dear little Mother Stewart, I feel very tender toward her. Junior is the pride of her heart. She would not allow us to bring him on this trip, so she is at the ranch taking care of my brown-eyed boy. Every one is so good, so kind, and I can do so little to repay. It makes me feel very unworthy. You'll think I have the blues, but I haven't. I just feel humble and chastened. When Mr. Murry pauses I can hear the soft spat, spat of the falling snow on the tent. I will be powerfully glad when we set our faces homeward.

Good-night, dear friend. Angels guard you.

Elinore Stewart

PART FOUR

Trophies

THE IDEA OF HUNTING FOR TROPHIES, LIKE THAT OF HUNTING "FOR sport," strikes a negative chord for many people, some of them hunters themselves. The impulse to stalk and shoot an animal for food, they argue, is one thing. But can one really justify turning the head (or the entire animal) into a static representation of its once-vibrant self and putting it on display?

Actually, one can, and for several reasons. First of all, taxidermy is an art, akin in many ways to sculpture. A skilled taxidermist can capture something of the animal's lived essence, preserving its strength and beauty in ways that inspire appreciation, contemplation, even awe. This can serve a healthy psychological, as well as an aesthetic, purpose. The late environmental philosopher Paul Shepard argued that there is something in us that needs the non-human animal "other" in order to be our human selves. In some senses, we more or less unconsciously inhabit a world of "trophies": We wear the skins of animals, held together by buttons of horn or bone, trimmed with feathers or fur. We are at considerable psychological risk when the animals who keep us fed and clothed become faceless. There is much to be gained by meeting an animal's gaze head-on: even, perhaps especially, if its eyes are made of glass, a clear reminder of its and our own mortality.

There are, to be sure, trophy collectors who care about little more than the accumulation of species for their game rooms. But for most hunters who value the trophy, it is as part of a much larger experience. It is a symbol of the hunt itself: the memory, the story, the lesson learned about one's relationship with the world beyond the merely human. It is also, as the stories in this section demonstrate in various ways, a testimony to the fact that hunting, good hunting anyway, is invariably hard work.

In the days before television and widespread tourism, trophies additionally formed the basis of museum displays which were the only way, other than pictures in books, that most people learned about the wild animals of their own and other continents. Adventurers like Carl Akeley and Bernard de Watteville were also naturalists with scientific training and interests. The animals they hunted were primarily specimens, intended for artful display, scientific inquiry and public education. (This did not mean, of course, that they did not enjoy hunting them!) Both men died in Africa, in pursuit of their work, respectively, for New York's Natural History Museum and the museum in Berne, Switzerland: Akeley died of fever and de Watteville was mauled to death by a lion. Akeley's wife, Mary, and de Watteville's daughter Vivienne were both thrown into the role of carrying on the men's work and completing their projects. And each woman rose to the task. The excerpts here convey the feel of safari hunting, which, while an adventure in itself, simultaneously has a purpose beyond itself: Mary Akeley's story of lion hunting dates from happier times before Carl's illness and death; Vivienne de Watteville's tale of a white rhino hunt is the wrenching climax of her struggle to complete her father's mission.

By contrast, the more contemporary selections here, by Sheila Link and Eileen Clarke, present unalloyed depictions of the way trophies can encapsulate the thrill of the chase. They also help to illustrate the conventional hunting wisdom that the most important trophy that any satisfying hunt yields is the memory of hard work, well done.

Daylight Stalker

(2002)

SHE TURNED ON THE LIGHT AND LOOKED AT HER WATCH. IT WAS 3:19 A.M. She shoved the blanket aside and got out of bed. Swiftly, silently, she donned the drab-colored garments laid out before going to sleep. She put the face mask and gloves in a pocket, picked up the gun and slipped out of the house.

Her pickup was parked beside the porch steps. She climbed in and drove for twenty minutes before slowing down to search for the nearly hidden narrow dirt road. When she found it, she turned in, cut the head-lights and stopped. She sat for several minutes until her eyes became accustomed to the darkness, then touched the accelerator pedal lightly. Four hundred yards from the highway she pulled over to the edge of the narrow road and turned off the engine. She reached overhead for the dome lightswitch and slid it to off so no light would show when she opened the door.

Stepping out, she pushed the door gently until a faint click told her it was shut, then stood silently, making certain her approach was unno-ticeable. Satisfied, she loaded the gun, pulled on gloves and face-mask and strode into the woods. Not a loner by nature, for now she wanted to be alone.

Although the sky was still murky-black, a sliver of grey light was edging along the eastern horizon. The ground under her feet was soft and she welcomed the quiet it afforded as she breathed the familiar scent of damp, muddy leaves. She noticed the sky becoming softer, lighter. Intent on her mission, her face was expressionless as she mentally sorted the data she'd collected, going over the facts she'd studied in preparation for this undertaking.

"I've got him this time," she told herself. "I know the bastard. I've learned his routine. I know where he'll be at full daybreak—when he makes his move, I'll be there and I'll be ready—there's no way he can escape." Impulsively yet unconsciously, she quickened her stride. As she walked she thought about the adversary she'd sought for so long and was about to confront.

"He's smart," she mused, "and maybe he's been tipped off . . . I know someone was in here last week, because I saw those tracks . . . and when I was scouting the other day and stumbled over that damn dead limb, it made a racket . . . He probably heard that . . . But I don't think he knows that *I'm* after him. Well, I'd better be extra cautious today—I'm running out of time . . . "

Hours later, disgusted, she returned to the pickup, pulled off the face mask, and drove home. Her carefully contrived plan had failed. The face-off she yearned for hadn't materialized. Occasionally she cursed softly, shaking her head from side to side. "I've gotta give him credit," she brooded, "he's a crafty S.O.B . . . but so am I!"

Before going to bed that night she repeated the preparations of the previous night, laying out clothes and boots, wiping down the gun and working the action. "I'll get him tomorrow," she muttered, pulling the blanket up over her shoulders. "I *know* he's there . . . hell, *heard* him this morning . . . He outwitted me all right, but he's *there* and I'll get him! . . . I'll get him . . . "

When she awoke a bit after 3 A.M., she followed the same routine as the day before but, just before leaving, she slipped a tiny object into her breastpocket, patted the pocket, and smiled grimly as she pulled the door shut behind her.

When she reached the location she sought, she carefully brushed dry leaves and twigs away from the base of a big oak tree and sat down with her back against the tree's broad trunk. She'd been there nearly twenty minutes when she heard, off to her right, the morning's first sound, the "Whoo-who-awhooo-aagh!"of a barred owl. Instantly the response she'd waited for came: "GOBBLE-GOBBLE—GOBBLE-GOBBLE!"

The hunter grinned. Reaching into a pocket on her pants leg, she pulled out a piece of slate and a spindle and began pushing the spindle across the slate to make a soft purring sound, throwing in an occasional contented little cluck. After a few moments she heard a muffled flurry as the tom flew down from his perch. The hunter took out a cedar box-call and began making a series of yelps. She was rewarded with another, louder gobble-gobble, this time definitely closer.

Very carefully, the hunter laid her cedar box on the ground and slipped a hand into her breastpocket. She brought out her Old Faithful diaphragm-call and placed it in her mouth. Drawing her knees up, she rested her elbows on them to support the 12-gauge pump and proceeded to give out a series of flirtatious, importuning yelps.

The tom responded immediately, advancing toward the allure of a promised rendezvous and announcing his amorous attentions as he came, with ever longer and louder gobbles. When he reached a small clearing, some fifty-five yards away, he stopped. Slowly, majestically, turning this way and that, he drummed his wings on the ground and fanned his tail, strutting and gobbling to tell the whole world that the biggest, baddest, handsomest tom turkey ever, was available for admiration.

The hunter's breath came faster. She could hear her heart beating as she watched the ancient courting display. She continued calling, softly now.

Suddenly the bird switched from narcissism to the urgency of spring. He gave out a low, booming, "GOBBLE-GOBBLE-GOBBLE-GOBBLE!" and broke into a run, straight for the hunter.

The shot was true. The hunter rose, shotgun in hand, and walked to her downed prey. It was an old tom with a 12-inch beard and long, curved, time-dulled spurs. The tips of his wing feathers were worn ragged from drumming. This was a real trophy, and hard-won.

"Well, I can sleep late tomorrow," the hunter thought, smiling as she walked back to her truck with the feathered foe over her shoulder. After a moment, though, her smile faded. "But I'd rather have the hunt ahead of me . . . it's not all that tough getting up early . . . in fact I like being in the woods at daybreak . . . and I wasn't all that tired . . . Of course, I might not see or even hear another gobbler . . . And sure, it's great to get a big old tom like this one . . . but damn—now my hunt's over . . . "

As she laid the bird in the back of her truck and climbed into the cab, the hunter murmured aloud, "It's gonna be a long wait 'till next season . . . " She shoved the truck into gear and headed home.

MARY L. JOBE AKELEY

Playing with Friendly Lions

from Carl Akeley's Africa *(1929)*

EVER SINCE I HAD FIRST TALKED TO CARL'S OLD GUNBOY, BILL, IN OUR Lukenia camp he had announced more or less frequently that he wanted "Memsahib to get a lion in Tanganyika," the country he knew so well, and now that we were actually in Bill's country, he often mentioned casually that he knew a valley where there were *"Simba mingisana"* (very many lions) and that he thought no one had ever shot there.

But in three weeks in Tanganyika, spent largely in hunting and camera work, I saw sufficient lions at close range to feel quite content not to take even one natural history specimen from Africa; vivid sounds and pictures indelibly impressed on my mind seemed quite enough. For many nights lions close to our camp had made the world reverberate to their roaring, and so close were they that as I lay in my cot, I could hear the long drawn intake of their breath, and when they later went out to kill, the stampeding zebra tripped across the guy ropes of my tent!

Shortly after dawn we started for "Bill's country." The indescribable blue of the morning sky was streaked with rose; the whistling wind was crisp and chill; and as we drove our little open camera car across the level stretches of the veldt, we felt grateful for warm sweaters and topcoats for the sun had not yet touched the summit of the eastern hills. Two secretary birds, rare and beautiful in form and color and of amazing dignity of motion, were sitting by their nest on the top of an acacia tree, feeding their young. Herds of wildebeest, quietly grazing in long lines across the landscape, stampeded noisily at our approach. Statuesque grown-up Tommies looked us steadily in the eye without giving an inch, the flick, flick of their little tails being the only indication that they were living and not sculptured animals. Their little ones, for all the world like the little wooden animals in a toy Noah's ark, shy as young fawns, went jumping across the landscape, stiff-legged, and on all fours.

Topi stood gazing quietly in groups of twos or threes, their brown, satiny coats gleaming in the morning light. A cheetah walked cautiously through the tall grass, herding her two little cubs ahead of her toward the shelter of a low growing tree. Two fennec foxes playing on a brick red

141

anthill, whisked their fawn-colored bodies suddenly out of sight, only large ears and little beady eyes showing that they watched us as we passed. Three or four miles from camp, a large band of hyenas—we counted thirty-eight—were fighting over the half-devoured carcass of a wildebeest, apparently their recent kill. They moved by slightly at our approach and we photographed them in motion pictures to our heart's content.

It would be hard indeed to describe adequately our course through the obscure valley we now entered. On the African veldt it is more than difficult to determine distinguishing landmarks. This is due largely to the lack of outstanding hills and mountains with distinct topographical characteristics. Few stand in vivid outline against the sky and you find a familiar landmark repeated again and again in the course of a day's journey. I could certainly go again to the long chain of hills which marked our entrance to this valley but our devious way thereafter, the crossing of deep dongas, and wide plains is a matter of Bill's exclusive and unparalleled knowledge of this big Tanganyika wilderness. To see him steering our course through the maze of thorn and scrub and high grass, you would think him traveling by some unseen star, and I firmly believe that Bill has his star that guides him into strange places and leads him to disclose to us the mysteries of landscape and wildlife which would never otherwise be revealed; and that his almost supernatural alertness of sense affords him a deep and quiet joy, in the realization of his own resourcefulness— approximating the high spots of human intellectualized emotion. His own unequaled native intellect, his quick absorption of all "his Bwana" had taught him, his pride in his own ability and achievement, his loyalty and steadfastness of purpose, his insight into the minds of other men, black and white, make of Bill an outstanding personality.

For two or three miles we drove across an extensive plain filled with high grass which for lion concealment is equal to donga or forest. Once a lion is seen, or sees you in this deep grass country, all he has to do for self protection is to travel a few feet or rods as he may wish, crouching close to the ground, and then lie down in the grass. There he will wait until you are upon him, and the chances are very good if you surprise him by quick and close approach that you will have the lion's share of the "surprise."

On a little rise in this deep grass country we soon saw two hyenas and near them a lion. We approached cautiously to the spot where they evidently had finished their early morning kill. The hyenas were still there but the lion had vanished. We went on a little further to the crest of the next rise, and there we saw the lion and another hyena. The lion was sitting in the grass waiting for us. Bill using his glasses, said, "Lion not big, no mane." We watched him quietly. He soon got up, turned a broad side to us and walked deliberately away. I counted off his paces—one-two, one-two—in just the time of a measure ticking of a clock. We had not even interested the lion. We went on down through the valley. It was well stocked with small game—Granti, "Tommies" and one fine herd of impala. Bill climbed the side of a hill and herded the impala down towards the camera, and as they jumped and vaulted and ran as only impala can do, Carl made a motion picture of them.

We next turned down into a still wider valley and traveled not far from the rim of a donga filled with dense bush, large trees and deep grass. Carl was driving the car and intermittently watching the donga, an almost impossible feat in this country of many pigholes, foxholes and anthills. We soon came upon a fine herd of giraffe, seven beautiful adults and five totos, but they were between us and the sun in a small thornbush so it was impossible to photograph them. We stopped to watch them. We saw one of the little totos take his breakfast and we finally got so close to the big old bull that we could see him wink his eyes. How easy it would have been to spend the whole morning watching these fascinating, prehistoric creatures.

We continued on down the valley, still keeping as close to the donga as possible. Here a recent fire had burned off the high grass and the going was much better. Soon Carl saw something moving across the donga. The sun was now high and the great heat waves were beginning to roll in and suffuse and distort the whole country in a shimmering mirage. "They may be only 'Tommies,'" he said. But soon we saw they were three lions sitting in the grass watching our approach. We went nearer. They dropped down a little in the grass as we advanced and then two others, a little farther on, sat up to watch us too. Right between the two groups a big, dark-colored lioness suddenly appeared. She was determined to get a close-up of us. She came up the slope of the donga, and through the tall grass, traveling straight toward us. When she reached the edge of the deep grass, where it abruptly joined the burned veldt, the big cat lifted her paws high, stepping out full into the open with the grace and assurance of a queen. As she came into the open Carl seized his .475 and I had presence of mind enough to grab my Goerz and photograph her, but unfortunately there was no chance for Carl to move back to his motion picture camera to make the photographs that would actually count.

It was the most thrilling sight I had ever beheld. The lioness slowly but steadily stalked us with lowered head, keeping a slender green thornbush, about three feet high, but no bigger than a cane, between us. Every now and then before she left the flimsy shelter of this bush she looked back to the others, doubtless to see if they were coming too. Then she left the thornbush, stepping out quite boldly and with head still held low, she sat down a little to one side and back of a large tree. This survey of us was not satisfactory. The lioness got up and deliberately moved on, reached the tree, walked back of it to the other side and came directly toward us. Not once did she take her eyes off us; not once did she hesitate. I was indescribably thrilled and fascinated. "If she comes five steps nearer I'll have to shoot," Carl said. With his gun on her, he tooted the motor's horn. She paid no attention and came a step nearer. He next started the engine but she paid no heed. I photographed. Finally Carl and Bill both shouted at the top of their lungs. She stopped for twenty full seconds, gave us one long look, turned, and as slowly, deliberately and gracefully as she had come toward us, she retraced her steps to the tall grass, and then jumped into the donga where her five companions still waited for her only half concealed. We all gasped audibly with our pentup excitement. "Oh! I'm glad I didn't have to kill that big beautiful cat. But I gave her only two more yards. Then I should have had to shoot," Carl said. We paced it off; she had turned at *exactly thirty paces.*

We took ten minutes to get our breath again, and to realize what had happened. The sheer courage and audacity of this superb, feline huntress preparing to investigate, perhaps if stampeded, to attack a living something, as we and our motorcar were to her, twenty times her size! She was, of course, backed by at least five other lions in the donga, who would have been swift and efficient seconds had she decided to attack what may have looked to her like a gigantic rhino, but we were quite certain that, had she been so inclined, would not have hesitated to install herself as an uninvited passenger in our little touring car. "You have seen one of the biggest things anyone can see in Africa," my husband said. The sheer thrill of the moment's experience brought me a conviction past any doubt.

We traveled on, through thorn-scrub and grass, through tall growing hibiscus plants, dead since the passing of the rains, until we reached a veritable network of dongas with deep-cut banks, and holding pools of fetid water throughout the year. With much difficulty we made our crossings, our car often sticking in the process and having to be pushed up the last grade. In one place the natives had built their hunting blinds of thorn and grass and from them lawlessly killed their game with bows and poisoned arrows. Our eyes were now alert for buffalo and rhino, but we saw only a big troop of baboons—I counted forty in the open, while half a dozen romping youngsters watched us from their perch on a big dead tree stub. One baby, sitting close to his mother's side, was left alone when she decided that a closer investigation of us was necessary. The baby foolishly clung to the tree, instead of to his mother, and too tiny to keep his balance, he fell off into the grass. But he was a nervy little fellow and climbed back after his fall. A little farther and we came to a troop of monkeys scampering about in the big yellow acacias. Our eyes glimpsed them as they figuratively flew from limb to limb, but it was impossible to focus our field glasses on them so swift were their movements. Next we saw big herds of zebra. I counted a hundred in one near-by group, with many more in the background. Distorted by the highlight of approaching noon, some looked pure white, others seemed covered with long shaggy fur, others shimmered and shifted as if constantly moving, but they were actually standing stockstill gazing at us under the trees.

We next came upon a herd of eland. One big cow eland had followed behind us from where the lioness had stalked us until now she joined this herd which consisted largely of cows and young calves. On our approach they stampeded in a cloud of dust, the calves racing in front and the big cows vaulting five feet into the air like frisking calves and looking for all the world like the picture in our nursery books of the "cow that jumped over the moon." These antics are one of the sights of Africa, and one not to be expected from such large antelope. A few days before we had seen a herd of one hundred behave in just the same way, and had got a good film of it. An old bull will weigh about fifteen hundred pounds—as much as a big Holstein bull. He has a deep dewlap, a satiny coat and beautiful, spiral-shaped horns that terminate often in an ivory-tipped spike.

The sun was on the meridian. Except for the cries of a flock of small green parakeets the stillness of noon enveloped everything. "When we find a good tree, we'll stop for lunch," we had agreed. Suddenly, Carl remarked casually, "Do you see that lion over there under the tree?" And as I looked for it, "It's probably a stump and will stay until we get there," he laughed. The whole world was enveloped in heat waves but as I looked at the stump I distinctly saw it turn its head. A little farther on we stopped and looked. It was a lion, sure enough, and a big one. We studied him through our glasses. He was near the donga, the securest refuge any hunted animal could wish. An alarm, a bound or two and he would be permanently safe. Although a lion had been the only thing I had even dreamed of killing, I had felt again that morning, as I had many times before, that I had no desire to kill. Then there seemed no chance that fortune would tempt me to change my mind. Now the most unexpected of all things happened. Exactly as if it had been staged, planned and timed for me the old lion walked deliberately into the open two hundred yards away to a small tree with dense shade. There he stood gazing out on the veldt at a small herd of wildebeest, dozing under small thorn bushes. He had an impressively fine, dark mane.

"He big lion. You take picture Bwana? You shoot?" asked Bill, all tensed with suppressed excitement. "You think he has a good mane, Bill?" Carl asked in deference to Bill. It was Bill's day we both remembered. "Yes, *mazuri* (good). He *kubwa sana* (very big)," jerked out Bill. "Memsahib's lion," said Carl as we crawled to a fair shooting range. And so it was ordained. Bill handed me my .275 Hoffman and Carl covered the lion with his .475. "Shoot when you are ready," Carl said very quietly. Conscious of an absolutely new sensation in my fingers I pulled, and the lion bounded back twenty yards, and stood facing us. At my second shot the lion took a nose dive into the veldt, lit on his back with his feet in the air and lay silent. We approached cautiously. "Can you see him breathe through your glasses?" Carl asked, still covering him with his gun. We could not. Bill walked toward the lion with my little gun. "Don't get between me and the lion," Carl shouted. The wise hunter knew from experience how easy it is for a "dead" lion suddenly to come to life. Bill cautiously threw rocks at the lion. No response. And as a final test touched his eyeballs with a long stick. There was not even a reflex. The old lion had surely gone on to another hunting ground.

It seemed unreal to me that the *only two shots I should fire in Africa* would bring such a prize. The first shot in line for the heart had struck directly on the humerus, and shattered it; the second at one hundred and thirty yards, had severed the aorta from the heart.

The lion which measured nine feet six inches from tip to tip and weighed about four hundred and seventy-five pounds was an old warrior. His coat was a dark silvery gray; his mane, silver-gray with a deep full frill of black—the brush on his tail was jet black. His face above his eyes was grayish white. Not only was he one of the largest lions my husband had ever seen, he told me, but never before had he seen such a rugged leonine countenance, so marked with age and battle scars, nor one which possessed such marks of personality. He had evidently been in a battle as recently as that morning; one hind leg was deeply cut; his upper lip was bleeding; both nostrils were freshly scratched, and there were three or four smaller wounds higher up on his face. In a conflict for food or perhaps for the favor of some lady feline, lovely as the one who a few hours before had stalked us, the old monarch had had his punishment.

He was probably ten or twelve years old. Four of his incisors, and one bicuspid were missing. His stomach, although of a capacity sufficient to contain half a zebra, was entirely empty, and now in death contracted to a long pipe-like organ hard as sinew. Further observation of his alimentary tract showed that he had probably not eaten for three days. When we first saw him he was doubtless about to lie up until the heat of the day should have passed, and then make his kill. The skinning of this superb animal revealed the marvelous strength and beauty of his muscles, ending in sinews like tempered steel; the masses of shoulder muscles; long rope-like chest muscles—those used in striking and rending; strong hooked claws of needle sharpness, that rend the hide of a rhino or break the neck of a zebra.

The revelations of the anatomic structure of the lion made me realize more than I ever had before how the pursuit of taxidermy had opened to my husband another source of joy—his sculpture—and why sometimes he was tempted to desert all else for that alone. And so for more than two hours, Carl and Bill worked in the care of the animal that I might have perhaps the most unusual specimen in all the world, and finally as my husband worked to photograph and get the last detail of measurement and sculptural characteristics, my appreciation of it all knew no bounds as he told me, "You know I am going to mount him as a complete animal, as a natural history specimen for you."

Now the finding of these lions in Bill's country, so apparently unmolested and unafraid was a discovery which Carl wanted by all means to share with Martin Johnson, so that a permanent record of these lions in motion pictures might be made. Accordingly, a second trip to the valley was made the following day, and there not far from my "Silvery Simba's" last stand, Bill showed them a colony of seventeen lions, fourteen of which were massed in one big family. Of course all we did for the next few days was think, feel, see and hear lions. Certainly the sights we saw almost made us believe that it would only be a matter of time until, as Phil Percival's little boy had said, we could "just go up and pat their big, shaggy heads." All our other lion experiences were fading into oblivion.

Carl took the wheel of Johnson's camera car and by skillful manipulation got him in excellent camera range of the big group where he made hitherto undreamed of records of peaceful lions in their home.

First, four grouped themselves on an ant hill, observing us carefully, and nine more watched us from the other side of the donga through a flimsy screen of grass. Not one manifested a sign of anger or of fear—only wonder and curiosity. As a reward for posing for us, we gave them a zebra for their supper.

The next day Carl drove Johnson and his camera up to within twenty-five feet of a group of eleven, which in the middle of the afternoon we found lined up in a row, this time on our side of the donga, quietly watching a herd of zebra out on the plains. As we approached, three that were a little hidden by the grass moved nearer and out in plain sight. Those in front and nearest the camera were for the first half hour alert, sitting up on their haunches and letting nothing escape them, consequently Carl not only maneuvered the car with great care, backing it farther away at the psychological moment when the lions showed a little nervousness and might have vanished from the scene, but at the same time kept his elephant gun ready for action. Once the engine went dead and the car had to be cranked. When the beasts quieted down, he drove nearer and nearer, where they could watch and photograph every movement of the lions.

Those farthest away from the camera, and, as it happened, near to where Bill and I waited, were entirely unconcerned. One big old lioness with yearling cubs licked their faces and fondled them playfully. Two grayish white young lions, who each day had kept side by side, played with each other standing on their hind legs and "strengthening their claws" on a near-by tree. Yawning sleepily they came over to the mother and yearlings and all five rolled about in the grass with paws in the air, displaying a wide expanse of white belly.

An old male with a fair mane, somewhat apart from the rest, took little interest in the others. He would nap for five or ten minutes, would then get up and stretch himself, change his position and lie down to sleep again yawning enormously. At one time seven of the lions were lying flat on their sides apparently sound asleep. Even those nearest the camera became indifferent to what was happening and, finally relaxing their watchfulness, meandered about and dozed or rested.

After two hours of "playing with" these lions, and as the sun was dropping low and a storm was brewing in the west, they manifested signs of hunger, became a little restless and showed great interest in the zebra herd. They now stretched themselves, yawned frequently—a time or two I thought I heard the click of their closing teeth—but they remained aloof and politely ignored our presence. It seemed time to leave, and as we had done the night before, a zebra was killed and brought to them as a reward for their patient posing.

What a day it had been! As we drove home in the thick blackness of the early night, and with a thunder storm breaking in torrents over us, Carl said, "It is the most wonderful lion show I have ever seen." Strangely enough the lion family was not seen again in the valley on this expedition. When looked for they had disappeared as suddenly as they had been discovered. They were doubtless following the departing wildebeest.

This story we had witnessed of lions at peace with the world, is the same story which my husband has told in his taxidermic lion group mounted in the American Museum of Natural History just before leaving for Africa—the story of family life as he had witnessed it in smaller groups of lions on the slopes of Mt. Elgon. Certainly here we all had a remarkable demonstration of my husband's creed that the "lion is a gentleman"; that if a given room he will go his own way without aggression.

VIVIENNE DE WATTEVILLE

Semliki Valley and White Nile

from Out in the Blue *(1937)*

NOT UNTIL THAT AFTERNOON TOWARDS THE END OF NOVEMBER WHEN the sun gilded the foothills of Ruwenzori and the Semliki plains stretched out drowning in distance, could I believe in this last trip. Not till I scrambled down the escarpment into that fond immensity of breathing earth and trees and stone, the voices of the little doves melting into the silence that fell around me, could I realize that I had been allowed to come back to it. In fact it was not until night returned, and the old throbbing song of crickets, and the tent was once more pitched against the stars, that I understood how overwhelming had been the kindness shown me, how it was alone by that strong help and because every one had wished it, that this last expedition had been made possible.

The Ituri forest had been ruled out. There were sufficiently good reasons against it, chiefest of them that it was not on British territory.

The white rhino was a quite big enough task. I had gone on doggedly maintaining that I could manage it, yet now that I was to go ahead, all difficulties swept aside for me but the natural ones, the enterprise grew suddenly daunting. It was no longer the collection alone, and success or failure my own affair; for I had been backed up, helped on every side and believed in; so that it was now doubly and trebly vital to succeed.

There was no hazard about it, no beast alive is more docile than a white rhino, no shooting poorer sport. The difficulty would be to find a good specimen, and much more, to remove the whole skin. Its bulk would be enormous, for rhino hide is thicker than elephant's. Months ago we had heard what an undertaking it was likely to be, how the horn alone cost a day's labour to remove. As with the elephant skin, it would be a race against time, and the climate would not be an ally, for the heat on the banks of the Nile is the damp heat of the Lorian in the rainy season.

But the boys were keen, that was the chief thing; and in the meantime there was nearly a fortnight in which to secure a good Sing-sing water-buck in the Semliki valley.

Just where the best heads were to be found, how to hunt the banks of a little stream called the Dura, Captain S who knew every acre of this district had already told me, and he had even furnished me with a rough map; so that if I failed to lay low that big waterbuck it was not for want of knowing where to look for him. On the other hand, a worse time of year could not have been chosen; the grass, still too green to burn, was a jungle that in some places reached higher than one's head, so that one might have walked within five yards of the record and been none the wiser.

It was like hunting in the dark, fighting one's way through those rank walls, and every now and then climbing a tree for a look out; and twice at least I should have literally stumbled upon buffalo had not the tick birds flown up and warned me.

This special licence which had been granted me allowed two water-buck. Two chances for a good head, and at the end of three days one of these chances had been thrown away.

It was after a long march, and I had reached a waterhole and pitched camp. The boys had seen a bull, we spoored but never came up with him, when just before dark we saw him making back for the waterhole. Posting myself, I saw him come slowly towards me picking his way across the open. His horns made me tremble with excitement, and the bullet sped all too true, for I had to beat thirty-two inches and when I laid the steel tape over them it would give not a fraction over twenty-eight.

With one chance left, I was determined to hunt the banks of the Dura systematically until the time was up and then take the best that offered. But it was disheartening work, for the boys especially, for when after hours of tramping we could at last find a herd, looking it over in vain for something good I invariably turned away.

Not only that, but the Dura was salt, and I had not been encamped there twenty-four hours before I began to have the symptoms of dysentery. It became obvious that it was only a matter of falling ill enough and I might not collect the second waterbuck at all; so when one morning three days before the ship was to call for me I had seen and passed by at least eight fairly good heads and I came upon a single beast which the boys declared was the best we had yet found, I decided to risk all upon him.

He gave me a great hunt, always crashing off among the trees as I was coming up, so that I too began to prize him. The chance came as he paused between two bushes, and the sun catching his horns in a wide arc above his head put to flight my last doubt, and I fired. But the steel tape marked inexorably thirty and a half inches.

Regrets were now unavailing and so I pretended to be pleased, for the boys were delighted, and they had worked for him with unflagging patience for what had seemed more like weeks than days. He was a fine specimen and I took the skin.

Comparing the measurements of both these bulls with the bull of Kinyonza, I found there was a considerable difference. The Kinyonza bull was nearly six inches higher at the shoulder. The kob on the contrary seem to be larger in the Semliki than in the Congo. As they appeared to have more white round the eyes and ears I collected a pair, the ram measuring three inches more at the shoulder than our largest Congo specimen.

The time of day I loved best was that hour before sunset when taking the shot-gun on the chance of a guinea-fowl I could wander off alone. Moving quietly among the buses I once came upon a waterbuck within a few yards. We both halted gazing at one another, he burnished in sunlight; and then he bent his head to nibble the grass as though reassured I was no enemy. There was no sweeter solace in my loneliness than these gestures of trust, as if Nature admitted me, nay, claimed me for one of her own. Then, knowing how surely I belonged, I was alone no more.

Between the Semliki and Rhino Camp, the *Baker* broke her voyage for a long week at Butiaba, a station on the shores of Lake Albert, built at the end of a desolate tongue of sand; and since it could provide neither porters nor food supplies, there was no hope of escaping from it. As a matter of fact I was very lucky to reach it at all, for I had foolishly allotted November thirty-one days in my diary, and only by an extraordinary chance happened to notice an almanac on the back of my writing-block. That was at three o'clock in the afternoon, it was a day later than I had reckoned, and between camp and the lake-shore was a day's march. I made Ntoroko sometime after sunset, and the *Baker* arrived in at sunrise. It was a near thing, and had I missed her there had been no white rhino, for it would have meant the loss of a fortnight and the licence expired at the end of the year—a heavy price to pay for learning that November has but thirty days.

In the semi-civilization of Butiaba there was nowhere to pitch the tent and I was obliged to sleep in a rest-house. Beyond studying the birds along the lake-shore and trying to paint sunsets of unimaginable beauty there was nothing in the world to do there, till the D.C. arranged for the hire of a canoe and paddlers and I spent days and nights in unsuccessful hippo hunts. I had done better to look upon that week as a reprieve, but I could neither pause nor rest, and I yearned to redeem our failure to collect a hippo on Lake Victoria.

And at night while the moon looked down into the lake, and infinitely far away the Congo hills rested like a veil of silver upon the horizon, there came the exultant beat of tom-toms. On and on they throbbed, while the distant voices rose and fell in haunting repetition of a phrase so wild and weird and sad that one could have gone mad with melancholy.

Thus the week at Butiaba eventually came to an end, and after a trip of eighteen hours the *Baker* steamed round a bend of the Nile and drew in alongside under the trees at Rhino Camp.

I now more than ever longed for the solitude of the real wilds, and hoped to trek to the nearest waterhole as soon as everything was put ashore. But inland there was no water, so there was nothing but to pitch the tent in the rest-camp by the river. It was Captain W who told me this, and he had come down to meet me, being under orders to remain at Rhino Camp until the white rhino had been safely disposed of.

Had I been alone I should have striven after B's example and worked for a good trophy if necessary until New Year's Eve. But although one might tramp day after day perfectly happily when it was for one's own great object, I had not the heart to ask Captain W to tramp too, and had I been alone, the rhino would doubtless be roaming through the bush to this day. As it was, I had only three days' hunting, and I was now humble enough to be deeply grateful for help, for fear dogged me that I might not stay the course. To have overcome what had appeared the greatest difficulties, and to fail at the eleventh hour merely because I was physically at the end of my resources, was a kind of defeat that could never be outlived.

The grass was as high as in the Semliki, and a couple of hunts convincing us of the unlikelihood of chancing upon rhino in such cover, we fired it. Fortunately it was dry enough to catch and spread, and there were soon bush fires great enough to throw up a light into the night sky. After this the country was a blackened prairie and the ashes rose underfoot in choking clouds, but one could at least see.

Setting off by starlight—and how reminiscent was the smell of ashes under the dew!—by the time the east warmed, we came to the place where we had last seen rhino spoor. The boys went off to reconnoiter, but the sun had climbed into the heavens and the dew and freshness had gone long before any word came back. Another day wasted, I thought, but after all, it was not likely that a white rhino was to be had without working pretty hard for him. Besides, I had seen two or three bulls already, and decided that they were not good enough. But presently the askaris came to report a rhino feeding close by.

The wind was shifty, for it was that time of day when it is still undecided which way to blow, and tries alternately from every quarter. Three times we retraced our way, and when we reached the spot the only indications of rhino were his retreating footsteps through the ashes.

It was past midday when we saw three rhino standing in the shade of some bushes, a cow and calf, and the bull a little way behind them. Then began again the business of deciding upon the length of his horn. As he lifted his head, the horn in profile, black in the shadow against the glare beyond, looked immense, at another angle indifferent, yet again a good sweeping curve to make my heart beat. I held up the thirty-inch stick which H.E. told me would serve as a rough guide, but even then I could not make up my mind. Captain W was doubtful; the boys swore it was huge, but then they always do, and they had never before seen white rhino. Finally exchanging the rifle for the camera, I crept up. The rhino saw me and bolted and I dashed after him to get a photograph, till round a bush I almost fell over the cow and calf, and they all galloped off in a cloud of ashes.

We had not continued far when we came upon another bull, and this time everyone was unanimous that he carried a fine horn.

A patch of long grass necessitated a standing shot, and as I edged up and he began to look round uneasily, a hundred reasons for not shooting flashed across my mind. As I was still hesitating, Muthoka whispered that the rhino was about to move off, and it was now or never. To let him go meant more endless tramping, and I might not find anything as good; but I suppose it was being half-hearted over it and not willing the shot, for leveling on that unmissable target I missed it clean.

He spun round and lumbered away, and seeing that in another moment he would be gone for good and all, I pulled myself together and put a bullet into his stern.

He made a stand, and I stalked close up, sat down and took long and steady aim for the middle of his chest. But as he galloped by in that last mad rush his horn appeared to be about a foot long, and I had not the heart even to go and look at him.

However, since he was dead, the next thing was to get off his hide. It was interesting, too, to see a white rhino, his curious square mouth without the prehensile tip, his large ears fringed with stiff black hair, were all unlike the common black rhino, and he seemed also to be lighter in colour. After the excitement of the hunt, the measuring had always been the tedious part, and in this instance tunnels had to be burrowed under him for the circumferences.

We hauled him over on to his back, and he was such an unwieldy mass that ten boys a side were only just able to steady him. Climbing on top of him I made the cuts; Muthoka had put a razor-edge to the knife, and it needed that, for the skin even on the belly was almost an inch thick.

By the time the skinners arrived, we had made good headway, but the horn proved an arduous business and the sun went down upon us still hacking and hewing. By good fortune there was a gang of road workers eager for the meat; they made a frame of saplings and thirty of them shouldered the skin and brought it back to camp.

When we reached the road, it was again under the stars, but these homecomings, even if one has been only moderately successful are fine enough and fatigue does not enter into them. And a few inches one way or the other in the length of the horn does not lessen the difficulties of removing the skin. There had been a gnawing anxiety of doubt over that, whether with only four experienced skinners it could be achieved.

The whole skin had to be pared down, and a dozen local natives were induced to help, so that we were twenty to work on it; and we worked next day without intermission from six to six. It was hard straightforward labour, and for the past weeks the actual getting to work on that white rhino had been the summit of my desire.

On the following day, H.E. and Lady Archer were to pass Rhino Camp on their way to the Sudan, so Captain W sent out his askaris to cut stacks of papyrus, and we amused ourselves all the morning decorating the rest-camp. Over the seats of honour we drew a shield with a large snow-white rhino rampant, bearing the motto "white is might," and above the landing-stage I hung a blanket on which, cut out in calico, was a rhino, and CAMP. This rhino could be seen with the naked eye for miles, so that the *Baker* could not possibly steam past Rhino Camp and forget me.

The other rhino was spread out on a platform under the trees, and as the time drew near I went to give the horn a final polish. I had scrubbed off the mud with soap and water, and a fresh coating of Vaseline brought out the amber lights in the horn, in fact one might have been almost tempted to admire it, that is if it had been just three inches longer. Confessing these twenty eight inches was going to be a bad moment, for H.E. had told me not to look at anything under thirty inches and I was afraid that he might regret all the trouble he had taken in arranging this expedition for me. So that when after all he did not look disappointed but admired the horn for its exceptional thickness round the base, I had not thought of that, and I rushed to our tattered copy of Ward's *Records* at the first opportunity.

The *Baker* continued her voyage, Captain W returned to Arua and I had just ten days left of Rhino Camp.

Throughout the trip, even in the early days, I used to dream that it was over, but always I awoke again to the V of sky beyond the green roof, an awakening so full of gladness that every succeeding dawn brought back the same impulse to run out to meet the sunrise and hail it. Now the dream would be the reality, I should wake to the prison of four walls where nature would be out of earshot; and each day brought nearer the time when I must tear myself from her healing and tender keeping and return alone in the numbness of sorrow to the loneliness of civilization. Little did I guess how much I owed to the white rhino, for he had stood like a strong hill between me and the end. I moved in the coma of a fatigue so immense that I could only go on ceaselessly working or sink for ever into the deep well of sleep; there was no middle course. Yet even now he helped to stave off the future from which I shrank, for the skin threatened to "slip"; and it gave me such an anxious time of thinning and pasting and overhauling that thought was held at bay.

During those last days I was drawn back again and again to the river, till with the hours of watching its slow soothing current my very mind was woven into the deep serenity and purpose of its flowing; and I lay beside the Nile as one might lie beside the waters of Lethe, gazing out in a deep abstraction that was almost forgetfulness.

It flowed by so tranquilly, neither hurrying nor tarrying, and the little Nile cabbages floated past eddying in the current and slipping by and out of sight. Thus might you muse upon it for a few brief hours or for a thousand years; and it might stand for a symbol of Time itself running down through the ages; here still in its beginning, its banks wild and untrodden, its people primitive as the first man; anon flowing through the desert till it flows at last under bridges and past great civilizations old and new. About it and about the natives who sat watching it there was the same strong patience that would finally conquer all. It is this very patience that is at first so exasperating about Africa and Africans, a kind of apathy and indifference that is callous, and a fatalism that enrages one. Yet there, perhaps, lay the solution. Africa, and life itself, is too mighty for anything so brittle as impatience, and one's strength lies not in pitting oneself against it, but in ranging oneself upon the same side.

During all those months of hunting, what might most have struck you was the stoicism of the beasts; how they would fight to the last inch always, no amount of pain subduing their spirit, nothing but death itself. The boys were stoic too, and though they may have had a hundred failings, loss of patience was not one of them.

And after all the "blue" did not end with Rhino Camp. The Nimule-Rejaf trek at this season, so far from being a highroad of tourists was as deserted as any of it, and I met never a white man. Except one, a missionary who overtook me on a bicycle on New Year's Day and sympathized over my having to walk. I could not tell him that not for all the bicycles in the world would I have foregone a step of that last march. It was splendid hard marching too, for the *Baker* was late and the boat at Rejaf was not, so that there were only six days in which to cover those ninety-six miles.

It was the Sudan now, and desert heat, so that I trekked during the small hours. There is little game, but it is nevertheless a fine road, stone-strewn and lonely, and each dawn the sun rose above it in fiery splendour and the wind went blowing deep-voiced among the rocks.[1]

At Rejaf there was much to do, import permits on the rifles to obtain, money to be changed, Customs to go through, heaven-sent occupation, for it left less time in which to dwell upon the rest—on selling up our tent and equipment—though at the last moment on a sudden impulse I unpacked the saw and cut through the tent-pole below the ferule, for it was that same piece of wood we had cut in Meru forest and I could not let it go.

Jim and the cook, who had accompanied me to the end of the safari, had also to be discharged, and at length the steamer hove in sight. Since it had been a race and I had arrived first, there was a faint hope that something might still prevent her coming. But even though each turn of her paddles and the very current itself would conspire against me, it was all for the best, for much as I yearned for that trek over again, I was on the eve of a bad attack of fever and I was not good for another march.

She did not weigh anchor till after nightfall, and there was yet time to climb the Rejaf hill. Up there the kites went circling and the granite smouldered in the dusk. Below me the Nile stretched lazy coils of turquoise spanning the horizons. Earth arched round the sky, darkling bush with here a hill and there a light ribbon of road—leading whither? Somewhere toward the sunset or out to the dawn, like all African roads. Happy are they who wander in them.

Herr Guide

(2000)

H E WAS CHARLES BOYER–HANDSOME WITH DISTINGUISHED GRAY HAIR, elegant bearing, and that continental education which makes a person comfortable in two cultures, three homes and many languages. Except it wasn't the usual suspects: French, Greek, and Latin. It was his native German, then Afrikaans, Ovango, English, and two varieties of Bushman, to name a few. Oh, yes, he told me that first morning as we headed down a two-track road two inches deep in red Namibian sand, "I talk the Bushman talk." As well as ten other languages within walking distance of this ranch. And he ticked off the names on his fingers as a fifth grader recites his state capitals.

But, with all his language, he had not asked me what I wanted to hunt. And to be honest, my list wasn't set in stone. There was the kudu. That had been on the list right from the beginning. And the blue wildebeest, which as far as I was concerned, defined Africa. From there, I'd grown intrigued with gemsbok—the harlequin duck of African antelope, I thought, though both of those giants of literary Africa, Hemingway and Ruark, considered shooting "oryx" little more than killing time.

Most days, warthog made the list. I already had a Russian boar hanging over my fridge, and fancied a warthog head over the dishwasher. Then zebra. Maybe. The rest of my little hunting party, my husband John and our friend Tom Brownlee, knew exactly what they wanted, and headed off that first morning with definite pictures in their heads. But my list was fuzzy as ever as I headed out with my own personal, elegant, and multilingual guide.

Forty-five minutes later, we parked beneath an overhanging acacia tree and set out silently cross-country. Fritz in the lead, me behind trying to adapt to a cornucopia of unfamiliar thorn bush. The first thing that struck me was the easy walking. For a person "used to" climbing the Rocky Mountain Front for elk, bighorn sheep, and grouse, as well as stumbling over wheat-stubble for birds, this was a piece of cake. Perfectly flat. No rocks, no grade, no clumps of hard dirt to sprain an ankle, wrench a knee, or noisily trip over. The second thing to strike me was a long wait-a-bit thorn branch that penetrated deeply into my shin then some-how wrapped around my leg.

As I peeled the branch off, Fritz slowed to a crawl just ahead, walking up behind a white thornbush and peering slowly through a gap. He whis-pered something back to me, then waved a hand behind his back signal-ing we would go left. I followed, and soon we were on our knees. "We do the leopard crawl," Fritz told me, and we slithered on our bellies through another fifty feet of brush and peered over a dirt embankment.

Through the last layer of cover, I could see a herd of thirty or more glossy red animals the size of large mule deer, lounging in the mid-morning heat around a well-used waterhole. Fritz pointed one animal out of the crowd of cookie-cutter bulls, cows, and calves that he said was a fine trophy. They all had horns. The same horns, it seemed. A combination of ridged bases that grew forward, then a smooth upper horn that bent back into a sharp point. But the more I sat there watching, trying to figure which horn was which, the more confused I got.

"What are they?" I finally asked.

"Hartebeest," he said. "Red hartebeest. You should shoot that bull. He is a fine animal."

"I've never seen one before," I said, which wasn't technically true. Tom had one mounted on his living room wall. And had tried to turn me on to them, saying that Namibia was the best place to get a "good" red hartebeest. If I wanted one. They just never appealed to me.

"Are you going to shoot him?" Fritz asked impatiently.

"No. I don't want a hartebeest. Aren't there any kudu or gemsbok here?"

"Yes, of course. Is he too far for you to shoot?"

"No, of course not. I just don't want him."

The hartebeest herd paid no attention to us, continuing to sleep, graze, and rise languidly, one by one, to take a drink.

"Yes, it is very far," he said, seemingly agreeing with someone else.

"I can take him, no problem," I insisted. "If I wanted to."

He turned to me, enunciating very carefully. "If you want to hunt, you must hunt like a man."

We were both silent for a few minutes, sitting there over the water-hole watching the hartebeest scratch their ears, dog-style, with a hind hoof. Then the wind changed. The hartebeest herd bolted a split second after I felt the gust on the back of my neck.

"We will come back. But that bull was very nice."

Sure, I thought. That would be a lot of fun.

We saw little but hartebeest the rest of the day, and I began to see the difference between males and females in the herds. I refused two more bulls at the next three waterholes; hartebeest not as big as the first one, I was told, but still very respectable trophies. As we walked from the last waterhole, Fritz turned to me and said, "I carry your rifle," as he grabbed it off my shoulder. "Ah, it is light," he said, as he nestled the sling across his shoulder.

"Yes," I answered. *"Ultra Light,"* a brand name, not an adjective. Designed and built by a man who shot groundhogs at 600 yards to keep his eye tuned; that I had used to take pronghorn antelope at over 400 yards. *When* I wanted to pull the trigger.

We emerged from the thornbush and crossed a fence onto a piece of two-track road. Fritz looked up and down the road in annoyance.

"No truck?" Fritz said, as he turned to me. "Where is my driver? He is maybe sleeping, I think." He looked back down the two-track.

In short order, the truck showed up. And Fritz took Johannes, our young black driver, to task in his native language. I glassed for kudu, biting my lip hard, but surprised with the in-your-face vehemence of Johannes' response. Finally Fritz was done, letting young Johannes have the last word.

"He was 'thinking,'" Fritz exclaimed in English. "He 'thought' we'd be somewhere else. He 'thought' we would come out 'later' he said. Very dangerous thing, to let the black man 'think.'" Fritz paused and looked down the road. "Now, we go up here a little bit," pointing past the front of the truck. "Then we have some breakfast."

I held my tongue and got back up into the raised safari seats as Johannes drove to our breakfast spot. As we drove, Fritz climbed over the safari frame and stood, feet braced, on the hood of the cab. With the higher vantage point, he spotted gemsbok horns a half mile off in the thornbush. He tapped the driver's open window with his branch but Johannes didn't stop. Fritz leaned forward over the windshield and rapped it hard with his stick. Johannes hit the brakes just as we hit a stretch of deep sand. In an instant Fritz had slid off the roof of the cab, down the windshield and onto the middle of the little bit of a Mazda hood, knees bent, arms outstretched, taking what balance he could grasp from that absolutely dew-less Namibian air. Miraculously, he stopped at the lip of the hood—looking like a gnarly old surfing dude. He smiled wryly and reached with one hand to the small of his back as he straightened back up.

"You mustn't *drop* me," he said in English. Johannes' English was as good as my Ovango, so what Fritz said, he'd said just for me. Silently, not wanting to give him any momentum in this war with Johannes, I had to agree: It's not a good thing to be dropped off the front of a moving vehicle. Even if it's an under-powered Mazda mini-truck. Even if it isn't moving very fast. And even if you've just been a jerk.

"We go for the gemsbok," Fritz said, looking back up to me.

"Okay," I said, not even daring to ask about breakfast.

I am grateful for not knowing beforehand the reputation of gemsbok. That they are very hard to kill. That they will go forever with a lethal wound, taking out wire fences, farm after farm, as they run. So with the bliss of total ignorance, when we got up on this guy after miles of thorn-bush interactions, Fritz spotting the horizontal black marking on his belly first, I catching the blink of an eye emerging from thick cover, I placed the shot perfectly and he fell in the split second of recoil. Fritz saw him go down. I never did. Quartering to me, I'd put the shot in his near shoulder, and the Fail Safe bullet had lived up to its hype, traveling diagonally the length of his body, and almost exiting the far hip. The bullet took the jugular, too; in revenge, the gemsbok ripped the petals completely off, leaving only a pencil stub under the hide.

Fritz congratulated me, and in my total ignorance of gemsbok lore, I thanked his praise a little less than I should have. We ate breakfast, finally, and delivered the gemsbok to the meat handlers at camp. John and Tom had been in earlier in the morning and left an eland, which they'd already quartered and was being hung in the cooler as we retired for a well-deserved noon break.

By two, Fritz was ready to go again, with no obvious ill effects from his surfing adventure. Johannes took the wheel, and the three of us headed out again, content with our gemsbok, but looking to add more trophies to this day.

We saw more gemsbok, of course. And warthog sows with young, all on to us before we saw them, and all running away with their tails straight up like lightning rods. But it was the hartebeest that began to weasel themselves into my consciousness, imprinting their weirdly ridged horns on my imagination, their gaudy red coats on my retina, and starting to make my trigger finger twitch. Fritz approved of none of the bulls we saw.

Finally it was the witching hour. In Namibia, that first week, the moon was coming full. And as the sunset, the moon burst huge over the horizon—bathed in the vibrant crimson-orange wash of the swiftly disappearing African sunset. It was a powerful distraction, I'll admit, watching this miracle, and in the orange glow of sunset, Fritz saw the kudu bull first.

We had taken another "little" walk through the thorn bush. Five miles, this time to a waterhole which ended up deserted. Not even a warthog. As we cut across the trampled shoreline to cross more miles of thornbush, he spotted the horns. At the same instant, the kudu saw us. Quartering to me, the bull offered the same shot as the gemsbok. I took it and he fell. But soon as he hit the ground, he bounded up again, gathering himself for a quick getaway. I'd already jacked a second shell into the chamber, and as the kudu ran behind the first bush, I instinctively plotted his trajectory. Just a few feet ahead was an opening in the thick white-thorn, if he didn't change direction. I held shoulder high in the open space and he ran right into my crosshairs, dropping for good this time.

Unlike the gemsbok, I'd read about the kudu voodoo. The kudu mystique. But this was beyond what black and white words could imprint on my brain. My kudu was incredible. Like the moon, his wide, massive horns faced the failing sun and reflected its golden light in my hands. I was stunned by the hand-dwarfing mass of them, the shadows on his hide, the sheer luck that he had not veered from his course. In this one day, I had taken both the most elusive and the toughest of all African plains game. Cleanly, and in front of witnesses.

"How did you learn to shoot like that?" Fritz said, positively glowing all over me. I didn't tell him: It was simply that kudu looked like elk to me—from the rocking gait to their gawky, shoulder-heavy profile—and almost every elk runs downhill despite a perfectly lethal shot, when the trail home is clearly *up*hill. Even with the flat terrain, and more hands than we needed back at the ranch, the instinct remained: Don't let him run downhill. Having no downhill to point to, I kept all that to myself.

As the moon climbed higher in the sky, shrinking to its usual size and pale silver color, we drove back to the ranch. We were both still looking for game. Both half-heartedly.

Tom, John, and their guide were not yet back from hunting. The kudu was the only game now waiting for skinning and quartering.

"You will join me for a drink?" Fritz asked as we admired the kudu one last time.

"Yes," I said. "A cold beer would taste very good right now."

I started to walk around to the back of the house, where the table was set for dinner, but Fritz stopped me.

"We go in this way. It's closer." He took me in through the kitchen— the family entrance.

We sat in the cool of the ranch house, enjoying the smugness of a hard day's work done well, and the two trickiest animals on my wish list safely in the cooler.

I thanked Fritz for his trophy eye; he bragged some more about my shooting. Then we ran out of things to say. I was about to finish my beer and go back to my room to shower, when Fritz pointed at his shoes. I'd noticed them before. Them and the fact that he always went sockless in the thornbush. I was wearing 8-inch Russell Bird Shooters with duct tape wrapped around the laces to keep them free of free-loading burrs and seeds.

"Before you leave Africa, you should buy a pair of these. Kudu leather," he said. "They make the best shoes. All the guides wear them. Gemsbok is too thick. And giraffe. Ach. It is thickest of all. So tough that when the giraffe dies, the vulture can't break the skin with their beak."

"They need the jackal to take the first bite?" I asked.

He laughed, pulling his folding knife out of his pocket. "They need the white man. To use his knife."

I heard the other truck pull up with the rest of my party, and excused myself. With only twenty minutes to get cleaned up, John, Tom, and I decided to wait for the dinner table to catch up.

Fritz was expansive at supper. Gathered around the table, over South African wine, hartebeest curry, and good Namibian bread, we three hunters, our guides, and their family, Fritz boasted broadly of "his" hunter, and announced to everyone that I was the "real shooter" of our hunting party. I was almost beyond worrying about the effect this would have on John and Tom. The teasing I would take once we were alone. Almost.

Afterward, walking back across the ranchyard, our stomachs full, I started by telling them about Fritz's surfing safari to deflect their attention. Then I asked my husband, How did you do today?

"Oh, I got my eland."

"I saw that," I said. "Did you get him with one shot?"

"Two," he said. "He stood broadside, but the first bullet hit a twig or something and turned sideways. The second shot landed point-on."

"It dwarfs my gemsbok. And the kudu. *Together*," I said.

"How kind of you to notice," he grinned. "But you also bagged Fritz. He probably adds another 200 pounds to your bag."

"That's true," I nodded.

"And nothing you do from now on," Tom pointed out, "will change his opinion of you. You could miss completely and he would defend you to the death."

"So what are you and Fritz going after tomorrow?" John asked. "Your blue wildebeest or a dishwasher warthog?"

"Hartebeest," I said. "A red hartebeest. I've taken a liking to them."

PART FIVE

Predators and Prey

W<small>E ARE A PREDATOR SPECIES. OUR EYES, FACING FORWARD, SEE COLOR</small> and depth. Our teeth are designed to bite and tear. Our brains are wired for action: We make tools and weapons, we follow signs and tracks, we anticipate and make connections between seemingly unrelated events, we search for hints and possibilities, we act rather than react. Being a predator means being fully attuned to one's surroundings, paying attention with all five senses. It means being keen-eyed and quick-witted, stealthy and smart, confident and capable. It means knowing how to be patient and when to take action. It means inhabiting the moment and trusting one's own instinct.

It does not, of course, always mean being on top of the situation, or the food chain. There are other predators out there, too, who are sometimes in the hunt for us even as we stalk them—witness, particularly, Mary Hastings Bradley's chilling account of a lion hunt below. Or Agnes Herbert's close encounter with a she-bear, with its tragic consequences for the sow's orphaned cub. Even non-predacious prey can be deadly, as Beryl Markham recounts about her hairbreadth escape from a bull elephant. And yet, hunters are drawn to the danger inherent in stalking dangerous quarry, perhaps because, especially when those quarry are predators like ourselves, they sense a deep if sometimes ironic kinship with them—another point that Herbert makes, as Gretchen Cron does more elaborately.

Being a predator also means, of course, participating in the cycle of life and death and life. It is surely no accident that Artemis, the hunting goddess at the dawn of Western cultural history, was also a goddess of births and deaths, of creation and destruction in their manifold natural guises. And so Durga Bernhard, painter and writer, muses here on the deep connection between killing and nurturing nascent life.

AGNES HERBERT

On Killing a She-bear

from Two Dianas in Alaska *(1909)*

. . . WE WERE NOW EXCEEDINGLY CLOSE TO THE ALDER PATCH, AND FAIRLY in the way of the oncoming she-bear. With a sort of beautiful and refreshing trust in Providence, we both imagined that her ursine highness would turn aside and avoid us. A she-bear with a cub to protect is a big thing to tackle in any country, in Alaska she is a fiend let loose.

With a short sharp yell of rage, voicing the fury of her rage and offended majesty, she came straight for us. How she traveled! And the very small cub ambled behind as if nothing untoward was afoot. The front claws of the bear appeared to take a real grip of the ground as she propelled herself in great gallops over the coarse, knotted grass, through the make of blazing buttercups.

"I leave it to you," I said, hardly knowing the tone of my own voice, it was so huskily excited.

The Leader threw up his rifle, fired, and for a moment the oncoming bear certainly checked her speed. I saw, in a kind of dazed wonder, my companion wrestling with his rifle, hurriedly, anxiously, feverishly—something was wrong—the cartridge would not rise into the magazine.

"Kill her!" said the Leader laconically, with the greatest *sang-froid*.

Of course it had to be. I was using my old 12-bore—best of friends—a terrifically hard-hitting, heavy weapon, and had just time to get in a shot at a near thing of thirty yards, but it was well in the forehead. Still the game and courageous animal came on, her head dipping low to earth, and as I danced backwards she crashed over, so close to me that I could have touched her as she fell. A brave and gallant beast!

"Thus she passed over, and all the trumpets sounded for her on the other side," the Happy Hunting Grounds.

To have had to kill a she-bear! 'Twas the way luck went. Would that it had gone some other way.

The poor little cub stood bewildered a little way off, and presently he advanced to the great prone form and stood beside it, with his quaint little feet, and tiny growing claws, set in a faint trickle of blood. My heart-strings were tugged with the pity of it! What a brute I felt! I took out my very grimy handkerchief.

"You aren't going to cry about it, Agnes, are you?" the Leader asked apprehensively.

"You know I'm not," I answered indignantly; "I'm going to wipe the cub's feet, if I can catch it. I do think it is dreadful for it to be standing in the blood of its own mother."

"What a woman you are!" laughed the Leader. "Killing one minute, and healing the next. I wonder you have acquired your wonderful collection of trophies at all."

"You're jealous," I said calmly.

We played "You're another" until we managed to catch the little cub, a most beautiful little thing, very young and furry. As soon as the Leader saw that I did indeed mind very much having helped to make an orphan of the cub, he gave over chaffing, and did all he knew to comfort me. It was the truest fellowship. In countless tender ways he made the deed of blood seem less gory and revengeful.

Tendernesses are so dainty, so delicate, they are the work of Nature's genius. So long as a man can bring himself to give a woman tenderness— and I use the word in its highest sense—then she may know she has his love safe.

"I wonder who the little beggar takes after," said the Leader meditatively, as he held the little animal, struggling fiercely, in his arms; "its father or its mother?"

"Neither. It is just like Lord Kitchener."

And so it was. An amazing likeness. I often notice the extraordinary resemblance of expression which some animals have to some people. This cub was an excellent photograph of K. We christened him Kitchener in consequence. And the small animal who had crept so unexpectedly into our lives crept into our hearts as well during the three short weeks he lived aboard the *Lily* with us. We so hoped to be able, somehow, to get him home, for he was evidently on the way to being a fine specimen of *Ursus dalli gyas;* but, alas!, it was not thus to be. Kindness killed him. Or indigestion. The crew, though forbidden to do so, would feed the cub, and one morning we were greeted with the sad intelligence that our Kitchener lay dead. But I anticipate, as the novelists say.

DURGA BERNHARD

The Gift of Artemis:
A Hunting Mother's Perspective

(2002)

AN HOUR BEFORE MY ALARM WAS SET TO GO OFF, MY GROWLING STOMACH and full bladder roused me from restless sleep. In the dim light of the setting moon, I could barely make out the outline of my cat curled up in the folds of my bedspread.

Squinting in the light of the refrigerator, I reached for a container of goat milk and poured myself a bowl of cereal. The clock on the windowsill read 3:30 A.M. I was eight weeks pregnant and famished.

Instead of going back to bed, I switched off the alarm clock and reached into an ice chest near the door. It was full of camouflage hunting gear, safely stored away from household odors. Above the chest hung my compound bow, its quiver full of razor-sharp arrows. I pulled on insulated pants, a silk undershirt, a turtleneck, and a jacket. Over my clothes went a layer of camouflage, followed by camouflage facenet and hat. As I fastened my climbing safety harness around my waist, my cat rubbed against my legs, begging to be fed. Hastily I scooped some food into his dish, then sprayed my hands with scent eliminator. Then I took my bow down from its hook and slipped out into the clear moonlit night.

The cold November air brushed my face as I strapped my climbing tree-stand to my back and entered the nearby woods. Enveloped in silence, watching carefully for familiar shapes, I picked my way through the darkness. Stepping over logs and pausing whenever I felt a twig underfoot, I tried to step quietly through the dry leaves. Slowly I made my way up the mountain. The black silhouette of a young hemlock told me where to turn, and soon the land leveled off.

Twenty minutes later, I was climbing the straight trunk of a tall maple that I had picked out weeks earlier. Moving slowly and deliberately as a tree sloth, I eased my treestand up through the darkness, stopping just beneath the first large branching limb. Cautiously I settled into the tree-stand seat and hauled my bow up on its rope.

Fifteen feet up in the air, I breathed the predawn air and looked around.

The forest was a tapestry of black trunks and interlocking branches that stood like sentinels in the dark.

It was forty-five minutes before sunrise. Scarcely an hour since my last meal, my stomach was already growling. Surrounded in the immense silence, I leaned back against the trunk of the tree and waited.

Soon the sky began to lighten in a notch between the mountains to the east. I watched as the autumn landscape, coarse as wool, slowly took shape around me. As the morning birds awakened, the forest seemed as pregnant with hidden life as my own body. I took an arrow from the quiver and clipped the nock in place on the bowstring. I sat up straight and felt my aching breasts press against my camouflage, noticeably tighter than a week ago. Preparing to draw back, I began to scan the forest floor for prey.

Time passed, and the timeless cloak of silence slowly wrapped itself around me. As I sat motionless against the great tree, I felt myself almost disappear, drawn as a single strand into the living tapestry of my surroundings. How easily this trance came over me in my dreamy first-trimester state . . . how quickly I found my own presence blending into the forest. A great sense of privilege came over me; this was the most peaceful part of hunting—and what most predators, both animal and human, spend most of their time doing: waiting, watching, and listening.

Again my stomach growled, interrupting the silence. A wave of nausea followed. This was not the ordinary hunger I had grown used to ignoring while out in the woods. Normally I could quell my body's cravings for hours at a time. Now there was an urgency to this hunger that I knew would drive me out of the woods within an hour or two. Already this pregnancy was making its mark upon my habits; already I was changing.

The sound of rustling leaves turned my attention to the right. It was more defined than the swish of a squirrel's tail, so familiar to all deer hunters of the northern woods. These

"Night Cathedral." Gouache painting.
© 2001 Durga Bernhard.

steps came in succession, with space between that suggested the lifting of feet. Holding my breath, I waited for the deer to come into view.

The footsteps stopped and started as the two deer paused in exquisite alertness to the world around them. Ever watchful for predators, these animals of prey never failed to awe me with their fine senses. As if in slow motion, the silhouette of a doe moved through the space between the trees. A second doe followed some twenty yards behind.

The fiberoptic sights on my bow had barely begun to glow. It was not yet light enough to shoot. I clipped my wrist release to the bowstring, waiting for the gaining light, hoping the deer would move within range. Would I be able to pull off the shot? Six months of preparation hung in balance as I watched the two animals.

When the deer began to amble away, I took a fawn bleat call from my pocket and released the sound once, cutting the silence with the sudden noise. The larger doe stopped, turning her ears and lifting her nose. A minute, two minutes, five minutes passed in frozen silence. Barely visible behind a tree, she raised and lowered her head. With a flick of her tail, she began to walk toward me, circling round and stopping behind a young sapling that stood between us. The deer turned broadside less than twenty yards away—well within range—but a branch, still sparsely covered with brown leaves, clearly stretched in front of her vitals. The shot would be too risky. Ready to draw back, I dared not move a muscle. My heart pounded; I could feel the blood pulsing through my swollen womb. Time vanished as I waited breathlessly for her to step out from behind the tree, hoping she would offer herself, praying for the gift of success.

Then as if a spell had been broken, the deer simply turned her white tail toward me, and walked straight away, never emerging from either side of the tree. I exhaled involuntarily and slouched back against the trunk. Within a moment, the doe's footsteps had faded into the silence, and the forest was still.

It was my last opportunity to shoot that season.

I waited another hour in my treestand, watching the sunrise turn the forest from blacks and grays to the golden hues of autumn. I considered the doe who had *not* offered herself to me on this day. Had I sought to prey upon another mother? It was too early still for the rut; she would not be pregnant yet as I was. But if she lived through this year's hunting season, she would almost certainly give birth in the spring, at the same time my own baby was due.

My cravings for protein had been steadily increasing every day. Even as my nausea and fatigue also increased, making it harder and harder to get out of bed before dawn, my drive to hunt was never greater. For me, there was no commercial meat that matched the richness and vitality of wild game. I preferred to take my meat directly from the land, rather than delegate the responsibility of killing to someone else. And even as new life spun itself into form from my own flesh and blood, there was something just as fertile, just as embryonic in the exchange of wild flesh to feed new life.

But my pregnancy had its own agenda. As with my two older children, I soon found it was not up to me what sacrifices I would make for this child. Two weeks later, a threatened miscarriage (unrelated to hunting) nearly aborted the rest of my hunting season, forcing me to stay close to home and avoid exertion. After a week of rest, I hunted from the ground only, wandering in the woods mostly on private land near a friend's house. As the weather grew colder, I exchanged bow for shotgun, venturing out for short spells before sunset, and arriving home just in time to cook dinner.

"Did you get anything?" my teenage son asked as I peeled off my gear.

"Not today."

"You smell, Mom." He waved his hand at the rank odor of my cover scent—raccoon or fox urine, depending on the terrain.

My daughter bounced into the kitchen. "What's for dinner?"

"Venison pizza," I said, pulling a package of defrosted meat from last year out of the refrigerator.

"Yum! My favorite. Well, I'm glad you won't be up late butchering tonight."

What did my children learn from watching their mother bring home meat directly from the forest? For them, it was not unusual to see blood on my clothes, bones on the kitchen counter, heart and liver soaking in the sink. Whenever a dead deer was hauled into the garage, my daughter would come and look. She crouched down to look at its lovely eyes that always turned mysteriously blue after death. In our era of mass manufacturing and food production, how many children have the experience of running their hands over the soft fur of an animal that would soon become food on the table? Always, her words would sketch out the same paradox: "I'm glad we get to eat this meat, Mom, but I wish the deer didn't have to die."

Her words echoed the age-old quandary expressed in *The Yearling*, the classic story of a boy growing up in a southern homesteading family, written in 1938 by Marjorie Kinnan Rawlings. Halfway through the book, young Jody expresses his feelings forthrightly after witnessing a kill:

"I hate things dying," Jody said.

The men were silent.

Penny said slowly, "Nothin's spared, son, if that be any comfort to you."

"'Taint."

"Well, hit's a stone wall nobody's yit clumb over. You kin kick it and crack your head agin it and holler, but nobody'll listen and nobody'll answer." [1]

"Mountain Buck." Gouache painting on rice paper collage. © 2001 Durga Bernhard.

As Jody grows up, he learns to accept death as a natural and inevitable part of life. His father, however, does not teach Jody to harden his heart. In fact, he allows his son to take in an orphaned fawn, whom Jody learns to care for deeply even as he participates in the hunt.

The same paradox is still faced by all hunters today—all hunters, that is, who rightly respect their chosen prey. Whether hunting for sport or subsistence, whether meat is taken directly from the land or purchased in a store, the truth remains the same: One way or another, life feeds upon life. If children can be comfortable with death, if they can learn to take their place in the natural scheme of things with reverence and grace, that is a valuable lesson.

Life and death have not always presented the contradiction that we struggle intellectually to come to terms with today. In ancient mythologies, they were woven together as one. Artemis, the ancient Greek goddess of both the hunt and childbirth, is a prime example. Bearing the emblem of the crescent moon, she skillfully presides over the affairs of women. It was only natural that she should usher life both in and out—both of which were accompanied by the threat of death. Known also as "Lady of Wild Things" and "Mistress of the Animals," her ministrations were considered kind, not cruel.[2]

Not only does the beauty of wildlife *not* contradict the purpose of the hunt—it is an intrinsic part of it. To me, the deer is unspeakably beautiful: Its grace and agility, its quiet dignity and exquisitely fine senses always find their way into my work as an artist. The more intimately I come to know their patterns and habits, the more I am privileged with direct observation, direct contact, and direct consumption of their flesh, the more reverence I feel for these incredible wild creatures. Every kill is a priceless gift of both experience and nourishment. Apart from childbirth itself, I could not think of a greater blessing, or a more immediate way to participate in the process of life and death.

The blessings extend far beyond the actual hunt, too. From its conception, this fetus was growing on the meat of not only deer, but black bear—shot in the backwoods of Maine just weeks before the pregnancy began—and wild turkey as well. Sometimes, a fellow hunter would gift us with pheasant, or extra venison in a season without success—an experience that almost every hunter has to face. Occasionally, I would even take a fresh road kill. More often than not, the deer was killed by a blow to the head; I could not bear to let so much undamaged meat go to waste. One way or another, our family frequently had some kind of wild meat on the table. In our area, away from the pesticides of orchards and farms, the meat was completely organic. Wild animals, especially browsers, live on an incredible variety of wild plants, nuts, berries, insects, barks, and roots. They are hardier, leaner, and possess greater strength and vitality than domestic animals. All of this translates into the meat. And unlike animals raised in captivity for slaughter, hunted prey live wild and free in their natural state—provided they are taken by a skillful hunter—until the moment of death.

The hunt also brings home other bounty: wild plants for both food and medicine, foraged while scouting and tracking; ideas and inspiration for paintings; photographs taken during every season; and a sense of connection and intimacy with the surrounding mountains that roots us deeply to our environment and gives an immediate sense of place in the web of life.

All of this is naturally understood by my children, and at the same time seems to foster respect in them for wildlife. Although they haven't yet participated directly in the hunt, they are deeply affected by it. Through the seasons, they are witness to endless target practice, scouting and planning, and final sighting in and preparations, followed by the excitement of opening day. Later, with a little luck, they see the whole process of gutting and skinning, quartering, butchering, and finally the cooking of game into meals. They share the bounty of the season and through the winter, sleep with deer pelts on their beds. They watch paintings come to life that memorialize animals sighted, animals taken, and animals let go. My daughter, with her more sensitive nature, seems to mourn the loss of beauty in the sacrifice of every innocent creature, even as she is equally fascinated and amazed. The inevitably two-sided nature of hunting touches her very deeply. My son, for his part, accepts the sacrifice of life more readily, and seems more interested in the nuts-and-bolts process. The aerodynamics of arrow trajectory and bullet drop, mastering aim under pressure, and the critical monitoring of wind direction and scent all fascinate him. I try to teach my children that hunting is both a challenge and a sacrament; both modern and poetic; an opportunity for both skill

"The Death Flower," gouache & acrylic painting. Created as a one-of-a-kind target to raise the stakes of a single shot in preparation for the hunt, this painting was shot in mid-progress by the artist's hunting mentor, Jerry Duffin, with an RB3 broadhead at a distance of 14 yards. The flower "wound" was then completed around the triangular hole left by the arrow. Caught in its destiny that both encircles and blooms within the deer, the animal of prey surrenders to a skillful heart shot with dignity and grace. © 1997 DURGA BERNHARD.

and inspiration—and above all, for communion with the natural world we live in.

That world includes all the demands and responsibilities that every mother has to juggle in order to pursue *any* passion. My attempts to weave hunting into my busy work and home life are not always successful. Even though it puts meat on the table, hunting often has to take a back seat to our family's needs. My goal is to integrate hunting into daily life just as any other activity that claims personal time and attention. I do not want it to be separate; this is not the pursuit of an obsession or ideal, but the integration of something ancient into my ordinary, contemporary life. Some of my hunting friends—mostly men—shun this attitude as lack of dedication. But hunting more moderately also makes each success that much more precious and rewarding, and it keeps the sense of competition out of it that can so easily creep into sport. If hunting is truly meant to nourish my children, then it will have to serve their priorities, too—and takes its place beside school plays, music lessons, baseball practice, and homework.

With the coming of a third baby, an entire hunting season will probably have to be sacrificed for the sake of my child. But the infant, born in the time when the does birth their fawns, will be laid on the most beautiful pelt of a black bear, and will grow up with her little fingers close to the pulse of life and death. To whatever degree hunting finds it way into my life and the lives of my children, it all seems worth it.

King, Sultan, or President?

from The Roaring Veldt *(1930)*

EVEN IN THE AFRICAN WILDERNESS THE MALE SEEMS TO HAVE AN IDEA that he rules the roost. No matter how independently or bravely the female may act, if a male happens to be present he stands around looking as though he were the master-mind behind it all and that it was done under his personal supervision.

It is well known that the lioness kills oftener and more unerringly than her mate. She is the more agile, the more gifted by nature to make a stalk and swift rush. But when it is all over, the male calmly assumes command. I really think he begins to believe he has done the whole thing himself.

Time after time, when we dropped a zebra near a group or pair of lions, the lion himself lay safely up in the bush and expected his lady not only to take the risk of investigating the kill, but after that to wait on him hand and foot into the bargain. And sure enough, before very long she began to cater to his whims. To our own infinite annoyance she would come out and start dragging the zebra towards the covert where he lay concealed, and then the pair would feast on it out of range of our cameras.

But during the last five days of our lion safari we were lucky enough to be aided by an instinct in the fine old maned lions which was even stronger than hunger, and which brought them into the open with more than usual abandon. It was "courtin' season," and on several occasions we came across a pair of ardent honeymooners that allowed themselves to be photographed as readily as a pair of proud newly-weds posing hand-in-hand at Niagara Falls or Atlantic City. Nevertheless, I believe that the pictures we got of actual lion courtships are rather unique, for it is not often that one happens to run across them in such numbers at just the right season.

In the lion world, it seems that even though a lioness has consented to be the mate of her chosen one it is up to him to guard her continually from the approach of a rival gentleman. It is just as though she had bestowed on him, along with her heart and hand, the dubious consolation of knowing that her heart would always be true—to one lion at a time! And he feels he must act accordingly.

You have never seen such jealousy in your life! The mere sight of a shaggy old male trailing his lady-love around wherever she went was funny enough. But when the rival appeared on the scene, even at a distance of a hundred yards, the growling and spitting indulged in by the lady's jealous consort were really uproarious. At least they were to us, and I hope the female enjoyed them as much as we did. However, she affected such a blasé manner that it was hard to tell.

If the unhappy rival were near enough to get within striking distance, the snarls would change quickly to short jabs with the front paws which usually sent him skulking away like a cowed puppy. We never saw a really serious battle. Interesting developments seemed always about to begin, but always they ended in nothing much more than a moral victory for the lion in possession. Nevertheless it was fascinating to watch.

The lioness never failed to look simply bored to death. Instead of watching the proceedings like a wide-eyed maiden for whom two valiant knights were doing battle, she seemed to be thinking: "There isn't much to choose between those two sillies! Neither of them are exactly worth writing home about. All I hope is, they won't be too long with this nonsense."

And when finally the conqueror came to her proudly she would walk away; and his every attempt to show his affections would meet with a rebuking cuff in the face that might have discouraged the most ardent wooer in all lion land. But then, if he ceased his attention even for a moment, she would be true to the eternal feminine by playing up to him suddenly, cuddling against him and nuzzling him until he was won over.

Through every act of their love-making they never paid the slightest attention to us. Why should they? Like the other lions we had seen, they probably had an idea that we were some sort of rhino; and what stupid short-sighted rhino would ever take notice of their indiscretions? I think that is why we were able to get our pictures of large lions under these conditions.

Another thing that entertained us in the big males was their *penchant* for showing off. After all, even if they tried to make the lioness do the bulk of the work, was it not they who made the largest and most important kills? Didn't their strength, when they chose to show it, entitle them to a whole retinue of admiring wives? At any rate, whether it did or not, they often took more than one wife unto themselves and sat around showing off and enjoying the luxury of it like a modern King Solomon.

Once we saw a quaint example of this which photographed splendidly.

I had been terribly anxious to secure a real "close-up" of a lion, so one morning we took the light truck and went out determined to get it. Alfred Klein did the driving; and Herman and I sat on the front seat with him. Herman was in the middle, because I was the one who was anxious to get a picture. Klein had his gun; and Herman had his own gun and a movie camera. I sat clutching another camera as though my life depended on it, determined to secure a fine lion portrait this time or "bust."

For an hour or two we zigzagged through the bush. Sometimes we had to cut down trees to open up the way; and sometimes we sagged into deep holes that we just managed to climb out of. But something told us we were on the way to a splendid picture, so nothing else seemed to matter.

All of a sudden, as we were threading our way through a bit of particularly thick bush, we saw a lioness break from cover yards ahead of us and rush away with tremendous speed. For some reason she seemed unusually frightened. She was merely a tawny blur against the bushes as she ran; and in a few seconds she was swallowed up in the twisted scrub.

We wondered why she was in such a hurry. But in a little while, after we had worked our way into the next clearing, we found the answer.

There in front of us, about a hundred yards away, we saw a truly idyllic sight. A majestic old lion, flanked on either side by a lovely lady of his harem, reposed on the top of an anthill and blinked lazily in our direction. He looked the picture of a contented sultan basking in the adulation of two of his favorite wives. And we were positive that one of those wives was the lioness which had just scampered away from us in the bush. Apparently she had run to tell her lord that a visitor was approaching.

Slowing the car down as much as we could, we barely crawled over the veldt towards them. Here was our wonderful opportunity for a "close-up," and we weren't going to let anything spoil it. Once I thought we had stopped altogether, and glanced inquiringly at Klein. But he nodded his head encouragingly and I felt the car creep on again.

Soon we were only fifty yards away. Then forty. Thirty-five. We could see that old Sultan Leo was very much aware of us now. Suddenly he rose to his feet and thrust his splendid shaggy head very positively our way. His ladies got up too, and stood beside him like ladies at court waiting with their ruler to receive an ambassador from some far off land.

Then the old monarch actually sneered. With a low snarl he twitched his lips back in one of those subtle but menacing expressions of which every lion is a past master. Nothing in the world could have registered his contempt of us more forcibly. I could almost hear him saying to one of his wives: "So this was the thing that frightened you a little while ago! Well, I must say, it certainly doesn't look like much. But you'd better both leave till I find out what it thinks it's doing. And anyway, maybe it's here on business and wants to see me alone!"

Nevertheless I could hardly believe my eyes when he came deliberately down from the anthill and began to walk slowly towards us. Only that lifted lip of his and slight twitching of his tail showed that he was the least bit concerned. And the two lionesses, evidently only too willing to allow him a certain amount of privacy for this interview, slid quietly down

"*A Monarch Investigates. Here is 'George Washington,' the lion which was sitting with his two ladies on an anthill when we found him. When he came forward to look us over, his wives hiding the grass behind him. Their heads are just visible in this picture, beyond the range of my focus. He got to within twelve yards of us before he stopped and lay down with an air of calm bravado.*"

FROM CRON, *THE ROARING VELDT.*

the other side of the anthill and watched the proceedings from the cover of the grass. We could just see their heads craning up out of it, like those of two cats hunting birds in a field.

By this time I was frantically trying to get my focusing device and lens aperture ready for a picture. Herman, a little further inside the car, was already grinding away with his movie camera. I kept as still as I could, but as I was sitting sideways with my legs hanging over the side of the door, I was terribly afraid I would spoil things by moving too much. My fingers felt like thumbs on the delicate apparatus that had to be so minutely adjusted.

Still the old lion kept coming. He wasn't in a hurry. In fact, I even suspect he was little bored. He looked as though he felt like turning back to the peace of his anthill, but had decided that with the admiring eyes of the ladies upon him it would be more impressive to go on a little further. And he did.

He was twelve yards from us before he stopped. Then he squatted down in the grass and began to study us carefully. The sound of the movie machine apparently didn't bother him. But the slight movement of my legs as I shifted my own camera seemed to fascinate him particularly.

He appeared to be thinking: "Well, this thing beats me! If it wants anything why doesn't it come to the point?"

I was taking pictures for dear life now. After each exposure I had to raise my camera and adjust it again for another. It seemed to me I was moving so much that I must look to the lion like a whirling commotion of hands and legs. But I guess I really kept pretty quiet. In fact, I managed to keep so quiet that His Spoiled Majesty got more bored than ever. He expressed it by yawning impolitely in our faces.

Luckily I had the camera ready for action just at that moment. My picture of a king committing a social blunder turned out beautifully.

All at once the royal husband seemed to remember that his two wives were watching him. He glanced around at them to be sure they were still properly impressed by his nonchalance. But he must have read disappointment in those cat-like countenances that peeped up out of the grass, for suddenly he looked at us again and then, with a deep snarl, took a determined step or two in our direction.

Out of the corner of my eye, as I was trying to get another picture, I saw Herman and Klein quietly raise their guns and draw a bead on him.

"Too Bored for Words. After looking our way and puzzling things over for a little while, 'George Washington' apparently lost all interest in us. He pretended to gaze around the landscape for something more worth while. I think he had a feeling that the two lionesses were admiring him from their retreat in the tall grass." From Cron, The Roaring Veldt.

"A King Committing a Social Blunder. Pretty soon 'George Washington' yawned. He didn't try to stifle it politely. He opened his mouth as wide as he could and yawned right in our faces. It may have been only another gesture to capture the flagging attention of the ladies, but it certainly was a good one!"

FROM CRON, *THE ROARING VELDT.*

They told me afterwards that they had really been good and worried at this moment, for there is no accounting for a lion's capriciousness. I was so busy with the camera that I didn't really appreciate the tenseness that was in the air. But I realized later that we should have been in a very tight place if our regal acquaintance had suddenly decided to declare war. There wouldn't have been much time to place a shot, for when a lion makes up his mind to come on, he comes fast. And this one was only a few feet away.

I've heard a number of people say that lion hunting isn't very exciting because it is so easy. That is because they have always been able to get ready to meet a charge beforehand. Backed up by a couple of powerful guns in strategic positions, they naturally have not felt much danger. But every once in a while comes a time when you aren't given a chance to get all ready, or when you happen to be crowded together as we were now, without any elbow room.

However, we acted in the most cautious way we could under the circumstances. Very, very slowly Klein began to back up the car, while I took up my own gun and joined Herman in keeping an eye on the lion. Then, when we had retreated a few yards, Klein snapped the gear out of reverse and into second, swerved to one side, and away we went—leaving a very surprised monarch standing supreme once more in his kingdom of thorns and grass.

It was only after we had gotten back to camp, all keyed up over the prospect of the pictures we had taken, that we remembered a fact that helped put a finishing touch to our morning's experience. It was February 22—Washington's Birthday! And so, in spite of the fact that the lion had looked like a sultan, with two wives into the bargain, we decided to name him after a president. We began to call him "George Washington"; and it is as "George Washington" that we shall always remember him.

I'm glad we left him unharmed and heroic in the eyes of his ladies. Doubtless they thought he had chased us away—and he had! Probably they are still complimenting "George Washington" on it to this day; and telling their children to grow up into fine brave lions like their father—and never, never to forget to tell the truth!

Lion Hunting at Night

from On the Gorilla Trail *(1922)*

T HE MOON WAS BRIGHT NOW, A TROPIC MOON DIRECTLY OVERHEAD, casting inky pools of shadow beneath our feet. Every night we heard the distant roaring of lions and that hungry hunting grunt of theirs. Their hunting noise is really a series of grunts, beginning with one low one, followed by six or more hurried ones, ending, after an instant's pause, with about three long-drawn-out grunts, generally increasing in loudness. Um—um-um-um-um-um-um—*um*—*um*—UM!

It is almost impossible to tell how far away those grunts are. Whenever you hear them you are always inclined to think the lion is behind the next bush. To hear them from our camp made us eager to spend a night in the brush and see the night life of the jungle and try for lions.

The way to try for lions at night is to kill an antelope about half a mile from where you want to use it and have it dragged that half mile to leave a good trail; then you stake it down in front of the thicket where you conceal yourself and wait.

You try to arrange the scene so the moonlight will be on the bait, with a clear background against which the lion will show up well when he comes to dine. You pile as much fresh brush as you can artistically upon your thicket or "boma," as the hiding place is called, for the lion can see as well by night as by day, and you leave a peephole for outlook and your gun. You have to get into the boma by sundown for the moment the first gray shadows creep over the plain comes that hoarse grunt. And then you sit perfectly still and wait for twelve hours.

Before Monsieur Flamand left us Mr. Bradley went out one night with him, but though they heard lions all night they had no chance at a shot, except at mosquitoes. We had no mosquitoes at all in our camp, but this boma was six or eight miles away from camp, by a waterhole in the brush. However, a waterhole was a good place for game, so the next night Mr. Akeley, Miss Miller, and we two Bradleys went again to the same boma to try our luck.

It was a natural thicket, reenforced with greenery so the lions wouldn't see us too easily, and the clearing within the thicket was so absurdly spacious that we spread boughs for any weary ones to lie upon during the night.

We had our porters carry out a chop box and blankets to this retreat. Then the porters left and we ensconced ourselves and dined sketchily within it. I had a foreboding at the time that the flavor of green onions and cheese was not likely to help conceal our presence. We were surprised, as always, by the swiftness of the tropic night, for at five-thirty by our watches the sun dropped behind the mountains, and at six o'clock Martha, Herbert, and I were sitting in the dusk, guns in hand, peering out through loopholes in the boughs at the mournful nose of a poor dead topi.

The moon rose, the dark turned silver clear, the lions grunted and roared but not one came near us. But the mosquitoes came. They came humming in swarms and settled on every vulnerable inch of us. But for the strangeness of the scene, I could have believed myself back in dear old Wisconsin on a June night. But we were handicapped here as we were not in Wisconsin. There we could at least attempt to protect ourselves. Here to lift a hand and deal a slap was to bring reproach upon yourself from your fellow, and equally tormented, hunters. With grim self-control we learned to blot mosquitoes in slow silence.

Mr. Akeley was not trying for a lion. He reposed peacefully most of the time upon the boughs, and from time to time the two weary Bradleys took their turns, but Martha Miller sat unstirring upon her camera box for nine long hours until the moon sank and the morning light began to steal over the far-away mountains.

We decided that the location was not a happy one, and that we would abandon the neighborhood of the waterhole. A day later, Mr. Bradley took out the tiny pup tent, at Mr. Akeley's suggestion, and squeezed it into the center of another thicket some distance away, cut three portholes in the sides for guns and set up three steamer chairs within it which filled it to repletion. Then, leaving a porter to guard the antelope he had killed and staked out in front, he came hurriedly back across the plains for Martha and me.

We dined at five and at five-thirty we started off. Our camp was encircled by such a deep ravine that we had always a sharp scramble down and then a long climb up the perpendicular sides of it before we gained the opposite plains. Three luckless porters carried our bicycles up for us and once on the plains we mounted them and set out along the tiny ribbon of native path running out to the western mountains.

The world was bright with color when we started; we were riding straight into the mountains of azure through fields of grass that seemed like waving golden grain. Here and there the scattered trees and brush glimmered with that lovely green that comes just after the sun has gone.

We cycled as fast as we could but the light went faster. The mountains grew darkly purple, then coldly gray. The grass lost its gleam of gold and became vague and mysterious with blotting shadows of forest reaches. The path ceased to glimmer whitely. The world was spectral gray.

At our left we heard a lion grunt. Um, um-um-um-um-um-um—*um*—*um*—UM!

It was uncannily near. We cycled a little faster, remembering that there was but one gun in the group and that was on Herbert's wheel and difficult of access. There was no use getting it out until we stopped cycling. Martha's wheel and mine were a little short for carrying guns so we had left our Springfields for the porters to bring on, and the porters were trotting after us somewhere out of sight. It was but a few minutes after six but the mountains had shouldered the day so quickly out of the way that it seemed like midnight at home.

The lion was keeping right up with us, grunting away, somewhere out on those plains at our left. It was no use for us to tell each other that he was probably a mile, a half mile, away—he wasn't. And he could see us. Probably on our wheels he took us for a new species of antelope. It seemed to me that our crouching pose, our apparent flight, would just naturally invite him to the chase, and I realized that being on horseback was no bar to an attack by lions; I had heard innumerable stories of men set upon when riding casually homewards. Even with my frail memory for names I could remember there was a Mr. Pease, a former magistrate in the Transvaal, who had been pulled from his horse by a lion.

I wished I hadn't remembered his name. It seemed to make it more real.

And, then, at our right, another lion grunted. There are people to whom a lion's roar is the most terrifying thing in the world, but I think that a lion's grunt, that businesslike hunting grunt, is the most chilling sound that I have ever heard. And these grunts, hard as they were to place, sounded unmistakably close.

Just why the lion grunts when hunting no one knows. One theory is that it is done to start up the game and I can easily believe it—that sudden reverberating intimation of a lion's presence would send every panic-stricken little hoof flying in revealing clatter. Later, when the lion has his prey located and is ready to strike, there is never a warning noise from him.

We cycled so fast that we soon reached the brush and in a few minutes we thought we had come to the right place to leave the path and our wheels and strike off for the boma. There was a lone tree to our left, the landmark that Herbert was watching for, with a bush at the right, and beyond the scattering of thickets. We abandoned our wheels at the pathside and Herbert got out his gun with a speed considerably accelerated by the increasing concert from the lions, and then we plunged into the grass towards the thicket where the ambush ought to be. Herbert had left a boy to see that nothing made off with the bait before we arrived and we began to whistle to this boy. No boy responded. We tried again. Then we called. He couldn't be asleep—not with those lions about. My immediate theory was that he had been eaten by lions—not the present, grunting lions, but other previous lions, now silent and replete.

We stared about in the darkness at the dimly looming thickets. They were all utterly unidentifiable. Any one of them might be our boma. Any one might be the retreat of some lion lying up during the day and just ready to sally out afresh. I remembered the lions I had seen starting from thickets just two days before on the plains, the day I had killed my lion. And when Herbert began plunging briskly about up to the black thickets to find the dead antelope and the ambushed tent I remonstrated feelingly, while keeping close to him and protecting my gun. I reminded him that the Foster brothers, back to back with two guns, had not been able to ward off a lion in broad daylight.

But Herbert was not concerned with warding off lions. He was only afraid that our conversation would frighten them away before we found the boma. The boma was apparently a little further on. It was certainly not here.

We stood there in the sinister gray dark with the snuffling grunts coming a little closer all around us. I carried Mr. Akeley's little flashlight worked by a dynamo which threw a spot of light a few feet ahead, but I did not feel that it was bright enough to annoy a lion—it was nothing but a little wink of light. As I stared out in the vague reaches beyond us something moved. It melted quickly from bush to bush.

I said in an extremely flat and quiet tone which I trusted indicated perfect calm and absence of tremor, "There is a lion just ahead of me. Point the gun that way."

And then in a similarly unmoved and casual voice Martha remarked, "There's a lion on this side, too. Better keep the gun circling."

We sounded as if we said, "Why, there's Mrs. Brown-Jones coming for tea. Better put on an extra cup."

"They won't come near while you're talking," said Herbert, and he added in a discouraged way, "Now they probably won't come near us all night."

I thought his discouragement was premature. Those two lions were calling across us to each other in a more and more intimate understanding. I can jest about it now—I could jest about it then—but I had a very perfect understanding of what terror was. It was in the helplessness of it all—not having a gun, not having a revolver, knowing that if anything did come I hadn't the defense of a stricken antelope. And the whole situation was shot through and through with a feeling of responsibility for Martha.

Wholeheartedly I advocated abandonment of the brush and a return to the path. Back we went and as we stood there in the path between the grass fields and a stubble of burnt ground, where a heap of bleached bones glimmered with wan reminder, I felt a surge of remorse. That very morning I had laughed lightly at runners who wanted to go in threes instead of twos—I had been skeptical of their tales of a lion attacking them the previous night and felt they were trying to make a social excursion of their errands.

Now I knew that three runners were none too many. Not three times three. And I knew why they kept such fires at their camps.

I tried a little fire myself but the grass would not burn, so we kept the searchlight swinging and talked in loud, nonchalant tones, while the lions grunted back and forth, apparently heartening each other to have the first go at us. "No, you have the first choice . . . After you . . . "

Then we heard another noise, faint, far away . . . More lions, I thought for a moment, but it was the babble of the porters coming on down the path towards us. Nothing was ever such music to my ears.

There, on those backs, were our guns. And there in those black heads, was the native geography to lead us to our boma. The men came on, half a dozen of them huddled together in a din of talk. We knew then why porters are so conversational. It is their life insurance policy on lion nights.

Paddling swiftly along they soon reached us, in the lead a wizened old mite, spear in hand, my camera strap across his forehead, my camera bumping his bare back. We clutched our guns and a blessed peace enveloped us. That awful helplessness was gone. We fell in behind the leader and that grizzled mite led us on and on for half an hour, then struck into another stretch of shrub.

There was extraordinary similarity of marking—the same tree at the left, the same bush at the right, the same scattering of thickets. We went farther and farther along, then the guide gave a hyena call which brought a swift echo from the boy on guard in the ambush.

There was our dead topi and there, in the thicket, our waiting tent. Martha and I squeezed in, thrusting our breakfast box and bags with coats and sweaters under the chairs; Herbert hurriedly dragged the kill to a spot a little more in view, staked it down so no lion could drag it away—and the porters fled.

Before we could get comfortably settled, the lions were roaring around us. We crouched in the chairs trying to peer out the peepholes, which were sagging too much with the weight of the brush piled outside and the drag of our guns in the apertures, and wished that we had necks like flamingoes.

It was seven-twenty when we were inside, black dark, with the kill scarcely discernible. We heard constant grunting . . . we heard the whistle of a reed buck leaping with alarm, then a hard patter of racing antelopes flying for their lives. A lion must be near. We maintained a positive torture of silent, neck-breaking attention.

The moon slipped out from the clouds at last, a blood-red circle bringing the foreground to something like distinctness. And then I relaxed, leaving the watch to the others. I was at the right end and my view was very circumscribed. Martha was in the middle. The first lion was to be hers, and after she fired the first shot we were all to fire as fast as we could to give him all the lead we had.

I was just resting my neck, which had been curved like an Arab steed, when I heard Martha's gun go off into the stillness like the incarnation of all noise. I got a glimpse then of a huge lion, heavy maned, looming before us at an angle to which I tried in vain to jerk my gun, and that same instant the roar of Herbert's big gun followed Martha's Springfield, and the white smoke from it obscured the scene.

Then was a thud of galloping feet. When a lion stalks in to you he is silence itself, but when he gallops off his padded feet hit the ground as hard as a horse's. And then we heard roars, horrible roars. He was at our left, in the brush, evidently badly wounded. The roars became groans, dying down spasmodically. It is a wretched thing to hear a wounded beast groan, but one can fortify oneself by remembering the violence by which he lives, the ruthless clawing down of antelopes. And to-night, remembering those encircling grunts, those dim shapes gliding from bush to bush, I knew just how the poor antelopes felt, milling about bewilderedly, their noses strained, their flanks quivering with fearful expectation.

We heard fainter and fainter noises from the wounded lion and shrill above them the vixenish yelping of jackals teasing him. Then the groans died away. We pressed Martha's hands excitedly. She had her lion, we felt sure. And he was a big fellow with a fine mane.

This was at nine o'clock. One by one the other hours went by, with lion calls now far, now near. The moonlight was marvelous. We saw jackals steal out to the kill and hyenas and two swift cat-like creatures, either leopards or serval cats. Out in the brush a hyena laughed horribly. All the night noises and all the night life of the jungle went on about us as they had been going on from the beginning of time.

It had a wild fascination that stirred the blood. It was Beauty and Night and Violence. . . . Every time a lion sounded near, excitement held us tense. . . . At twelve I was holding the watch alone and I waked the others silently to see two leopard-like forms running in about the kill. They suddenly fled and then we stiffened.

At our left a lion appeared, walking past the thicket to the kill, as silent as a picture on a screen. He seemed tremendous. The dark outline of him against the moonlit grass and sky was a perfect thing, a great, calm, arrogantly assured presence. Majestic is the word for lions. They appropriate it.

Herbert waited till he had sure aim and shot. The lion never knew what struck him down. The guns drowned his roar.

There is no way to tell of the tense excitement of such a moment. The nerves thrill with the old, primitive passions of the time when life was cast on a die. The countless generations that have stalked their prey stir through us. And the blood that loves to race and thrill is tired of beating tamely through a safe life quickens to exhilaration.

Night shooting has not the danger of the daytime, for unless the wounded beast happened to charge directly at our ambush we had nothing to fear. But it has the element of uncertainty, and the constant edge of expectation that any moment will come the instant upon which all your chances of success are staked.

We saw other lions that night, but far away. One that we took to be the faithful lioness kept running back and forth in the dim distance and calling her dead mate. She flitted by again in the morning dark and Herbert risked a sudden shot, but we couldn't see what happened.

About dawn a terrific roaring sounded on our left, and we feared that Martha's lion was coming to life again. Then the roaring grew farther away. As soon as we could see in the dimness, Herbert squeezed out of the ambush and glimpsed a lioness off at the left making into a thicket. He fired, but without result. There was no sign of the wounded lion. He had apparently revived, like Anthony, and made off.

Out in front lay Herbert's lion, a very fine male, and behind him, so directly in line as not to be visible from the thicket, the creamy, soft-furred, graceful creature whom I christened Nellie, the Faithful Lioness.

In each case Herbert's bullet had penetrated the heart, severing the arteries. Death had been instant.

I felt a little sentimental, looking down on Nellie. Her faithfulness had cost her her life, but I was glad that she had gone with her mate and not been left to mourn. . . . But the jungles are ruthless to illusion. Naturalists have no pity. Nell was Nimrod—a young two-year-old male, who had hung about, not from sympathy but for his dinner, and run in for a snatch at the antelope.

Lions are strangely indifferent to other dead lions on the bait. We heard of five that had been shot over the same kill and here we had three that came in, one after another. Several young males often hunt in bands with one or two older, and the apparent lioness that Herbert had seen making off at dawn might have been another such young maneless two-year-old as the erstwhile Nell.

We never did get that first lion of Martha's although we searched the coverts and watched for days to see if the vultures gathered.

For three more nights we went out again, with one night in between for sleep, but, though lions roared all about us, not one stepped out where we could get a shot until that third night.

That night the moon was not due until after one. From six to twelve-twenty we had been watching steadily and uselessly through the dark. A lion had been grunting on our right, and apparently coming in towards the kill, but for some time we had not heard him. We had alternated tense concentration with relaxing disappointment.

Then, just at twelve-twenty, from the right came a great shadow, black against the lightening night, still as silence itself. Not a twig cracked under the padded paws. Not a leaf rustled.

It was Martha's lion. I held my gun on him waiting for her to fire first. It seemed an eternity until she shot; she chose her aim with care. Then I followed. There was a tremendous roaring and the lion was down. We saw the great bulk of him in the shadow before us; his roaring filled our ears. He was fatally wounded—Martha's shot had penetrated the brain—but, to prevent an escape and a difficult chase, we flashed the searchlight out one peephole while Herbert gave him the big gun in the heart.

He was a splendid lion. I think he had really the finest mane of all. It was our last lion. Herbert and I went out again and we took out Priscilla Hall, who had reached us now with Alice. We sat up in vain. Though we continued to hear lions every night, we got no more shots at them here—the moon gave us only an hour or two of light now, and the lions were more wary.

BERYL MARKHAM

I May Have to Shoot Him

from West with the Night *(1942)*

ISUPPOSE, IF THERE WERE A PART OF THE WORLD IN WHICH MASTODON still lived, somebody would design a new gun, and men, in their eternal impudence, would hunt mastodon as they now hunt elephant. Impudence seems to be the rod. At least David and Goliath were of the same species, but, to an elephant, a man can only be a midge with a deathly sting.

It is absurd for a man to kill an elephant. It is not brutal, it is not heroic, and certainly it is not easy; it is just one of those preposterous things that men do like putting a dam across a great river, one tenth of whose volume could engulf the whole of mankind without disturbing the domestic life of a single catfish.

Elephant, beyond the fact that their size and conformation are aesthetically more suited to the treading of this earth than our angular infirmity, have an average intelligence comparable to our own. Of course they are less agile and physically less adaptable than ourselves—Nature having developed their bodies in one direction and their brains in another, while human beings, on the other hand, drew from Mr. Darwin's lottery of evolution both the winning ticket and the stub to match it. This, I suppose, is why we are so wonderful and can make movies and electric razors and wireless sets—and guns with which to shoot the elephant, the hare, clay pigeons, and each other.

The elephant is a rational animal. He thinks. Blix and I (also rational animals in our own right) have never quite agreed on the mental attributes of the elephant. I know Blix is not to be doubted because he has learned more about elephant than any other man I ever met, or even heard about, but he looks upon legend with a suspicious eye, and I do not.

There is a legend that elephant dispose of their dead in secret burial grounds and that none of these has ever been discovered. In support of this, there is only the fact that the body of an elephant, unless he had been trapped or shot in his tracks, has rarely been found. What happens to the old and diseased?

Not only natives, but many white settlers, have supported for years the legend (if it is a legend) that elephant will carry their wounded and

190

their sick hundreds of miles, if necessary, to keep them out of the hands of their enemies. And it is said that elephant never forget.

These are perhaps just stories born of imagination. Ivory was once almost as precious as gold, and wherever there is treasure, men mix it with mystery. But still, there is no mystery about the things you see yourself.

I think I am the first person ever to scout elephant by plane, and so it follows that the thousands of elephant I saw time and again from the air had never before been plagued by anything above their heads more ominous than tick-birds.

The reaction of a herd of elephant to my Avian was, in the initial instance, always the same—they left their feeding ground and tried to find cover, though often, before yielding, one or two of the bulls would prepare for battle and charge in the direction of the plane if it were low enough to be within their scope of vision. Once the futility of this was realized, the entire herd would be off into the deepest bush.

Checking again on the whereabouts of the same herd next day, I always found that a good deal of thinking had been going on amongst them during the night. On the basis of their reaction to my second intrusion, I judged that their thoughts had run somewhat like this: A: The thing that flew over us was no bird, since no bird would have to work so hard to stay in the air—and, anyway, we know all the birds. B: If it was no bird, it was very likely just another trick of those two-legged dwarfs against whom there ought to be a law. C: The two-legged dwarfs (both black and white) have, as long as our memories go back, killed our bulls for their tusks. We know this because, in the case of the white dwarfs, at least, the tusks are the only part taken away.

The actions of the elephant, based upon this reasoning, were always sensible and practical. The second time they saw the Avian, they refused to hide; instead, the females, who bear only small, valueless tusks, simply grouped themselves around their treasure-burdened bulls in such a way that no ivory could be seen from the air or from any other approach.

This can be maddening strategy to an elephant scout. I have spent the better part of an hour circling, criss-crossing, and diving low over some of the most inhospitable country in Africa in an effort to break such a stubborn huddle, sometimes successfully, sometimes not.

But the tactics vary. More than once I have come upon a large and solitary elephant standing with enticing disregard for safety, its massive bulk in clear view, but its head buried in thicket. This was, on the part of the elephant, no effort to simulate the nonsensical habit attributed to the ostrich. It was, on the contrary, a cleverly devised trap into which I fell, every way except physically, at least a dozen times. The beast always proved to be a large cow rather than a bull, and I always found that by the time I had arrived at this brilliant if tardy deduction, the rest of the herd had got another ten miles away, and the decoy, leering up at me out of a small, triumphant eye, would amble into the open, wave her trunk with devastating nonchalance, and disappear.

This order of intelligence in a lesser animal can obviously give rise to exaggeration—some of it persistent enough to be crystallized into legend. But you cannot discredit truth merely because legend has grown out of it. The sometimes almost godlike achievements of our own species in ages past toddle through history supported more often than not on the twin crutches of fable and human credulity.

As to the brutality of elephant-hunting, I cannot see that it is any more brutal than ninety percent of all other human activities. I suppose there is nothing more tragic about the death of an elephant than there is about the death of a Hereford steer—certainly not in the eyes of the steer. The only difference is that the steer has neither the ability nor the chance to outwit the gentleman who wields the slaughterhouse snickersnee, while the elephant has both of these to pit against the hunter.

Elephant hunters may be unconscionable brutes, but it would be an error to regard the elephant as an altogether pacific animal. The popular belief that only the so-called "rogue" elephant is dangerous to men is quite wrong—so wrong that a considerable number of men who believed it have become one with the dust without even their just due of gradual disintegration. A normal bull elephant, aroused by the scent of man, will often attack at once—and his speed is as unbelievable as his mobility. His trunk and his feet are his weapons—at least in the distasteful business of exterminating a mere human; those resplendent sabers of ivory await resplendent foes.

Blix and I hardly came into this category at Kilamakoy—certainly not after we had run down the big bull, or, as it happened, the big bull had run down us. I can say, at once with gratification still genuine, that we were not trampled within that most durable of all inches—the last inch of our lives. We got out all right, but there are times when I still dream.

On arriving from Makindu, I landed my plane in the shallow box of a runway scooped out of the bush, unplugged wads of cotton wool from my ears, and climbed from the cockpit.

The aristocratically descended visage of the Baron von Blixen Finecke greeted me (as it always did) with the most delightful of smiles caught, like a strip of sunlight, on a familiar patch of leather—well-kept leather, free of wrinkles, but brown and saddle-tough.

Beyond this concession to the fictional idea of what a White Hunter ought to look like, Blix's face yields not a whit. He has gay, light blue eyes rather than somber, steel-grey ones; his cheeks are well rounded rather than flat as an axe; his lips are full and generous and not pinched tight in grim realization of what the Wilderness Can Do. He talks. He is never significantly silent.

He wore then what I always remember him as wearing, a khaki bush shirt of "solario" material, slacks of the same stuff, and a pair of low-cut moccasins with soles—or at least vestiges of soles. There were four pockets in his bush shirt, but I don't think he knew it; he never carried anything unless he was actually hunting—and then it was just a rifle and ammunition. He never went around hung with knives, revolvers, binoculars, or even a watch. He could tell time by the sun, and if there were no sun, he could tell it, anyway. He wore over his closely cropped graying hair a terai hat, colourless and limp as a wilted frond.

He said, "Hullo, Beryl," and pointed to a man at his side—so angular as to give the impression of being constructed entirely of barrel staves.

"This," said Blix, with what could hardly be called Old-World courtesy, "is Old Man Wicks."

"At last," said Old Man Wicks, "I have seen the Lady from the Skies."

Writing it now, that remark seems a little like a line from the best play chosen from those offered by the graduating class of Eton, possibly in the late twenties, or like the remark of a man up to his ears in his favourite anodyne. But, as a matter of fact, Old Man Wicks, who managed a piece of no-man's-land belonging to the Manoni Sugar Company, near Masongaleni, had seen only one white man in sixteen months and, I gathered, hadn't seen a white woman in as many years. At least he had never seen an aeroplane and a white woman at the same time, nor can I be sure that he regarded the spectacle as much of a Godsend. Old Man Wicks, oddly enough, wasn't very old—he was barely forty—and it may have been that his monkish life was the first choice of whatever other lives he could have led. He looked old, but that might have been protective colouration. He was a gentle, kindly man helping Blix with the safari until Winston Guest arrived.

It was a modest enough safari. There were three large tents—Winston's, Blix's, and my own—and then there were several pup tents for the Native boys, gun-bearers, and trackers. Blix's boy Farah, Winston's boy, and of course my Arab Ruta (who was due via lorry from Nairobi) had pup tents to themselves. The others, as much out of choice as necessity, slept several in a tent. There was a hangar for the Avian, made out of a square of tarpaulin, and there was a baobab tree whose shade served as a veranda to everybody. The immediate country was endless and barren of hills.

Half an hour after I landed, Blix and I were up in the Avian, hoping, if possible, to spot a herd of elephant before Winston's arrival that night. If we could find a herd within two or three days' walking distance from the camp, it would be extraordinary luck—always provided that the herd contained a bull with respectable tusks.

It is not unusual for an elephant hunter to spend six months, or even a year, on the spoor of a single bull. Elephant go where men can't—or at least shouldn't.

Scouting by plane eliminates a good deal of the preliminary work, but when as upon occasion I did spot a herd not more than thirty or forty miles from camp, it still meant that those forty miles had to be walked, crawled, or wriggled by the hunters—and that by the time this body and nerve-racking manoeuvre had been achieved, the elephant had pushed on another twenty miles or so into the bush. A man, it ought to be remembered, has to take several steps to each stride of an elephant, and, moreover, the man is somewhat less than resistant to thicket, thorn trees, and heat. Also, (particularly if he is white) he is vulnerable as a peeled egg to all things that sting—anopheles mosquitoes, scorpions, snakes, and tsetse flies. The essence of elephant-hunting is discomfort in such lavish proportions that only the wealthy can afford it.

Blix and I were fortunate on our very first expedition out of Kilamakoy. The Wakamba scouts on our safari had reported a large herd of elephant containing several worth-while bulls, not more than twenty air miles from camp. We circled the district indicated, passed over the herd perhaps a dozen times, but finally spotted it.

A herd of elephant, as seen from a plane, has a quality of an hallucination. The proportions are wrong—they are like those of a child's drawing of a field mouse in which the whole landscape, complete with barns and windmills, is dwarfed beneath the whiskers of the mighty rodent who looks both able and willing to devour everything, including the thumbtack that holds the work against the schoolroom wall.

Peering down from the cockpit at grazing elephant, you have the feeling that what you are beholding is wonderful, but not authentic. It is not only incongruous in the sense that animals simply are not as big as trees, but also in the sense that the twentieth century, tidy and svelte with stainless steel as it is, would not possibly permit such prehistoric monsters to wonder in its garden. Even in Africa, the elephant is as anomalous as the Cro-Magnon Man might be shooting a round of golf at Saint Andrews in Scotland.

But, with all this, elephant are seldom conspicuous from the air. If they were smaller, they might be. Big as they are, and coloured as they are, they blend with everything until the moment they catch your eye.

They caught Blix's eye and he scribbled a frantic note; "Look! The big bull is enormous. Turn back. Doctor Turvy radios I should have some gin."

Well, we had no radio—and certainly no gin in my plane. But, just as certainly, we had Doctor Turvy.

Doctor Turvy was an ethereal citizen of an ethereal world. In the beginning, he existed only for Blix, but long before the end, he existed for everybody who worked with Blix or knew him well.

Although Doctor Turvy's prescriptions indicated that he put his trust in a wine list rather than a pharmacopoeia, he had two qualities of special excellence in a physician; his diagnosis was always arrived at in a split second—and he held the complete confidence of his patient. Beyond that, his adeptness at mental telepathy (in which Blix himself was pretty well grounded) eliminated the expensive practice of calling round to feel the pulse or take a temperature. Nobody ever saw Doctor Turvy—and that fact, Blix insisted, was bedside manner carried to its final degree of perfection.

I banked the Avian and turned toward camp.

Within three miles of our communal baobab tree, we saw four more elephant—three of them beautiful bulls. The thought passed through my head that the way to find a needle in a haystack is to sit down. Elephant are never within three miles of camp. It's hardly cricket that they should be. It doesn't make a hunter out of you to turn over on your canvas cot and realize that the thing you are hunting at such expense and physical tribulation is so contemptuous of your prowess as to be eating leaves right in front of your eyes.

But Blix is a practical man. As a White Hunter, his job was to produce the game desired and to point it out to his employer of the moment. Blix's work, and mine, was made much easier by finding the elephant so close. We could even land at the camp and then approach them on foot to judge more accurately their size, immediate intentions, and strategic disposition.

Doctor Turvy's prescription had to be filled, and taken, of course, but even so, we would have time to reconnoiter.

We landed on the miserly runway, which had a lot in common with an extemporaneous badminton court, and, within twenty minutes, proceeded on foot toward those magnificent bulls.

Makula was with us. Neither the safari nor this book, for that matter, could complete without Makula. Though there are a good many Wakamba trackers available in East Africa, it has become almost traditional in late years to mention Makula in every book that touches upon elephant-hunting, and I would not break with tradition.

Makula is a man in the peculiar position of having gained fame without being aware of it. He can neither read nor write; his first language is Wakamba, his second a halting Swahili. He is a smallish ebon-tinted Native with an inordinately wise eye, a penchant for black magic, and the instincts of a beagle hound. I think he could track a honeybee through a bamboo forest.

No matter how elaborate the safari on which Makula is engaged as a tracker, he goes about naked from the waist up, carrying a long bow and a quiver full of poisoned arrows. He has seen the work of the best rifles white men have yet produced, but when Makula's nostrils distend after either a good or a bad shot, it is not the smell of gunpowder that distends them; it is a kind of restrained contempt for that noisy and unwieldy piece of machinery with its devilish tendency to knock the untutored huntsman flat on his buttocks every time he pulls the trigger.

Safaris come and safaris go, but Makula goes on forever. I suspect at times that he is one of the wisest men I have ever known—so wise that, realizing the scarcity of wisdom, he has never cast a scrap of it away, though I still remember a remark he made to an overzealous newcomer to his profession: "White men pay for danger—we poor ones cannot afford it. Find your elephant, then vanish, so that you may live to find another."

Makula always vanished. He went ahead in the bush with the silence of a shade, missing nothing, and the moment he had brought his hunters within sight of the elephant, he disappeared with the silence of a shade, missing everything.

Stalking just ahead of Blix through the tight bush, Makula signaled for a pause, shinned up a convenient tree without noise, and then came down again. He pointed to a chink in the thicket, took Blix firmly by the arm, and pushed him ahead. Then Makula disappeared. Blix led, and I followed.

The ability to move soundlessly through a wall of bush as tightly woven as Nature can weave it is not an art that can be acquired much after childhood. I cannot explain it, nor could Arab Maina who taught me ever explain it. It is not a matter of watching where you step; it is rather a matter of keeping your eyes on the place where you want to be, while every nerve becomes your eye, every muscle develops reflex action. You do not guide your body, you trust it to be silent.

We were silent. The elephant we advanced upon heard nothing—even when the enormous hindquarters of two bulls loomed before us like grey rocks wedded to the earth.

Blix stopped. He whispered with his fingers and I read the whisper. "Watch the wind. Swing round them. I want to see their tusks."

Swing, indeed! It took us slightly over an hour to negotiate a semicircle of fifty yards. The bulls were big—with ivory enough—hundred-pounders at least, or better.

Nimrod was satisfied, wet with sweat, and on the verge, I sensed, of receiving a psychic message from Doctor Turvy. But this message was delayed in transit.

One bull raised his head, elevated his trunk, and moved to face us. His gargantuan ears began to spread as if to capture even the sound of our heartbeats. By chance, he had grazed over a spot we had lately left, and he had got our scent. It was all he needed.

I have rarely seen anything so calm as that bull elephant—or so casually determined upon destruction. It might be said that he shuffled to the kill. Being, like all elephant, almost blind, this one could not see us, but he was used to that. He would follow scent and sound until he could see us, which, I computed, would take about thirty seconds.

Blix wiggled his fingers earthward, and that meant, "Drop and crawl."

It is amazing what a lot of insect life goes on under your nose when you have got it an inch from the earth. I suppose it goes on in any case, but if you are proceeding on your stomach, dragging your body along by your fingernails, entomology presents itself very forcibly as a thoroughly justified science. The problem of classification alone must continue to be very discouraging.

By the time I had crawled three feet, I am sure that somewhere over fifty distinct species of insect life were individually and severally represented in my clothes, with Siafu ants conducting the congress.

Blix's feet were just ahead of my eyes—close enough so that I could contemplate the holes in his shoes, and wonder why he ever wore any at all, since he went through them almost in a matter of hours. I had ample time also to observe that he wore no socks. Practical, but not *comme il faut*. His legs moved through the underbrush like dead legs dragged by strings. There was no sound from the elephant.

I don't know how long we crawled like that, but the little shadows in the thicket were leaning toward the east when we stopped. Possibly we had gone a hundred yards. The insect bites had become just broad burning patches.

We were breathing easier—or at least I was—when Blix's feet and legs went motionless. I could just see his head close against his shoulder, and watch him turn to peek upward into the bush. He gave no signal to continue. He only looked horribly embarrassed like a child caught stealing eggs.

But my own expression must have been a little more intense. The big bull was about ten feet away—and at that distance elephant are not blind.

Blix stood up and raised his rifle slowly, with an expression of ineffable sadness.

"That's for me," I thought, "He knows that even a shot in the brain won't stop that bull before we're both crushed like mangos."

In an open place, it might have been possible to dodge to one side, but not here. I stood behind Blix with my hands on his waist according to his instructions. But I knew it wasn't any good. The body of the elephant was swaying. It was like watching a boulder, in whose path you were trapped, teeter on the edge of a cliff before plunging. The bull's ears were spread wide now, his trunk was up and extended toward us, and he began the elephant scream of anger which is so terrifying as to hold you silent where you stand, like fingers clamped upon your throat. It is a shrill scream, cold as winter wind.

It occurred to me that this was the instant to shoot.

Blix never moved. He held the rifle very steady and began to chant some of the most striking blasphemy I have ever heard. It was colourful, original, and delivered with finesse, but I felt that this was a badly chosen moment to test it on an elephant—and ungallant beyond belief if it was meant for me.

The elephant advanced, Blix unleashed more oaths (this time in Swedish), and I trembled. There was no rifle shot. A single biscuit tin, I judged, would do for both of us—cremation would be superfluous.

"I may have to shoot him," Blix announced, and the remark struck me as an understatement of classic magnificence. Bullets would sink into that monstrous hide like pebbles into a pond.

Somehow you never think of an elephant as having a mouth, because you never see it when his trunk is down, so that when the elephant is quite close and his trunk is up, the dark red-and-black slit is by way of being an almost shocking revelation. I was looking into our elephant's mouth with a kind of idiotic curiosity when he screamed again—and thereby, I am convinced, saved both Blix and me from a fate no more tragic than simple death, but infinitely less tidy.

The scream of that elephant was a strategic blunder, and it did him out of a wonderful bit of fun. It was such an authentic scream, of such splendid resonance, that his cronies, still grazing in the bush, accepted it as a legitimate warning, and left. We had known that they were still there because the bowels of peacefully occupied elephant rumble continually like oncoming thunder—and we had heard thunder.

They left, and it seemed they tore the country from its roots in its leaving. Everything went, bush, trees, sansivera, clods of dirt—and the monster who confronted us. He paused, listened, and swung round with the slow irresistibility of a bank-vault door. And then he was off in a typhoon of crumbled vegetation and crashing trees.

For a long time there wasn't any silence, but when there was, Blix lowered his rifle—which had acquired, for me, all the death-dealing qualities of a feather duster.

I was limp, irritable, and full of maledictions for the insect kind. Blix and I hacked our way back to camp without the exchange of a word, but when I fell into a canvas chair in front of the tents, I forswore the historic propriety of my sex to ask a rude question.

"I think you're the best hunter in Africa, Blickie, but there are times when your humour is gruesome. Why in hell didn't you shoot?"

Blix extracted a bug from Doctor Turvy's elixir of life and shrugged.

"Don't be silly. You know as well as I do why I didn't shoot. Those elephant are for Winston."

"Of course I know—but what if that bull charged?"

Farah the faithful produced another drink, and Blix produced a non sequitur. He stared upward into the leaves of the baobab tree and sighed like a poet in love.

"There's an old adage," he said, "translated from the ancient Coptic, that contains all the wisdom of the ages—'Life is life and fun is fun, but it's all so quiet when the goldfish die.'"

PART SIX

Food

BEFORE THE ARRIVAL OF THE WHITE MAN, THE BLACKFOOT INDIANS, LIKE the other Native peoples who populated the High Plains and Rocky Mountain regions, subsisted as hunter-gatherers. They fished and foraged, they hunted deer and elk, moose and pronghorn antelope, birds and small game. But their primary quarry, the animal that occupied the center of their ritual life as well as their economy, was the buffalo or bison. The Blackfoot word for bison meat translates as "real food." They knew, as all hunters do, that on a very essential level, we are what we eat.

The majority of people in developed Western societies have not simply forgotten this fact; they have gone out of their way to evade its implications. Living at ever-farther remove from the sources of their sustenance, most people prefer not to think in too much detail about the circumstances in which a domestic food animal like a pig or chicken lives and dies, about the amount of pain and suffering—and, increasingly, hormones and antibiotics—required to transform a bovine into a burger. Most people are relatively complacent about letting the blood be on someone else's hands, even if, as Eileen Clarke points out below, maintaining one's supposed "innocence" as a meat-eater entails no small degree of self-delusion.

Hunters know better, of course. They cannot help but know, as poet and environmental activist Gary Snyder has phrased it, that "if we do eat meat, it is the life, the bounce, the swish, of a great alert being with keen ears and lovely eyes, with foursquare feet and a huge beating heart that we eat, let us not deceive ourselves."[1] Participating in the cycle of life and death, the hunter experiences an intimate, and intensely personal, relationship with her or his food—a relationship at once symbolic and practical.

Because of the traditional connection between women and nurturing, between mothering and feeding, what female hunters have to say about this relationship is particularly intriguing. The stories in this section are about church suppers, Christmas and Thanksgiving dinners, and other meals celebratory and routine. But they are about so much more, as well: Marjorie Kinnan Rawlings delineates the way hunting and cooking define a rural culture. Osa Johnson offers a Kenyan Christmas reverie of surprising depth and resonance. As both her fall hunting season and her marriage appear to be imploding, Gretchen Legler takes solace in recollecting the sheer lavishness of nature's table, the reason she cannot help but continue to be a hunter. And Clarke approaches the intricacies of communicating with one's loved ones with a generous sense of humor.

There is real food, on many levels, in all these stories.

MARJORIE KINNAN RAWLINGS

Our Daily Bread

from Cross Creek *(1942)*

ISPEAK WITH SOME TREPIDATION OF MY BLACKBIRD PIE, FOR IT MIGHT have brought down on me Federal dishonor, or roughly speaking, jail. I began the shooting of the blackbirds and the making of the pies in a spirit of innocent experimentalism. I sat in a blind on Orange Lake on my first duck hunt. Around and beyond me the good shots were bringing down their ducks. I had not touched a feather. Nearby, hundreds of red-winged blackbirds were stirring in the tussocks. I thought of the four and twenty blackbirds baked in a pie and wondered if these grain and seed eating birds might not be the edible one of the rhymed fable. I slipped No. 10 shells into my shotgun, and two shots brought down a dozen birds. I made the dozen very secretly into a pie. It was utterly delicious. For the next few years, when game was scarce, or I had not been to market for meats, I relied on blackbirds to make a tasty dish. I dressed the birds whole, but skinned, dipped them in flour and browned them in butter, along with tiny whole onions and tiny whole carrots. I covered them with hot water, seasoned them with salt, pepper, a bay leaf or two, sometimes a little of the Greek herb originon, and simmered until tender. I added small whole new potatoes, chopped parsley and sherry, placed them in a baking dish and covered them with a thick rich pastry crust, and finished the dish in the oven. The blackbirds were exquisite morsels of sweet and tender dark meat. Then I began to be ashamed of shooting the cheerful chirruping things that were so ornamental in the marshes. I decided I would do no more of it. And then I discovered that they were listed on my hunting license, by a name I had not recognized, among the birds protected by Federal game laws and forbidden to the hunter. I wondered what I should have done if the game warden had walked in on one of my blackbird pies. I decided that there would have been nothing to do but follow in Fred Tompkins' ways. He and his wife, the Old Hen, and I were dining at his house one day. She went to the door and returned nervously.

"Honey," she said to him, "there's a carful of law at the gate."

"Why, if it's the law," he said, "invite 'em in and give 'em a snort."

It was in the Big Scrub that I had roasted limpkin. The Ocklawaha River is one of the two or three remaining haunts of the strange brown crane who cries before a rain. I lived above the river with my friend Leonard and his mother Piety, and often slipped down the high bluff to the swamp along the river, to see what I might see. I walked there one summer day and beyond me saw a slow, long-legged bird with a mottled breast and long bill, feeding on crayfish. It could only be a limpkin, the old timers had spoken of its flavor, and Piety's kitchen would welcome it. I crept closer in the swamp, among the cypress knees, and shot with my .22 rifle. The bird dropped in the water, and only then I realized that it was out of reach. I believe in killing game only for one's needs and it distresses me to leave dead or wounded game unfound. I waded toward the floating limpkin, above my ankles, above my knees, at last waist-deep. A moccasin swam in spirals in front of me. I found myself at the edge of a deep slough. I reached forward with the rifle and drew the limpkin in to me. Leonard and his mother rejoiced, and we parboiled the bird and stuffed it and roasted it in the wood range, and I have never eaten a more delectable fowl. I shot another while I was there, and then I heard of their vanishing history, and would not shoot another.

Mistress Piety would have cooked anything I suggested. Leonard caught a raccoon in a trap, and though I had heard that "'coon has a foolish kind of taste," I knew that it was eaten and set to work. I parboiled it, as I had done the limpkin, then roasted it, and it was so inedible that one by one the three of us were obliged to head for the open door. I found later that the raccoon has a musk-sack that must be removed before cooking.

Leonard said, "We hadn't never been hard put to it enough to try to put down one of the jessies, but we wouldn't leave you to try it alone."

I am of a divided mind about 'possums. Zelma's mother had one waiting for our supper when we came in one night from the census taking. It was roasted with sage stuffing, with sweet potatoes roasted around it, and it was more delicious than any roast pork. Then I baked one myself at the Creek, and it was completely inedible. I found, again too late, that 'possums are scavengers and must be penned and fed clean food for a week or two before they are fit to eat. It explained why Martha rejoiced whenever I capture a 'possum alive on the road at night, but silently buried it when my car had hit and killed it.

Bear meat is good according to the condition of the bear and the manner in which it is cooked. A male in the mating season is almost inedible, like a boar hog. If mast has been scarce and the late fall and winter have offered poor forage, bear meat is lean and inclined to stringiness in the early spring. But under proper conditions, a Florida bear may be fat and sweet at the end of winter. The Florida bear goes very late into hibernation, emerges early and the hibernation is never absolute. If acorn mast and palmetto berries have been plentiful and he has fed late, piling on layer after layer of fat; if the winter is warm and feed still abundant, he comes out often, lazily, feeds close to his den, sleeps again, rouses to stuff in a few mouthfuls of feed, and goes back to sleep. Under these already favorable conditions of established avoirdupois, sleep, continued feeding and no ranging, early spring may turn him out in plump condition.

The finest bear meat I have eaten was at a church meeting at Eureka. One of the village inhabitants had shot a bear along the Ocklawaha River a few days before and an enormous roast had been hung in the smoke-house just long enough to be tendered and aged in time for the church dinner. It had been cooked as a pot roast, browned in its own fat, sim-mered half a day in an iron pot on a wood range. It was served in cold slices and was the first dish on the long loaded plank tables to melt away. The flavor was that of the choicest prime beef, with an added rich gami-ness. I gave thought to a second slice, but so many little Eurekans were holding up their plates for it that I retired.

I heard a mother say to a small overalled boy, "Now son, you savor this good. This here's bear meat, and what with things changin' outen the old ways, and the bears goin', you're like not to never get to taste it again."

Leonard's mother cooked it equally well. She also sometimes cut very thin slices from the rib steaks, dipped them in flour and fried them in deep hot bear fat. They were crisp and brown and tender. The steaks I ate came from a very large fat bear that Leonard's bride noticed lumbering down the scrub road. She called him casually to its dispatching. The meat, some fried and put down in its own fat, some smoked lightly, lasted the family for many weeks. The golden liquid fat filled two lard tubs and pro-vided a sweet nutty cooking fat for the whole summer. The bear was the one creature for which Bartram did not have a kind word. Although he developed "gratitude and mercy" toward the rattlesnake, and regretted the killing of a young wolf, he protested in 1773 that there were "still far too many bears in Florida." He would find them very nearly gone today.

My elderly friend Cal Long, a famous hunter, told me that wild-cat liver was a tasty dish, especially in lieu of anything better by the campfire.

But Leonard said, "I don't want anything to eat my old hound won't eat. I tried him on a piece of wild-cat liver once, and he spit it out and just looked at me."

But Cal had old-fashioned tastes in general, and had even given up hope of curing his rheumatism, since panther oil was no longer available. All his way of life in the last of his nearly eighty years irked him. This was especially because a Federal game refuge had been established in the scrub, taking in his clearing. He was no longer allowed—he was no longer ostensibly allowed—to kill deer on his own land. But I noticed that veni-son continued a staple meat on his table.

"The law says I cain't shoot a buck in my own potato patch!" he raged. "The law says I cain't kill me a wild turkey scratchin' up my cow-peas. The law this, the law that! Why," he snorted, "I'm too old a man to begin obeyin' the law!"

I have a glass jar of venison in my icebox, of Cal Long's killing. After it is gone, I think I shall eat no more of it, for I have lost stomach for the meat of animals that I once studied, to use for an emotional purpose in a book. I have never killed a deer, holding my shot several times in wonder at their beauty and fluid grace of movement. Long ago Leonard and I hunted deer together in the swamp below his clearing on the Ocklawaha. He put me on a stand on a narrow island, to which the deer came, some-times to feed, sometimes to rest before crossing the river when pursued.

I stood shielded behind a clump of ash trees, where I might watch and cover the crossing. Leonard's Indian-soft steps faded and I strained my hearing for other steps. There was no sound for a long time but the wind in the cypresses and the rushing of river current on both sides of the island. In the distance I heard a light pounding, then running steps so rapid that the two creatures were breaking cover in front of me before I understood that they were deer. They hesitated on the bank for an instant that was only a break in a musical rhythm, a change of beat, then plunged smoothly into the swift arm of river between mainland and island. They passed so close to me that I might have tossed the pointed ash leaves on the beautiful tawny bodies. I do not know whether they saw or scented me. The great liquid brown eyes turned anxiously, for the fear of man, the great killer of all killer animals, is always on them in the hunting season. They emerged from the water, bounded up the bank of the island, lifted their white scuts and were gone like ghosts of deer into the cypresses. As they went, I remembered Piety's waiting cook-pot and the empty smoke-house. I lifted my gun and fired half-heartedly far behind the deer, afraid on the instant that by an accident I might not have missed them. In a few minutes Leonard crashed through the bushes and jumped to the island.

"I missed," I said, and did not tell my story.

He bent down to examine the tracks.

"Just as good you did, I reckon," he said. "They was an old doe and a maiden doe."

He led the way back soberly.

"We'll cut us a swamp cabbage up the trail a ways," he said, "so's not to go home to Ma empty-handed."

Many a hardened hunter has told me that he is done with his deer killing. When a clean kill is made, he takes pleasure in the sport, but when the fallen deer is yet alive when he comes up to it, and he must cut its throat, he cannot face the big eyes turned on him with a stricken wonder. Such use as Leonard and Piety make of game is an ancient and honorable and necessary thing. The meat is needed and none of it is wasted. It is eaten gratefully. The sportsman often comes to feel that he might better buy a roast of beef at the butcher's. Venison is seldom as good as beef.

I am still torn on the matter of bird-shooting. I dread the day when conscience shall triumph over palate. There is no more delicious food than quail or dove, the one meat white, the other dark. I dress them whole, and they must be picked, never skinned. I stuff them with buttered crumbs and pecans, dip them in flour and brown them in butter. I place them then in a casserole, pour over them the browned butter to which a little hot water has been added, add an eighth of a cup of sherry for every bird, cover and bake slowly until meltingly tender. I prefer as accompaniments a Chablis or even a Sauterne for quail, and Burgundy for doves. I like to serve with them soft-cooked grits, small crisp biscuits, wild grape or wild plum jelly, whole baby beets warmed in orange juice and butter with grated orange peel, carrot souffle, a tomato aspic salad, and tangerine sherbet for dessert. I make the tangerine sherbet by any good orange sherbet recipe, substituting tangerine juice for orange juice, and using more lemon juice and less sugar syrup. I cannot recommend the dessert, delicate as it is, unless one has one's own tangerine trees. It takes two large water buckets of tangerines to make sherbet for eight.

In the matter of cooking ducks I am in violent opposition to the pretendedly Epicurean school of raw bloody duck whisked through a duck press. The advice to "run your duck through a very hot oven" leaves me shuddering. I prefer my thoroughly done, moist, crumbling duck to any dripping, rubbery slices, fit only for the jaws of a dinosaur. When my flock of Mallards has unusually successful season, so that I am fairly over-run with ducks, and the feed-bill equals that of four mules, I am sometimes obliged to decimate their numbers. My friends hint the year around that I have too many ducks. When I give in to them and announce a duck dinner, I find myself unable to eat, and must have a poached egg on the side. But on these sad occasions, I am certain of the age of the ducks, and I roast the young ones quickly. When I am uncertain, as one must be, with wild killed ducks, I take no chances, and steam them until tender, then proceed with the roasting, basting often with butter if the wild ducks have little or no fat. The rest of the menu is: claret; fried finger-strips of grits; sweet potato orange baskets; small whole white onions, braised; hot sherried grapefruit; tiny hot cornmeal muffins; a tossed salad of endive dressed with finely chopped chives, marjoram, basil, thyme and French dressing made with tarragon vinegar; for dessert, grape-juice ice cream.

To make the sweet potato orange baskets, I mash peeled boiled sweet potatoes, add beaten eggs, butter, cream, salt, a few spoonfuls of orange blossom honey and a little grated orange peel. I cut oranges in half, scoop out the contents, serrate the edges so that the half-shells look as though a large and accurate fox had bitten them; fill the shells with the potato mixture, dot with butter, and place in a hot oven to brown. A handle of orange peel may be added, but this is only elegance and gets in the way. The hot sherried grapefruit that I serve with the duck makes also an excellent first course on a cold night, or a dessert when something light is needed. I prepare grapefruit halves as for breakfast serving, turning them upside down to drain off the excess juice. I sprinkle the fleshy part with brown sugar, powdered clove and dots of butter, and fill the centers with them piping hot. The grape-juice ice cream is pleasantly acid after the rich duck. To a pint of grape-juice I add the juice of one lemon, half a cup to a cup of sugar, and a pint or so of heavy cream, and freeze. This meal sounds simple and well-balanced, but somehow it is deadly. I have very nearly killed people with it. I keep hoping that it will teach them not to hint for my ducks.

The pilau is almost a sacred Florida dish, and for making a small amount of meat feed a large number, it has no equal. A Florida church supper is unheard of without it. Bartram found the dish here those many years ago, and called it "pillo," and once, "pilloe." We pronounce the word purr-loo. Almost any meat, but preferably chicken or fresh pork, is cut in pieces and simmered in a generous amount of water until tender. When it falls from the bones, as much rice is added as is need for the number to be fed, and cooked to a moist flakiness. The flavor of meat and gravy permeates the last grain of rice. Fred Tompkins once cooked a coot liver and gizzard pilau at the Creek. It was very good, and the only time I have been able to down coot in any form. The rest of the Creek considers coots almost as edible as ducks. I have followed Martha's directions faithfully, soaking the coots overnight in vinegar-water and parboiling with soda before roasting, but they still taste rankly of the marsh mud on which they have fed.

We are all in complete agreement on squirrel meat. Fried, smother-fried with a rich gravy, or made into a pilau, we esteem it highly. There are, however, strong differences of opinion on the edibility of the head. I saw this disagreement flare up violently at the doing at Anthony.

Word came that Fatty Blake, a snuff and tobacco salesman, and Anthony's richest citizen—wealth at Anthony, as elsewhere, is relative—was having a big doings on a certain Thursday night. The world was invited. Fatty himself stopped at the village store to verify the invitation. He was inviting two counties to his doings, and all was free. There would be squirrel pilau and Brunswick stew. Fatty couldn't likker folks, as he would like to do, but if you brought your own 'shine and were quiet about it, why, he'd meet you at the gate for a drink, and God bless you.

"I got boys in the woods from can't-see to can't-see," he said, "getting me squirrels for that pilau. I got a nigger coming to stir that pot of rice all day long. And my wife, God bless her, is walking the county, getting what she needs for Brunswick stew, the kind her mammy made ahead of her in Brunswick, Georgia."

Cars and wagons and lone horses and mules began coming in to Anthony long before dark. They brought women in homemade silks and in ginghams, men in mail-order store clothes with stiff collars and men in the blue pin-checks of the day's work. Children screamed and played all over the swept sand about Fatty's two-story house. The wives of Anthony bustled up and down a forty-foot pine-board table. Each had brought her contribution, of potato salad made by stirring cut onion and hard-boiled eggs into cold mashed potatoes, of soda biscuits and pepper relish, of pound cake and blueberry pie. Back of the house a Negro stirred rice in a forty-gallon iron kettle with a paddle as big as an oar. It grew dark and the crowd was hungry.

At seven o'clock Mrs. Jim Butler played three solo hymns on the Blakes' parlor organ, moved out to the front porch for the occasion. Then she lifted her shrill soprano voice in the opening strains of "I know Salvation's free," and the crowd joined in with quavering pleasure. At seven-thirty the Methodist preacher rose to his feet beside the organ. He lauded Fatty Blake as a Christian citizen. He prayed. Here and there a devout old woman cried "Amen!" And then the parson asked that any one so minded contribute his mite to help Brother Blake defray the expense of this great free feast.

"Will Brother Buxton pass the hat?"

The hat was passed, and as the pennies and nickels clinked into it, Fatty Blake made his address of welcome.

"I've done brought all you folks together," he shouted, "in the name of brotherly love. I want to tell you, all at one great free table, to love one another.

"Don't just stick to your own church," he pleaded. "If you're a Baptist, go to the Methodist church when the Methodists have preaching Sunday. If you're a Methodist, go help the Baptists when their preacher comes to town.

"Now I want to tell you this meal is free and I had no idea of getting my money back, but as long as our good parson here has mentioned it, I'll say just do what your pocket and your feeling tell you to, and if you feel you want to do your share in this big community feed, why, God bless you.

"Now, folks, we've all enjoyed the entertainment, and I know you're going to enjoy the rations just as much. There's all you can eat and eat your fill. Don't hold back for nobody. Get your share of everything. I've had a nigger stirring the pilau since sun-up and it smells the best of any pilau I've ever smelt. It's got forty squirrels in it, folks, forty squirrels and a big fat hen. And my wife herself made that Brunswick stew, just like she learned it at her mother's knee in Brunswick, Georgia. Now go to it, folks, but don't rush!"

The crowd packed tight around the table, weaving and milling. The pilau and stew were passed around in paper dishes. The passing hat reached a lean, venerable farmer just as he had completed a tour of exploration through his pilau.

"No!" he shrilled, with the lustiness of an old man with a grievance.

"No, I ain't goin' to give him nothin'! This here was advertised as a free meal and 'tain't nothin' but a dogged Georgia prayer-meetin'. Get a man here on promises and then go to pickin' his pocket. This food ain't fitten to eat, dogged Georgia rations, Brunswick stew and all. And he's done cooked the squirrel heads in the pilau, and that suits a damned Georgia Cracker but it don't suit me.

"I was born and raised in Floridy, and I'm pertickler. I don't want no squirrel eyes lookin' at me out o' my rations!"

OSA JOHNSON

Christmas at Lake Paradise

from Four Years in Paradise *(1944)*

" . . . *Our friends think we're having a tough time out here, and I suppose it isn't any bed of roses by some of their standards, but to Osa and me it is Paradise in every way. We are doing the work we want to do, living in the great sunny, healthy out-of-doors, enjoying good food from our own garden, accomplishing what we believe is useful and important work, and we feel richer than anyone we know . . . "*

—Martin Johnson

"Do you know what day it is tomorrow?"

Martin looked up from his porridge, a little puzzled.

"Sure, it's Tuesday."

"Oh, shoot! You mean you don't know tonight is Christmas Eve?"

His eyes widened. "By George, if we stay out here much longer I won't even know what year it is. By that time our money will be gone and we won't be able to get home. We'll have to stay here and live on the fat of the land."

Then and there I made up my mind that I would give him a Christmas surprise such as he had never had before.

I had my mule, Lazy Bones, saddled, and with Boculy and three boys I started off to shoot our Christmas dinner. Although I knew how Martin felt about my going off alone, he would be busy in his laboratory and wouldn't miss me.

For some unaccountable reason Lazy Bones was very irritable. It was quite unlike him, because he usually had a sweet and gentle disposition, and I wondered about it. I dismounted, and carefully examined his legs to see if he had been hurt. I looked at the saddle, but everything seemed in order, so I mounted once again. We rode along the trail and still the mule fidgeted, and seemed greatly disturbed about something.

As we came to a steep ravine, Lazy Bones suddenly stopped, then bucked. I hung on a moment, then lost my grip and went over his head into the stones along the ravine. I landed head-first and was dazed for a few minutes. When I opened my eyes, Boculy was standing over me with a canteen of water.

"Did you hurt your head?" Boculy asked, his eyes popping.

"I got a little bump. But I'm all right. It's Lazy Bones. What's the matter with him?" I asked.

Boculy shook his head. The mule was standing beside him, peering down at me with big eyes, looking very forlorn and sympathetic. I think he was trying to explain to me what was wrong. The native boys said it was a puff adder that had frightened him. But I had had enough riding for one day, so I sent him on home with one of the boys leading him. Later on they reported that they had found a tick the size of a shilling under his saddle blanket!

We pressed on, and the boys spread out and watched for birds. Suddenly I spied a long, feathered neck showing above the grass. It would be just the thing for our Christmas dinner—a giant bustard. I raised my rifle, and fired. There was a short rustle, then no movement save the slight sway of the grass in the warm afternoon wind.

There lay the giant bustard. Thirty-five pounds of delicious African turkey. I held him up. He was a beauty. The feathers of his tail were spotted, his handsome chest a pearl-gray. His long beak and the proud little white pompom crest on his head were splotched with red where the bullet had entered. As I looked at him, I realized as never before that there was more joy in shooting with a camera than a gun. But this wild African turkey would taste mighty good on Christmas Day, so with two native boys carrying the prize, we turned back along an elephant trail.

As we emerged from a bit of forest, Boculy suddenly grasped my arm. We stood motionless, hardly daring to breathe. Ahead, at the top of a ravine, was a leopard. He was sprawled out majestically in the golden grass among the tiger lilies, sunning himself. I raised my gun and slipped the safety. The leopard lifted his handsome head towards us, stared for a moment, then sniffed and gracefully slid away into the grass.

But that wasn't the end of our adventure. Just as we neared the entrance to Lake Paradise and our little village, we heard the unmistakable crunching sound of elephants. Boculy listened for a moment, held up one finger, which indicated that there was just one animal, and promptly fell to his knees. I followed suit, and so did the native boys.

We began crawling off on a detour, just as the elephant came into view. He halted, got our scent, looked in our direction, and began "rocking," which I knew to be the prelude to a charge. When we looked again, the elephant was quietly feeding. He must have thought us baboons, for I am sure that is how we looked as we crept along through the grass on all fours.

At the edge of the crater we met Martin. He seemed very worried. He had his .470 rifle under his arm.

"Osa brings home the dinner." From Osa Johnson, Four Years in Paradise.

"Osa, where in heaven's name have you been? I saw an elephant wandering up from the Lake and I was afraid you might meet him."

"We did meet your elephant," I laughed, "and what's more we met something else."

"Something else?" he snapped.

"Yes. Our Christmas dinner. Look, Martin! We're going to have a feast that will equal all the Christmas dinners you've ever had back home in Kansas."

"Equal? Why, Osa, I bet it will be better than any Christmas dinner back in Kansas."

Martin looked at me delightedly as the boys helped me lift the bustard.

"Just hold that pose," he said. "I'm going to get the camera and snap you—standing there and holding that bird. And we'll get Lazy Bones into the picture too."

"Hurry up!" I shouted to Martin as he focused the camera, and as the boys helped me hold up the prize. "This bird is heavy. It's almost as big as I am."

Of course, there was a little matter of cooking the thirty-five pound bird for the Christmas dinner.

First of all, the barbecue pit had to be prepared. The pit was about three feet deep, four feet long, and three feet wide. I had the boys line it with stones which were fired to a white heat, then covered with moist earth.

Then I cleaned and rubbed the bird with olive oil. Of course, there would have to be stuffing. What is a Christmas dinner without stuffing! And wild mushrooms from the forest would be just the thing to put in it.

These preparations completed, I stuffed the bird, sewed him up, rolled him in banana leaves, then wrapped him in a damp cloth, plastered with clay. He was then ready to be placed in the pit, and the pit filled with earth and a layer of coals on top. There I left him to cook for eight or nine hours, a process of steaming his own juice—a "natural" fireless cooker.

What else could we have to make this a Christmas dinner without precedent? Our two-acre garden would solve that.

I went to the garden to get a couple of bunches of celery. This had been one of the problem children among my garden family and it was amazing what lovely white and tender stalks we now had.

In the forest, where I went to gather asparagus, I found a clump of beautiful stalks, which for some unknown reason the baboons hadn't touched. I was just about to cut them when a cobra raised its head out of the center of the cluster, ready and poised to strike. I screamed and the native boys, always on the alert, killed it. I particularly hate snakes, and the incident upset me a good deal, but not for long. I had too much to do.

Finally my menu was complete:

CHRISTMAS DAY MENU SPECIAL
LAKE PARADISE
*

ANCHOVIES
WILD BUFFALO OXTAIL SOUP
(with garden vegetables)
WILD ROAST TURKEY
(bustard)
WILD MUSHROOM STUFFING

WILD ASPARAGUS   CANDIED SWEET
(Hollandaise Sauce)   POTATOES

CELERY HEARTS

MIXED GREEN SALAD   WATERMELON PRESERVES
STRAWBERRIES AND CREAM
COFFEE
NUTS & RAISINS

I draped Spanish moss to look like bows over the fireplace, and above our chintz curtains at the window. In the forest I had found a bush laden with small red berries. It wasn't holly, of course, but I tied little bunches of it together to make wreaths and hung them all about the house. And, little by little, things took on the atmosphere of Christmas.

Lake Paradise was an Eden for every sort of flower. I gathered armfuls of them and arranged the room and the table until we looked as though we were having a real party.

There were tiger lilies from the plains, sometimes with one red and one yellow blossom on the same stalk. And orchid which would have cost a fortune in America bloomed on the trees in the yard. There were clusters of heatherspray, wild yellow poppies, wild gladiola, carnations and cosmos. There were no poinsettias, but we most certainly could say "Merry Christmas" with a house full of flowers.

And then it was Christmas morning at Lake Paradise.

Overlooking the great desert, I felt as if I were living on the roof of the world, as if I dwelt in a wind-swept tower, never before inhabited by man.

It was about seven thirty when I called Martin to announce that our Christmas dinner was on the table. He came into the room, and for a few minutes he just stood there and stared at everything.

"Osa, it's wonderful!" he cried. "Watermelon preserve, too!"

"This beats that Christmas dinner we had in London. The Savoy hasn't anything on you, Osa."

We said no more but just pitched in and ate. I had never before been so proud of a table, and I had done it all from the jungle. When we had finished, Martin pushed back his chair and came over to my side of the table. He took my hand in his. I looked up at him. Neither of us could say a word. It was one of those times when no words could convey our feelings.

We went into the living room. By this time night had fallen. Stars shone in the sky; the moon sailed into view, cold, distant, and serene. It poured a smooth river of silver light into the garden and left the forest in shadow. The same moon would be shining down on Kansas this very Christmas night. Time and space seemed close. I could feel the brisk chill of the African night, as the cool breeze stirred the chintz curtains at the window.

After we had finished coffee, Martin suddenly jumped up, nearly knocking over the tiny coffee table.

"Osa—the presents!" he cried. "The Christmas presents!"

I hadn't forgotten about them. Bukhari, who had kept most of the presents hidden under a pile of straw in his hut, had brought them in before dinner.

Martin was as excited as any small boy expecting a new bicycle. He went over to the table in the corner where I had carefully arranged all the gifts and began to look at the various boxes.

"Holy smoke! What a lot of them! We did pretty well for ourselves, I think."

He was busy unwrapping the packages. There were ever so many, all sorts, sizes and shapes. Packages from our friends all over the world—packages from friends we didn't even know personally—packages that had arrived at Paradise many, many weeks before Christmas, some even months before, all carefully marked: *Do not open until December 25th.*

There were our own special surprise packages that Martin and I had prepared for each other—things bought months before, ordered from America or Europe.

"What's this?" Martin was opening a small box. "It's from home—from Kansas."

"It's from your father." I had noticed the Independence postmark on the brown wrapping paper.

Martin turned to me. "Why, Osa—what's the matter?"

"Nothing."

"Nothing! Now, you can't fool me, honey. You were thinking about something. I know what it was—Kansas! When I opened that package from Dad."

"Yes, I was thinking of home. After all, it's Christmas, you know, and it *is* nice to think of home at Christmas."

"I wonder if it snowed in Kansas this Christmas, Osa. Remember how all the kids used to get out their sleds and go coasting down-hill? That was the best fun in the world."

I laughed as I thought of all the things we used to do as children back in Kansas during the Christmas holidays—those happy childhood days in Chanute when my brother and I would hitch our little yellow sleds to Mr. Jerome's grocery wagon, and go gliding along the avenues of snow, shouting with glee as his chestnut bay trudged through the deep drifts, and clapping our red mittened hands to keep warm. I shall always remember the trees, burdened with snow, and the doorsteps of every house in town chocked with the soft white stuff. The trees were crisp, sparkling, and white, and the air on Christmas morning quivered with the pealing bells of the Episcopal Church on Main Street and the music of the early morning carolers. I thought of the houses in Chanute, delicately frosted, with their gables and chimneys. Why, we hadn't hitched our sleds to an old grocery wagon at all on Christmas mornings; we had hitched them to the Star of Bethlehem.

I could hear Martin speaking. "I remember . . . I remember . . . "

Yes, "Remember!"—certainly one of the loveliest words in the English language.

After a bit, Martin lit his cigar, and we sat by the fireplace. Every flickering flame was a memory. I could see the store windows in Chanute, Kansas, brightly lit. Everything one could dream of had found its way to the counters of the stores. There was Main Street, hung with garlands and wreaths. And, right there in the middle of Main Street, stood an enormous Christmas tree, shining with colored lights and hung with ornaments and red and green ribbons. Santa Claus had come to Kansas!

And he was here in Africa, too.

Martin puffed away on his cigar. I looked up at him, and he smiled. He rose and came over to me.

"You know, Osa," he said, "I think that we must be the two happiest people in all the world."

"I'm sure of it, darling," I said.

"What do you say if we go out and take a walk?"

I got our coats, glanced at the mountains of Christmas cards and packages—from home, from Sir Harry Lauder, Mr. Eastman, Chic Sale, Mr. Pomeroy, Will Rogers, Mr. Wilcox, and many others. There's nothing in the world quite like knowing that your friends haven't forgotten you.

The scene was peaceful and lovely. We could see the black outline of the forest. The Lake was alive with moonlight, and Martin and I watched in silence as the animals came to the water to drink—elephants, baboons, rhino, leopards, and buffalo.

We heard the sounds of the elephants as they cracked down branches, lumbering their way through the denseness of the forest. We saw them at the water's edge, listened to their trumpetings.

As the animals wandered about, the ducks and the birds flew up from the surface of the Lake, and we heard the quick frightened beat of their wings in flight.

I huddled into my coat, and took Martin's hand in mine.

Stretched out before us, surrounding us on all sides, was a primeval world. I felt very close to the beginning of life.

As we looked up to the peak above us we saw a star twinkling at its very top like the star the Three Wise Men followed to a manger in Bethlehem.

We felt that here at Lake Paradise, deep in the heart of Africa, we had really found the timeless peace on earth, goodwill toward men. I nestled closer to Martin. Neither of us spoke. And we sat there into the dawn.

GRETCHEN LEGLER

Gooseberry Marsh, Part Two

from All the Powerful Invisible Things: A Sportswoman's Notebook
(1995)

THIS FALL ON GOOSEBERRY MARSH THE WEATHER IS WARM AND THE water is high. As Craig and I load the canoe on the grassy shore of the marsh, the sky is turning from rosy-gold to gray-blue. The blackbirds that make their homes in the reeds are singing by the hundreds, a loud, high, rocks-in-a-bucket screeching. Above us, lines of geese cross the lightening sky.

This is the first fall of our not living with each other, of living separately, of living apart: Craig in the big house, me in a small apartment. But we decided to hunt together anyway, hanging onto this sure thing, hunting at Gooseberry Marsh, this thing we have shared for so many years, this activity that has defined our relationship.

We try in a polite and partly exhausted way to pretend that nothing is different, that we still love each other, but something subtle has shifted beneath us. It is something more than the details, the awkward rearranging of our lives that this separation has necessitated. In preparing for this trip, I bought *our* supplies with *my* money and brought the food to *Craig's* house. When we get *home* from hunting I will unpack *our* decoys and *our* coolers full of wet birds, do *my* laundry, and then I will pack *my* bags and leave for *my* apartment. These are uneasy adjustments. We are unused to being apart. We both feel embarrassed and sad when we catch ourselves saying, "Next time. . . . " Next time we should leave half an hour earlier. Next time we should wear waders. Next year let's buy more bluebill decoys. We both know there probably will be no next time.

But something even more huge and silent has changed. It is hard for me now even to reach out to hold his hand. The intimacy we had, the warm space between our bodies, has stretched so that it feels like nothing. Between us now is only this coolness, as we stand so close together on the shore of the marsh. Something feels terribly wrong.

Even with the high water this year, we have to pull our canoe through the faint, watery channel between the forest of reeds that separates the two parts of the marsh. We both lean forward, grasp bunches of reeds in our fists and on three we pull.

"One, two, three, pull," I call. "One, two, three, pull." We inch along.
This is maddening. I can't steer the bow. Because Craig is pulling so hard
in the stern and not watching, the canoe gets jammed nose-first in the
reeds. We have to back out and start over. I twist around in my seat in the
bow and glare at Craig.

"Don't pull unless I say so," I say.

"Just shut up and do it," he says, angrily, wearily, coldly. "This isn't a
big deal."

A sourness rises up in me. The nape of my neck bristles. He has never
said anything like this to me. Ever. He has hardly raised his voice to me in
seven years, not even in the midst of my most dangerous rages. I am so
startled I fall silent. As we move out of the reeds into the pond again, I say
quietly, "You were a jerk. You should apologize."

"Okay," he says mockingly. "I'm sorry I hurt your feelings."

On the far end of the pond we see frightened mallards and teal rise
up, quacking. We know they will come back later. The sky around us now
is a faint pink. The day is fast coming on. We open the green canvas packs
in the middle of the canoe and one by one unravel the lead weights and
string from around the necks of our plastic mallards and our plastic bluebills, placing the decoys carefully in a configuration we think will draw
ducks close enough to shoot—one long line to the right of the place where
we will hide in the reeds, a bunch to the left, and sets of three and four
scattered about. I reach into the pocket of my canvas hunting jacket to feel
the hard, cold wood of my duck call. It has always been my job to do the
calling.

After our decoys are set and we have paddled the canoe into the reeds,
pulled reeds down over us, stretched a camouflage tarp over us, we wait.
We hear sharp echoes from hunters shooting far off on other ponds. The
first ducks to come to us are teal. They are small and tan, only as big as
a grown man's fist. They land on the water and we can see by the tinge of
powdery blue on their wings that they are blue-winged teal. We have set
some ethical guidelines to stick to, as we have every year. We will shoot no
hens, and no birds sitting on the water. We don't shoot the teal on the
water, but I rise up to scare them into flight so that we can take a shot. We
miss.

The next birds are mallards and we shoot a hen. She falls into the
water and flaps around, dipping her head in and out of the water, slapping
her wings. Then she sits up, confused and frightened, and paddles toward
the reeds. We know that if she gets into the reeds we will never find her
again, that she will go in there and die, probably be eaten by a fox or a
weasel, or, eventually, by the marsh itself. But I will still see our shooting
her as a waste. My heart cramps up as we follow this bird in our canoe,
chasing her, paddling fast, trying to mark where she entered the reeds. We
look for her for nearly an hour, straining our eyes for curls of soft breast

feathers on the water among the reed stems, standing high up on the bow, one foot on each gunnel, looking down from above. I engage in this search with a kind of desperation. I must find her. I must. But she is gone.

"If it's still alive, it'll come out," Craig says. He is impatient to get back to our blind. While we have been looking, another flock flew over and flared off, seeing us plainly in the water.

I feel defeated and sad. We paddle back to our spot in the reeds, drive our canoe into the grass, pull the long reeds over us to hide again and wait. Half an hour passes. The sun is out now and I am sweating in all this wool and cotton underneath my canvas hunting jacket. I doze off. I am bored. I take my duck call out of my pocket and practice making quacking noises.

Quack Quack Quack

Craig rolls his eyes. "Stop it. You might scare them away."

I throw the call to him at the other end of the canoe. "You do it then," I say, stuffing my hands back in the deep pocket of my coat.

The next birds to come over are bluebills, and I shoot one as it is flying away over my right shoulder. The momentum of its flight carries it into the reeds behind me. Again we spend forty-five minutes looking for the bird. We don't find the bluebill either. I want to keep looking. I insist we try again. Craig says, "We'll never find it. Give it up."

The next birds to come in are wood ducks, mostly males. We shoot at them just as they have set their wings and two fall in a mess of feathers and shot, the pellets dropping like hail on the water. We paddle out to pick them up. One is breast-down in the water and when I reach with my bare hand and pull it up by the neck, I gasp. Its breast has been shot away. I shot away its breast. The white feathers are laid wide open, dark red breast meat split open, gaping, the heart smashed, the beak smashed, the head crushed. I swallow down something nasty rising in my throat. We pick up the other wood duck and head back into the reeds. I hold the broken wood duck on my lap. What is left of its blood is soaking through my tan pants onto my long underwear. The warm heavy body lies across my knee. I am stroking this bird's elaborate, feathery purple and orange and white crest, bitter tears come up to the surface and roll down my wind-chapped face.

Craig says, "Let's get the camouflage back on the boat, and then you can play."

"Play?" I ask him. At this moment I hate him fiercely. I vow that I will never hunt with him again. I wonder why I ever did. Why I married him, stayed with him. Why I hunt at all. "I'm not playing," I whisper hoarsely. Later, after we have been quiet for a time, I say to him, "Maybe you want to hunt with a man, someone who doesn't cry." He doesn't answer me.

Still later, when we are cleaning the ducks onshore and I reach my hand into the cavity of the ravaged wood duck, scraping my hand on the broken bones such that I bleed, I ask him, "What would a man hunter do about this bird? Would he cry?"

Craig says, "No, he would throw it away." And there is a hardness in what he has said, so that I barely recognize his voice.

After the ducks are emptied of their hearts and livers and green, reeking, grass-filled crops, we line them up as before on the banks of the marsh and sprinkle cornmeal on them, in front of them, beside them, behind them. This time I complete the ritual with a sick resignation, as if there is nothing now that I can say or do that will make amends for this—for this hunting gone all wrong, for this hunting when the love between us has gone all wrong.

There is nothing I can do for this now, except take this wood duck home, save its skin, and give the lovely feathers to my father, who will make beautiful dry flies out of them to catch trout with in Montana. I will salvage what breast meat I can from this wreckage and make a soup or a stew, something good to eat, something hot and rich to share with my friends, or to eat alone.

Hunting with Craig has never been like this. My heart aches and I am afraid. I hate what we have done this year. It feels like murder. In the beginning, when Craig and I were first in love, everything was different. I wonder if I will ever hunt again. I wonder if I can make sense of what has happened here. I think now that hunting for us has everything to do with love, with the way we feel about ourselves and each other. The heaviness or lightness of our hearts, our smallness or our generosity, show in the way we hunt; in the way we treat the bluebills and mallards and teal that we shoot and eat; in the way we treat each other. I want to correct this imbalance between Craig and me and inside myself. I want to go on hunting but not this way.

Part of what hunting meant for us, when we were together, was feasting. It wasn't the shooting that mattered, but what we did with this food we gathered: how we prepared the ducks to eat, how we shared them with friends, how we raised our glasses before we ate, at a long table lit by candles, covered with a lacey white cloth, and thanked the ducks for their lives. Several times a year, at Easter, at Thanksgiving and at Christmas, Craig and I prepared banquets for our friends. Nearly everything we cooked for our feast was from our garden, or collected from the woods, or killed by us. This, I think now, was why I hunted and why I still want to. Because I want this kind of intimate relationship with the food I eat.

There were some things—flour, sugar, oranges, walnuts, chutney—that Craig and I served at our feasts that we could not grow or collect ourselves. And for these items I would shop at our local grocery store. To get to the checkout counter in the store, I usually walked down the meat aisle. There was hardly ever a whole animal for sale, only parts. There were double-breasted cut-up fryers with giblets. Three-legged fryers and budget packs—two split breasts with backs, two wings, two legs, two giblets and two necks. There were boneless, skinless thighs; packages of only drumsticks; plastic containers of livers. There were breaded, skinless, boneless breasts in a thin box—microwaveable, ninety-five percent fat-free, shrink-wrapped, "all natural" and farm-fresh. The meat cases were cool, so cool I could hardly smell the meat, only a sanitary wateriness. The smell was different from the smell of wet ducks and blood in the bottom of our canoe. The smell was different from the smell of the warm gut-filled cavity I reached my hand into when I cleaned a bird. The smell was different from the smell in the kitchen when we pulled out all the ducks' feathers, piling them up in a soft mound on the kitchen table, different from the smell when we dipped the birds in warm wax, wax that we then let harden and pulled off in thick flakes along with the ducks' pinfeathers.

The birds in the store were pared down and down and down so that what was left had no relationship to what these animals were when they were alive. They were birds cut and sliced until all that was left was grotesque combinations of named parts. It always felt obscene to me. What were these birds like whole? It was hard, standing amid the dry coolness rising up from the meat cases, to imagine any life; hard to construct a picture of these birds flying, walking, making morning noise, pecking for insects in the grass, fighting over corn, laying eggs. Hard to imagine them in any way but stacked in their airless cages.

The Russian philosopher and critic Mikhail Bakhtin tells us that the ritual of feasting serves to bridge humans' most basic fears. In writing about banquets and feasting in the novels of sixteenth-century French author François Rabelais, Bakhtin says that in the act of eating—as in the act of drinking, of making love, of giving birth—the beginning and the end of life are linked and interwoven. In Rabelais's novels, eating celebrates the destruction of what humans encounter as most threatening, that which is not us—nature. Humans celebrate their interaction with the world through food and drink, through sex, through laughter. This is how feasting bridges fear.

In modern culture, Bakhtin says, where what we eat is so separated from our own labor, hardly anything remains of these old connections. Nothing is left of our encounters with food, tasting the world, but a series of artificial, meaningless metaphors.

In Rabelais's work, eating is a victory, a joy, because in the act of eating, the body crosses over its own limits—the body becomes part of a larger world. Because of this, Bakhtin says, "No meal can be sad. Sadness and food are incompatible (while death and food are perfectly compatible)."

One year, two weeks before Christmas, Craig and I invited twelve of our friends to our house for a feast. We spent all day preparing for this meal. I sliced through the dense brilliant layers of three red cabbages and set the purple shreds to simmer in a pot with honey. I stuffed our ducks with apples and oranges and onions and raisins, and spread the slippery pale breasts with butter and garlic, sprinkling on thyme and rosemary. We took handfuls of dried morel mushrooms from a coffee can above the refrigerator, quarreling over how many we could stand to give away. I dropped the mushrooms into a baking pan with white wine, where they would gain their moisture back before we sautéed them in butter.

Craig scooped out the insides of a pumpkin from the garden for a pie. He walked to the freezer on the porch and brought back a jar of frozen blueberries. Another pie. He took from the same freezer a jar of cut up frozen rhubarb. Another pie. The squash from the garden was piled in a cardboard box in the basement. I walked down the stairs into the dark cool, turned on the light, collected four acorn squash, carried them upstairs into the steamy kitchen, peeled off their tough green and orange skins, chopped them, added butter and onions and carrots and cooked the mixture. And then I puréed it for soup.

We were drinking wine and dancing as we cooked. We were full of joy. We felt generous. To feed all of these people, our friends, with food that we knew in some intimate way, food we had grown or animals we had killed ourselves, was a kind of miracle. The meal we concocted was nearly perverse in its abundance.

Appetizer: venison liver pâté and hot spiced wine.

First course: acorn squash soup sprinkled with fresh ground nutmeg.

Second course: spinach and beet green salad with chutney dressing.

Third course: barbecued venison steaks, wild rice, morel mushrooms, buttered beets and honeyed carrots.

Fourth course: roast duck with plum gravy, new potatoes in butter and parsley sauce and sweet-and-sour red cabbage with honey, vinegar and caraway seeds.

Dessert: rhubarb pie, blueberry pie, pumpkin pie. Ice cream.

Then brandy. And coffee. And tea. And as we sat and talked, we ate tart, green and red, thinly sliced apples, slivers of pear and cheese and grapes.

In eating these foods—these ducks that we shot out of the sky, that fell, tumbling wing over head, with loud splashes into the cold pond beside our canoe; pumpkin pie that came from a pumpkin that grew all summer long in our backyard garden, surviving three weeks of me cutting open its stalk, scraping out squash borers with the tip of a paring knife; these mushrooms, collected over April and May in the just-leafing-out Minnesota woods full of cardinals, scarlet tanagers, bloodroot, new violets, nesting grouse, and baby rabbits; this venison, from a big-shouldered, spreading-antlered, randy buck Craig killed in November, which we tracked by following the bloody trail it left on bushes and dried grass and leaves—in eating these foods, in this passing of lives into ours, this passing of other blood and muscle into our own blood and muscle, into our own tongues and hearts; in this bridging we were taking up not only food for our bodies, but something that is wild that we wanted for ourselves. Perhaps it was our own power we were eating. Perhaps it was our own ability to grow, to shoot, to find food for ourselves, that we were eating; our ability to engage creatively with the world. We were eating what we wanted so much. We were eating life.

Poet Audre Lorde has written about what she called "the erotic" and its potential to help us redefine our relationships with ourselves, with each other, and with the world. Lorde, who died from cancer in 1992, writes about using the erotic as a way of knowing the world differently, as a source of power that is unlike any other source of power.

We live in a racist, patriarchal and anti-erotic society, Lorde writes in "Uses of the Erotic: The Erotic as Power." We live in a pornographic society that insists on the separation of so many inseparable things; that insists on ways of thinking that separate the body from the world, the body from the mind, nature from culture, men from women, black from white; a society that insists on bounded categories of difference.

But we can use erotic power to resist those splitting forces. The erotic is the sensual bridge that connects the spiritual and the political. It has something to do with love. The word itself comes from the Greek word *eros*, the personification of love in all its aspects—born of Chaos and personifying creative power and harmony. *Eros* is a non-rational power. *Eros* is awareness. *Eros* is not about what we do but about how acutely and fully we can feel in the doing, says Lorde. Its opposite, the pornographic, emphasizes sensation without feeling. Pornographic relationships are those that are born not of human erotic feeling and desire, not of a love of life and a love of the body, but those relationships, those ideas born of a fear of bodily knowledge and a desire to silence the erotic.

Everything we have ever learned in our lives tells us to suspect feeling, to doubt the power of the erotic and to confuse it with the pornographic. But the two are at opposite ends of the world. One is about parts, not wholes. One numbs us to the irrationality, the comedy, of eating animals that are strangers to us, who come to us as perverse combinations of wings and breasts.

I understand the horror among some people I know over my shooting and eating a duck. But while I have become accustomed to hunting and eating wild duck, they are accustomed to buying and eating chicken from the store. Our actions are somehow similar yet also fundamentally different. Buying and eating a shrink-wrapped fryer feels to me like eating reduced to the necessities of time, convenience, cleanliness.

Lorde asks when we will be able, in our relationships with one another and with the world, to risk sharing the erotic's electric charge without having to look away, and without distorting the enormously powerful and creative nature of that exchange. Embracing the erotic means accepting our own mortality, our own bodiedness. Embracing the erotic means not looking away from our relationships with what we eat. And that can turn hunting into a relationship of love; at least not something brutal. Accepting our own bodiedness means acquiescing fully in our own temporariness, and seeing that we are somehow, all of us, deeply connected.

One spring I was walking around Lake of the Isles in Minneapolis with a friend. We were walking fast, dressed in sweatpants and tennis shoes. She would rather have run, but because I was recovering from knee surgery, I could only walk. We took long strides and when I stretched out my leg I could feel the scars there, the manufacturing of new tissue that gave me a strong knee.

We were talking about nothing in particular, about her job as an editor with an agricultural magazine, about running, about lifting weights, about books we had read. Suddenly I shouted, interrupting her. "Look at that!"

She looked to where I was pointing and turned back to me to see what it was I was so excited about.

"Look at those ducks," I said. "All those ducks." As we came upon a gaggle of mallards, feeding on broken tortilla chips a woman was tossing to them from the grassy bank, I insisted on breaking our stride, stopping to stare.

I was fascinated by the greenheads, how when they moved their heads turned violet and emerald in the light. How there was one duck with a broken bill and a goose with only one foot. There was one female among the group of males. Two of the males were chasing her. It was mating season.

My friend and I moved on. She talked to me about her lover who teaches writing and literature at a local college. We stopped again because I'd seen a wake in the water, a silvery V streaming out behind a fast-moving muskrat. "Where?" She squinted.

"There," I said, pointing.

"What is it?"

"A muskrat," I said, watching it as it moved toward a small island, its whiskered nose in the air.

I notice everything. I hear geese honking outside my window in the middle of the city. I used to track the garter snake in Craig's and my garden from its sunny place in the bean bed to its home under the house, its entryway a pie of bent-up siding. I watch squirrels in the trash cans at the university. I pay attention to spider webs.

I want to know if I can call this love. I want to know how I can say I love the swimming greenheads in Lake of the Isles, when every fall I make an adventure out of killing them. I am full of questions. How can I say that killing has anything to do with love? What kind of language do I live in that allows me to embrace this paradox? This tragic conflation of violence and love is part of what I try to resist in the world, yet here I am, in the midst of it. How is my love for the greenheads, the swimming muskrat, the Canada goose different from the feelings other hunters have for the animals they kill? Can I have a relationship with these animals alive? Or is the killing, the eating, that magical bridging, a crucial part of my love, part of my relationship with these animals, with the world?

What does it mean, that in my body, helping to keep me alive, to make me joyful, to share joy with people I love, is the breast of a greenhead mallard that I shot down on a cool autumn day and scooped from the cold water with my hand?

In the Eye of the Beholder

(1998)

I COME FROM A LONG LINE OF SHOPPERS. A&P, GRISTEDES AND GRAND Union as a young girl in New York City, then Albertson's, Buttrey's and IGA when I came to Montana at 18. My sister takes after my mother and father's side of the family. To her, wild animals are either pests or diversions, occasionally both: She never noticed bears lived in the woods until one of them ate her hummingbird feeder.

But I eventually grew out of shopping and became first a gatherer, and then a hunter. Whitetail, elk, waterfowl and upland birds in the fall and winter. Black bear and turkeys in the spring. When it comes to trout, bass, walleye and pike I'm an opportunistic feeder.

And while I've told my mother of this life change, forsaking the ancestral shopping line of my family and adapting to the hunting and gathering tradition of my new home—a sort of *when in Rome* conversion—she's always been in denial about it.

Seven years ago, she and my step-father came west to visit. My in-denial mother is married to a man from Pennsylvania, who hunted every year of his life. He's also a man of immense curiosity——and delights in teasing Mom good naturedly. So this first time he came to visit John and me, he was very curious about everything around him, especially us, and started walking through our house looking at the trophy-game snapshots on our Wall of Fame and the refrigerator—friends, family, business associates, fishing, hunting, camping and playing outdoors. And very quickly he found the picture of me with my first big game animal—a 14¾-inch antelope buck.

I was in the living room with my mother, Doc was walking around with my husband John, and he said to John:

"Is that Eileen with an elk?" Even then his eyes were starting to fail him.

And John said, "Yes, it's Eileen. With an antelope."

And Doc said, "Cece told me Eileen didn't hunt."

And John said, "Yeah, Eileen hunts. Do you want to see her gun?"

Doc's eyes lit up with the potential there. They went into John's office and John pulled my .270 off the gun rack and handed it to Doc.

"This is Eileen's gun?" Doc asked with a grin. And when John said yes, Doc turned and made a beeline for my mother in the living room.

"Look, Cece. This is Eileen's gun," he said, holding it up as if he was a Greek bearing gifts.

The thing is, Doc knows how to carry a .270. And he's pretty good shooting it, but only if you let him stand up. He carried a J.C. Higgins FN Mauser .270 into the woods every hunting season of his teen and adult life. But either because of his curiosity or his gregariousness, he could never stand to go out to the woods when it was too dark for him to see—be it deer or other people. He would sit all day long, from an hour after sunrise to an hour before sunset, and he said, "I saw lots of deer but always when I was walking out or in. I never shot one." They were always running fast.

But thanks to Doc, at least Mom's not in denial anymore. Now she's in the "Oh, it's okay but I wish she'd grow out of it" stage. She calls up during hunting season to ask if I've "caught" anything yet, and rewards me with small gifts if I lie to her. She's even accused me of cheating when I describe trying to bugle in an elk, or rattle up some poor unsuspecting whitetail.

She went directly from denial to rooting for me to lose. In the meantime she would harass me with "How can you kill those beautiful animals with those big brown eyes?" Or alternately, "How can you eat that meat? You don't know where it's been."

It's not like she's a vegetarian. She loves beef and lamb, eats sausage at breakfast, and when I was a child she took me with her to the kosher slaughtering house to get really fresh chickens. I remember the kosher slaughtering house: They take chickens and stick them upside down on a conveyer belt that takes them first to a defeathering station before killing them. But we've been all through that, including my accusing her of cheating by not killing her dinner herself, and, in The World According to Mom, it's simply not the same.

Then one day we were visiting her and Doc over lunch when she said: "Doc and I have been trapping crabs and making crab cakes, and they're absolutely wonderful."

I looked at my Mom with new respect. *"You're* catching crabs???"

"Actually, Doc catches them, I make the crab cakes."

So I asked the most obvious question. "Who kills them?"

She said, very quickly and surely, "Nobody kills them."

"Then how do you make them into cakes?"

"Well, Doc goes to the Winn Dixie and he gets day-old meat, and puts it in the crab pots and sets them out one morning along the banks of Chesapeake Bay—which is where they live in the summertime—and goes out the *next* morning and picks up the pots that are full and sets out some new ones. And I pick the meat off and make crab cakes and put them in the freezer."

"Okay, wait a minute. He brings them in the kitchen and you pull the meat off? While they're alive?"

"No silly. They're dead."

"All right. Tell me again how this works. Doc goes out and traps the crabs in the crab pots."

"Yeah."

"Then he goes out in the morning and collects the crabs, resets the pots, and brings the crabs back to the kitchen where you're waiting for him."

"Yeah, yeah. That's right."

"And then does he kill them?"

"No. Nobody kills them."

"Okay, but then you pull the meat out of their bodies. Somebody had to've killed them."

"No, no," she said, and at that point, Doc took over. I was starting to feel like an anthropologist in a Far Side cartoon.

Doc said: "Eileen, dear, Nobody kills the crabs."

"Okay, so *you* bring them into the house. What happens to them?"

"Well, your mother has a pot boiling. Your mother pulls the meat off the bones and she makes these delicious crab cakes."

"Doc. Back up to where you brought them into the kitchen."

"Eileen, you're a smart girl, why aren't you getting this?"

"All right, you come in the kitchen and take the crabs out of the pots."

"No, I've already done that down on the beach."

"Okay, so you plop them on the counter and mom's got a pot of boiling water. Then what happens?"

"Your mom takes the meat out of the chest cavity, they're not like Alaskan crabs with those big claws, you know. So she takes the meat out of the chest and makes it into cakes."

"No, Doc, wait. She takes the meat out of them while they're lying there screaming on the counter?"

"No Eileen, no, no." He shook his head in frustration.

"Okay Doc, so you brought them into the kitchen. Closed the door, put your Irish tweed hat on the table. Now what? Mom's got a pot of boiling water going?"

"Of course she does. I told you that."

"Does anything happen with the pot of boiling water?"

"Yeah, your mother puts the crabs in it. And then she pulls the meat off and makes the crab cakes and a delicious tartar sauce with lemon and a bit of sugar."

"So MOM kills the crabs."

"No no, your mother doesn't do it. The STEAM kills the crabs."

Perhaps after all, I don't kill the deer. John Nosler kills the deer. Or John Moses Browning.

In my sister's kitchen, it's the owls that do the killing. Katherine has a recreational cabin in the woods, where she has been fighting back nature since she drove up with the first load of nursery plants. Her husband and grown son, Tom and Mathew, bought a tractor and use it to clean the woods each weekend, tearing out grapevines and dead trees. Now she is planning to clear a pasture for alpacas, and she already runs a herd of guinea hens. Twenty-seven of them, until this past Christmas morning.

I was stuffing our holiday turkey when the phone rang.

"I wish you were here *right now*," she said, desperation in her voice.

"What happened?" I asked.

"I have twenty-six guinea hens," she said.

Busy with the trussing, I said, "That's nice."

"I had twenty-seven last night."

"Oh, one's missing?"

"Headless."

"Headless?"

"I was taking my morning walk, and went by the pen. Then I noticed one of the hens was lying on the ground, with its head chopped off. Tom wanted to cook it, but I made him bury it."

"Bury it? Was it fresh?"

"Yes, the blood was dripping out of it's neck, and it was warm. They were in a pen with fences eight-feet high, and I thought nothing could get them. So I called the fish and game guy who lives down the road, and he said it was an owl. It's a mating ritual of male great horned owls to offer a head to the female they are courting."

"Weird," I said.

"So the problem is, how to cook it."

"But you made Tom bury it."

"Yes. But then Matt showed up and his dad told him what had happened, and they went out and dug it up. And now they want to cook it."

"It's a delicacy, you know."

"What, guinea hens?" Incredulous. As incredulous as when I told her that wild turkeys fly. She never did believe that strange tale. But she had obviously accepted my hunter/gatherer status.

"Isn't that why you were raising the guinea fowl?" I asked. She had made her own leap from the family tree: Rather than shopping for chickens, she was domesticating wild fowl, though I wasn't about to start telling her more strange tales, even though John had hunted those same guinea fowl, in the wilds of Africa.

"No. Of course not. Anyway, I wish you were here right now, so you could gut it. Tom's making a mess of it. How much do you have to take out anyway?"

"Just pull out anything that's bloody. And rinse the cavity out with cold water. You don't even have to do that. Just breast it. He knows how to breast a chicken, doesn't he?"

"I think we've gone too far already to do that."

I finished stuffing my turkey, listening over the miles as Katherine instructed Tom in cleaning the guinea hen.

"So how do we cook it?"

"It's a delicacy, Katherine. Pretend it's a Cornish hen you got for a free coupon."

"So what are you having for Christmas dinner?"

"Butterball turkey," I said, putting it in the oven.

"From the store?"

"Yeah, but don't tell Mom. I told her I was fixing a Canada goose with pheasant sausage stuffing I made myself, and mashed potatoes and Brussels sprouts I grew myself, and huckleberries I gathered and canned last summer. Oh, and bread I made myself this morning."

"That's cheating."

"That's one way to look at it."

PART SEVEN

Family Ties

IKNOW A BIG FARM FAMILY IN MINNESOTA WHO ANNUALLY MARK DEER season as an occasion to celebrate the ties that bind them all together. As many family members and close family friends, male and female, as are able converge on the farm—some of them traveling hundreds of miles to get there—for a long and intense weekend of hunting. They always manage, one way or another, to fill out all their tags before noon on Sunday. Then they set themselves to the communal tasks of skinning, quartering, butchering, wrapping the meat. By weekend's end—and it always ends in high spirits—each member of this extended family has bagged her or his year's worth of venison. They also have renewed their acquaintance with kith and kin too seldom seen, garnered the latest news about births and marriages and graduations, and stored up another year's quota of gossip, political chinwagging, and new venison recipes to try. Without hunting, this family might well come together in other ways, for other reasons. But it wouldn't be the same.

Those mostly rural Americans who grew up in hunting families know the deep and often subtle ways in which hunting shapes the rhythm of family life and the structure of relationships. Indeed, several writers in this collection evoke the extent to which hunting serves to unite or to divide family members. The selections in this section, however, focus more specifically on the manifold ways in which hunting is for the authors a family affair. And they suggest, in various ways, that the most important gifts parents and siblings give one another, the most profound of life's lessons, are generally the things which cannot be put into words.

BARNEY NELSON

My First Daughter Was an Antelope

from The Wild and the Domestic *(2000)*

M Y PETS WERE USUALLY WILD: BABY TURTLES, FLYING SQUIRRELS, FAWNS, coyote pups, or cottontails. I once raised a red fox who liked to sleep curled around a blaring TV speaker. I had a little red harness and a leash and would take Freddie walking when I went to town, just to watch people. Freddie was very well behaved on a leash and would trot out in front of me, his give-away tail floating on the breeze. People would smile at me, walk past us, stop in their tracks, spin and say, "Hey! That's a fox!"

The trouble most people have when trying to raise young animals is failing to do their homework: studying animal ways and finding out what they eat. A baby Vermillion flycatcher, for instance, will starve without flies, and no amount of birdseed or habitat will help. I always fed young mammals some combination of Carnation Evaporated Milk and white Karo syrup. Too much syrup produces diarrhea, too little produces consti-pation. Another problem most people have is performing only half of an animal mother's duties. Nests and dens are kept clean because baby ani-mals only defecate and urinate when stimulated by the mother's tongue. So after a feeding, the surrogate mother must "lick" her baby's butt with a damp cloth.

I've always been a sucker for beady black eyes. No bird or animal ever came to my door hungry and left the same way, although I'm careful not to make welfare cases out of them. After my divorce, I once even adopted a spider who set up housekeeping between the window and screen in my air-conditioned apartment where flies couldn't go. I tried to talk him into either moving on into the house to catch flies for me, or going on out into the wide world. But he was a very independent little spider and preferred his spot.

So, occasionally, when he looked hungry, I'd open the window and chase a fly in his direction. He had no idea I was helping him. Technically, I suppose I wasn't, I just made his hunting possible. He had to catch the fly all by himself, and he had an ingenious method worked out. Flies always seem to crawl up a window screen and in a fairly straight line. So he would wait in a dark crevice at the top of the screen, creeping along

233

until he was directly in line with the fly who was crawling up toward him. When the fly got close enough, he'd jump out and grab it, sort of like a bulldogger—so I named him Harley May after an old rodeo cowboy I know.

Sometimes Harley missed, but in just a few minutes, the fly would be crawling up the screen again. I imagined the fly trying to count coup, like I've heard Indians used to do when it was considered more honorable to risk their own life to touch an enemy than to kill. Lots of times the spider came right out in plain sight and crawled toward the fly who kept crawling toward the spider. Sometimes the fly lost his nerve and flew, but after a few deep breaths, he would try to count coup again—or something.

What kind of person has flies and spiders for friends?

I'm choosy too. I don't like spiders who have to build webs to catch flies—they are too messy to live with. And I don't like those fancy, shiny spiders with the long, skinny pointed legs that might like to bite me. I don't like those female spiders who eat their men and build crazy Picasso-looking webs that feel like nylon. I don't like great big hairy, slow moving spiders with deep voices either or the kind that set up long thin trip ropes across trails. Those ropes must be intended to blind or decapitate humans because they can't catch flies. So I imagine that the ropes come from glory seeking spiders who want to hang a human. I've even been around some spiders who were after cowboys. Their trip ropes were just about a foot higher than a horse's head and stretched between trees. I always wondered just what those spiders intended to do with a cowboy if they caught one?

But back to my personal preferences. I don't even like all little black and white spiders. Harley was short and chunky and fuzzy and looked like a cross between a teddy bear and a spider, so he was easy to love, but some of his relatives liked to hide and jump out and scare me. When I opened a cupboard door, jumped, and screamed, I imagined that I could hear them giggle. So I didn't make friends with them. I don't like to be laughed at.

That's why I liked Harley so much. I always knew just where he was and he never tried to scare me. If I wanted to feel very, very secure, I could shut the window and he couldn't come in my house even if he had wanted to. If I was bored and needed some entertainment, I would open the window and chase a fly in his direction. Maybe he was the ideal friend for a selfish person: there when I needed him, tucked away when I didn't.

I also liked the fact that Harley jumped on his fly and grabbed it. That seemed to be a much more honorable way to catch flies than spinning a big nasty web, tying a line around a toe, and taking a nap until the float bobbed. And since flies go to bed at sundown, I felt sure Harley went to bed then too. That made him much easier to live with than those kind who prowl around in the dark while I am sleeping.

Socrates, the guy who started rhetoric, said a writer should be a gadfly. To Montaigne, the father of the essay, writing was undefinable. In French, his native language, the word essai means a test, an attempt, or a trial. Montaigne insisted his essays were based on ignorance. Shakespeare seemed to agree and called his own essays "looking at truth askance." Hemingway said the secret was going to Paris, Langston Hughes recommended the rhythms of jazz, and Chekhov favored dung-heaps. On the other hand, Samuel Johnson said a writer should strive to make the world better, and Kafka said writing was the reward for service to the devil. But all of those old men are dead.

I am a teacher. I study literature with my students and teach college freshmen how to write essays: five paragraphs, a thesis, topic sentences, support, audience awareness, and standard English usage. Tell me what you're going to say, say it, and then tell me what you said. That's my job.

I usually begin the semester with a motivating lecture, explaining that writing an essay is like planting grass. First you make a plan, then you prepare the ground. You loosen the soil by digging, enrich it with fertilizer, and fill uneven spots. You buy seed for the kind of grass you want to grow. Each kind of grass, I explain, has its advantages and drawbacks: some can handle more traffic, some needs more shade, some more water. Once the seeds are sown, keep the ground moist—watch it carefully so it won't dry out. Keep the weeds pulled. Mow it.

"Do you have a yard, Miss?" asks a voice from the back of the room.

"Well . . . no." I stammer.

I stare at the student for a moment. I always seem to have at least one of these in every class. The student who is never paying attention, who asks stupid questions in the middle of a good lecture, the student with the cowboy hat and sun glasses, desk tipped back against the wall, no pen.

No . . . I don't plant grass, don't mow anything, don't water anything, don't even pray for rain anymore. I like my grasses wild. Sometimes, when I'm walking, I might strip a seed stalk between my thumb and first two fingers and fling the tiny seeds into the wind, like shooting dice. Maybe that's planting, but I don't look back. I trust its fate to quail or packrats, or some cow to grind into the rocks.

I like my grasses mixed. I want black grama on west facing slopes, *sacaton* along creek bottoms, and *tobosa* in rotten flats to warn me to slow down. I want some bear grass, some bluestem, some sprangletop. I like it weedy with *loco* catclaw, *tasajilla, sacahuista*, Mormon tea, and *sotol*. I want some whitebrush for the bees and some creosote to smell after a rain. I like it ragged, windblown, parched; tough, patient, and fast. I've seen West Texas gramas shoot up, bloom, and produce seed in two weeks after one last minute October rain.

I just don't respect green grass. Mowed grass never moans or blooms. The tiny orchids in shades of lime green, white, orange, yellow, and blood red, dangling from the seed heads of wild grasses are my favorite flowers. Mowed grass never spun a spur rowel. But if mowing must be done, then I prefer critters or wind and lightning—20 sections at a time in thirty minutes—whoom!

I stop to catch my breath.

"Jeeze," says the student with the sunglasses, smiling now, "You coulda just said no."

Like most daughters, I keep a framed picture of my mom and me on the bookcase. However, unlike most, my bear-slayer mom and I are both dressed in camo. I hold a Remington 12-gauge automatic shotgun; mom's scoped .243 Savage lever-action hangs from a sling over her shoulder. Stretched between us is a dead bobcat. We each hold one hind leg and grin at the camera like Hemingway wannabes. Behind us stretches an endless expanse of Southern Arizona desert, the only kind of playground I ever had. Until lately, I never realized how unconventional my boring old polyester-clad parents were.

My dad didn't hunt with "buddies" but with his wife and kids. He never drank whiskey or owned the latest hunting fashions or gimmicks. Hunting was not a virility-thing in my family, it was a domestic chore. We were pothunters. Our rifles were sighted-in on the money, but there was no fancy checkering on the stock or engraving on the barrel, seldom any varnish or bluing left.

My dad was a teacher. At night, after his day-job, he taught gun safety courses to kids for the American Rifle Association for many years. Pointing a gun indiscriminately, climbing through a fence with one in hand, or shooting without knowing my target would have been grounds for even more severe child abuse than I was used to, but I don't remember ever not knowing those rules. I was whipped for lots of things—giggling in church, catching trout with my hands, playing with bait, making my little brother eat mudpies—but only once for the way I handled a gun: When I got my first BB gun, I shot all the windows out of the barn while shooting pigeons. Mostly, I always thought what I got whipped for was worth the whipping. I'm quite proud of the fact that I once made a man who has addressed a joint session of congress eat mudpies, and for reasons I've never analyzed, I've always been proud of shooting those windows out of the barn. I've told that story a thousand times.

Like Huck, I grew up barefoot. I fished the Mississippi River, built fires and picnicked on its islands, swam in it—but only under strict guidance. I don't remember ever being afraid, but I deeply respected that old river and knew that just under that smooth, quiet, milk chocolate surface beat a bloody heart. I read a modern story once written by a man who had recently taken a boat trip down my old Mississip. He complained about the flood control dikes, the locks and dams, the way the U.S. Army Corps of

Engineers had tamed the river, making it conform to the needs of society. He said we have stripped the river of its power and its will and its natural dignity. I smiled to myself. He didn't know my river.

Samuel Clemens did. He wrote some great essays about it and said only the naive see the Mississippi as tame and beautiful. To a river boat captain, every sun-glint, every dimple on the surface revealed some hidden snag, reef, shoal, or undercurrent. Clemens wrote, "that silver streak in the shadow of the forest is the 'break' from a new snag and he has located himself in the very best place he could have found to fish for steamboats." But that would also be the best place to fish for fish. Those same dimples and slanting lights that talked to river boat captains, my grandfather read for food. Instead of backing off with warning bells ringing, our little boat would quietly slip its way in deep, among the snags, and my grandpa couldn't swim.

The river was always changing: on the surface, along the banks, in the channel, and around the islands. Sandbars, snags, whirlpools, and undercurrents would be here today and gone tomorrow. Clemens said that once he had truly learned the river, "All the grace, the beauty, the poetry," had gone out of it for him. Yet no one else ever wrote about it with such grace, beauty, and poetry. I think Sam Clemens sometimes lied.

Probably because my father's DeGear side of the family was illiterate until my father's generation, and because my father refuses to consider alternative spellings for the family name (like Duger or Daguerre), we haven't been able to track his family back past Illinois pioneer and War of 1812 soldier, Peter DeGear (1786–1835). All we know is that they were never far from a river. I've heard it said that no modern family actually needs to hunt in order to provide food. But I think my family did.

Before plastic buttons were invented, my dad, uncles, and aunt hunted washboard, sand, and papershell clams with their bare feet in shallow water, feeling around on the muddy bottom. They slept in their boat at night, their backs so sunburned from bending over and pulling up clams, they had to sleep on their stomachs. If the water was too deep to wade, they rigged a trick to catch clams on bare hooks. Once loaded they'd pull ashore and cook the clams in a big vat until the shells opened. Then they'd scrape the meat out, save it to ferment for fiddler net bait, and sell the shells to the button factory—by the ton. During the depression, my dad, uncles, and aunt did everything from hunt snapping turtles to spear carp to gather black berries and sell what they couldn't eat door to door. They also can-fished, ran 100-hook trot lines, seined for their own minnows and crawfish, hunted turtle eggs with a stick, sculled for ducks, and sawed down bee trees. In their spare time they cut fence posts and firewood. Their dad, my grandfather Bill, was a commercial fisherman, driving carp, sheepshead, and buffalo into nets like cattle. After a life on the river, he'd found enough freshwater pearls to give one to each of his three granddaughters. A freshwater pearl ring is one of the few pieces of jewelry I've ever owned.

During my own childhood, my dad's blue-collar wages stretched only so far. We made every tank of gas, every fishing license, every bullet count to produce meat, furs, or bounty. I don't remember ever coming home empty handed. But we often rose at 3:00 A.M. to be the first fishing boat on a lake or to be hunched in a wet duck blind before daylight. At 10:00 P.M. we would still be at it, again struggling in the dark to clean fish or singe pinfeathers. If there was a heavy dew, we'd hunt nightcrawlers with a flashlight until well past midnight.

"Sleep? Goddamn it, you can sleep when you get old."

My skills were good one day and bad the next. I learned what kind of fish I had on the hook by the way one took my bait, how to play and land one that weighed 10 times what my line could handle. Then I'd go for days without a nibble. To keep my spirits up, Mom would make a bet that I would catch the next fish. But if I also caught the most, then Dad reminded me that he and Grandpa spent half their time filing my hooks or dipping my fish. Once, after I was grown, fishing ranch creeks while the experts fished a trophy lake, I beat all the old pot-bellied bass fishermen in a stringer-weight tournament. Yet, on another occasion, also after I was grown, just wanting to look, I let my dad's full stringer swim away to die a wasteful and agonizing death.

"Je-sus-Christ!"

I'm still surprised I didn't have to dive until I found it.

Up until I left home at about 17, I had eaten more wild meat than tame. Today when I read that Native American hunter/gatherers led an idyllic life of leisure, I laugh. Those who think hunting is easier than herding, or that herding is more sedentary, have never done both for a living. We have a secret saying in my family which is often recalled when the moment requires heroic stoicism—"Let it drip." The saying evolved during child-hood instruction periods spent watching a snowy deer trail, waiting for some blundering town hunter—who thought hunting was hiking—to start the deer moving. A whispered conversation between me and my father during a six-hour period on an agonizing 10 degree below zero morning might go something like this:

"Daddy, I have a cramp in my leg."
"Be still."
. . .
"My toes are frozen."
"Shut up and be still, Goddamn it."
. . .
"(sniff)"
"Let it drip."

One day, riding choppy waves on a Minnesota lake, my little brother, suffering from terrible seasickness, threw up regularly all day (Dad called it chumming), but he was never allowed to stop fishing. I cut my feet pollywogging Mississippi sandbars for freshwater clams and was kicked on my butt by a single-shot 12-gauge shooting my first squirrel. I'm sure I've walked around the world a couple of times, carrying guns and dead animals. I never had a boyfriend in high school because weekends were spent calling coyotes, tramping after javelina, scouting elk bedgrounds, or loading and unloading a boat. Neither rain, sleet, nor human exhaustion were excuse enough to let a rod tip droop or make noise sniffling up a runny nose.

"What, you have to go to the bathroom? Je-sus-Christ!"

The first house my newlywed parents owned was underground, buried in the side of a slippery steep bank on the Mississippi. Maybe that makes me part muskrat. Actually, the "house" was the basement to a normal house we never quite got around to finish building. Pregnant, my mother used to sit hunched over her swollen belly there, holding a dead muskrat between her legs, her elbows resting on her knees, while my father skinned off the pelt. Twice during the same pregnancy, she broke out up and down the insides of her legs with poison ivy rash, contracted off the muskrats' hides. She'd catch poison oak trying to go to the bathroom on some island where Dad would grudgingly finally let her out of the boat. If she didn't go with him, Dad would come home and throw a dead goose in bed with her.

Mom, the Mayflower descendant in the family, eventually became a vice-president for the Arizona Bank, but she wasn't much of a storyteller. When hunting stories were told, she just listened and laughed. "You lie, and I'll swear to it," she'd tell Dad. The only story I ever heard about her successful bear hunt, I read in the newspaper: "his wife also shot a bear." Mom chattered like a dang squirrel, but she didn't tell stories.

"The hell you say."

I'm the female storyteller in the family. I like to tell stories about Dad calling in a mountain lion when he was trying to call in a bear. He prefers to tell stories about hunting with my brother. I like to tell that I once killed six deer with six shells over a six year span; my dad prefers to tell about the day I forgot to load my gun (we always carried them unloaded in a vehicle). I like to tell about Dad bagging all but the buffalo (which he thought was a stupid hunt) in the Arizona grand slam and being the second highest-point (2 points for a coyote, 6 for a bobcat, 100 for a lion) varmint hunter in 1964, one of those predator hunters Edward Abbey cusses so eloquently. Dad likes to tell the story about the day I got "buck fever" and couldn't shoot a big deer in Blue River Canyon. He always forgets to tell that after three days of skunked hunting, I found the spot, led him in there, and helped him drag the damn deer out. I've also corrected him a thousand times, explaining that I expected him to shoot and was just waiting. I didn't know he was waiting on me.

"Yes, dear."

One other time, too, I couldn't shoot. I was grown, married, and hunting alone. I had glassed a rocky side ridge and spotted a mule deer buck laid up under a big Spanish dagger near the rim. Checking the wind, I made a long sneak and came down on him from above. When I got within range (300 yards for my custom glass-bedded .270) and not wanting to be caught unprepared, I laid down behind a rock, got a good rest, held my breath and whistled. Nothing happened.

I waited, then whistled again, then tossed a little rock. Still nothing.

So, I got up and crept closer, repeating my strategy of rock, rest, whistle, rock. Again nothing happened. The buck must be sound asleep. My sneak somehow turned into a game to see just how close I could get before the buck woke up. I got so close I could see him breathing and finally actually hit him with a rock. Then the dagger exploded with antlers. He just kept on getting up. He was the biggest deer I'd ever seen. He ran straight away from me down the side of the mountain, and I had him in my sights the whole time, my finger on the trigger.

But I couldn't shoot.

"What the hell was the matter with you, anyway?"

I told that story at a Terry Tempest Williams round-table discussion and my fellow environmentalists nodded knowingly. They thought the moment had been a conversion for me and that I had given up my sinful life of blood lust. Creeping close enough to see the deer breathing, they thought, made me realize that I was killing a living animal. I let them think they understood my story and never explained. But in truth, it was a difficult down-hill, running shot and wasteful. My only vital choice would ruin the best meat. Besides, with all those antlers, he wasn't going to be very good to eat. It was a shot a pot hunter's kid would be whipped for taking. I didn't shoot because I had been raised better.

"Well, I'll be damned!"

I do remember once, though, when I didn't shoot because I was just overwhelmed with the moment. I was hiking along the rim, trying to get a glimpse of some wild barbary sheep which had once been imported by a neighboring rancher and eventually gone wild all over West Texas. The sheep ranged in the high, unfenced country and I hoped to get a picture of one. My dog, *Perro* (a very creative name meaning "dog" in Spanish), was with me. An Australian shepherd, *Perro* was a frustrated working dog because I didn't allow him to work cattle. I didn't want the cattle trained to let a dog bluff them because I was afraid that then the cows would stop fighting predators off their calves. So, *Perro*'s job was mostly to be my best friend. The ranch raised a little band of Spanish goats that he was allowed to play cowdog with. Whenever I came home from town, he'd gather his goats into a tight wad and make them greet me. I'm sure they hated him.

On this particular day, *Perro* trotted beside me. I spotted some of the wild sheep across a canyon about the time he did, and my normally well-behaved dog took off barking. I figured that was the end of my chance to see any wild sheep, so I concentrated instead on picking my way through the rocks, down toward a pour-off I liked to visit. Suddenly, I was face to face with a full-curled, panting barbary ram. *Perro* had brought me one! I was so shocked that I completely forgot the camera dangling from my neck until the sheep, realizing its close proximity to a human, had bailed off the side of the rimrock to what I expected to be its certain death. Of course, to my amazement, it found tiny hoofholds on the side of the rim. I have the story, but I missed the picture. So, I guess my dad is right—I have suffered from buck fever.

For twenty years, I lived in old ranch houses at the end of long dirt roads. As Annie Dillard noticed in the Galapagos, critters always seem to want to be close to humans. At the 7W Camp on the Nail Ranch, water from the Clear Fork of the Brazos came out of the tap black, and rattlesnakes denned under the house. There was seldom a moment during the summer when I couldn't find one somewhere in the yard if I looked. A warm day in winter would bring the thousands of yellow jackets who denned in the walls and attic down into the house in a sluggish stupor. I slept on a screened-in porch and every night would holler at the frogs to, please, go to sleep, but they never did.

They'd croak, "Sex? Sex? Anybody want Sex?" all night long.

Lightening hit the tin roof regularly. The 7W Camp doesn't exist anymore. The ranch bulldozed it off the face of the earth because no one but me ever liked to live there.

My second home on the Tippit Ranch had been abandoned for twenty-five years before I moved in and stands abandoned now. The house water was all spring fed, so somehow, a little frog had taken up residency in the toilet. I'd flush him away and in a few seconds, he'd pop back up. It was always fun to listen to guests shriek when they went in the bathroom and then holler out, "Hey, there's a frog in the pot!"

I'd holler back, "Yeah, I know. It's OK. He lives there."

I tried not to think about what he ate.

At the Willow Springs Camp on the o6 Ranch, skunks denned under the house, and we killed a rattlesnake in the living room, in the bathroom, and two on the back porch. If I found rattlers in the pasture, I always let them live—I liked to joke that they helped keep away tourists—but if I found one inside the house, that was crossing the line. Snakes always return.

I learned that once trying to rescue some baby phoebes from a red racer. I had been sitting on the screened porch with a cup of coffee, trying to write. Before I could begin, some Say's phoebes, who had built a nest out in the carport, started crying and carrying on, so I went to investigate. A big red racer was laying along a pipe wall-brace and across their nest. He hadn't eaten any of the baby birds yet, but I knew that was his plan. About that time, the teenage cowboy who worked for us on the ranch walked by and since boys always want to kill something, I asked him to kill the snake. But he talked me out of it and suggested we just scare it real bad and maybe it would go away. We did, and I went back to the porch and my notes.

In a few minutes, the phoebes were crying again. Sure enough, the racer was back. His hunger had outweighed our scare. This time I talked the teenager into making the kill and went back to my writing feeling compassionate. But that feeling didn't last long. I got to thinking about the snake. Who did I think I was deciding a baby phoebe was worth more than a red racer? Did the racer have a nest of babies somewhere too? Would my house be overrun with mice this winter as just punishment?

Before I could soothe my conscience, the phoebes were crying again. The racer had damaged the sides of the nest and one of the babies had fallen out. I picked it up, put it back, and once again went back to the porch.

I'd hardly sat down when the birds were calling me again. This time my cat, who had followed me out to the carport on my last trip, found the baby phoebe first. After a few "Here Kitty, Kitty, nice Kitty"'s, I grabbed her and took the rescued baby bird back to the nest.

Well, now I really had troubles. My cat wasn't going to forget where she found a nice juicy baby bird and in few minutes, she had another one. This time she wasn't about to let me sweet talk her out of it either. I couldn't bring myself to kill my cat, even though her motives weren't nearly as noble as the snake's. She had a bowl of cat food available at all times and a bowl of milk most mornings. She didn't need to hunt and kill for her survival. But she was my cat! She sat on my lap when I was lonesome.

So, I gave the phoebes a good lecture. I told them I was sorry, but that they needed to think about where they built a nest next time. That, sure, the carport was out of the rain, but phoebes can raise a lot of baby birds between rainstorms around here. They were safe from raindrops that might never come, but the pipe where they built their nest could support the weight of a snake and a cat walked through that carport a hundred times a day. I also told them about a little hawk I'd seen dive-bombing a badger and that they needed to toughen up, peck the cat on the head or in the eye, fix their nest, and keep their babies from jumping out. They had some responsibility around here too. I was not going to keep coming to their rescue.

Well, of course, the cat got the rest of the babies one by one. The phoebes did try to chase her once, but they weren't very good at it. They cried pitifully when their nest was empty. I told them I was sorry and plugged my ears with my fingers, being real thankful I don't have God's job.

School districts in rural areas are too poor to send busses long distances after one kid, so when my daughter started to school, I had to take her. After some serious rains, we were often stranded on one side or the other of a creek. I would park the ranch pickup on one side of the creek and my own on the other. My daughter and I would hike back and forth in the dark, through the raging black water, in order to get her to school on time. Instead of feeling sorry for ourselves, we almost regretted dryer weather because once the motor was turned off and we were out in the dark, cold air, the morning changed.

For the first few steps I would hear only silence. Then I would hear rubber boots swishing through water and déjà vu would sweep over me. The air was cold and smelled wet. It was that time of day just before grey dawn when no one is awake except birds, animals, and my family. A killdeer would screech at us for invading her domain. Somewhere in the dark ducks would mutter softly, whispering in duck talk. They probably said something like "Listen to that racket, will you. They just don't make hunters like they used to." My father could mutter just like that and talk ducks down out of the air. These ducks thought my daughter and I couldn't hear them. They just don't make ducks like they used to.

My daughter's school called one day to let me know she qualified for free lunches under migrant labor relief. I guess I spent most of my life in abject poverty and never knew it. The houses where we lived were always old; the electricity went off at the first hint of a storm and the phone too. Nobody picked up the garbage. I fed scraps to the wild critters, burned what I could, and carefully washed cans and broke glass jars so animals wouldn't get their heads caught trying to reach food. I thought everyone did.

My first daughter was an antelope. She was a wedding gift, blind with pink-eye and so tiny I could fold her match stick legs and hold her in the palm of my hand. I named her sappingly "Dolly." I got up every two hours a night for a month to warm a bottle and "lick" Dolly's butt. Like a new mother, I rushed her to the vet every time she sneezed. The first time, when the vet squirted a line of clear salve across her tender diseased eye, she groaned with pain. Me—a tough old hussy who had assisted with C-sections to deliver dead and rotten calves, baited catfish hooks with stink bait, and field dressed deer—I fainted dead away.

The fainting spell reminded me of Ka-nook. During the '60s I found myself the first female ag-major in my college and also the only female in most classes. A loud-mouthed, hard-drinking, cussing Canadian we affectionately nick-named "Ka-nook" teased me unmercifully every time there was blood, shit, or slime. Once, during an especially nasty C-section on a sheep, the seven foot, 250 pound obnoxious ape, to the surprise of the class, hit the floor in the feminine swoon he kept waiting for me to display. When he woke up, I smiled my most condescending Apache smile. But, this time, empathizing with the pain of an animal I cared deeply about, I found myself on the floor too. Maybe I had misjudged Ka-nook.

Dolly was gentler than any dogie calf I'd ever raised. When feeding time came, I simply opened the screened door and she would tap-tap into the kitchen like a little girl in high heels. Although her bottle always stimulated a rattle of antelope "pellets" across the floor and a flood of urine, like any doting mother, I found it easy to clean up. Her fluffy white rump was just too cute to cover with a diaper, and I hated to make her stay outside.

The night a pack of coyotes had her trapped in the yard fence, she let out one sharp little bleat which I had never heard before, but it woke me from a sound sleep. I was running before my feet hit the floor. The coyotes got her tail and a patch of skin off her ribs, but nothing more. From that night on, I left the yard gate open, knowing that her only defense was running, and confining her put her in more danger.

Although I kept the yard watered and green, she never took a bite but preferred instead the ugliest, most dried-up looking weed stalk she could find—and dogfood. When her pellets started looking like dog shit, the vet said maybe I should feed the dog behind closed doors to keep her out of it. I had a very small mongrel yeller dog and Dolly would try to stomp him in order to get more dogfood. They fought like brother and sister and yet took naps together.

We lived on a long eighteen-mile dirt road from town and could see visitors coming for several miles. The day I recognized the local game warden's truck, my heart caught in my throat. I gathered Dolly in my arms and raced toward the creek, folding her legs and bidding her to "stay," which sometimes she did. The game warden had just stopped by to swap stories, and of course, he needed a glass of tea. We sat on the porch and rocked while he, for some reason, turned the talk to antelope.

"Yessiree, the last antelope I ever saw in this country was running on those hills right out there," he said and pointed toward what locals called "The Antelope Hills."

As if on cue, Dolly stood up right under his pointing finger, her unmistakable white antelope rump shining in the sun. He choked on his tea and sputtered, "Is that an antelope?"

What could I say? No?

"She's a pet," I confessed and threw myself on the mercy of the court. Luckily, he was an old game warden and quite merciful. He said he guessed there was no law against having her as long as she wasn't in captivity.

"Oh, no!" I said hurriedly, "She's free to come and go at any time." He finished his tea and drove back to town.

One day, while I was watching Dolly graze, she suddenly began to run in circles. I tried to catch her and calm her, but she was wild! Her eyes shown white around the edges and her tongue lolled. Round and round she ran, sides heaving. Frantically, I talked soothing talk and tried to stop her. Then, as quick as she had begun, she stopped on her own, puffed a second, and returned to nibbling dry weeds. After that, her "fits" gradually increased in frequency, duration, and effort. I finally figured out that she was simply building her stamina for flight.

When Dolly turned two, I began to worry about her love life. Since I had moved her from the country she was born in, no males were available. I wondered if she was lonely. I worried that even if I took her back to the land of her birth and turned her out, the other antelope might not accept her or she them. I had seen how antelope bucks treated their women and wasn't sure I wanted my Dolly to be subjected to harem life. Did I know anyone with a nice fat hand-raised buck who might prove monogamous?

I never had to solve the dilemma. Dolly disappeared one night during a fierce hail and thunder storm when the creeks flooded and several jackrabbits were found stoned to death. I couldn't track her because of the heavy rains. Sometime later a neighbor told me that he'd heard some oil-field roughnecks say that when they finished that job, they were going to take the tame antelope with them. The roughies were gone, but I never knew if coyotes got her, if she drowned, was stoned, stolen, or what. And I never tried too hard to find out. It was easier somehow not to know.

My real daughter's first kid was a white-tailed deer fawn she called "Little Bit." She let him drink cokes out of a glass until I spanked them both. I didn't spoil my second kid.

Although I've lived in mountain lion country all my life, the only live ones I've ever seen were asleep under a friend's livingroom couch or held in the arms of a child. I have slept like a baby in grizzly country, right after the first thaw, when bears emerge from their dens very hungry and very crabby. After a life around animals, I can only remember being truly terrified once—one midnight when I switched on a light in my own bathroom.

For some reason, it had been a good year for miller moths and they had invaded my old ranch house by the millions. That sounds like exaggeration, but anyone who came to see me during the moth crisis knows. For a month, I never turned on a light after dark—except once.

The moths hung in big dark bands, like bats, around my ceilings, behind picture frames, behind curtains. Chalky pink moth excrement painted my windows opaque. Furniture, walls, clothes, food, everything was covered with pink moth shit. I tried chasing them away, spraying them away, vacuuming them away, but nothing worked. I remember once, after battling them for several hours, just sitting in the middle of the floor and crying. I don't cry often.

Just at dusk, when the house became darker than the world outside, the moths would congregate on the windows. I would dash around, removing screens, in order to turn them loose. But they only crawled back inside through the many cracks after twilight. Turning on a light after dark stirred them into a frenzy of fluttering paper wings, each headed in a different direction.

The night I woke up sleepy, shuffled to the bathroom, and snapped on the light without thinking—I thought they were going to smother me. Nothing in Edgar Allen Poe or Alfred Hitchcock has ever been so terrifying as being caught inside that whirling cloud of flying moths, feeling the wet drips of pink excrement hit my face and arms and hair. I was so disoriented by the sense of suffocation and panic, I couldn't find the light switch for several long minutes. I couldn't get enough air to scream.

I can snore in grizzly country, but one moth inside my house will keep me awake. Nothing I've ever read about moths tells this side of them. I've often wondered if Annie Dillard or Virginia Woolf ever really knew moths.

I was kissed by a wolf once, too. It was part of the entertainment for participants in the 1993 Environmental Writing Institute at the Teller Wildlife Refuge in Corvallis, Montana. "Koani" was a black female wolf. Her owners used her to educate the public about wolves. Prior to her visit, we were primed with a slide show explaining wolf behavior and taught how to "greet" a wolf before Koani was brought out of her cage on a leash.

We all got down on our knees in a circle and the wolf went from person to person, licking us in the face. When she came to me—possibly the smell of cow was still faint—she licked and licked and licked until the handler finally pulled her off and I could breathe again. My fellow environmental writers were delighted. My face burned from something in her saliva. I was amazed to find a full-blooded wolf more affectionate than most dogs. The handlers said they had to build a special pen which allowed the wolf free access into their home because, due to the loss of her pack social life, she needed much affection and human contact.

As Koani drug her thin vegetarian handler around the yard like an old woman with a spoiled poodle, we were told about the wolf's amazing strength. The handlers said Koani made a very bad dog because she would revert to her wild prey-based attack nature when a child or another animal ran from her.

Shawn Young, Co-owner and Seamstress of Babe in the Woods Inc., with Daughter Cheyenne at the Buckarama, Forest Hills, Georgia, 1997.

"With turkey hunting, my favorite time is in the morning. It's just about completely dark, I mean there's just enough light to see in front of you. When you get settled wherever you're going to be, you have the opportunity to watch the sun come up. It doesn't take very long, it's just a matter of a short period of time and all of a sudden it's kind of like magic. The sun is up before you've even realized that it's come up. It's a very magical feeling that you experience. In the dark you don't see the wildflowers growing and the birds haven't started chirping yet and the squirrels aren't stirring around yet and all these things, they just kind of open up and come to life and then all of a sudden when the sun is really out, you know, it's entirely different. You see many, many shades of green, dark brown, black come to life when the sun comes up and that's something that if you haven't ever been out in the woods and experienced that alone, you need to have that experience at least once in a lifetime. You really do. I get emotional about that because it really means a lot to me to see that and that's what I want Cheyenne to be able to experience."

When I was four, a coon dog grabbed me by the back of the neck and tried to shake me dead. Royal Grabel loved that hound as much as I loved Dolly. He also knew that I had been raised never to tease or torment any dog, and he knew his dog knew me well. All I had done to provoke the attack was wear a fuzzy grey, raccoon-looking coat and knock on their door to ask if the Grabel kids could come out and play. Without a bark, the dog broke its collar chain and grabbed me. It was a registered red-boned hound, famous among local hunters and worth $300 in 1951. Royal thought briefly about shooting the dog while I was in the hospital. My dad and the rest of the county thought he was nuts.

"Je-sus-H.-Christ, Grabel?"

I never thought the dog should have been shot either. Why? Well, after I was grown, I was helping with a saddle-shop booth next door to an old East Texas hog hunter at a folklore festival. A fancy lady, dripping with diamonds, stopped to chat with the old man. I eavesdropped on their conversation when she asked for what kinds of hunting his dogs were good.

"They're hog dogs, Ma'am," he said politely.

"Hogs? Don't they hunt anything else?" she asked incredulously.

"Jeeze, Lady," he answered, quite indignant and defending his dogs, "cain't everbody make a welder!"

Even at four, I knew that not all dogs were coon dogs, and a good one was rare indeed. Kids, on the other hand, seemed fairly common and easy to replace.

Some of the things I know and some of the things I don't know make me wonder about school. I have studied sonnets time after time after time during my twenty-one or so sporadic years of learning and teaching college literature, yet I still have to stop and look up the difference between Shakespearean, Spencerian, and Petrarchan. In contrast, I was nine years old the last night I stumbled after Herb and Eldon Hueneke's pack of hounds through invisible wet miles of corn stubble and briared timber, hunting coons. Yet, when I am 90, I might be sitting on my porch some black moonless night and faintly hear coon hounds baying in the distance. Of course I won't know the dogs and won't be able to pick out their different voices, but I will know whether or not they are cold trailing; I will know the moment they start barking treed.

I will still know, at 90, which direction to look and how long to wait for a bobcat to come in to a call or how to tell by a single drop of blood if a deer is lung or heart shot. I will always know how deep to fish for largemouth, sunfish, crappie, perch, walleyes, stripers, rainbows, browns, fiddlers, bullheads, flatheads, or channel cat; when to use spinners, shiners, flies, or salmon eggs; leaders, floating line, sinkers, or bobbers; when to release the drag or set it, how to file hooks, tie knots, or hold the line softly between my fingers, and when to set the hook. I will never, however, remember for more than an hour, the difference between those three kinds of sonnets.

NELLIE A. O'BRIEN

The Muskrat Trapper

(1997)

BEFORE FARM SUBSIDIES, SOIL BANKS, SOCIAL SECURITY, AND WELFARE payments came the age of survival, maybe even survival of the fittest. Nature was to be conquered, a living wrested from her. Every predator was an enemy to be shot on sight. Wild animals fell into two categories: those that could be used for food or profit, and competitors.

Teenaged boys living on the edge of cities or in the country trapped beaver and other water dwellers to earn money.

But I was only a girl. My two brothers had first claim on any trapping rights on our Wyoming ranch, no one questioned that. But one year some beaver made a dam in our irrigation ditch where they could be legally trapped. After selling a few beaver furs for fabulous prices, my older brother, Tommy, disdained trapping muskrat. "That's for kids," he said. "I'm big enough to handle beaver trapping. Walter can trap the muskrats when he gets a little bigger."

When Tommy bought himself a new saddle with his fur proceeds, I really became envious of him. Our friend Katherine, who lived on the next ranch and had her own saddle, made snide remarks like, "How can you stand to ride bareback all the time?"

The fall I was ten years old the muskrat were plentiful in the streams flowing through the pasture where we kept the milk cows. One family even bravely moved into the back of the round pool we called the swimmin' hole, less than two hundred yards from the house. I tore into the house yelling, "Mama, I saw a muskrat in the swimmin' hole. I'm going to set a trap!"

"You don't know how to trap," Walter sneered.

Walter was just enough younger than me to feel I was a rival, even if he was a boy. He was a rather frail child, and Mama probably encouraged him not to be too aggressive; I was far more venturesome.

"You just wait and see," I said, heading for the blacksmith shop where the small steel muskrat traps hung by long chains on a spike. With three traps, I went back to the house, heading for the cellar where the garden vegetables were stored for the winter. "I guess I'd better get a carrot for bait," I said.

Seeing I was serious, Mama said, "We'd better all go with you." Of course she couldn't go off and leave the younger children alone, but she was afraid I might fall into the pool.

Deeply eroded by the little stream that fed it, the pool was about fifty feet in diameter.

The muskrats had moved into the roots of an enormous willow tree overhanging the pool. Fresh grass was strewn around the muddy slide that led up to the hole, an ideal place to set a trap. But I couldn't reach it as the giant tree hung out over the water on either side of the hole, and there were no banks. Mama and I studied the situation.

"There's no way we can get near that hole to set a trap," she said. I know she breathed a prayer of thanks that she had insisted on coming with me; alone I might have been daredevil enough to try.

"We'll have to find another," I said.

We walked up and down the bank and finally set traps in the shallow ripple leading onto the pool. Both sets were baited with a carrot stuck on a stick just beyond the trap.

Mama let me run the trap line by myself. Early in the morning I hastened through the dew-damp, sweet-smelling grass to where the traps were set. As I approached the first one I saw a round ball of fur sitting dejectedly on the bank, fur fluffed out as a bird puffs its feathers. It looked twice its real size, beady golden eyes looking at me balefully, but with no plea for pity.

I knew the moment of truth had arrived. Was I a trapper or not? It all depended on whether I could kill the muskrat. I'd witnessed the killing of chickens, held them firmly by their feet and wings with their necks stretched out on the chopping block. I knew if you had to kill, you must do it quickly and with the very first blow, to crush the skull instantly, preventing suffering for the animal and the trapper. I hesitated, but knew I had to be a trapper. I made sure I had a stick big enough and that my blow was well aimed.

When I tore back to the house, carrying my prize by its snakelike tail, everyone gathered around. "Now you'll have to skin it and stretch its hide," Mama said. Evidently, if I was going to be a trapper, there were a lot of things I'd learn to do alone. "I think there's some stretching boards in the shop," Mama said.

Before long I was trudging farther afield in search of favorable muskrat sets. I learned that they preferred to live near moving streams rather than in stagnant swamps of the sloughs. They like a certain tall, sweet-smelling grass, young willow shoots, and aspen bark. I learned to make sets close to deep water so the muskrat would dive in and drown. In a couple of years my trap line was two miles long. Very early every morning, I rode my pony to cover it, earning a great deal of money for those hard times. Told I had to share either my profits or my trapping territory with my younger sibling, I shared my earnings since I loved the excitement of seeing what would be in my traps each morning.

We shipped our furs to Sears and Roebuck and spent our money on school clothes ordered out of the catalog. Store-bought clothes were a rare treat. Mama was a good seamstress and hand-me-downs from our older sibling were always available. I didn't buy myself a saddle as I had originally intended, but I remember buying a dark green and black checked jacket. When I looked in the mirror and saw how nice it looked with my red hair, I decided it wasn't so bad to be only a girl after all.

KIM BARNES

from *In the Wilderness*

(1996)

*M*y father's arms encircle me as he snugs the rifle into my shoulder, pressing me against his legs. He steadies my left elbow, extended and trembling with the barrel's weight. I lay my cheek on the cool wood, breathing in the camphor of gun oil.

"Steady," my father says. "Don't hold your breath. Aim like you're pointing your finger."

The target—a red circle crayoned on butcher paper and tacked to a stump— seems more distant with one eye closed. I know in a moment my arms will collapse, that the rifle will fall from my hands. Imagining the lovely brown stock caked with mud makes me shudder. I focus on the wavering bead and touch the trigger. The still afternoon explodes into pain, sharp and burning, spreading from my shoulder to the tingling tips of my fingers. My ears ring as the shock reverberates across the meadow.

He moves from behind me, loosens my hands, cradles the rifle against his chest. He pulls a Camel from his pocket and smiles, a full, eye-wrinkling grin, holding the cigarette between his teeth. He is proud of me.

He nods toward the target. "Let's go see," he says, and I move after him, my shoulder numbing, still feeling at my back the cool air of his absence. It is 1964. I am six.

I am twenty, my father's age when I was born. He, my brother and I sit in the pickup, parked somewhere in the Clearwater National Forest, drinking sweet tea from a thermos, waiting for dawn. Nearly a decade after moving to Lewiston, we have come back to hunt my father's country.

It has been two years since I left home on graduation night, and we have barely spoken since. Two years on my own have given me the courage to believe that I'm independent enough to forge a new relationship with my father based on love and respect rather than on authority and obedience. I want to be welcomed into his home again. I want him to stop getting up from the table when I sit down. More than anything, I want a family that will not shun me.

I know that our truce will not come via apology—we both hold firm to the decision we made that day—and so I've found another alliance: I've asked him to hunt with me, to show me the land he knows. He logged it, punching through skidroads now grown over with chokecherry and alder. The thicketed draws, the stands of cedar, the meadow lush with tall grass and lupine are landmarks he lived by, familiar beyond simple memory. He has moved through this landscape, taken it inside of him, worked in the bone-deep cold of its winters, hauled from its heart millions of board feet. He has found the water sprung from rock and filled his hands with it, so cold it seemed molten.

I crave his intimate knowledge of the woods and want to show him what I have learned. I'll point out the deep-cut track of a running deer (*twin divots at the back—it's a buck, then*), name for him the birds that cross the sky (*flicker, evening grosbeak, pine siskin, and that one you call "camp robber"—it's really only a gray jay*). Given the chance, I'll prove my marksmanship, but not with the rifle I've carried for the last year. I've given the Winchester 30.06 back to him, cleaned, oiled and polished—a token of peace. Maybe here, I think, in the woods, we can come to some understanding of the ways we share.

Sitting next to him in the pickup's cab, I feel light-headed and girlish, once again a visitor in my father's territory, beset by the need to act properly, to show myself worthy of his command. I try to keep my arms and legs close, conscious of every brush of cloth between us. I try not to breathe too fast and give away my nervousness. Greg sits on my right, six-foot-three and solid, touched by the light coloring of our Grandfather Barnes—dark blond hair that will prove itself red as he matures, his beard and mustache the color of fox. Between the two men I feel both protected and diminished, the daughter, the sister, always in need of safeguarding. When the silhouettes of trees notch the horizon, we pull on our hats, savoring the last of the heater's warmth before stepping out into the frosted morning air. My father checks for matches, drops a few shells into his shirt pocket. He turns a slow half-circle, squints at where the sun colors the clouds, smiles at us and heads for the cover of timber.

For a time, we keep to an old dirt road, then turn onto a game trail that leads us along the flank of a high ridge. My breath wisps out and evaporates, and I keep my eyes on the path, intent on keeping up. Already, my shoulder is numb with the weight of the Marlin—a lever-action 30.30, heavy and homely compared with my father's Winchester. I swing it around, cradle it in the crook of my left arm.

My father is a tall man, long-legged and lean, unhurried and efficient in his movements. He keeps our pace steady, as though he has no intent of simply hunting but will lead us directly to where the deer stand exposed, stunned by our arrival into stillness. We should slow down, I think, listen.

There might be bucks stripping alder only a few feet away. The farther we get from the rig, the farther we have to carry what we kill. The thought of half a carcass on my shoulders makes me groan. The muscles in my thighs ache with the climb. Sweat wicks into my long johns, and I am thankful for the overcast sky, gray and cool as gun metal.

I've been told my father can outwalk any man, can walk for days without tiring. Beneath a towering larch, he stops just long enough to strike a match. Golden needles drop around him, catching in his hair. His hands seem sometimes possessed of their own grace, like the wings of a raptor, finely boned and beautiful. He is strong, his chest and arms surprisingly large, so that when he rolls up his sleeves I find myself staring, seeing the muscle there tense and release, and I feel all that he has held back and is capable of.

No matter how carefully I step over twigs and loose rock, my presence is betrayed by the thud of my boots, the crack of dry limbs echoing through the quiet. A raven flies before us, calling its disgruntled warning. I watch its blackness against the sky and see the head pivot to follow our movement. He knows something we don't, I think. I think that ravens are our attendants through the forest-dusky harbingers, impartial jurors, marking our progress, patient as fate.

I see my father's back, the straight shoulders, the way he moves: in the swing of his legs the hint of a swagger. I sense the rhythm of his stride and begin to hear its song, its smooth cadence. I bring the rifle around to rest behind my neck and drape my arms across its barrel and stock, like a woman carrying water.

Only a few miles into our hike and already I want to stop for a drink of tea. I want to rest. I try to discern the hour by the muted light of clouds. I hum out ragged bits of old songs—"Going to the Chapel of Love" and "I'll Fly Away" and something by Bobby Goldsboro.

My father's sudden stop startles me. I nearly run, thinking we've surprised a cougar or bear. He points to me, freezes me in my tracks, motions me to his side. My eyes follow his to a dense jumble of slash and tall brush.

Even with his direction, at first I cannot see the light-dappled back of a deer, motionless in the frosted undergrowth. My father's hand is a brush-stroke through air as he silently traces the hidden head and legs. I nod, finally able to see the doe where she stands fluid as mercury.

I step back to give him room, but he shakes his head. He has given me the shot. I should be grateful, but instead I feel patronized, instantly aware of his expectation, his judgment of my every motion. This will be his test of me, his way of making me prove up. The action, which normally comes easy—*snug the butt of the rifle tight against your shoulder, elbow up and out*— seems awkward as I lay my cheek to the stock. The deer raises its head and I think she has sensed us, but she dips again, browsing in fern and the shriveled leaves of mullen.

I aim for the killing spot, just behind the shoulder, a point at which I know the bullet might puncture the lungs or pierce the heart, but now I'm not sure I want to kill the doe. We're not here for meat; we're here because a daughter and her father can speak to each other only in a code made up of action and reaction. The forest, the trail, the deer are backdrop and props for the little war we wage, and if only a few hours ago I believed our outing an innocuous attempt at reconciliation, I feel our roles settling upon us: the powerful father, the willful daughter, each intent on gaining some edge over the other, even here, in the wilderness, in this ritual of blood.

The shot echoes across the ridge. I lever in another cartridge and aim again, waiting for leaves to move, for shadows to separate. What I see is the deer's white flag of a tail disappear into the thick undergrowth. I turn to my father pulling smoke deep into his lungs. He looks at me above the still-lit match and raises one eyebrow. I glance at my brother, who is studying his boots.

Before I can protest, my father turns and moves away. Greg shrugs his shoulders and follows him. I want to tell them I meant to miss, or that anyone can miss a shot. I think, Quit walking, listen, but the distance between us lengthens until I fall far behind.

I hate my weakening legs, my slow finger against the trigger. I hate the doe, who believed us trees solidly planted in the bank, and I hate that I made of her some symbol of resistance. I think I might hate the man in front of me, my father, who carries his burden so easily, as if it were nothing, the rifle slung over his shoulder. I wonder what he is thinking, and as has always been the case between my father and me, I think he can discern the reason for my every action. He wanted me to shoot the deer, and because he wanted me to, I wouldn't. *But it was you who started it*—I want to say—*you're the one who insisted I take the shot. It wasn't a gift, it was a test, a trial.*

By the time we crest the ridge, I'm somewhere between tears and fury, both unacceptable shows of emotion. I swear silently that I'll never subject myself to this again. My father slows, then stops. He pulls a cigarette from his pocket with two fingers, lights it, scans the ridge. I long for a cigarette of my own, but I cannot imagine smoking in front of my father. I kick mud from my boots, glad for the moment's rest, already planning a hot bath when I get back to my apartment, where I can be free of my father's reckoning.

He turns his gaze on me. "Now," he says, "you lead."

For a moment I feel between us the steel-blue shock of recognition: He is the father, I, the daughter. His job is to teach, mine to be taught. No matter how many years pass, no matter what conciliatory gestures I make, nothing will change. I look to my brother, who shakes his head and looks away.

I hate this, this *lesson.*

It was *I* who had thought to save *him,* to rescue him from his television and easy chair, to remind him of the life he had left behind. I wanted him to remember what his life was like before his all-night runs hauling wood chips from one mill to another; before his stride of open country turned to the cramped steps of a man shuffling from bed to table, from the door of his house to the door of his truck, between the close boundaries of manicured hedges, back and forth, cutting the same swath so it might be watered and grow to be cut again.

But now it is I who must walk for hours toward what I think might be our beginning. The men follow me, my father half-smiling, my brother wary and observant, knowing that he might be called upon to take my place. If there are deer, I do not see them. The air darkens. How long will he let this go on? "Learning the hard way," he'd say, "makes them remember."

What I learn is this: I am lost, and he will not lead me out.

We could walk for miles, spend the night shivering in our clothes beside a fire of pine branches, more smoke than warmth. He'd let us, I think, just to prove . . .

I want to spit my anger at him. I want to cry and sink to the ground. I want him to gather me up in the circle of his arms and carry me to a place of comfort, as he did when I was a child. I stop, close my eyes, take a deep breath: "I don't know where we are," I say.

He settles onto a log and unwraps a chocolate bar, breaks it into thirds. I crouch on my heels, unwilling to give in to exhaustion, to let him see me beaten. Greg walks a little ways off to pee, an excuse, I think, to give us all the room he can. My own bladder is full, but I can't bear the thought of fighting my way off the trail and into the brush to gain the privacy I would need to squat.

"You haven't been watching," my father says. "The treadmarks on the road run a certain way. Notice that."

I nod, tired beyond remembering. I let the chocolate melt on my tongue. He crosses his legs and points, his cigarette deep in the V between two fingers.

"See the ridge? That tallest snag? Tamarack. Been there as long as I can remember." The dusky horizon seems a solid wash of trees, none distinguishable from the other.

"You look down too much. You've got to see it all, forward, backward, sides. You get lost in here, it'll be a long time before someone finds you."

You could, I think, but I keep my eyes on the blank sky and say nothing.

"You won't always have the sun, or even stars. You have to make your own map. Memorize it." He rises, unhurried, lifts the Winchester to his shoulder and begins to walk us out.

In the late heat of August, I stand with my mother at her kitchen window, watching my father mowing their lawn. He is nearly sixty now and paces himself, pausing to pull a cigarette from his pocket before pushing toward the next turn. My mother worries about his heart, but I still believe he could march for miles. When he stops to empty the bag, he sees me and nods, the distance between us only a few yards—a distance we still cannot cross.

I think of that hunting trip, the dark way back, without horizon, without stars, the bead of my father's cigarette our only light, his face luminously floating. I could barely lift my feet as I shuffled through downed limbs and stumbled over rocks, yet he moved through the night as though his life depended on silence. I wonder if he would remember the walk out as I do, those places where he slowed so that we might rest: beside the antler-stripped alder; along the bank of a creek rimed with ice; beneath the drapery of a single cedar missed by the sawyer or left to seed, a tree so large the tips of our fingers would not touch had we measured its girth. During the silent drive home, the road a dark ribbon unfurling before us, we drank the still-warm tea, sweetest at the last. If he had touched me then, reached across and patted my knee or squeezed my arm, the wall between us might have fallen, his rigid authority and my bitterness dissolve into the shared and necessary experience of the elder and his charge. I might have come away from that trek in the wilderness believing my father's instruction a map I could follow. I might have believed the hand that held fire could heal any wound.

Earl

(2002)

M Y FATHER-IN-LAW, EARL, IS A MAN OF TRADITION AND HABIT. HE IS the sort of man who backs his car into the driveway on the night before every trip. Who hunts with his brother every year on Thanksgiving Day morning from the same deer stand, and then in the afternoon, sits in his chair watching football, working and sucking the after-dinner tooth-pick. He is the sort of man who stubbornly insists on driving—at age seventy-eight—across four northern Plains states to shoot upland birds with his only son, Jeff. Jeff has grown of same resistant rootstock, and there are things we do in our home because *that's how I've always done it.*

This year, we are sitting three-across in the Ford, three Labs in the back. The weather's hot and turning hotter, sending the sharptails elsewhere. Earl tells a story of hunting pheasants in '46. He had a friend, Eddy, and his friend's father told the boys as they left for the war that when they made it back, he would take them pheasant hunting in South Dakota. Earl never speaks of the war, but you can tell it saddened him in a permanent way. He was a gunner in the air force and refuses to fly now. "Well, Eddy and I made it back and there were thousands of birds in those fields," Earl croons. "There were so many pheasants we couldn't help stepping on them. You see," and he turns to look at us, a big beak of a nose at close range, his eyes bright and the lines of his face softened, "no one hunted those birds during the war, so afterwards there were pheasants every-where." He shakes his head slowly. "Just everywhere! Ho boy, that was something."

Jeff is driving and only half-listening as Earl tells the old stories, but I've just joined their annual hunt in these last few years. Once when Earl was recalling the time Jeff shot his first buck, I asked if he ever took Jeff's sisters out hunting. His bald, pointy forehead drew down into wind-rows. "No, I never did. Don't know why not," Earl said, shaking his head. "Guess I never thought of it."

I never hit many birds when I first hunted and those times when I missed, and we were all together for that week in September, Earl would happen to walk by me and say a gracious word or two. He eased my gloom. But when I knocked down the rare bird I could hear him calling from across the field, "Well, now, you'd better leave one or two for us." Later, Earl would brag about my minor success, which was never half as grand as he made it sound. And when I took up big game hunting and shot my first antelope and first deer, in one weekend, and each with one shot, I phoned Earl first and told him. I told him I squeezed the trigger with the hinge of my index finger as he suggested. Then Jeff told the stories of my hunts to Earl, again, with different details and new pride.

But last year, Earl didn't drive out West. His health, and Jeff's mother's health, are on a roller coaster course and each roaring decline threatens to permanently diminish their quality of life. Yet, remarkably, they recover again—first one and then the other, increasingly inter-dependent like soldiers under fire. This spring, we traveled to Wisconsin to visit Earl and Gladys when neither of them had been feeling well and the list of their ailments had grown long and serious. "Try to make it out to Montana for hunting in September, Dad," we said, leaving. "You could take the train," I suggested. But the unspoken truth was we all feared that Earl had made his last trip.

He tells another hunting story as we bump along in the Ford on drought-dry tracks. The stories flow like the water of a river and Jeff and I are rocks in mid-current as the words bend continually over and around us. The air conditioner cools, and the hot sun wavers above, and the sound of his voice merges one dusty day with the others. Climbing in and out of the truck, Earl makes small sounds of effort and pain which Jeff and I don't comment upon. We look for places to hunt that require neither a long walk nor much up and down. But the unseasonable heat, more than anything else, is defeating us.

Earl is hunting with our dog, Beta, again this year. She's between three and four years of age, now, and has recently acquired ideas of her own. She is maturing with the familiar willfulness that runs among the females in our kennel. Jeff hunts with her mother, the old drama queen. Just the day before, Jeff killed a sharptail and Jazzy charged out for the retrieve but didn't return. When Jeff found the dog, she was laying in a water hole with no bird in sight because she'd thrown it into the cool mud before lounging on top of her prize. I've thought that Beta's brother, Cooper, would be a better companion for Earl—slower and mindful—but Coop has never hunted with anyone but me. So I watch Beta as she beelines out ahead of Earl at rifle distance and wish that I had trained her better, or at least could now reach across the distance of bleached-blond alfalfa and whoa her with muffled threats and stern gestures. Yet Earl has only good words for the athletic dog, as he says her name again and again in that sonorous, sing-song voice, "Bay-tuh." And again at day's end, without having fired a shot.

Earl recalls the time our son, Jack, shot his first whitetail on a trip with Jeff and Earl to the Marias Breaks. "Jeeze, that was a big whitetail buck," he coos, and then makes a goofy face. "A big four by five." Later, Earl adds that not one of his grandsons hunts now. "Not Jack, Mike or Jessie," he says, thinking about this as we ride the hard-scrabble road back to the motel and showers.

"But I can understand it," Earl tells me later at dinner, "it's hard for a young person to kill an animal. I felt that way too when I was a boy, walking up to the deer I'd shot and wishing I could take it back so the deer would live. And feeling so sad. Over the years, I've felt that way several times. But boy!" he says, and makes that sweet, goofy face again, "I sure do like to eat 'em."

In the late-spring of this year, Earl's brother, who has been his deer hunting companion and best friend all their lives, died in six weeks time of liver failure. Jeff's sisters told us it was hard for Earl and he hasn't been the same since. Now, driving around Montana, Earl wonders aloud if he'll go deer hunting during Thanksgiving—he doesn't know if he'd be able to get a deer out of the field by himself. But he's thinking about it.

A year and a half ago, even before his brother died, Earl didn't expect to hunt deer again. Earl had developed macular degeneration in his right eye, his dominant shooting eye, and with that eye he could only see a black hole surrounded by peripheral images. Then Earl practiced bringing the rifle up to his left shoulder—revising sixty years of habit—and sighting through the scope with his left eye. He had told us the story of his clean-kill with modesty: He and his brother were sitting in the stand last year where they usually hunt, the story began . . .

"This is beautiful. What a place!" Earl declares, looking across the prairie where we are about to hunt. He savors it all, moving slowly, smiling. He is less concerned about the lack of shooting opportunities than Jeff and I are; we would like, more than anything, to put him into some birds and then hope for the best.

The macular degeneration has forced Earl to give up his old, reliable Browning automatic for a new SKB over-and-under and to try and learn to do the far more difficult thing of wingshooting left-eyed, left-handed. It seemed impossible. But before coming to Montana, Earl shot sporting clays for the first time and knocked down thirty of one hundred targets. "Pretty good, Pops," Jeff tells him. "I only hit three out of fifty the first time I shot clays." Like his father, Jeff is gracious and bends the truth at times.

By the end of our day, Earl has fired only one ridiculously long shot. "To see if the gun still works," he said with uncharacteristic sarcasm. Under the looming heat, we call it quits and make plans for an earlier morning.

An hour past the rosy dawn Earl looks tired and older. He had a rough night, he concedes, after the greasy hot-beef sandwich he ordered for dinner, and he hasn't faced a breakfast. But ducks and geese are flying and sandhill cranes are rattling their strange ancient songs, and Earl brightens up. "Listen to that," he says. Smiling, and with his *frenchie*-voice, he adds, "And the mal-*LARDS*."

Down the road we go and Earl is quieter than usual. We return to the same place we hunted the day before and I question the wisdom of beating the same bushes thrice, saying *I wouldn't do this*, but the two men are already locked on to the objective. Jeff is dropped off at his usual spot. Earl and I drive up the road and park at the usual gate. Earl is going to hunt the same cover he circled the previous day, and in previous years. This habitual retracing of hunting ground—making the same circle in the same direction—seems lacking of imagination. So I head off for new, distant alfalfa fields beyond the weather-stunted limber pine and aspen groves, deeper into grizzly country.

Earlier in the week, as Earl and I sat on the tailgate waiting for Jeff at the usual parking place, a rancher and his wife, Ora and Tiny, drove up in a slow whirl of dust, turned off the ignition and visited for a spell. Among the interesting bits of local knowledge they imparted was the fact that thirty-six grizzly bears had been counted recently in this vicinity between the mountain face and the reservoir a couple miles east. "Thirty-six," we repeated.

"Be careful," Tiny implored just before their old Caddy pulled away.

I have often wondered if at the moment of being charged by a grizzly, while bird hunting, would I shoot my 20-gauge at *very very* close range or pull the trigger on my canister of pepper spray. Believing I could not juggle both the shotgun and canister in those critical seconds, I would have to choose just one. So could I factor the wind's direction swiftly enough to choose the gun if, by chance, both wind and grizzly came from the same direction? Or, on the other hand, does 7½ shot punch a big enough hole in a 300-plus-pound grizzly to halt the forward momentum of its charge in time to save my life?

Perhaps as a way of answering the question, I had stopped carrying pepper spray except in new territory. I'd thought of giving Earl a canister on the first day of hunting, then decided against it. For all the years of repeating the hunters' circles, we had never seen a bear in these limber pines and stunted aspens or even their sign. The thirty-six grizzlies must follow traditional trails to traditional feeding grounds—although among those ursine creatures of habit there might also be one errant, imaginative hunter.

As I walk west into a large meadow, I hear a mute shot and hope that it's from Earl's gun. Cooper and I continue quartering silently at the

limber pine edge when I see a single sharptail flush a quarter-mile off, rising from the thin standing, drought-stressed alfalfa. Cooper hasn't seen
the flush, but he's birdy. We continue on in minatory silence and I circle
casually toward the flush. No matter. The birds are not holding and the
balance of the covey suddenly, noisily, up and leaves the country.

Back at the truck, Earl and Jeff are leaned into the shade waiting for
me. No birds. Jeff reports a wild shot taken through the trees and Earl
hasn't seen a thing. The black dogs are in the shade, too, with big pink
spoons for tongues sawing in and out. At ten o'clock, the temperature is
in the eighties. We decide the heat will soon end our hunting and that
we should try a place nearby, up the road, where we've sometimes found
birds by a spring creek, and where we can drive close to the cover for Earl.

Jeff has been dropped off down the road a ways. He'll swing a wide arc
through the limber pines to join us. The sharptails go to the trees for shade
in the sun's heat, but they won't hold for some reason, and not one of us
has ever shot a sharptail there. Still, Jeff wants to try it. I park the truck in
the middle of the prairie, near the spring, and with a hint of resignation,
Earl and I unload our guns and the dogs.

"Come on, Be-ta," Earl calls, and moves slowly, steadily across the
cinquefoil prairie toward a likely patch of willow and buffalo berry. I wander in another direction to give Earl the best cover and some solitude. Dis-
cretely, at a distance, I watch him circle the brush without putting up a
sharptail, and wonder where else we might go, as I turn and quarter away.
Then the shot sounds. And a second one when I look and see Earl swinging hard on a sharptail that flies on without missing a wing beat. But he is
calling Beta, and I'm sure I hear him say, "Give."

"So you got one," I comment, by way of asking, when I get over
to him.

He stands up taller, then, and smiles. "Got two."

"Earl!"

"Yeah. I kind of surprised myself. But then I tried to get that third bird,
thinking I had the automatic." He grins—and is twenty years younger.

Earl told the whole story of circling the brush and deciding to walk
another green bit of cover, of the dog work, of the flush and of shooting;
and he told it again when Jeff caught up with us and the two men cleaned
the birds side-by-side at the clear-running creek. And again that evening,
while we were fishing and catching rainbows. Next year, he'll be telling
it in September, bumping down the dirt roads three-abreast. Then some
year, we will tell the story for him. Of how an old man switched from
shooting right-handed to left-handed after a half-century of habit and
then knocked down a double—which seemed to us to say more about
how he chose to live than how much he wanted to hunt.

My Mother's Shotgun

(2002)

I CAN BARELY SEE THE POND IN FRONT OF ME. THE CLOUD COVER HAS blocked out what little bit of moonlight could have illumined it for me. I had to find it with a flashlight after walking nearly a quarter-mile from my parked truck across a pasture knee deep in grass, carrying my gun, a shell bag, and a backpack of decoys. Even then, I didn't know I'd found it until the water started splashing up on my waders.

Now I'm sitting in it. The seat of my stool rises just a few inches above the water level at the edge of the pond. Sitting here, I'm in good cover. Between the camouflage face mask, gloves and shirt I'm wearing, and the stalks of cindybeans that stand in the water and form a canopy under which I sit, they'll never see me as long as I sit still until the second I decide to pull up and shoot with my lucky gun. The mosquitoes are buzzing my ears and trying to bite through my waders. I can feel the sweat running between my breasts and the bug repellant burning my eyes. My heart is racing from the pot of coffee I had on the drive here, and my stomach churns a bit from the late bedtime and early alarm. But, I don't care. At this moment, there is no place on earth or in life I'd rather be.

You see, today is the first day of teal season in Texas. And I'm hunting with my mother's shotgun.

This gun is not my usual gun. Normally, I shoot a Beretta 12-gauge semi-automatic called the Pintail. I use the Pintail for every bird I hunt: dove, quail, ducks and geese. I don't have a gun for every species, every weather condition, every time of day. I hunt with one gun, and I hunt everything with it. This morning, however, I packed my mother's shotgun, a 20-gauge Remington Model 11. She abandoned it a while back for a muzzleloader and a high-powered rifle. So, I borrowed it indefinitely a few years ago and decided to use it this morning for luck. My mother could fill a large meat locker with everything she's killed with this gun. And anyone who hunts teal knows that you can use all the luck you can get to bag your limit of the fast little ducks.

I have about fifteen minutes until shooting time. My mother's shotgun lies across my lap and I finger the safety on it while I wait. I'm not loaded yet, so I push the safety in and out a few times, getting used to the feel of it again. My left hand caresses the barrel, scratched and dull from years of use. My right hand moves from the safety to the stock, smooth overall but notched here and there where it's been dropped, or banged against trees, or knocked into the bumpers of pickup trucks or the sides of aluminum duck boats. It's a gun with a lot of history, a lot of success, and a lot of attitude. It takes after my mother; or maybe she takes after it. Either way, I'm going to do well with this gun today, I just know it.

My father bought this gun for my mother in the late '50s from a friend who ran a pawn shop. My mother grew up around hunting, but not until she married my father did she enter into hunting as a family tradition, as the only real way to spend vacation weeks, as the closest thing to religion except, well, religion itself. The gun was in great shape (practically new), would serve as a good all-purpose gun, and would fit my mother's small frame. Plus, the recoil wasn't too bad, even when firing buckshot or slugs. So, Daddy bought it for my mother and she began to hunt as a member of the Carroll family.

My oh my, did she hunt. My mother is good at nearly everything she tries, but hunting is in her blood. After honing her natural shooting talents with a few lessons from my father, a police officer and fire arms instructor, she took to the woods in southeast Arkansas and northwest Louisiana. And killed her limit of everything she hunted. Every season. Every year.

It started in September with squirrel season. I accompanied her several times as she stalked the crafty rascals from cypress trees to beechnuts through the river bottom along the Little Missouri River. Others used a .22 rifle, but mother filled her game vest using her shotgun. She would stop beside a hollow stump or a fallen tree, pull me close to her (usually in her shadow, if there was one), and would stand statue still, peering into the treetops. For the life of me, I could never really see what she saw, but suddenly she would raise her gun and fire. A patch of treetop would explode and clatter down onto the leaves, a part of it thudding as it hit the ground. There would be the squirrel, perhaps not quite dead yet. Mother would put her foot on its head while she reloaded. I got to pick it up by the tail and slip it into the back of her game vest before we resumed the hunt.

Soon, I could no longer hunt with my mother. No one could. No one in our family hunted with as much attention to detail, as much obsession for basic hunting skills as she did. Standing on the ground, in a makeshift deer stand of fallen limbs, some scraggly trees and, perhaps, a stump, she would take nearly thirty seconds to even blink her eyes. She took a full minute or more to turn her head to the left or right, and even more to look behind her because that required something of a body turn. She stood still as a fencepost, gun at an angle, hands in shooting position on it, fingers on the safety and the trigger, for hours without moving significantly. She didn't scratch an itch. She didn't adjust her stance or her parka. She just stood there, frozen and fully camouflaged, waiting for her quarry to come up to her as if she were a pin oak.

They came routinely. She has dozens of stories of deer coming within fifteen feet of her, craning their necks toward her, sniffing and looking, trying to determine if she was a tree or something to be afraid of. They snorted and stomped at her. Stepped away, then came back to stomp and sniff again. Sometimes, if the deer were out of season, she finally dissolved into giggling, broke her cover and watched the whitetail flags disappear into the woods. Other times, however, she waited for the buck to look away just once more, then in a seamless, smooth, instinctual motion, raised her 20-gauge to her shoulder, hugged its stock to her cheek, switched off the safety and fired. One shot to the heart. The deer, most often, fell dead in its tracks.

Deer weren't the only ones. Squirrels came careening down the trunks of the very trees against which mother leaned. She heard their claws on the bark, waited until she heard them move back up a bit, or onto the leaves, circled around the trunk with her back, raising her gun as she went, and fired. Rabbits would step right out into the road where she sat like a stone in a clump of brush. They would stop to eat a frost-nipped leaf, and she would fire. One shot to the head. Wood ducks or mallards would come gliding in to decoys she and Daddy set out amidst flooded timber, with her sitting only 20 feet away, knee deep in water, pressed flat against a mossy oak or crouched down among bald, gnarly cypress knees. One shot, two shots, even three. And there on the water, upside down, their feet still paddling, floated one, two or three ducks.

My mother and her shotgun were deadly. Everyone knew it and praised her for it, despite their good-natured jealousy. When no one else killed anything, she got a limit. When deer were hard to come by, she got a freezer full. When ducks were shot up and wary at the end of the season, she got them in range and killed them. She rarely missed, and when she did, she brooded about it for days, going over what she did wrong, how she could've positioned herself better, or waited a few more seconds, or gotten her gun up a second faster or with more precision. She was—and still is—relentless. She is a hunting hero, my hero. And this morning, I'm using her gun so that I may hunt like her and have her success.

About five minutes remain before shooting time. I can make out the pond in front of me and the dozen or so decoys I've placed on it. The coastal breeze coming from the south is rippling the water and moving the decoys, which is good. I hear the steady swoosh of a flock of teal passing overhead. I feel the hair on my arms raise and a chill run from the back of my neck. Those teal are the first I've heard in over eight months, since the close of last year's season. My heartbeat quickens. My soul opens.

Suddenly, another group announces itself, this time much closer, with a prolonged "Sssshhhhhhh" of beating wings. They buzz the decoys on my pond like a swarm of oversized bees. I can make them out, about thirty of them, as they dip down, skim the surface of the water, then veer off and up to disappear into the graying sky. Within moments, they are back in a flurry of sound and motion, checking out their "friends" on the water. After a few elliptical sweeps, they settle into the decoys. Shooting time still lacks a few minutes, and I'm not loaded. I sit still, relishing the close presence of so many wild and wondrous beings, and the fact that I lured them to me. I smile at the first one-note whistle that rings out from the pond. He is calling to another group that I hearing swooshing overhead.

I have to load up, and as I reach into my shell bag, the flock leaves the water with a splash. Every 15 seconds or so now, I hear flocks overhead. As I stuff the third shell into my mother's gun, I hear gunshots at the far end of the pasture. It's shooting time.

Another group of teal buzz my pond and my arms stiffen involuntarily, eager to raise the gun. I place my fingers on the safety button and the trigger, my other hand ready to raise and fire. I can see and hear the tiny ducks coming back at an alarming speed. If I hesitate even an instant after the best moment to fire, they'll be in the next county before I can get my gun up. They're coming straight toward me, like a formation of mini fighter pilots, lowering to the surface of my pond. They lower, lower, and I see the first indication of landing, fanned wings and lowered feet.

I raise my gun and fire, in one continuous motion, at the bird on the left edge of the group. He folds and falls while the rest wing away. I can see him floating among the decoys. He's not moving, so I feel safe in letting him float there while I reload and get ready for the next flock. I am breathless. Breathless that I made my first shot, breathless that my mother's gun has done its work. I'm breathless with gratitude. Grateful for this pasture and this pond, for fast teal and this quickly lightening morning, for the world, and that I get to be in it.

Gunshots ring out from across the pasture. Teal are everywhere. The next group swoops in from behind me. They nearly clip the cindybeans under which I sit as they lower to skim the pond, then raise and circle out over the pasture. As they turn to re-approach, I sink lower and prepare to fire. I see the blue patches on their wings as they blaze toward me. I fire at the lead bird. He and the bird behind him fall into the water. One of them swims upside down in a death circle, his head hanging in the water. I watch him, ready to shoot him again. He stills just as I click my safety button.

I reload my mother's gun quickly. As I load, a flock of over 40 birds nearly knock me from my stool as they pass by, low and determined.

Almost instantly, another group wings in from the opposite side and, without thinking, I raise my gun and fire. Nothing falls. I fire again, twice, chasing with my barrel the bird that brings up the rear. He doesn't fall. My gun is empty. Good grief, these ducks are fast.

More shots resound from across the pasture. Shooting time is now about ten minutes old, and I've got one bird left to fill out my limit. I see flocks of teal virtually everywhere in the sky around me. Some large, some small. Some low enough to disappear into the grass as they swoop a distant pond, some high and tiny in the sky, furiously flapping, their little necks outstretched.

I find my birds again on the pond. The breeze has moved them closer to the edge. Within minutes, a swarm of ducks blows over my pond and I take my last bird from the back of the group. He falls into the grass on the edge of the pond. Quickly, I leave my seat to retrieve him, never moving my eyes from the spot where he fell. My waders sink into pond sludge, and I almost lose my balance as I make my way through the flooded grass, gun angled and ready. I reach the spot and stop, looking, listening for anything. I can smell the blood, the unmistakable scent of a shot bird. The water splashes a bit a few feet to my right. I lunge and grab the duck before it can skitter away into the grass.

He's a shiny, blue-winged drake. He's shot in the breast, and will bleed to death within minutes. His heart purrs in his chest. His wings quiver. His eyes blink, but are beginning to glaze. He doesn't struggle against my hand. I marvel and almost swoon, my own heart thumping. He's so beautiful, so perfect, exactly as he's meant to be in the world. I cradle my gun under my arm, and gently place my free hand across his mottled breast. I ease my fingers into his feathers to touch his hot skin. I grip his breast and squeeze, to stop his heart and hasten his death. I feel his body quiver, and his feet paddle once. His eyes fade and begin to close. I say "thank you" as he relaxes into death.

I relax now, too, and walk back to my stool. I unload, lay my gun across the stool, and step into the pond to retrieve my ducks and decoys. Several flocks buzz me in the fifteen minutes it takes me to load up and begin walking to my truck. I feel the warmth of the birds through the back of my game vest. My decoys bang against my calves as I walk, and my mother's shotgun balances lightly across my shoulder.

I study my shadow as I walk. I'm a little bit taller than my mother, but I look a lot like her in shadow. The boxy hip waders, the slightly bulging game vest, the shell bag on my right hip. I turn my head slightly and see the outline of my hat brim. I turn the other way and see the sharp outline of her shotgun. I am my mother's daughter today, offspring of my hunting hero mother. I earned my place in her lineage. I earned her gun. I am walking in her footsteps, and her shadow stretches out before me.

PART EIGHT

Guides, Companions, Significant Others

THIS SECTION BEGINS WITH ANNIE OAKLEY, WHO ESTIMATED THAT IN HER lifetime she personally taught fifteen thousand women how to shoot. And she has, since her death in 1926, served as an inspiration and role model—a guide in spirit, if not in fact—for countless others, who have seen through the cartoonish heroine of *Annie Get Your Gun* to the genuine hero that Oakley, in fact, was. Despite the Broadway version's complaint that "You cain't get a man with a gun," the real Oakley not only "got" her man by outshooting him, she also championed every woman's natural right to hunt, to shoot for fun, and to bear arms in self-defense. One can tell, from the straightforward advice in her "Notes on Shooting" below, that she must have been a patient and generous instructor for the women fortunate enough to learn to shoot under her tutelage.

Not all markswomen have been so lucky. Nellie Bennett, *Outdoor Life* magazine's "lady representative" in the first decade of the twentieth century, writes about her grouse-hunting guide "John" with far more grace and good humor than he evidently showed her. Suffragist and free spirit Alberta Claire holds her own with her male compatriots afield, yet one gets the feeling she would vastly prefer hunting in the company of the sister-outdoorswoman she knows only through her letters. Writing far more recently, Erica Fresquez finds in adult life male friends who are willing to teach her the hunting skills and lore her father didn't think appropriate for a girl-child. And Marilyn Stone, a mostly solitary hunter since childhood, having despaired of being taken seriously as an equal by male hunters, discovers what it means to find a man who is willing to trust her to "come out of the dark woods alone."

ANNIE OAKLEY

A Brief Sketch of Her Career and Notes on Shooting

(1913)

DURING THE YEARS I HAVE BEEN BEFORE THE PUBLIC GIVING EXHIBITIONS of shooting, I have received innumerable requests for information in relation to shooting.

They have come in the form of letters, and by personal requests from the many people I have met, and they number in the thousands. These requests I first thought came from curious people, and I treated them lightly, but later I saw those who wrote me and those who questioned me were in earnest and really wished to be enlightened, and I felt anxious to enlighten them if I could, but I was at a loss how to impart that information. I told my trouble to a friend, and he told me that those thousands of inquirers all sought about the same information, and I might tell briefly my career and give what points about shooting I possess in a booklet, and thus answer most of those questions. I have acted on the suggestion, but I would state at the beginning I can tell in comparatively few words what has taken me many years to learn.

I was born in Woodland, Darke County, Ohio. My parents are Quakers, and I never could see they were at all interested in firearms or any kind of shooting; in fact, they objected to it.

I believe I was born with a fondness for shooting. My earliest recollections are of the times I would smuggle my brother's musket away to the woods and shoot game, and I feel certain that I shall never lose that fondness. I am, too, quite sure that I have a preference for game shooting, a sport that seems to increase as I grow older. I began my shooting career on wild game when scarcely twelve years of age, with a muzzle-loading gun, and killed a great deal of game with what would now be called a very homely gun.

Two years later I was presented with a 14-gauge muzzle-loading gun, which was a better arm than my first gun and my marksmanship improved greatly. I acquired quite a local reputation, and was surprised one day with a proposition to give exhibitions of shooting.

I had always taken a pride in my shooting, believing no one could be successful without such pride but I hesitated about giving public exhibitions, but my love of shooting influenced me to accept the proffered engagement, and I determined that I would study shooting, as every one should study the profession they choose to follow, and I also made up my mind to show the world that shooting was a healthful exercise and pastime that might be followed with benefit to health and without detracting from a lady's qualities.

When I decided to appear before the public, I determined to acquire skill with the various types of firearms. I studied and practiced with gun, rifle, revolver and pistol, and, while my friends tell me I took to shooting all those arms naturally, I know myself that were it not for the love of shooting born in me and the determination to acquire skill by practice, I would not have reached the degree of skill I am accorded.

My shooting career has probably brought me in contact with the best living shots of the world. Beginning as a little, wild Quaker girl in the then wild part of Ohio, I first came before the public in the nearby towns and cities. Then I appeared in the large cities of the United States. When I though I had reached the limit of my shooting sphere I was asked to go abroad. I went first to England, then to other foreign countries, until I had given shooting exhibitions in fourteen different foreign countries and with the different types of firearms I have mentioned. During the years of exhibition shooting I have met the enthusiastic shooters of different lands, from the titled nobleman to the person occupying the humblest station in life, and, too, from the lady of royal blood to the rancher's daughter. All, I may say, were infatuated with that love of shooting which makes an equality among the shooting fraternity far and near.

I think it safe to say that one and all of these persons asked about the same questions, namely, What style of firearm to choose and how to learn to shoot; so I will try to answer here the questions I am so often asked.

Guns, rifles and pistols are of many styles, and to declare that any one make is superior to all others would show a very narrow mind and limited knowledge of firearms. It is probably true that no one make of firearm has all the best points. The fancy of the shooter, his or her physique, and the kind of game to be hunted, should govern the choice of intelligent shooters. The various forms of mechanisms will always appeal differently to persons of equal intelligence. I am firm in the belief, however, that cheap guns are undesirable.

First, strength and safety should be considered; then balance and symmetry; and, finally, mechanism that suits best. When I say high-priced guns are best, I do not mean that the expense should be found in engraving and ornamentation. I mean that one should pay enough to secure in gun, rifle, revolver and pistol the foregoing points, namely: strength, safety, balance, fit and ease of manipulation; not considering embellishments. After that, if you have that love for firearms such as the art-lover has for paintings, embellish with such ornamentation as you fancy; but, remember, the embellishments don't improve the shooting qualities of the arm.

As to my own collection of firearms, I have many shotguns, most of them hammerless. They weigh about six pounds. I use 12-gauge guns chiefly, because of the readiness I can procure ammunition for such gauge. I have, however, used with success the smaller gauges. With rifles I use the caliber best suited for my work. My exhibition work is chiefly with .32 caliber.

With revolver I use the various calibers from .32 to .44. With pistol I use the .22 caliber.

Ammunition is something I am more particular about. I believe if one secures good results with a particular make of ammunition, it is wisdom to continue to use that ammunition, if it is procurable. The amount of ammunition I have consumed during my shooting career I imagine would appall most persons; the various shells, primers, wads and metallic cartridges I have used would supply an army. And what a number of experiments I have made to secure the best load! I can truthfully say that I have seen ammunition develop from the crudest kind to that which it seems impossible to improve.

After what seems to me to be exhaustless experiments, I have selected Union Metallic Cartridge Co. ammunition as the most satisfactory to me. For my guns I use U.M.C. Smokeless shells loaded with thirty-nine grains of Schultze Smokeless Power and an ounce of shot. In my rifles and revolvers I use U.M.C. Metallic Cartridges.

It has occurred to me as I reply to these queries in this necessarily brief form, am I not giving advice without warning, so I am impelled to add some words of caution, for I should regret very much if my replies to those seeking information about shooting should lead to accidents and consequent unhappiness.

Aside from the pecuniary returns from shooting I have realized, I have found shooting a healthful exercise, a great training, morally and physically, and very entertaining. I regard it as an accomplishment beneficial to any lady or gentleman. But from my earliest experiences with firearms I have always looked upon them as dangerous instruments if handled by careless persons, both to the handler and every one about, and, therefore, I feel this little work would be incomplete if I did not warn every one handling firearms to handle them with the greatest care. I have for years made it a practice to never take a firearm into my hands, unless with the knowledge that it was loaded, without turning away from every living person about me and opening the action to see if it were loaded. I would never hunt with or shoot at targets with any person who exhibited carelessness in handling firearms; and if any person ever pointed a firearm at me, or any living person that person did not intend to shoot, I would forever shun that person. I have the greatest patience with a painstaking poor

Annie Oakley in the field, Leesburg, Florida. Previously unpublished photograph of Oakley hunting. Courtesy of the Annie Oakley Foundation, Greenville, Ohio.

shot, but no patience with a careless shooter, however brilliant a shot that person may be.

Many persons who address me for information ask me to tell them how to aim to kill a flying bird. I can truthfully say that I have tried for years to frame a reply to that seemingly simple question, but have not been able to settle upon a fully satisfactory answer yet. With all my experience and after consulting the best shots of America and Europe, I can find no better answer than to say: You must shoot until you overcome confusion at quickly sighting on a moving object. At first you are likely to shoot wildly; you many not have the butt of the gun at the shoulder, not even pointed at the moving game, and you will probably miss the game. If you continue to shoot, however, you will sooner or later become calmer; you will not be so flurried; the confusion will disappear, and you will bring the gun properly to the shoulder; the eye will align its vision along the rib of the gun; you will direct the aim at the game and make the proper allowance ahead, over, or under the game, if necessary, press the trigger of the gun, and then realize the delights of shooting with ecstasy, but with calmness. You are likely to realize that you have made a successful shot.

After much thought I have come to the conclusion that this is the second stage of shooting, because a little later you are likely to declare truthfully that you cannot tell how you make your shots. This is because shooting has become a habit with you; that is, when the game is flushed you naturally bring the gun to the shoulder, glance along the barrel, aim directly at the game, or make the proper allowance ahead, above, or below, according to the direction the game is going, press the trigger and feel that you have finished your effort, regardless of the result. This is quite different from the novice, who is likely to think: I will shoot any way and make haste to get in as many more shots as possible: for the more shots I make, the greater number of pellets I fill in the air, the more likely I am to get the game. This is downright folly. Strive continuously to make a deliberate shot; remember, too, deliberation does not necessarily mean a slow, pottering shot; that is a bad habit to acquire.

I do not think I can better illustrate shooting than to refer to music. The musician, from training, knows just how to strike a note on his instrument; the successful shooter, even if he be the most illiterate person, knows how to bring the gun to the shoulder, align it, make the proper allowance for a flying bird or running animal, press the trigger. I might write a thousand pages on this subject, but could not say more than I have said in the foregoing remarks, especially as applicable to wing shooting with a gun.

With the rifle the same principles apply when snap shooting or shooting at moving objects is done, but, when shooting at the target, deliberate aim can be cultivated. The object in this style of shooting is to acquire by practice extreme steadiness. It is impossible to hold a rifle or revolver absolutely still so long as pulsation exists in the body, but the degree to which steadiness may be acquired is astonishing to most persons. Some persons are naturally steady, others are very unsteady. Every one will realize the difficulty of holding a rifle still when they aim on a small object at a long distance away.

Practice in rifle, pistol or revolver shooting, however, will usually make steadiness, and therein is the chief charm of shooting these arms of precision.

I have referred to the wonderful improvement in arms and ammunition. This is particularly noticeable in rifles, pistols and revolvers and ammunition for these arms. Most persons with normal health and vision may acquire proficiency with these arms, and in a comparatively short time. If persistent in practice, they will in a short space of time perform what was regarded by them heretofore as impossible. This is largely due to the improvements I have mentioned. I have found the ammunition now made so reliable I no longer make my own cartridges. The Union Metallic Cartridge Co.'s metallic cartridges for rifles and revolvers are in every way equal to its shotgun ammunition, and I feel that with guns, rifles and revolvers as made today, and the excellent ammunition I have mentioned, the art of shooting is within the reach of almost anyone who desires to acquire it.

NELLIE BENNETT

A Colorado Outing

from Outdoor Life *(August 1904)*

Spring has fled and summer bright,
Autumn leaves are falling;
The wild duck southward wings his flight,
The Elk to his mate is calling.

Weary Nature soon will creep
'Neath her fleecy cover;
Spring shall wake her from her sleep
When the Winter's over.

Memory only, ever green,
Clings to pleasures flown,
Lives again in vivid dream,
Joys that we have known.

Years are fleeting swiftly by,
The leaves of life are falling,
And ever with a plaintive cry
The past to me is calling.

Forgetful quite of care and strife,
I sit and idly dream,
Or read the pages of Outdoor Life,
And the past comes back again.

I know it must be considered an unpardonable sin to begin a plain little story with a wretched little rhyme, but these are the melancholly days of autumn which are supposed to be conducive to poetic thought. One unhappy poet, whose name is to me unknown, thus mournfully expressed his impressions of autumn:

"The melancholy days have come,
The saddest of the year;
A little too hot for whisky punch,
A little too cool for beer."

We all know just how he felt, and we forgive him for the rhyme, as I hope you will forgive mine.

But to be serious—who is there so dull to nature's impressions as not to be somewhat affected by the solemn autumn days? The very haze which hangs over mountain and plain seems to whisper of the mysterious past, and the mind naturally turns to that which is gone, and dwells with dreamy pleasure over the events of the season, now swiftly fading from view.

Each of us who is fond of nature, and who finds great happiness in fishing or hunting, can recall some trip made during the past season over which the memory lingers with most pleasure. Some of us are so fortunate as to have made several excursions into the mountains during the season. So it was with me, but I think perhaps the trip which left with me the most pleasant impression was a visit to Almont, Colo.

To those who have never been at Almont, let me say that it would prove a revelation to them in the way of what can be made of a sportsmen's resort. Situated some ten miles north of Gunnison, in the very forks of the Taylor and East Rivers, which there join their waters to form the famous Gunnison River, its location, from a standpoint of natural beauty, is not equaled by any other resort I have visited in Colorado. Almont is owned and managed by Mr. Vernon Davis of Denver. From the short time he has been building up the place—this being only the second season— Mr. Davis has accomplished wonders. In a natural grove of pines he has built quite a number of rustic log cabins for the accommodation of guests. On the other side of the Taylor River are other cabins, dining hall, etc., and also a large cottage built of cobble stones along the lines of architecture adopted by Elbert Hubard in the Roycroft buildings at East Aurora, N. Y. Rustic appearance prevails throughout, but has not been obtained at the sacrifice of comfort. Then as to food, which to me at least is an item of some importance—it was served in abundance and of most excellent quality. I have often heard that "The good Lord sent food, and the Devil sent cooks," but at Almont I became satisfied, for the time being, that the Good Lord furnished both. As to Mr. Davis, I found him to be a thorough gentleman, and all that a good host should be.

At Almont I took my first lesson in hunting grouse, and found that what I didn't know about that particular bird would make a very long story. My hunting companion and tutor was John, just plain John. I should describe John somewhat in detail, and lay before my readers (some of whom are doubtless his friends) some of the quaint traits of his make-up, were it not for the fact that he is a vengeful mortal, and possessed of a very long memory. Suffice to say that he has the instincts, if not all of the qualifications, of a good sportsman. He did know a good deal about grouse, and I took lessons from him at the expense of great waste of shoeleather, and much wear and tear of my anatomy.

Early in the morning John and I started out on horseback to slay grouse, John being armed with a Savage rifle equipped with a bushing for shooting pistol cartridges, while I, as usual, had with me my Winchester shotgun. My horse was a gaited animal, but inasmuch as he used all of his gaits at one time in a most unhappy combination, I constantly experienced a series of jolts and vibrations which soon made me long for a saddle of softer material than mere leather. John was mounted upon a sad looking little pony, which soon transferred some of its sadness to its rider, although the latter, being somewhat stout and well padded at vulnerable points, did not seem to suffer as much as I could have wished.

We rode onward and upward, and upward and upward, the flat topped mountain for which we were making seeming to have a trick of receding as we advanced. But all roads have an ending, and finally after two and a half hours of riding we reached the level top and, dismounting, tied our horses. I had anticipated great relief upon climbing down from my steed, but instead became aware of numerous muscles whose experience I had never even suspected, but which now made their presence felt by their very soreness. John offered sympathy, which I rejected with the advice that he apply it to his own bruises.

We found the mountain top covered with a heavy growth of quaking aspen and underbrush. I found the first grouse, flushing quite a covey, from which I brought down two, but, alas, could find but one of them. Then I listened patiently to a long sermon from John on the folly of letting the eye wander for a second from a grouse when once brought down, and of the necessity of carefully marking down the dead bird. How a hunter can carefully mark down two dead birds which have fallen in different directions, unless afflicted with crossed eyes, I don't know, and John won't tell.

For the sake of covering more ground, and of greater peace of mind, we decided to hunt separately. Soon I heard the crack of my tutor's rifle, and overcome with womanly curiosity, and a lurking fear that John might have hurt himself, I hastened to his side. I found him gloating over an old hen grouse of quite venerable appearance. He had deliberately potted her from the top of a dead tree, and in response to my sarcastic inquiry as to why he had not shot for the head instead of the body, he muttered something to the effect that he was out hunting for meat—not glory.

At noon-time we ate our lunch by the side of a little brook, and discussed the habits of grouse and other wild game. John is a stubborn man, and quite sensitive to criticism upon his knowledge and ability in matters of hunting. When I asked him whether he supposed any of the older inhabitants of the country could trace the pedigree of a modern grouse back to the old hen he had killed, he really seemed quite hurt. But my good tutor could find grouse, even if he did pot that poor old fowl. He seemed to know intuitively just where they were, and in every instance but the first he was the one to discover our game, and either from motives of courtesy or prudence (let us hope the former) he always gave a signal whistle which brought me to the birds, and gave me the shot. I learned that he was right about the absolute necessity of marking down a dead bird without trying for a shot at another, and when I took three rapid shots at a departing grouse, dodging trees and looking for an opening to shoot, I realized that wing shooting in thick timber is of uncertain success. Sometimes I got my bird, sometimes I got a few feathers, and sometimes I got a derisive laugh from John.

The ride homeward was without incident except for numerous painful attempts on my part to find some portion of the saddle less obtrusive than others, and long lectures from John on matters in general, and women in particular. After eating a hearty dinner of grouse and other good things cooked by Mrs. O'Bryan—God bless her—the world seemed brighter and better. And now that time has healed my bruises; and has dulled the edge of my tutor's somewhat sarcastic hunting advice, I have stored this little hunting trip away in a bright corner of my memory, and as the whirl of events carries it swiftly backward into the misty past, I can meditate with pleasure even of John, and if I ever write of him again I may in kindness dub him with a more euphonious name—perhaps call him Algernon or Percival, or maybe Anthony.

ALBERTA CLAIRE

The Story of Two Girls (By one of them)

from Outdoor Life (March 1916)

We acknowledge we allus was strays at heart;
A-roaming all over the bloomin' chart
An' a-mixin' with herds of a hundred kinds,
The sort that a maverick critter finds.
Wherever we chance to take a stand
They sure pipe us off by our Western brand.

We never met, but thru a mutual acquaintance we heard of each other; and because Gladys Hardy was just starting out to ride horseback from Spokane, Wash., to San Francisco, and I had toured eighteen of the United States on the back of a buckskin cow pony during 1911 and 1912, we were quite naturally interested in each other.

So we each wrote the other a letter, and, strange coincidence of fate, the letters crossed, which apparently sealed the friendship, for such we decided it should be, genuine Western comradeship because we have so much in common.

A love of God's own out-of-doors and of Nature, rugged and rough in the great mountain regions, or stretching out in seemingly never-ending space on the vast plains and deserts, or perhaps gentle and placid in the hills and valleys, but always carrying her lesson of life.

And to me life always seems like climbing the high mountain peaks. There are long, steep slopes, deep, dark cañons with narrow, dangerous trails, level, monotonous mesas. To some the effort to reach the top is heart-breaking, but the crest of success is very sweet and well worth the hard climb.

A horse and a dog are Gladys' companions, as they are mine; we are both filled with a roving restlessness and a desire to see new lands and dip into that most fascinating of all studies—human nature.

When the sordid, prosaic, commonplace side of life begins to draw us into the force of its tide our refuge is the out-of-doors; the call of the wild. I think it must be, for Gladys Hardy says she feels like the dog in Jack London's book when the trail calls to her, and I have long known the irresistible call that sounds thru the voice of the wind in a winter's storm or the gurgling song of a creek in summer.

I've been guilty of smothering many a yawn while the pink tea society discussed Mrs. Dosnfetchit's new bonnet, but like Mr. Chauncey Thomas, whose camp-fire talks are one of my chief delights, I never weary of Mother Nature or wondering about the shooting stars!

Our friendship was still very young when I asked Gladys to describe her appearance—isn't that the woman of it?

She told me she was fair, but at that particular time the sun had burned her face unmercifully and left a blister on her nose, which didn't add to her attractions at all!

And then she added that she wasn't pretty, but she has mailed me a number of pictures at different times and I've decided that last remark was merely modesty.

She gave her height as a little over five feet and her weight in proportion and knowing that the outdoors is a sure prescription for health, also that it teaches us to be practical and self-reliant, it's a safe bet she is all three.

We have both rolled up in a blanket and gone to sleep in the flicker of the camp fire, where the wonderful stillness hemmed us in and only God knew how far away were all other human beings.

So we have come to know and love the vast stretches bounded only by the sunrise and sunset and to absorb a courage such as was born of pioneer stock.

What do I look like? Oh, yes, pardon me, I was sort of forgetting that!

Well, now, I'll just repeat the description given by the cowpuncher from whom I won my bald face pony (by "riding him and staying on"). "She's four feet eleven inches of doggone nerve, fellers, an' she tips the scales at ninety-six pounds—she's got a lot of black hair an' when them brown eyes a her's snap fire (which they do at times!) look out, 'cause she's on the war path.

"She ain't what yuh'd call pretty a-tall, but when yuh know her yuh fergit about that.

"I've knowed her since she was knee-high to a grass-hopper, an' 'fore they sent her to Europe to school she was the dog-gonest, cussingest kid as ever sat on a corral fence."

That's pretty much truth. I might offer some explanation of the last accusation, but I won't; my friends don't need it and my enemies wouldn't believe it, anyway.

Gladys Hardy was born in Divide, Colo., a small town in the Pike's Peak region. I was born in England, in the country made famous by Dickens in his Pickwick Papers, and we have both lived "most everywhere," tho my childhood was spent between a big Western ranch and the ocean liner of which my father was captain.

Mrs. Bertie Lord (Finetta) with coyote she shot near Eagle Rock on East Fork, after 1900. H. W. Bertie Lord, photographer. Bertie Lord Collection, Montana Historical Society, Helena, Montana.

Gladys makes no secret of the fact that she is "old enough to vote" (so she expresses it), but admits she never has, doesn't even know when woman suffrage was granted in the State of Washington, which is now her home, and tho she didn't say it in so many words, the fact glared out at me from between the lines in a most independent manner—she doesn't care, either!

How that will delight the hearts of Englishmen and antis. Yes, indeed, I am proud of the fact that I was able to cast my vote in favor of that splendid specimen of American manhood at present inhabiting the White House at Washington, for we women of Wyoming inherit suffrage, it was granted in 1868.

Then Gladys says her favorite pastime is "loafing," tho she likes to read and sew, and for her favorite occupation she gives "traveling."

Somehow I always designated my world-wide travels as my favorite pastime, and my favorite occupation anything which taxes my mental powers to the utmost, for nothing equals the joy of putting salt on the tail of an idea.

I love to study and to read deep books, but to sew only when necessity commands!

In the matter of dress we meet on the same footing, "neat and plain, with no pretense to show, yet of quality the best our bank rolls will permit."

My question as to her greatest ambition in life received a splendid answer from this happy Outdoor Life Girl, "to do the good I was put here on earth to do." So long as she strives to live up to that ambition her life will never be dark or dreary, for everything we give comes back to us in kind; thus if we give out love and good will those same will return to us.

Even as a little child this love of the out-of-doors held sway in Gladys Hardy's heart; she "played hookey" from school to wander thru the woods alone, preferring Nature's lesson to the others, and the people she has always wanted for her friends are those who know and love Nature.

Gladys prefers men for her friends: she isn't what could be truthfully termed a booster for our sex!

She's a young lady with many admirers and some few broken engagements shining out of the past, which she says were broken because she discovered she "wasn't really in love."

If more girls had the courage of their convictions the divorce courts would undoubtedly have fewer cases.

But Gladys is waiting for her "ideal man," and he must be an outdoor fellow, a regular pal as well as her husband. She has met just one who "almost" reached the ideal standard since she started out in search of adventure, but there's still a chance for the boys who want to qualify.

It was this almost ideal man who supplied her most exciting adventure so far, but that's her own story, which she'll no doubt tell some day for your approval, and when she does you'll quite likely say it was somewhat unconventional, but what did that matter? Mrs. Grundy was some few miles away and the gossips were not there to criticize.

> "Sometimes it seems to me I must
> Just quit the city's din and dust
> And get out where the sky is blue,
> And say, how does it seem to you?"

ERICA FRESQUEZ

Four Points Richer

(2000)

THE NEW DAY IS NO MORE THAN A SMEAR OF GOLD ON THE EASTERN HORI-
zon, the woods eerily silent, when I find my place beneath tall timber
on a frosty north-facing Colorado mountain slope. A stately old ponderosa
giant will be my easy chair for the morning, its trunk my backrest, its two
huge exposed roots like well-muscled arms, reaching out to cradle me.
Though not many women would want to trade places with me just now—
alone in the predawn dark, deep in the woods, on a sub-freezing mid-
November morning—I feel a sweet, familiar peace as I settle in to wait.

My hunting life grew out of a family tradition—or rather, out of my
exclusion from that tradition. My father, a sheep rancher, was the son of
a sheep rancher who was the son of a sheep rancher. Their home was the
Bar-Guitar Ranch in Picacho, New Mexico, a tiny village tucked away in
the Hondo Valley, a place of endless rolling hills creased by the Hondo
River and speckled with sheep and apple trees. The Hondo landscape is
to me a canvas painted with a thousand fond memories of my childhood.
With my mother, Lupie, at his side, my father returned home from the
Navy to run the family ranch and raise a family. I was born in 1962, fifth
of six children.

Five years later, while on duty as a reserve sheriff's deputy, Dad was
stabbed, almost killed and left temporarily incapacitated. The incident
was doubly heartbreaking in that it forced us to relinquish the ranch and
move to nearby Roswell.

Although no longer able to ranch, Dad remained a deer hunter. Venison was the richest part of many meals on our table, accompanied by
refried beans, fresh green chilis, fried potatoes and Momma's famous
hand-rolled tortillas—*ummm!* With elk replacing venison, this remains my
favorite meal to this day.

I always knew when autumn had arrived by the change in seasonal
colors, inside our house as well as out. With the approach of deer season came the annual appearance of Halloween—orange hunting clothes,
retrieved from the closet and scattered around on the furniture. More

poignantly, I recall my two older brothers' special bond with my father at that time, their voices a little more alive, their laughter a little more full and connected.

Since hand-me-downs were a necessity in our family, I waited until I could loosely fit into my brothers' cast-off hunting clothes before inviting myself along. My father's answer was no; in his view, hunting camp was no place for a young girl. "I can scramble a mean egg," I countered desperately. No.

These annual, all-male family hunting camps were a tradition that continued until my father died shortly after suffering an aneurysm on his forty-fifth birthday, in 1978. I was 16. I still needed him. We all did.

The morning light brightens beyond the eastern slope of the little side-hill valley I'm watching, sifting softly down through the aspens and conifers. Gradually, the forest comes alive: Ravens croak, gray jays fuss and scold, pine squirrels ratchet and leap about; a dawn breeze, like the sun yawning, whispers through the trees. Though the forest and understory here are so thick as to limit my vision to no more than fifty yards in any direction, I feel confident in my set-up, since several game trails intersect nearby, all freshly churned with elk tracks and dimpled with pellet droppings. Starting to shiver, I wriggle my fingers and toes in a futile attempt to generate some heat.

What an odd elk year this is! As usual, I've chosen to hunt the last of Colorado's three annual rifle seasons, counting on mid-November snow for tracking and quiet walking. But this year, rather than snow, we have cold, clear mornings and warm, crunchy afternoons. Yesterday was a prime example.

My guide for the day was David Petersen. Among my dearest friends, Dave and his wife Caroline are neighbors as well. Caroline and I have enjoyed grouse hunting and fly fishing together, and Dave and I have teamed up to chase not only elk but mule deer, turkey, pronghorn antelope and small game. With his elk in the freezer since archery season, Dave came armed yesterday with just a backpack and an excuse (me) to get out and about in the wapiti woods again. Dave is a veteran woodsman and a good one, a bonus on any hunt.

Our day started well before dawn as we crept quietly into a mixed conifer and aspen forest on a south-facing slope. Dave had seen "plenty elk" there during the September bow season, and thought it worth checking out. As if we were bowhunting, we moved slowly and deliberately uphill, stopping often to look and listen, trying not to make a sound and doing a pretty good job of it, at least for a while. But as the morning warmed and the night's dew evaporated, we found ourselves shaking our heads in frustration as dry leaves and branches crackled ever louder underfoot—nature's burglar alarms. Yet, with "no sign nowhere," as Dave put it, sitting on stand was useless; we had no choice but to keep moving, scouting more than hunting.

Dave is a funny, quick-witted man and always right-on with helpful hunting hints. During a break, for instance, he pulled what appeared to be a rubber pillow from his pack, unscrewed the cap and took a long drink. Then he smiled, and in a whisper said, "I won't offer you a drink, since I know you have your own water; I've been listening to it sloshing all morning." With that, Dave squeezed the air from his soft plastic bota— allowing the remaining water no room to slosh—replaced the cap, winked and whispered: "I'll get you one for Christmas."

As we crept along, the woods growing ever more dry and noisy, my sloshing water was lost in the racket. Nor did we ever find any elk, which Dave determined had moved to the cooler, moister north-facing slopes, like the one I'm watching right now. What I gained from the experience, reinforced by Dave's advice, was to come here this morning alone, fight my normal urge to walk around, find a good set-up, stay put and . . . "let the elk do all the walking and noisemaking."

A 737 whines high overhead, like some great silver mosquito, dragging its long white tail across an otherwise perfect sky. I greet the disturbance with a crooked smile, aware that next week, like last week, I'll be up there in one of those flying tin cans myself, earning my way in this crazy old world. But for now, I am hunting!

With the single exception of Annie Oakley, all of my outdoor exemplars and mentors have been men.

Following my father's death, I spent my $800 inheritance on a used car in order to return to the Hondo Valley as often as possible, visiting friends and family. In an attempt to recapture the good old days, I volunteered my help to every rancher I knew. I gathered and marked sheep. I rounded-up and branded cattle. I rode fence for my uncle Pete, an all-day job on horseback, which I felt honored to be trusted with alone at such a tender age.

But among all those good Hondo folk, there was one very special friend. His name was Sam Montoya, and he was 69 at the time. Soon, my father's former best friend and mentor became my best friend and mentor. It was Sam who taught me the gentleness required to saddle a spirited horse. He talked of the importance of an education and I learned by his example the joyful value of a warm heart. Sam taught me how to find my way home from the hills, and together, we rode those hills.

And it was Sam who took me on my first hunt.

One evening, after a long day of tending fence and livestock, Sam reached up high on a shelf, pulled down his old binoculars, placed them before me on the kitchen table and announced, "These are for you, Sweet. Next week, we go deer hunting, you and me!"

That same night, I got a crash course in handling and aiming a rifle. When I asked my brother Ralph to show me how to shoot one of Dad's rifles because Sam was taking me hunting, he chose an old Winchester Model 94, an iron-sighted, lever-action 30-30.

Ralph showed me how to center the front sight blade in the rear sight V, cautioning me never to cock the hammer or put my finger on the trigger until I was ready to shoot. After checking the chamber to be certain it was empty and picking a spot on his bedroom wall, the dry-fire practice began. When I brought the rifle naturally to my *left* eye, Ralph only shrugged.

After an excruciating week's wait, the hunt with Sam began. In fact, it was a working hunt, combining ranching with watching for and talking about deer. On the third day of the season, riding fence on horseback with Dad's 30-30 across my lap, a big muley buck jumped up from his bed, providing my first tangy taste of hunter's adrenaline. I leapt from my horse, tossing the reigns over the fence. Aiming quickly but carefully, I took the shot, by now a running shot. Instantly, incredibly, the buck went down.

Sam, who'd been riding 75 yards ahead of me, heard the rifle's crack, spurred his horse and came galloping back in a cloud of dust, a one-man Wild West movie. Sam looked at the deer, then at me, and for a long time said nothing, but only grinned a grin I interpreted as pride. At last he exclaimed, "You did it, Sweet!" grabbing me with both hands and pulling me into a hug.

My 4 × 4 buck was huge in my eyes, and killing him clean, on the run, with just one shot—my first shot ever with a rifle—was beyond good luck. (Please ladies, don't try this at home!) Yet, in Sam's retelling of the event, I became Annie Oakley reincarnate: "The deer," Sam bragged far and wide, "was streaking away fast as a mountain lion, when Erica made a perfect shot—over her shoulder, twisting in the saddle, aiming through a wall of dust churned up by the pounding hooves of her running horse."

Boy! What a word-picture he painted . . . Sam Montoya, my favorite artist.

Eight o'clock. The sun by now is full up. Yet, down here beneath the forest canopy it remains shadowy and cold. Resisting the urge to stand and stretch, I stay motionless, leaning back against my tree, a shivering bundle of heightened senses, hoping the noisy, tattletale squirrel above me isn't giving me away. Waiting, watching, listening . . . and when the squirrel finally shuts up, *hearing.*

But hearing what, exactly? A jay hopping around in a bush? A squirrel galloping through the leaves? Or something bigger, trying to walk quietly? I recall Dave's advice to "weigh" every sound, track its movement, anticipate its approach, be ready. Weigh every sound: This sound, in fact a patterned series of sounds, is coming from uphill to my right. Far too heavy for bird or squirrel. Deer? No, still too heavy and nowhere near dainty enough. Bears walk softly on padded paws and mostly have gone to den by now. That leaves only . . .

Again come the hard, heavy footfalls, but this time from my left. Whatever it is, there are two of them. Oh boy, here we go! I struggle to control my breathing, but with little luck. I can feel my heart pulsing through my entire body. The sounds continue: two big animals, coming closer, merging from opposite directions and likely to meet right in my lap!

Swimming hard against a flood of adrenaline, I bring my .30/06 to my shoulder, slip my left index finger into the trigger guard, flick off the safety and peek out around the 3× scope. With an either-sex tag in my pocket, the season half gone and my mouth watering for char-broiled elk steak, I don't intend to be picky.

Oh my God! Here *he* comes, closing fast from starboard . . . one, two, three, four points to the side and legal. Isn't it the way with hunting? You wait and wait, and then, it all happens so fast. I center the cross-hairs just behind the bull's left foreleg—at only 20 yards, he more than fills the scope—and squeeze. The rifle roars and pounds my shoulder, its echoes tumbling like bowling balls down the mountain.

Confident of my shot, I look up and wait for the bull to fall—but he doesn't fall! Rather, he brakes to a sudden stop and looks directly at me. As I bolt another round into the chamber he makes a sharp left turn and starts back up the hill he just came down. Refusing to believe I could have missed, I nonetheless bring my rifle up for another shot, find the bull in the scope—and, before I can squeeze the trigger, see him collapse. The great beast's stomach swells and falls with one last breath, then all is still.

I glance at my watch: 8:06 A.M.

After waiting a full minute, ready to shoot again if necessary, I click on the safety of my bull-barreled Model 700 Remington, open the bolt, place the dear old cannon gently on the ground, stand and go to the bull. My beautiful wapiti! Kneeling at his side, I stroke the rich black hair of his neck mane, oddly soft, like rabbit fur. His nose also is amazingly soft, feeling pleasantly warm against my chilled fingers as I hear myself saying, "Thank you . . . thank you."

Suddenly, my vision goes all blurry. What have I done? And why? The answer, as if spoken by somebody else, comes right back: If "necessity" is defined as something you cannot do without, then hunting is for me a necessity, tears and all.

Drying my eyes, I reach for my sheath knife and begin the hard bloody work of converting animal to meat, joyfully accepting my hunter's responsibility to my prey, and to myself. More than anything right now, I want to share this moment with David. I miss my father a lot, especially at moments like this, sitting here alone beside this great bull elk. I imagine his smile and how proud he would be—even though he always maintained that hunting was "not for girls"; well, with the deaths of loved ones, we are free to recreate them as we wish! I would love to have hunted with my father, even just once, and can't escape the disappointment that it never happened. Yet, I am blessed to have a friend like Dave, who has given me a place under his wing and admission to his very private world. I hang on gratefully.

The morning is middle-aged by the time the field dressing is finished and I've hiked down the hill and driven home, hoping to find someone to help me pack out my elk. As luck would have it, Dave is in town, so Caroline and I leave him a note and are about to head back up the mountain on our own when we run into Koby, a bowhunting, fire-fighting neighbor. Together, the three of us head back up the mountain to my prize.

Young and strong, Koby could probably pack a whole elk out in one trip. But before I can put that fanciful hypothesis to the test, Dave shows up, bringing a big hug of congratulations and a packframe. A few minutes later, I proudly lead my helpers down the mountain: Between Dave, Caroline, Koby and me, we get the whole animal out in less than two trips—meat, hide, head and "horns."

Next day, at home, out on the deck, while preparing my bull for a European (skull) mount, another airliner glints and roars high overhead, reminding me that tomorrow I must return to the jet-set reality of my workaday life. But thanks to a few good friends and a certain young bull, I'm forever four points richer . . . and already planning next year's hunt.

Some folks, women as well as men, have called it fanaticism, this passion of mine for the hunt. Others, echoing my father, have suggested that hunting is "unladylike." I just call it love. And just like love, it isn't always easy.

Time passed quickly following my father's death, and before I knew it I'd grown up, reluctantly trading horses for jumbo jets, swapping my chaps and spurs for a flight attendant's uniform. Even so, I returned to the Hondo Valley often, continuing to learn about life—including especially hunting and fishing—from my old friend Sam Montoya. In the spring of 1994, after 84 years on this Earth, Sam passed on. He was a true, old-time cowboy, among the last of a dying breed. More, he was my friend, my hero.

Today, my home is a cozy cabin beside a sparkling creek in a little mountain valley near a trout-filled river. The local scenery is enhanced by deep snow in winter, wildflowers spring and summer, golden autumn leaves and wildlife all year round. On warm afternoons I sit outside in the shade of cottonwoods, conifers and quaking aspens. Occasionally, a red-tailed hawk or bald eagle wings overhead. I am independent. I am happy.

But there's a price for everything, and mine is long commutes to work, endless hours in crowded airports and too many nights spent alone in hotel rooms, far from my beloved Rockies. When I first moved to Colorado, my challenge was to find someone to hook up with who shared my passion for horses, hunting, fishing and the outdoors in general. As it turned out, finding someone was easy. The hard part was being taken seriously. It was almost like being a child all over again, trying to get my father to take me hunting. Once again, I found myself being reminded that I am a "girl," trespassing onto traditional male turf.

My first Colorado elk-hunting mentor was a crusty mountain man character named Boyce. Boyce took one look at me (5' 2" and 115 pounds) and through a puff of cigarette smoke predicted, "You won't make it through your first winter up here." As if I were some frail deer! But looking back on it now, I don't recall being offended, only determined to prove him wrong. Soon enough, Boyce relented, showing me where and how to hunt elk— his way, at least, which is mostly from horseback.

Although I never came off the mountain with my own animal while hunting with Boyce—he was always quicker on the draw than me and gave no quarter—I learned many valuable lessons about wilderness survival, elk hunting, field dressing and loading meat for horse-packing down steep mountain trails. Though we had little else in common, elk, horses and wilderness bonded our friendship.

A little later, I met Tommy, another "she won't last" mountain man. The very first morning that Tommy guided me out to hunt elk, without Boyce there to shoot before I could, I took my first wapiti. A spike bull he was, and I killed him at 150 yards.

After that, I continued to hunt elk, though with the basics of where and how under my belt, I went out mostly alone and mostly without success, until I met "Roadkill Dave" Petersen.

My best friend, Karen Kebler, and I had just spent a week hunting deer near her home in Washington state, followed by an equally meatless week of chasing elk in Colorado. On Karen's last night here, I got a call from a neighbor who'd just killed a deer that had darted in front of her car. She'd tried calling Dave, knowing his insatiable appetite for roadkill, but he was in New Mexico hunting Coues deer. So she called me. The fork-horn buck was head-hit, its body undamaged, and Karen and I were thrilled to go out in the dark and cold rain to rescue the meat.

When David, a notoriously reclusive neighbor, heard about our midnight meat run, he stopped by to introduce himself and offer congratulations. His very first words to me were, "I heard about your roadkill save, and I'm *impressed!*" Before the conversation ended, Dave had offered to introduce me to camo hunting for wild turkey.

April finally arrived, and off we went to the spring turkey woods, which were also wintering grounds for local elk and deer. New to close-in, call-in hunting, I quickly became hooked on the wild turkey chase, which Dave calls "great training for bowhunting bugling bulls in rut." Better yet, a new friendship was developing, this one based on mutual respect, gender be damned, and bound by a shared love of all things wild and free.

And too, as a woman, a new "fashion statement" was evolving for me. As a rifle hunter, my field wardrobe consists of ugly orange, which I wear because I have to, not because I want to. But put me in camo and turn me loose in the woods, and I feel like I *belong* out there. This duality, between the mandated orange of a rifle big game hunter and the voluntary camo of a turkey hunter, strikes me as a metaphor for my double lives as prim flight attendant and gnarly mountain chick; one is a uniform, the other is me. Unlike humans, wild animals could care less about your sex, your weight, whether you wear earrings or the length of your hair. They only complain (by running away) when you make too much noise, walk the skyline or get upwind of them.

Being a woman who hunts, though challenging in many ways, especially at the beginning, has proven to be one of the most fulfilling aspects of my life. Today, I'm a capable and ethical hunter, fisher and "outdoorsman," with boundless enthusiasm for what I do and a solid understanding of why I do it.

And so, to my mentors—Annie Oakley and all the boys—to the four-legged others who lurk amongst the silent shadows of our natural world and, especially, to my fellow outdoors women . . . to you one and all, I tip my camo cap and wag my ponytail in camaraderie.

On Men and Hunting Alone

(2002)

IDIDN'T REALIZE HE WAS WATCHING ME. HE FIDDLED WITH HIS GEAR AS HE stood 100 yards away at the bed of his pick-up. I pulled my recurve bow from the truck and slipped on my glove and arm guard. As I swung my daypack over my shoulder, I hoped this other lone hunter wasn't hunting the same creek bottom. I had found fresh elk sign that morning, too late to ambush them. If I could set-up before the small herd rose from their beds . . . I sneaked a glance at the other hunter as I locked my truck. Good, he was headed into the national forest away from my new honey-hole.

I hiked out of the woods in the dark. I had smelled elk. I had seen elk. I was within 45 yards—too far for me with my bow. A shift in the evening breezes had exposed me to the vigilant herd cow. Camo clothing and stealth couldn't hide me from her nose. Maybe in the morning I would have another chance.

The full moon glinted off my truck's windshield, a welcome sight after climbing out of a Colorado mountain canyon. The other hunter was throwing his daypack in the truck bed. I ignored him. I didn't feel like a conversation. He blurted out, "I'm so glad you're back and OK. A woman out there alone, in the dark, well . . . you know." I just looked at him. I didn't know, but my aching legs and sore feet urged me to forego arguing with someone I wouldn't change. Still, I wondered what he thought gave him a survival edge. His pack was slack in its emptiness. The edge wasn't there. Mine bulged with water, extra clothes, snacks, first aid gear and other elements of the Ten Essentials. He must have something that enabled him to survive a couple nights in the woods, but he sure didn't carry it in his pack.

A combination store, gas station and post office marked the edge of civilization down in the valley. This one building, a self-contained mountain town, was a popular hunter pit stop. Hunters could buy the necessary snacks, hunting licenses, coffee and gas. A gregarious storeowner, who doubled as a meat cutter in the fall, ran the enterprise.

One day, bored and craving both chocolate and the sound of another human voice, I drove down to the store. The owner struck up a conversation with me. I let it slip that I was alone. On my next trip to the store, the owner said that he had asked every hunter who crossed his threshold if he had seen me. He apparently thought this would keep me safe. I was dumbfounded. My anger rose like the mercury in Death Valley. How dare he patronize me like a stupid child! How dare he broadcast to strangers that I was camping alone! Did he extend the same concern to an older gentleman from Minnesota who was also hunting alone? He righteously defended his parental attitudes. I stomped out. No more of my money ended up in his till.

I had been a solitary hunter for almost a decade. A boyfriend introduced me to bowhunting when I was in my late twenties. The boyfriend was no longer in my life, but bowhunting was. I saw no reason to give up one passion simply because another had died.

I've always loved September in the Rockies and I will always love bowhunting for elk. September is the swing month, ushering in fall. I love the feel, the sights and sounds of the changing season. The nights' coolness lingers late into the morning. Waning daylight spurs the aspens to turn gold. Lusty bugles of bull elk reverberate in the canyons. September helps me shed the incessant emotional demands of workaday life like an out-of-season, worn overcoat. In my work life, I've always taken care of everyone else. Camping and hunting alone reaffirmed my ability to take care of me—and only me. The feel of September and its bowhunting tradition, more than any other time, rejuvenates my soul.

A lone woman hunter has few choices of hunting buddies. Sister hunters spend their seasons with husbands and boyfriends. Married men bring too many complications, not to mention the ire of nonhunting spouses left at home.

Many male hunters have assessed my outdoor skills as deficient based only on my gender. They have predicted I will die tragically and alone in the woods. I refused to surround myself with men who believed so steadfastly in my incompetence.

Life is uncertain. Each September might be my last; I would not squander a single season on gloomy people who don't pull their own weight—or won't let me pull mine. Long ago, I had buried my hopes of finding a hunting partner who respected my competence. I vacillated in my peace with my compromise depending on whether I needed to be alone or I yearned to share my experiences with another hunter. Elk season was often tainted with loneliness as the second week stretched ahead of me with little human contact.

At the end of one morning's hunt while trudging past another camp, a simple hello turned into a conversation, followed by an invitation to lunch. Common passions can bridge differences if we let them. The two guys, Mike and Ed, were recurve shooters, too. We discussed our equipment and shared frustrations in getting within bow range of an elk.

As I approached their camp the next day, I heard Mike shout, "It's lunchtime and guess who just showed up?" Instead of my usual embarrassment, I just laughed. He was teasing me about panhandling, but I sensed it was devoid of malice or hidden agendas.

The next couple of days we planned daily hunts based on the elk sign we had seen. They didn't question my observations; I didn't have anything to defend. Lunch invitations turned into community dinners. We shared our hunting tales, which evolved into life stories as the hours passed. Both men lived in Ohio, although Ed was a West Virginia boy by birth. He managed operations at a waste management plant. Mike was trained as an engineer. He belied the nerdy, socially inept stereotype by telling engineer jokes well. They had met through an archery club. Both hunted hard and were equally satisfied with a buck or a doe, a cow, spike or bull.

Instead of bragging about the huge racks adorning his walls, Mike decried bowhunters who seemed unable to distinguish a stationary paper target from a flesh and blood animal. He sadly shook his head, as he recounted how one hunter could not fathom his perfectly aimed 80-yard shot going bad. The arrow flew fast, but the caribou still had time to take a step before the arrow hit its now-misplaced mark.

Ethics and a sense of humor, what an intriguing combination. I began to notice a nagging emptiness when Mike wasn't around.

One day I made a quick 4-hour round trip home to check on my garden and pay bills. I didn't get back to camp until Mike and Ed had gone out for the evening hunt. I left a note on their truck and drove down the road a half-mile farther before heading into the woods.

When I got back to my truck in the dark, I expected them to be waiting for me, but their truck was gone. What does this mean? I wondered. Were they mad at me? How could they be? I didn't see them all day. My concern for Mike's feelings toward me resonated a little deeper than I wanted to admit to myself.

I drove up to their camp. Mike was hanging up his camo clothes to air out on a clothesline. Ed had already started heating up dinner. I hesitantly approached Mike. He gave me an enthusiastic hug.

"Did you get my note?" I asked. It was the only way I knew to broach the subject of "why didn't you wait for me?" He grinned down at me. "Oh, yeah. Eddie wanted to wait for you, but I figured you would come up when you got back. If you weren't here by the time we were done eating, we'd come looking for you."

I stared at him. What kind of response is that from someone who says he cares about me? The big grin told me he did care, even if he didn't see why his dinner should be late on my account. Stunned and confused, I let him lead me to the table.

The next morning, Mike and I still-hunted opposite sides of a wooded ravine. I stared across at the camo-clad figure squatting to gauge the age of elk scat. In an "aha!" moment, I understood. Mike had given me exactly what I wanted. I wasn't a cute, harmless woman playing at men's games— I was another hunter, a hunter he respected for her skills even if she was a woman. He trusted my competence and treasured my independence as much as I did. And, I knew that he would look for me—all night if necessary—if I hadn't shown up by the time he had finished eating. I knew what I wanted from a hunting partner, but I didn't recognize something I'd never seen before.

September elk hunting still rejuvenates my spirit, but it's no longer tainted with loneliness. It is a season I share with my hunting partner and my husband, the man who trusted me to come out of the dark woods alone.

PART NINE

Death

IN HIS CLASSIC ESSAY, "THINKING LIKE A MOUNTAIN," ALDO LEOPOLD recounted how, having brought about the deaths of many animals over the years, his view on the place of death in the ecological scheme of things was ineluctably altered by one, very particular, death at his hands:

> In those days we had never heard of passing up the chance to kill a wolf. In a second we were pumping lead into the pack, but with more excitement than accuracy: how to aim a steep downhill shot is always confusing. When our rifles were empty, the old wolf was down, and a pup was dragging a leg into impassable slide-rocks.
>
> We reached the old wolf in time to watch a fierce green fire dying in her eyes. I realized then, and have known ever since, that there was something new to me in those eyes—something known only to her and to the mountain. I was young then, and full of trigger-itch; I thought that because fewer wolves meant more deer, that no wolves would mean hunters' paradise. But after seeing the green fire die, I sensed that neither the wolf nor the mountain agreed with such a view.[1]

Leopold went on to develop his idea of the "land ethic." Hunters like him, before and since, have similarly felt impelled to make moral sense of their lost innocence about the consequences of killing. All of the writers in this section share profoundly ethical concerns about the deaths they cause: about their necessity, their appropriateness, their place in the complex scheme of things.

All of these deaths are hard. They should be. Sometimes the world needs to break your heart.

They're Easy to Kill

(1997)

IBET I CAN JUMP FROM ROCK TO ROCK AND BRANCH TO BRANCH, CLEAR UP to the next corner without even touching the ground," eight-year-old Frankie said.

"So what. Anyone can do that," replied tomboy Julie.

I couldn't. I was not a tomboy and was scared of jumping from rocks or anything more than an inch above the ground.

"I bet I can run faster than you and beat you to that tree," Frankie yelled as he tore off running in that direction.

Julie, who was twelve years old, raced ahead and beat him.

I ran, but quit halfway because they were already there.

"That's no fair," I argued. "No one said, 'go.'"

We walked deeper into the canyon. Three explorers, equipped with the necessary walking sticks, plastic bread bag filled with lunch, and appropriate adventure attitudes.

"I'm hungry," I chirped, because I'd made lunch and wanted to eat it.

"Wait until we get to a side canyon."

Today's exploration centered around discovering side canyons, our term for washed-out gullies that wound from the hills behind our house to an immense canyon south of where we lived. We had named this immensity Spring Canyon for the spring that ran through it.

"There's a side canyon," I declared. "Let's eat."

"No, let's wait until after we explore it, then we'll eat our lunch where it comes to an end," Julie-the-leader commanded. Side canyons ended where they met the hills, some in abrupt cliffs, some sloping. Paradise Canyon, one of our favorites, mounted the hills in rock steps surrounded by beautiful red leaves we later discovered to be poison ivy.

We had stumbled into Paradise Canyon once—just once—and had never been able to find the mystical, moss-walled wonder again. Of course, we had found it from its ending, in the hills, and ended at its beginning, where it intersected Spring Canyon. To find it again, we should approach it in the same way—backwards.

This new side canyon was definitely not Paradise. Its walls towered twenty feet above us, seven or eight feet apart. As the walls tapered, we could see fifteen feet of sky.

We named all side canyons, as well as hills, rocks, and animals on our ranch. Cimmaron Hill was christened for a favorite television show; Pirate's Hill for a Hardy Boys book; Castle Hill because it looked like it should have a castle; and Dinosaur Rock because it looked like the head of a dinosaur. These were our playgrounds, and name-giving was an essential part of our life, an adventure, a ceremony.

"What shall we call it?" I asked.

"Let's call it Moss Canyon," suggested Frankie. "There's lots of moss on the walls."

"No," Julie said, scowling. "That's stupid. There's moss on all the canyon walls." She paused. "I like the name Rock Canyon."

"Let's go in farther," I replied. "Maybe we'll get some better ideas."

So on we went, the three sibling explorers, with Julie in the lead since she was the oldest and the least scared.

Noonday darkness closed in below overhead trees, the cold, damp walls encased us with eerie trepidation. The canyon narrowed, the walls got steeper.

"What if we see a snake?" I asked.

"We'll kill it," said Frankie.

"No sir," retorted Julie. "It might bite us, then we'd die."

"We'll run," I said.

"What if we see a porcupine?" Frankie said.

"We'll kill it," Julie said.

I thought of a conversation with our father earlier that week. We'd heard over the news of a man lost in the mountains who survived because he was able to kill and eat a porcupine.

"Why a porcupine?" we had asked, thinking his choice was foolish. After all, there were deer and elk and fish in the mountains, weren't there?

"They're easy to kill," Daddy explained. "A porcupine is easier to kill than any other wild animal. They are slow. You just have to knock them in the head."

"We'll kill it," Frankie repeated. His eyes sparkled, an adventurer thinking of the hunt, the glory of killing a beast, the power of man over animal, the wit of the hunter over the instinct and strength of the hunted.

The essence of all our explorations was to discover nature, to discover the power we had over nature's friends. Of course, we hunted only in our minds. But anticipation made us smile.

"Look!" screamed Julie. "We've found one!"

I gazed past her finger and saw it. The pudgy, horrible beast, the enemy of our pilgrimage, the easily killed porcupine.

We approached slowly, not knowing what to expect.

"Don't get too close," cautioned our leader. "This is a dangerous animal."

"They can throw their quills," I whined recalling a tale.

"Get your weapons," cried Julie. "We have to knock him over the head."

"They're easy to kill," said Frankie. "One thump and they're dead."

"Let's get out of here," I timidly trembled. "We'll get hurt."

"Not if we get him first," yelled Julie, throwing down the bread bag. She paused as the porcupine humped up to expose his quills and lifted his tail for defense. We didn't know how powerful his "sword," the tail, could be. We only knew that he was outnumbered and an easy victim.

We three explorers shouted and whacked the vicious animal with our walking sticks.

"Kill him!" became the battle cry.

"Kill him!"

Thump.

"Come on. Kill him!"

Whack.

"He's not dying!" I cried as the porcupine waddled quickly away.

"He's getting our lunch!" screamed Frankie. The bread bag was in the beast's path.

"Get him before he ruins it!" shouted Julie. She jumped ahead to save our lunch, since none of us had an appetite for porcupine, demanding, "Come on, help me!"

"I'm scared," I confessed. "He's supposed to be dead by now."

"His quills will hurt us," Frankie chimed, wide-eyed.

"But he's bleeding!" Julie screamed. "We've wounded him." Dread settled over the three explorers. No self-respecting hunter let an animal suffer; we had to finish the job we started.

Frankie and I joined in the rhythmical beating again. Whack.

Thump. "Oh, he's not dying."

We stepped back and looked at the leader, eyes imploring.

"Flip him over. He's getting away!" she said in a quiet but unmistakably frantic voice. Frankie helped while I retreated and fought back tears. Julie didn't try to hide hers as she beat the face of the porcupine with her stick.

Bash. I was close enough to hear the dull thud of his flesh receiving the blows.

Thump. I saw blood spurt from his nose as she hit him in the face.

"Oh, he's not dying," she sobbed.

"Daddy said they're easy to kill."

"Maybe you have to be strong to do it," Frank intoned.

"I don't know, but he's not dying," Julie moaned.

But then it was over. The porcupine stopped making his small whimpering noises. We continued making ours.

Meekly, we stood around him and watched the blood ooze out of his nose and from between his broken teeth. The small eyes which had blinked with every blow now stood open, glazed and accusing. After a few moments of silent graveside reverence, we were compelled to move.

We explorers had discovered the feeling of wastefulness, of taking a life that was not ours to take. But nature took something from us. No longer were we innocent.

At the mouth of the canyon we paused, looking back. "Let's call it Porcupine Canyon," I suggested.

LINDA HASSELSTROM

Reckoning the Cost of a Dead Steer

from Feels Like Far: A Rancher's Life on the Great Plains *(1999)*

I've OPENED ALL THE WINDOWS ON THE SECOND FLOOR OF THE HOUSE TO let the wind blow through, too hot for May and carrying car exhaust so thick I can almost see it. Out in the street, brakes squeal and an angry male voice yells, "Where did you learn to drive, lady?"

Sitting at my computer, I grin, wondering if the woman learned where I did—in pastures with no traffic lights, no competing cars, no drivers with cell phones at their ears yelling at her. My father started teaching me to drive when I was nine, letting me steer the pickup while he pitched hay off the back. I practiced in the hayfields and pastures as we worked. At that time, a South Dakota resident could get a driving license at fourteen, so in the spring of 1956, my father began reviewing driving rules as we drove, creating challenges to prepare me for the risks of driving on the highway. I failed a quiz on brakes just before my fourteenth birthday.

My father told me to drive him to the summer pasture. At the second gate, I couldn't find the brake pedal. I forgot about turning off the ignition and stomped on the gas pedal. All the while he sat utterly still. The gate wire sang as the pickup lurched through it. Then the top wire popped and the broken end ricocheted off the windshield like a bullet. He didn't duck.

He kept silent while he helped me untangle the wire from the front bumper. From the back of the truck, he took the wire stretcher, a little coil of new wire, and the fencing tools. Then he got in the driver's seat and said, "I'll be back when I finish checking the cows." I stared after the pickup as it disappeared over a low rise a mile off. Its speed never slackened. The sound of the motor drained into a breeze.

By then, I'd ridden my horse alone through the same pastures for five years, but I turned in a circle, staring as if I'd landed on a distant planet. Five miles west, near the faint blue line of the Black Hills, lay a highway and the ranch house where my mother was washing clothes, unaware that my father had abandoned me.

On the east the fence crossed a plowed field to disappear toward jagged pink Badlands peaks sixty miles away. The summer pasture was eight miles away, so even if the cattle were all right, he wouldn't be back for two hours.

My eyes were wet, but my mouth was dry. He hadn't left the water jug, but a dipper hung from a windmill a half mile away. At least I wouldn't die of thirst.

I sighed and said to a meadowlark singing on a post, "Tore hell out of that gate." I wasn't allowed to swear around my folks.

When my father came back, the gate stood tight and strong. I hadn't been more scared than I could handle. After the job was done, I'd walked to the tank for a drink and washed tear tracks from my dusty face. Now I leaned against the gate post, chewing nonchalantly on a piece of grass. Silently, my father slid to the passenger side, and I drove back to the ranch.

> *The shell is America's most active contribution to the formation of character. A tough hide. Grow it early.*
> —Anais Nin, *The Diary of Anais Nin*

The summer I turned fourteen, I developed into a tangle of hormones and growing muscles. Even my body was rebelling against my mother's plans for a delicate, ladylike daughter. I was already taller than she, and my feet had been larger since I was ten years old. Adulthood was so close I could inhale its musky perfume and dream of running my fingers through its hair. My father often reminded me that in his youth, both men and women were considered adults at ten or twelve years of age, but he still called me Child instead of using my name.

My birthday was in the middle of haying season, so we were all usually too busy to have a party. On every normal summer day, after breakfast at six, I mowed and raked hay while my father stacked. About mid-morning, we stopped in the field. Father drank coffee while I drank water and checked the bolts on my mower and rake. With a grease gun, I squeezed lubricant into zerks, nipple-like grease fittings leading to moving joints. Mother worked in the garden during the cooler mornings and brought lunch to the field around one o'clock. After she left, we lay down in the shade of a stack, heads on our jackets. Sometimes we napped until two. We quit work at dark, about nine, and ate cold sliced beef and salad for supper.

I loved the muscles growing on my skinny arms as I worked and sweated, sang songs, and felt myself growing up. The blood crooning through my body promised adventure. I loved my tractor, the danger and rhythm of the work. Daydreaming about a wonderful adulthood, I slid my hands over my body and imagined how good I'd be at adult stuff, like sex.

On the morning of my fourteenth birthday, Mother made a little speech about what a milestone this was: I was becoming a woman. "I think you ought to quit early and relax a little before supper. And we'll have birthday cake and ice cream for dessert." My father nodded without committing himself, but I hoped we'd shut off the tractors at seven. "Chocolate cake, please," I reminded her. Father made his annual promise that on the next rainy day—when we couldn't cut hay or work cattle—we could do anything I wanted. I always chose to go to the Black Hills. I loved walking on pine needles in dim, quiet aisles between the trees. I loved listening to singing streams, picking new wildflowers to identify. The trip was always such a joyous contrast to the ranch, where the only water lay in muddy stock dams, the ground was cracked and dry and the wildflowers tended to be prickly.

After supper and pink angel food cake from a mix, Mother brought out her presents, work socks and shirts in colors I didn't like. "They were on sale," she said. We sat at the dining room table while I unwrapped everything, trying to be grateful. Father tapped his fingers on the oilcloth while Mother refolded the wrapping paper, some of it printed with Christmas trees and snowmen, or pink bunnies. "This paper is older than you are, dear," she said.

When Father put the paper in the high cupboard for her, he opened the one next to it, where he kept an old .22 rifle. I expected him to get down a new horse blanket because my old one was worn so small it barely covered the horse's back. Instead, he brought out a gift I hadn't dared to hope for: a .22 rifle.

"Now, I bought this box of shells," he said, handing it to me with his tight little smile, "but from now on you buy your own, out of your allowance."

"Oh, you bet," I breathed. "Can we go over to the prairie dog town and try her out?" I knew even then that guns and other lethal weapons are always called "her," although I didn't know why.

"Right now?" he said, glancing at my mother. "I guess it's still light enough." Mother frowned and said, "Don't shoot yourself in the eye."

We went. Father helped me load it the first time with .22 long rifle bullets, saying I should never use anything else. He told me to put it down before I climbed through a fence and to leave an empty chamber, only that didn't apply to this rifle because it was a pump. As I jacked a new shell into the firing chamber, the old one was automatically ejected, fast and smooth. That first night I got five prairie dogs with eight shots.

My father shook his head and said he couldn't have done any better. All he ever used his rifle for was shooting skunks that got into the chicken house, or knocking off stray tomcats in the spring. Some guinea hens took up residence at our place once, and their squawking every morning drove him out with the gun, but it took him a long time to kill the last of them.

After that, I saved my money and bought a used scabbard to buckle onto my saddle and took the .22 with me everywhere. When Mother pursed her lips, Father shook his head at her. After I cut the prairie dog population, I shot three cottontail rabbits one day. Mother made me skin them and said the new rule was that I eat anything I shot.

My father approved. I got pretty good at skinning rabbits until I counted thirty in the freezer and realized I was sick of rabbit stew. I considered bringing Mother a prairie dog, but when I picked it up, forty fleas ran up my arm. I stopped shooting everything I saw.

But I still carried the rifle when I went riding and sometimes shot at posts or old pieces of wood just to improve my aim. I got very, very good, but because I was an only child and seldom saw the neighbor kids, no one else knew. I daydreamed about making impossible shots to save my father from a rattlesnake bite or my mother from a drunken burglar.

That winter, just before Christmas, my parents decided that I was old enough to stay alone for a few days while they took a short trip. They left me lists of instructions about the cattle, phone numbers to call if I needed help, notes about watering the plants. By the time they drove away, I had stopped listening to their directions, so they leaned out the car windows to repeat the important things: Don't use the rifle. Don't ride the horse. Don't drive on the highway.

"And if it snows, darling," my mother said, "Call your Uncle Harold to come do the chores. I don't want you to freeze to death." She always worried about things that wouldn't happen. I never mentioned the real dangers, like getting kicked while I was feeding.

That morning, I did the regular chores: scattered grain for the chickens, pitched hay to the milk cow and my horse, and grained the bunch of steers we'd sell next spring. I really enjoyed feeding things. The chickens clucked when I came and let me scratch their backs. The steers ate pieces of cattle cake out of my hands, wrapping their long tongues around my fingers to suck up the sweet blocks without biting. As long as I moved slowly and talked quietly, they stayed close, licking my pant legs, nibbling at my pockets, their big brown eyes making them look like astonished children.

I took my time doing chores, thinking that if the folks had forgotten anything, they'd be back within an hour. Carefully, I examined the steers, because it was the right time of year for waterbelly.

Minerals that plug the urinary canal of a steer—a castrated male—cause waterbelly. My father explained it to me in high-flown language, but I heard the vet use simpler terms. A waterbelly steer can't pee. If he's not treated, his bladder fills and breaks, and his own urine poisons him. If the condition is caught in time, the vet digs into the flesh of his haunch below his anus, finds the urinary tube, pulls it outside the hide and sews it down. Because the urine drains at the rear, vets call it "turning him into a heifer." The operation might save the steer's life, but he won't bring as much at the sale ring. To prevent waterbelly, we fed the steers salt, so they would drink enough water to wash the minerals out of their system.

I walked slowly around each steer studying the shape of his belly and watching for any that were switching their tails more than usual.

When I was sure my folks weren't coming back, I dug through the tractor repair manuals in my dad's shop until I found a magazine with pictures of naked women. I studied it awhile, catching up on fine points of anatomy. Then I gathered up the notes my folks had left all over the house and sat at the kitchen table to read them. They hadn't left much room for initiative. One of Mother's said, "Clean your room," and when I saw Father's list headed, "Things to do if you run out of things to do," I knew why he'd been chuckling to himself after dinner the night before: "Shovel manure out of the barn. Clean the chicken house."

For four days, I sang while I did the chores and still had time to study and clean my room. I shoveled out the chicken house, then dug out the old nesting material and replaced it with fresh straw, something neither of them had thought to mention. I considered breaking a rule by inviting some friends over, but a two-day blizzard saved me from temptation. I shoveled new paths to the garage, the chicken house, and the barn every morning.

Late in the afternoon of the sixth day, feeding the steers in the evening, I realized I was one short, the one that always licked my hip pockets until I fed him a piece of cake. I plodded over the only hill in the pasture and found him lying in the corner of the corral, switching his tail like the director of a marching band. His eyes were dull. I kicked him in the flank to get him up, but he just stared at me. "Damn. Hell. Jesus Christ. Crap," I yelled. He struggled to his feet.

His belly hung almost to the ground, grotesquely swollen. His bladder had burst. For all practical purposes, he was a dead steer, but he might walk around for days.

I went back to the house to fix supper and think. The job was simple, just like the day Father threw the fencing tools on the ground before he disappeared over the horizon. A vet wouldn't save the steer, only bill us for seventy-five dollars. My folks were due back in a few days, and the steer might still be alive then, but he'd suffer. If my dad were here, he'd "put the poor critter out of his misery." But I wasn't supposed to shoot the rifle.

All evening I picked up books, read a little and threw them down, wishing I'd found the steer sooner. The livestock paper beside my father's chair announced that nine-hundred-pound Hereford steers were cheap that year, selling for $20.10 per hundred pounds. He was worth nearly two hundred dollars. That meant my allowance for four years if I had to pay for him.

In the morning, I managed to cook two eggs without breaking the yolks, then did chores in the usual order: fed and watered the chickens, milked the cow, fed the horse. I dumped buckets of grain in the feed bunks without looking at the steers, then counted them. One short.

Over the hill, he was lying in the same spot, head down. His breathing was irregular. I swore at him until he moved ahead of me down the hill and into a corral. Too large for what I had to do, it was the only pen with a gate wide enough for the pickup. I'd need to back up close.

In the house, I loaded my .22. I had only ten bullets. Back in the corral, the steer stood, tail switching, his belly dragging in the snow. I leaned across the top rail of the fence, inhaled, and sighted on his left eye. I'd never shot anything larger than a rabbit but imagined the principle was to hit a vital spot. I always hit prairie dogs in the eye.

The first shot sounded like the wet slap the dishrag made when I swatted a fly. The steer shook his head and bellered. I jacked in another shell and pulled the trigger. Missed.

Faster, because he was shaking his head and bawling, I fired again, into his neck.

He swung his head and started to trot and I kept aiming and firing. Blood was trickling out of his eye, nose, and neck. He was trotting, staggering around the corral, bawling and bumping into posts on his blind side.

I waited until he turned toward me, sighted on his chest and fired three times before I heard a click: out of bullets.

The steer's left eye was only a pulpy hole in his skull. He ran and stumbled, spraying blood. I was crying hard, blinded. My hands shook as I groped in my pockets. No bullets.

I stumbled to the house and found an old box of .22 short rifle bullets in my father's gun cupboard. He told me shooting anything but .22 longs might ruin my rifle. I never thought of using his rifle.

"I don't have any choice," I sobbed as if someone cared. "I just don't have any choice." I fumbled with the shells, hoping the steer would be dead before I got back.

He was standing on the far side of the corral, turning his head, trying to see everything out of one good eye, trying to be ready to charge whatever was hurting him, smash it with his heavy head. But he couldn't see anything to chase.

Agitated by the blood smell, the other steers were pushing at the fence, roaring and pawing dirt. As I walked toward the corral, the steer bawled and turned his eye toward me. This time I had to get close since the .22 shorts had less power. I opened the gate and pulled it shut without fastening it, in case I needed to get out fast.

The steer was facing me, but I didn't want to shoot him in the forehead, where the skull was thicker. I waved, and he jumped sideways, looking toward the other steers. I pumped three bullets into his ear as fast as I could. He stood moaning, and then his knees buckled.

Kneeling in the snow, he stared straight ahead but wouldn't fall. He groaned hoarsely, continuously. The other steers screamed and ran back and forth by the fence, snuffling and blowing.

I sighted on the spot behind the shoulder where his heart was and stepped forward. One step. Two. Three. Four. The rifle muzzle nearly touched his shoulder, and still the steer didn't move. Bloody froth bubbled out of his nostrils.

I fired. Again. Again. I could hardly work the lever action. The shells were fouling the gun, maybe ruining my beautiful rifle.

Again. Again. The steer moaned and coughed blood on the snow. When he toppled, his head struck my foot. Blood poured out of his side and around my boots. His good eye grew dull, like a lead marble. He sighed and was still. Heat from his body warmed my face, manure pooled under his tail.

I knelt in the blood, put my face against his neck, and sobbed until I was dry inside, swearing to the steer that I'd never be so clumsy again.

The memory of shooting the steer still unnerves me, but beside it rises another memory. On a winter day a couple of years ago, my father and I went to the barn to load cattle cake for feeding and found dozens of fifty-pound paper sacks of cattle cubes ripped open. Thousands of cubes, easily a hundred dollars' worth of winter feed, were scattered and covered with excrement and urine.

"Badger's work," said my father grimly. "Might as well shovel it into the garbage. A cow won't eat that junk."

"I'll put it on my garden," I said. "Good mulch. But I don't think a badger made this mess." A badger is powerful enough—a twenty-five-pound badger no bigger than a beagle is stocky and bowlegged as a weight-lifter. But I didn't believe the destruction fit a badger's tidy habits. After we fed the cows, my father got a hammer and a few old boards and went around the barn trying to cover holes while I shoveled the ruined cake into a wheelbarrow and dumped it on my garden plot.

The next morning, another dozen sacks were ruined. "I think it's hopeless," my father said. "A badger could tear that barn down if he wanted in." I still disagreed, but I kept my mouth shut. That night I crept to the barn at midnight with my .22 rifle. When I snapped on the flashlight and opened the door of the feed storage room, a huge raccoon turned to face me. I fired twice and waited until the body stopped twitching, then went back to bed. In the morning, I dragged the corpse outside just as my father arrived. "What happened?"

"I shot a coon last night. But she's a nursing female. She probably has a dozen kits stashed in here somewhere."

"I hope they starve to death," he growled. "At least she won't be feeding them cake every night."

I returned to the barn with the rifle about midnight. This time when I shone the light inside, three tiny goggle-eyed faces turned toward me—baby raccoons. One by one, they put their paws over their eyes. I groaned, but shot them anyway. Having learned to scavenge, to forage destructively in human storage areas, they would never go back to hunting their own natural nourishment. In the same way, learning how to kill more efficiently had seasoned me, and I could never erase the knowledge.

JEAN KEEZER-CLAYTON

The Last Coyote Hunt

(1996)

I curled the barbed
wire in a loose spiral,
threading it down
the coyote burrow
until I hit pay dirt.

The barbs held
in the critter's fur
and I pulled, slow
and steady. Took
about ten minutes
to yank her out.
She whipped her head from side
to side, fighting
hard against the
wire, all the while
digging it deeper
into her sides
until the blood
puddled thick,
red on the ground.
Been pulling coyotes
twenty years without
thinking about
the sorry critters.

This morning, though,
I though about that she-
coyote—and bankers,
wires and mortgages.

Grabbed the wire-
cutters and vet salve.
Doctored that stupid
coyote an hour or more,
watched her crawl back
in her hole when
I let her go.

ASTRID BERGMAN SUCKSDORFF

Beloved Enemy and The Big Drive

from Tiger in Sight *(1970)*

BELOVED ENEMY

The tiger is the king of all jungles, the most beautiful beast on earth.

I have enormous respect and regard for the tiger. He is the most beautiful living creature that I know. With his strength and power and sinuousness he gives fresh dimensions to beauty. He is a perfect living being, a sovereign animal.

But I can kill the most beautiful creature that I know—because I happen to be on the side of the human race, to whom the tiger can be a terrible enemy. I have come upon a little dead boy, mauled by a tiger, out in the jungle. I have come to a village high up in the mountains where the very air was sorrow and where I met a mother whose grief at the loss of her only son burnt memories in my heart. I have stood in a clearing by a river bed and looked into an old man's face, streaming with tears, while vultures sailed in flocks above two buffaloes killed by tigers.

"What can you do now, Seile? Seile, they are dead, my beasts—they were all that I had, all. Now I have nothing. . . ."

The helpless face of the herdsboy, the tear-stained face of the mother and the old man are the reasons why I must kill tigers, and this is the way I shall always feel, for these faces are always with me. They can never turn pale or fade away at the sight of a tiger, however incredibly beautiful, however sovereign he may be as a beast, as a living creature.

THE BIG DRIVE

On the fifteenth of February there was excitement in the air. Today the District Commissioner accompanied by other high officials was passing through Narainpur on his way to Sonpur to a vast meeting. Thousands of Murias and mountain Márias would be assembled there, and the District Commissioner would distribute salt and clothes and give a "good will talk" to the natives—telling them how much nicer it would be if the women covered their breasts, how absolutely childish bead ornaments were, how the greatest happiness for children was to go to school, and that they ought to stop eating larvae and red ants. This sort of thing is known as social uplift, or the benevolent advance of civilization.

I had made up my mind to drive to Sonpur and photograph the spectacle. But my plans were completely overthrown.

The District Commissioner was very late. Thanks to this I was still there to receive the important news that "our man-eater" had killed the buffalo we had tethered beside the water hole in the river beyond Bengal. The tiger had dragged the buffalo away, which was just what we wanted it to do—we had tethered it with rather weak rope.

Now we had to act quickly; the drive must be held today. We drove to Gahr Bengal, where two of the men went down to look for tracks while the rest of us drove around to all the villages in the neighborhood to announce that the great tiger drive was about to be held, and that all the men were to come as quickly as possible with axes and bows and arrows and drums and hunting horns. Quickly, quickly!

The tracking showed that the tiger had dragged the buffalo a good three hundred yards, across the river bed close to the water hole and on into dense jungle. After that it had gone back to drink and now, presumably it was lying in the densest part of the jungle, perhaps no more than five hundred yards away.

Meantime, about a hundred and forty men had assembled. The area in which the tiger appeared to be was very suitable for a drive. To the south and west it bordered on open rice fields; to the north the jungle thinned out somewhat and gave way to little open glades. There were three of us marksmen. The first was to take his place on the machan just at the edge of the river bed, where the tiger's tracks were often to be seen in the sand. To the east lay the high mountains where the tiger had carried the dead boy. But between the mountains and the area of the drive ran the main road in a straight stretch almost five hundred yards long. Here two machans were swiftly erected at intervals of about a hundred yards.

The next thing was to place the beaters quickly and silently in a semicircle starting from the west. The drive was to work straight toward the road and the mountains, drawing together more and more, working the tiger as it were out of a sack, the opening of which gave onto our three machans.

Almost the most important part of a drive is the "stoppers." Fifteen men were to be placed up in the trees along each side of the mouth of the sack, close together so that if the tiger tried to slip out to the sides they would be there to turn it inward and forward again by a light cough or, if necessary, by clapping their hands. It is often thanks to the correct placing of stoppers that tigers have been shot in drives and not simply "run out" to the sides. The forester of Narainpur himself positioned all thirty stoppers and also gave strict orders to the beaters to maintain the proper distances from each other, so as to leave no open gaps behind.

We were all agreed that it was a cunning, vicious tiger, but we were almost sure we had it in the "sack."

Would the sack hold? I was on the middle machan. I could just see the next marksman farther down, and on the road at the corner of the "trap" where the southern rice field began, stood our green jeep, in which sat Arvind Shah.

Now the beaters were beginning to shriek and hoot. They struck their axes against the trees and blew their horns; two fiery trumpeters led the way at the outer edges. But how close they seemed! Were they on the wrong side of the tiger? Was the tiger really inside this area?

Strange—not a single wild cock or peacock, not even any monkeys came out onto the road. The trap seemed dead. No, come to think of it, that was probably good—I remembered now the police commissioner's account of a tiger drive: no deer, no birds had come out. Any more or less enclosed area in which a tiger is at large is normally empty of deer and other wild animals. This was actually a good sign. Only one solitary green parrot came flying past me.

A terrible roaring—I almost flew off the machan. In a flash I released the back cock of the quick-firer and held the gun to my cheek.

"Keep calm, Astrid, keep calm," I said to myself.

The roaring came from somewhere in front of me and to the right, where the first marksman waited.

I could follow the exact moments of the tiger from the howls of the beaters which, after that first roar, had risen to a surging crescendo, a continuous howl without beginning or end. Now he was straight in front of me but deep in the jungle; now he roared again, an eerie, blood-chilling sound like rumbling thunder, which was answered by howling men. Now he was down at the jeep end—would he break out over the road in spite of everything? No, in the end he must have turned. Back to the center again.

Now his roar came deadened—he must be down in the dense bamboo thicket beside the water hole. I could hear distinctly how the chain of beaters grew closer around the tiger. A man shrieked in terror. Had the tiger wounded someone?

A wary, vicious man-eater in a sack with walls of men. Would the walls hold? Would the tiger break straight out through the chain?

Without my being aware of it the barrel of my gun had followed the tiger's every movement. Now he was rushing in the direction of my shooting companion to the left. I squinted in that direction—he had his double-barreled rifle to his shoulder. Oh, if he would only fire! But no, the tiger turned and now, now he was coming in my direction. . . . I could see him for the first time—he was working along behind some bushes in an oblique line for the road, barely a hundred yards away. He stood still in a blind position—almost completely covered—listening to the cautious clapping of the stoppers to the right.

I expected him to move on toward the road. But he did not. He turned and trotted obliquely back to break out across the road on the left-hand side instead. Now his shoulder was free—broadside! I pulled the trigger. The tiger crumpled up—fell on his side. He did not stir. I knew that the tiger lying there, seventy or eighty yards away, would never rise again.

Quickly, too quickly, I tried to reload so as to be ready with a second shot in case. But the cartridge jammed. Even so, I felt sure enough to give a whoop of triumph, which was repeated by the nearest marksman, followed by:

"Fire another shot!"

"Can't," I yelled back.

Keeping one eye on the tiger, I managed in the end to get another cartridge in, took aim and fired another shot into my first tiger, lying there on the ground.

I shouted out that the tiger was dead. All the beaters and stoppers came running up rejoicing from every direction. I climbed down from the tree with my rifle, and we all stopped a little way from the tiger. Before going up, we threw some stones at it. But there was not a trace of life: The man-eater was dead!

He had a fine skin with unusually strong black stripes. He was no record in length—the forester measure him at nine feet, two inches—but he was big and broad.

The father of the tiger's forty-third and last victim, the little boy, was just bending over him looking at his nasty jaws. But not even his solemn face could dampen everyone's joy; it broke out everywhere. Many were the heroes of the hunt.

"I turned the tiger back twice," shouted Arvind Shah proudly. "He tried to break out beside the jeep, but I hooted as hard as I could, and he turned back!"

As for old Tangru Shikari of Koseranda, one of the stoppers, the tiger had rushed straight at him, roaring, trying to break out. But Tangru had roared back, he had, and the confused tiger had actually turned. Tangru, with delight, showed us time after time how he had roared as hard as he could.

For several minutes the tiger had lain crouched down in a deep, narrow ravine. The men had tried to "shriek" him out but in vain. Then they all started throwing stones and clods of earth down into the hollow, and with a roar the tiger rushed out. The fact that none of the beaters was injured in this dangerous and exciting drive seemed to me a miracle.

The forester had almost had a fit when he saw the tiger suddenly hurl itself at one of the beaters, who climbed up the nearest tree, quick as a monkey. The tiger had leaped after him, and the two great forepaws closed together only a few inches beneath him.

Yes, each link in the chain had equal glory in the man-eater's death. It had been a perfect, dramatic piece of teamwork.

All the men who were able to get near enough helped drag the heavy tiger's carcass out to the jeep and hoist it up onto the roof rack.

Then we drove home in triumph, followed through Narainpur by crowds of happy people running after the jeep.

All that evening, until long after dark, people came in a steady stream to look at the dead man-eater. There must have been six or seven hundred of them. I was given a garland of fiery-red hibiscus flowers, and a frail old woman brought me a coconut.

I was tired and hungry. Tea and something to eat were all that I wanted.

Before I crawled under the mosquito net to sleep I sent a telegram home to my father. It read:

FIRST MAN-EATING TIGER SHOT GREETINGS ASTRID.

MARY ZEISS STANGE

In the Snow Queen's Palace

(1996)

The walls of the palace were formed of drifted snow, and the windows and doors of the cutting winds. There were more than a hundred rooms in it, all as if they had been formed with snow blown together. The largest of them extended for several miles; they were all lighted up by the vivid light of the aurora, and they were so large and empty, so icy-cold and glittering! There were no amusements here . . . no pleasant games. . . . Empty, vast and cold were the halls of the Snow Queen.
—Hans Christian Andersen, "The Snow Queen"

The ancient Norsemen called her Skadi, "the Dark One," Goddess of Winter and Mother of the North. Only she could love the tundra expanse where, in her element, she danced snowstorms into being. Huge, furry white hounds pulling her ice-crystal sled across the drifted plains and through snow-canopied forests, Skadi aimed her icicle arrows with skill and precision. Huntswoman extraordinaire, she chose her quarry carefully, with an eye to the tender young ones. One chilling shot to the heart was all it took to make them hers forever.

Yet the Norse did not regard Skadi with fear or loathing, awesome as her power was in its glacial finality. No doubt they recognized that some darkness is the inevitable cost of human existence—as inevitable, indeed, as the blizzards of northern winters, as certain as death itself.

It takes a southern imagination, one trained in the seasonless sameness of the Mediterranean, to concoct a heaven of sweetness and light, an unnatural realm where death has no dominion. And so, early Christian missionaries turned Skadi, the benevolent rescuer of those too young or too weak to suffer the rigors of winter, into the malevolent Snow Queen. It was she, they said, who tempted children away from home, captivated them, turned their tender little hearts to ice.

The stuff of fairly tales, you say? Twentieth-century rationality would have it so. Yet a primal imagination still flickers in the heart of the modern-day hunter. There is wisdom in the ancient legend of the winter goddess. It

318

is a wisdom born of hunting in northern climes, where extremities shape experience, where nothing comes easily except, perhaps, the exhalation of a last breath.

The winter of 1985–86 brought record-breaking cold to the Northern Plains. Beginning early in November, an unremitting flow of arctic air swept down from Alberta into the Dakotas and eastern Montana, bringing early snow cover and daily high temperatures around ten below zero, when the sun was shining. At night the thermometer regularly plunged to thirty, forty, fifty below. On still days, the air itself felt frozen. When the wind blew, the congealed air shattered into myriad invisible particles, minuscule projectiles that pierced through layers of clothing and found their way through the tiniest cracks.

Skadi's arrows, a settler from an earlier time might have mused. The first Europeans who tried to make a living off this land were, after all, well-acquainted with the ways of the Snow Queen. Winters are typically harsh in this country. Today, long-abandoned homesteads dot the countryside, bearing mute testimony to the cold, dark, and often despairing wintertimes their inhabitants must have endured.

This landscape is scarcely more forgiving now than a century ago. Driving the gravel highway in the southeastern corner of Montana, one passes a reminder of the tenuousness of living in these parts. Before a cluster of now-vacant buildings that once formed a settlement with town hall, school, and post office hangs a large and carefully crafted wooden sign. It reads simply, "Albion: 1914–1964." Had Albion's demise had something to do with the winters here?

So I would have believed in November 1985, though the extreme chill of that season seemed oddly appropriate to me. My mother had died horribly the preceding spring after a long struggle with cancer. In the fall my thirteen-year-old cat also developed cancer; I'd had him put to sleep in October. I was overworked and underpaid, doing a one-year stint teaching English at a state college in western South Dakota. My husband, Doug, meanwhile, was between teaching jobs and frustrated about it. We were as near to a subsistence economy as we had ever been, or hope to be again, living close to the bone. Hunting had never been mere sport to me, but in these circumstances it took on a special urgency, not only because we needed the meat (we hunted for that every year), but because it leant some degree of normalcy, or sanity, to a world otherwise gone askew.

So the weather, brutal as it was, could not keep us indoors as the end of deer season drew near. It may have been a matter of not giving in when the conventional wisdom would have been to settle down by a cozy fire with a brandy and a good book. But the wisdom of hunters is in any case unconventional. Better to risk frostbite and endure what could only promise to be, in physical terms, an utterly miserable experience than to let deer season slip by for a year. With subzero temperatures the day-to-day norm, it seemed more reasonable to be out braving the same elements as the deer than to be shut up, unnaturally, indoors. There has to be, between hunter and hunted, more than a fair-weather kinship.

On the day before Thanksgiving we set out for a spot not far from Albion, some public land along the Little Missouri River where we had frequently seen mule deer in the trees hugging the shallow river bank. We drove, mostly in silence, in the pre-dawn darkness, our breath frosting the windshield. As we neared our destination, the day gradually came on, sunrise in the form of a soft shimmering light through the crystalline air. It would be an overcast day, and bitingly cold.

We were hunting antlerless deer, having both filled our "A-tags" earlier in the season. Since this was a hunt for meat, and since safety dictated limiting our outdoor exposure, this outing had a no-nonsense feel about it. Doug brought the pickup to a stop and cut the ignition. Staring ahead through the windshield, on which our suffused breath was laying a fresh veneer of frost, he sighed after a moment or two, "Come on, let's get this over with." Roused from the fairly comfortable reverie into which I'd slipped in the relative warmth of the cab, I reluctantly opened my door and, though I had known it was coming, was nonetheless stunned by the assault of numbing cold on my face.

As daylight increased, so did the wind. We would need to walk a broad arc across wide-open pastureland to get downwind of the deer we felt reasonably sure would be lingering along the creek that feeds the river there. Even with the wind at our backs, the cold was excruciating. Doug remarked that he thought the tears in his eyes must be freezing; my eyelids too, scraped when I blinked. Breathing was difficult, virtually impossible when facing into the wind. The sun, a translucent disk, was retreating into the frigid sky. Snow would be falling before long.

After several hundred yards of crunching through ice-encrusted grass, we sprinted along a fenceline toward the creek bed. Skidding down an embankment where the fence dipped toward the creek bottom, we were suddenly brought up short by what lay ahead: a little fawn, curled as if asleep, snugly nestled in the snow drifted against a fencepost. The tiny deer was frozen solid. It might have died days, or mere hours, ago. Doug knelt and stroked the fawn affectionately, as one might a cat or dog found napping by the woodstove. We kept a few moments' quiet vigil: A little death like this could not go unmarked, unmourned. Then we continued down toward the creek.

It was a relief to descend into a prairie cut, between the sheltering walls of the creek. Ordinarily, one of us would have walked the meandering creek bottom while the other walked the rim, on the alert for deer jumping ahead. But today was a day to err on the side of prudence, so we stayed together, the wind whirling overhead.

With miles of uninterrupted rangeland extending east and west of the Little Missouri, this waterway is a major deer-run, providing not only shelter, but also an escape route from danger. Yet there were surprisingly few tracks or other deer-sign here. We worked our way slowly, quietly, along. I became aware that, aside from the dead fawn, a couple of shivering magpies were the only wildlife I had seen.

At one point, where the creek doubles back on itself, there is a small grove of ash and poplar. Rounding a curve in the creek, we came within sight of this stand of thicker cover, and there we spotted four deer—a small buck, a rather large doe, and two fawns. They knew we were there, scarcely a hundred yards off, but they remained motionless, looking in our direction. We continued to weave cautiously through the creek bed toward them. When we were within fifty yards of them, we eased our way up the bank and into the open. Still, the deer stood as if frozen in space and time.

Stressed to the limits of endurance by so much cold so early in winter, the deer were conserving every bit of energy they could. This helped account for the absence of deer-sign in the creek; this little group probably never strayed from these trees if they could possibly avoid it.

We stopped perhaps twenty-five yards from them. The deer began edging away, clearly reluctant to expend the precious energy they would need to flee. They were, in effect, trapped by their instinct to survive. In such a situation, shooting was impossible. We stood as motionless as the deer. Then, exchanging a quick glance and a wordless nod, we turned away and tracked across the snowswept pasture in their full view, without looking back.

Circling back to the creek bed, we followed a different branch now. It was midmorning, and our own energy reserves were ebbing. Taking a shortcut back to our pickup, we started across a stubble-field toward the fenceline we had walked along earlier. Almost immediately, we spotted some deer at the far end of the field, several hundred yards off. No more than indistinct shapes, they appeared and disappeared, phantoms in the now thinly falling snow. With the wind in our favor, and the snow as much camouflage for us as for them, we proceeded along the fence until we were perhaps two hundred yards away. Steadying my .30/06 on a fencepost, I focused the scope on a doe, another doe, a fawn, another fawn.

Teeth chattering and my right hand burning with cold (I had to remove my deerskin mitten to shoot), I thought quickly about the fawn we had seen curled peacefully in the snow, about those deer paralyzed for sheer survival in the trees. "I'm taking the one farthest to the left," I whispered to Doug, who was also aiming his rifle. I placed the crosshairs for a heart shot, and fired. His shot came an instant later.

We had killed the two fawns.

from *Second Sight*

(1997)

On one thing at least, Valley and Gabe agree. Neither of them is a slave to fashion.

"I got these at the Salvation Army," Valley says, lifting both feet off the floor and holding her legs out straight in front of her to show off her black Mary Janes. "They're perfectly good. I hope they never wear out." Gabe never sees her wear any other shoes, though often Valley goes barefoot or wears slippers or borrows Gabe's dress boots.

The way their freedom from fashion plays out is entirely different though, Gabe dressing simply, for comfort and convenience, Valley not so much dressing as costuming. She has a collection of dramatic scarves and costume jewelry, vintage dresses and Eastern saris, but sometimes she puts on an old cotton housedress and still manages to look stylish.

Her secret, Gabe decides, is her willingness to exaggerate. If she wears a housedress, then she braids her hair and pins it in a peasant crown or adds a cotton babushka. Her look for after-bath is overdone frumpy. Until she dries and powders her feet, she keeps them wrapped in hideous multi-colored crocheted booties she got at a church bazaar. She wears a flowered cotton wrapper with hot pink rhinestone-centered plastic buttons, and pads around the kitchen, fixing herself tea, arranging crackers in a circle on a saucer.

She bathes frequently and likes to read in the tub by candlelight before she comes out to finish reading a chapter with Gabe at the kitchen table. Often she will read aloud some particularly important passage from one of her self-help books, as she does this afternoon. Already it's nearly dusk. She'd been complaining of feeling low. The days are so short, the nighttime so lonely, and now she has the antidote.

"You must envision your success now, just as you have always envisioned your doom in the past. Let go of those images that portray you as defeated, unsuccessful, disheartened. Paint yourself powerful now, see yourself move with complete confidence, addressing friends in wisdom and with assurance. Breathe deeply as you create this inner vision now."

Valley shuts her eyes then, taking a deep breath. The steam rises up out of the teapot's spout like a genie. She is no longer a girl in an old lady's cotton wrapper and slipper socks. She is a seer, a woman of mystical powers.

When she opens her eyes, she looks annoyed to find Gabe studying her, as if it were unthinkable that Gabe hasn't also shut her eyes, and has missed this moment. She breaks a single cracker in half. "You are so resistant to new ideas, Gabe. I worry about you."

She gets up, still nibbling and clearly irritated, though Gabe also sees embarrassment. Frowning, Valley undoes her hair and goes to fetch her comb. She sits down again, smoothing every tangle until her mane lies flat as a wide, shiny ribbon down her back.

She says, "You look like a lumberjack sitting there, do you know that."

She is trying to hurt Gabe's feelings. The girl gets up and walks past the kitchen window next to the door. Just outside is where Valley has been routinely dumping the parings and vegetable scraps from their meals. Gabe believes this a poor practice, but the first time Valley set out carrot peelings, something in the way she moved as she opened the door overtook Gabe—a memory of her mother doing this very thing, her one winter here. Her mother with the full mouth, the tense laugh, fighting with Pa about this one thing, frightening them all because she was usually not so fierce.

So Gabe has let Valley go ahead with her ill-placed charity, because other memories, or the possibility of them, still shimmer occasionally in some gesture Valley makes. Especially when she is quiet, Gabe thinks, wanting to soothe the girl, not particularly taking in the connection she's made.

There's a lot of activity out by the parings, and Gabe motions to Valley to come nearer the window. Their red squirrel, its tail flicking with a life of its own, is sitting upright on a branch of the maple tree, above the pile of scraps. A crow, wings spread wide, bumps down with a caw, makes a sharp jab with its beak, and, grabbing up a carrot end, flies off. But it's a field mouse Gabe wanted Valley to see.

It has come skittering across the clearing on important mouse business to find a hole under some tree roots where it disappeared. Through all of this, the squirrel keeps lookout on its haunches, holding food in its tiny, handlike paws, nibbling at a furious pace. Suddenly it drops down on all fours, tail jerking up in alarm. Gabe looks down, close to the glass, trying to see what's up, and sees a slim outline, a weasel, by the corner post of the porch. The thing must be starving because usually they hunt by night.

The weasel pauses a moment, then bounds across to the tree root, arching and extending, like a high-speed inchworm. It slips down the

mouse hole and then, very quickly, reappears with the mouse entrepre-
neur in its jaws.

Valley makes a small sound of discomfort as the weasel sits up with
the mouse dangling from its mouth, then, with prize still held high, disap-
pears with the same undulating hop. Valley looks stricken. "Poor mouse,"
is all she manages, her voice higher than usual. Her expression says she
has witnessed the death of a mouse martyr. "Why did I have to see that?"
she asks plaintively. "Was that why you called me over to the window? To
see *that?*"

"No. I didn't know that would happen. How could I? Honestly,
though, it's bound to happen. If you put food out and attract animals, why
then naturally you attract their predators, too, Valley. That weasel would
have to be stupid not to take advantage of a setup like that. I tried to tell
you it might not be a good idea to put out the garbage. You don't know
what you might get. It could be wolverine next time."

Valley only continues to look as if she's been dealt a blow.

"Look, don't feel bad. There must be a million mice out there. If it
weren't for weasels, we'd be overrun with mice. As it is, I have to trap
them in here by the dozens."

"Oh, you *trap* them? Don't you ever let me see that! I mean it, I
couldn't stand it, I couldn't *stand* it—oh, just the thought!" She puts her
hand over her mouth, looking sick.

"Valley. You can't spare every mouse in the world. I mean, we are talking about a little mouse here."

"Shut up. That doesn't help. That doesn't help. I am sick of your always
telling me stuff like that."

Gabe puts her hands up in surrender. "Okay, okay."

"I don't care what you say, I don't ever want to see that again. The
next time that weasel comes around, I am going to smash him flat with
the shovel, I am just going to smash him so he never does that again!" Valley says this with such venom Gabe has to look closer at the girl's face.
The mystical woman of spiritual power has her jaw set, her teeth on edge,
and the look in her eye might cloud the heavens, striking infidels dead
with a thunderbolt.

"Hello? This is Gabrielle. Who is it you're looking for, please?" She knows
that someone is on the line, but no one answers. "Valley, is that *you?*"

A click, then the line buzzes again.

"Very strange," she says, hanging up the phone. "Don't ask me why,
but I think it *was* for me."

"Well, the call earlier certainly was. I didn't want to alarm you, but
frankly she sounded beside herself. I had a hard time understanding what
she wanted exactly. She just wanted you very badly, I think."

"Oh," Gabe says, feeling her stomach turn over. "You know, I'm a little worried. I think I have to go home . . . my sister-in-law. Will you explain it to Professor Orbach for me? I'm scheduled to give my presentation tomorrow, but I'll have to reschedule. You can make him understand, can't you?"

"Sure," Jeannie says. "I'd do the same myself. . . ."

It is a good three and half hour dive back to Lake Nekoagon. Gabrielle diverts herself with memories of Valley that would explain the phone call—if it was Valley who called—she can't know that for sure.

Valley could get panicky over practically anything. She imagined her arteries clogging up just from breathing the steamy smoke from fried bacon. Swimming scared her to death. She was always frightened of finding a successful mousetrap, insisting that Gabe put them in out-of-the-way places where she couldn't possibly discover them.

The first month Valley had been at the cabin, they'd had a terrible scene over the buck Gabe had shot. She had needed the venison to get by for the winter, what with her not working except at Shub's. But what a commotion.

They'd had a second snowstorm, not long after Thansgiving, and were stuck again in the cabin together, both of them tense, feeling each other out. On impulse, when Valley was upstairs moving furniture around again, Gabrielle had decided to take care of the buck, a week earlier than would have been ideal for aging the venison, just so she could have something physical to do, to divert herself.

"I'm going outside," she'd called to Valley, not waiting to see if the girl had heard her or not. Gabe cleared the snow out in front from under the porch, so she could swing the door open to get to the cooler where she'd hung the buck. Her father had the room well set up for butchering—a table saw, a chopping block, another table for wrapping the meat in paper.

She would take the buck down, but first she had to skin him. Inwardly she addressed the deer, remembering the way her father had. A dozen times she had watched him stripping skin from muscle, murmuring instructions in a tone that was close as he ever got to worshipful. His deft hands had moved quickly, and she tried her best to do the same, as if sparing the buck.

"A lesson to us in purpose," she addressed him, guiding the knife with her finger close to the point, pulling, cutting. Shub used to say that like all good things, the deer's gifts were difficult to claim, only right to expect it to be hard.

Gabe stopped to sharpen her knife on the whetstone he had used and looked for the saw she needed to take off the buck's rack. She had decided to nail the antlers to the porch eaves overhead, where her father had put each of his. They were up there in a long row, a set of antlers for each of the years he'd hunted here, except the really big ones he'd had mounted for Boone and Crockett.

She went outside and nailed her six points into place, then stood back, studying them in context, comparing them with others for symmetry, not so much for size. Satisfied, she walked back down to the cooler, keeping the doors wide open so the light was better, and began to scrape the hide clean of meat and fat, and afterward, to salt the skin down, rolling it tight, fur side out. Her plan was to take the cape to Belle Nichols, who bought them if they were in good shape.

She was nearly done with the hide when she heard a small gasp and looked up to see Valley near the doorway. The girl was staring at the head of the deer, scalped of its antlers, which Gabe had propped upright against the open door, and at the four handsome hoofed feet which she had cut off and propped next to it, planning to have Belle convert these to a gun rack for Shub for Christmas.

The knife lay on the table next to her, the weight of the carcass swinging behind her. Still crouched over the hide, following Valley's gaze, Gabrielle looked at her handiwork with new eyes. In the winter's dimness, with a single bare lightbulb hanging next to the carcass, it was grisly, this stickum of blood, the blue-white of fresh-cut bone. The body was too red, its ribbons of muscles and ligaments shining and sheathed in a pearl-surfaced membrane—dreadful, what lies at the bottom of motion and power.

"What are you doing?" This was almost whispered, as if Valley were afraid to affront the demon corpse. But no, Gabe saw it then. She must have grown horns and a trident-tipped tail herself, *she* was the demon Valley saw.

"How can you?" she said next, and turned on her heel, going back up the hill to the kitchen porch where she came from, leaving Gabe blinking, trying to come up with an answer she could live with. She decided not to bother and picked up the salt to resume her sprinkling.

Valley came storming down to the door again, her face blotchy and red from crying, her mouth a puffy torn edge. She wore her ridiculous wool cloak and was carrying a garbage bag filled with her things. She attempted to say something but couldn't speak, then shot Gabe one resentful glance and stomped back up in the direction of her car.

Gabrielle heard the tinny roar of the VW's engine starting. She heaved a forced sigh and picked up her knife. Little idiot. How far did she think she would get on these roads? Let her go then, if she thought she could get anywhere. She heard the Beetle getting stuck, its tires whining and screaming, forward, backward, forward, backward. The car door slammed shut and Valley came stomping back into view again. "Where's the shovel?" she demanded.

"Over here, I used it earlier," Gabe motioned to the corner and went back to rolling the deer hide.

Valley grabbed the shovel and marched off again, calling, "I'll bring it back, don't you worry." Gabe didn't look up, but she had noticed Valley had her Mary Janes back on, along with the wool socks Gabe had loaned her.

A fury of chopping and slicing, the stinging sound of metal shovel on snow floated back to Gabe. She was trying to stop listening to the racket of Valley digging out the VW. The girl would never get out to the road, and even if she did, the lake road probably wouldn't be plowed for a good while yet. Gabe began wrapping cuts of meat in freezer paper, putting the packages in plastic bags.

More shrieking of tires and the painful sound of motor pushed too hard. More slamming and shoveling and, from time to time, words—Valley exclaiming, swearing possibly—though it was the tone Gabe made out, not the language. After awhile, she was certain the girl was crying again.

Eventually Gabe didn't hear anything, too engrossed in the work she was doing. When she was finished, there was only bone left of the deer, and even this would go into the freezer for soup stock, nothing wasted. She carted armloads of freezer-wrapped meat up the slope to take inside. Coming around to the kitchen porch, she could see Valley's car was still running. She realized then that the sound of struggle had been quiet for some time.

Gabe put her tools away and in several trips carried the meat to the room off the porch where the freezer chest sat next to a squat water heater. Then she took a single slender leg bone and walked to the nearest young beech tree, placing it as high as she could reach, in the crotch. This was something she had seen her father do, a goodluck charm he'd learned from his Koyukon friend.

Curious because Valley's car remained still, Gabe walked over to the driveway and approached the vehicle. Her shovel was buried in a mound of snow next to the car, the whole area ripped and spattered with ice and dirt. The car's windows were steamed up and clouds of white exhaust swirled at Gabe's feet and rose in spirals. Through a haze, she could see Valley sitting in the driver's seat.

She tried the door and when it caught on something, remembered it was wired shut, from the inside this time. She went to the opposite side of the car, yanked open the door and stooped over to look inside.

Valley didn't acknowledge her. She was hugging herself and rocking, staring at the dashboard and rocking, rocking. She had finished with her weeping, face streaked and blotchy from it. Her upper lip was swollen, its edges blurred and only a little darker red than her nose.

"Valley?"

The girl didn't answer. She kept on rocking.

Gabrielle used a harsher tone. "Valley, stop this and come inside. You'll be frozen again."

It was then that Valley looked at Gabe without turning her head. She looked with her eyes only, her eyes impotent and filled with sadness that spoke of broken things, a life filled with broken things that could not be fixed.

"Come inside now," said Gabrielle. "Come on."

Valley turned off the engine and lifted herself up over the gearshift. Gabe steered her by the arm, carrying her garbage bag. They walked back up the driveway and the porch stairs, past the crime of bloody bones. They went to sit in the living room where the couch faced the row of windows that looked out on a sky that was almost clear by now and blue, the color of indifference, its brilliance too vast.

Valley began rocking again, a tiny motion at first. There was something about it that cried out and, without thinking, Gabe put her arms around Valley and joined in the movement. Back and forth, back and forth, all the comfort they could find, this movement on and on, give and take, life and death, back and forth.

PART TEN

Body, Soul, and the Hunt's Afterlife

I N AN EARLY ESSAY CALLED "A THEORY OF THE VALUE OF HUNTING," environmental philosopher Paul Shepard mused about the cultural role that
hunting can, and should, play:

> What does the hunt actually do for the hunter? It confirms his
> continuity with the dynamic life of animal populations, his role in
> the complicated cycle of elements . . . and in the patterns of the
> flow of energy. Aldo Leopold postulated a "split rail value" for
> hunting, a reinactment of past conditions when our contact with
> the natural environment and the virtues of this contact were less
> obscured by the conditions of modern urban life. . . . Regardless
> of technological advance, man remains part of and dependent
> upon nature. The necessity of signifying and recognizing this
> relationship remains. The hunter is our agent of awareness.[1]

What the experience of the hunt means not only for the hunter, but also
for the broader culture, is the central focus of these final four selections.
Artist Sandra Dal Poggetto connects her evolution as a hunter to her
development as a painter. Page Lambert, herself a nonhunter, discovers
unfamiliarly primal instincts within herself, as she strives to articulate
the meaning of their father's hunting to her two young children. Geneen
Haugen explores her awakening as a hunter in light of her Buddhist belief
and practice. And Paulina Brandreth brings it all back to those "trails of
enchantment" that unerringly lead her and her fellow and sister hunters
home, to nature and its bounty and richness, and to themselves.

SANDRA DAL POGGETTO

Duccio in the Eye of the Hunt

(1996)

FOR MILLENNIA, PAINTING AND HUNTING HAVE BEEN AMONG THE MOST fundamental expressions of human culture, yet today their relevance is seriously being questioned in this time of radical technological change. In our modern world, one might ask why I, or anyone, would choose to be a painter of landscape—and a hunter.

To answer that question, I must begin in the manzanita groves where I played as a girl. Manzanita, chamisa and oak surrounded my home. The mild Mediterranean climate of the coastal California hills invited outdoor play, and I accepted the invitation with pleasure. Often I saw blacktail deer tracks in the powdered soil, or jackrabbits, and heard the call of quail during the quiet morning and evening hours. The smooth, taut skin of the manzanita I caressed. I pinched and ran my nails down the slender, flexible chamisa branch so that I could hold the stubby needles in my palm.

Within the concentrations of chamisa were a network of animal tunnels aglow with a diffused light. Through these I would crawl until I came to the wide trunk of a live oak whose coarse, gray limbs I would climb and, through the deep green of small, waxy leaves, look out over the valley. The slopes of chaparral, I knew, were shaped by fire, and the valley below was favored with river water. At times the voice of my mother would filter through the air, telling me it was time for my piano lesson, my ballet lesson, Mass. Always I was reluctant to go.

Years passed in this way until I reached adolescence, and I no longer followed the animal tunnels or climbed limbs but rather sought to extend mine to those of another. Something vital went dormant in me.

My grammar and high school studies included art courses, but it wasn't until college when I read Lord Byron's *Sardanapalus* and saw in reproduction of Eugène Delacroix's painting, *The Death of Sardanapalus*, that something reawakened in me. The pearlescent glow of the pasha's bedcovering, the opulent fabrics and twisting bodies, the powerful horse with flames approaching so stimulated my imagination that I wanted to see more. And I did.

Delacroix led me to Cézanne, who led me back to Poussin, black-figure, red-figure, white-ground. The Etruscans followed the Greeks, then Magdalenian cave painters, Beckmann's caves of horror. Donatello's mysterious bas-reliefs. Rothko.

Late nights at college, Giotto's fresco portrait of Dante on the page opposite would pull my eye away from the conjugation of Italian verbs: *devo, devi, deve, deviamo, devete, devono. Devo vedere:* I must see. In Padua, as I stood before Giotto's frescoes at the Scrovegni Chapel, I saw the life of Christ transmuted into luminous color rhythmically proportioned and felt the power of art.

Back at the university I drew the figure again and again, over and over, struggled with oil paint and then discovered pure, dry pigment. At the school art store were left-over bags of pigment ordered by the art conservation lab. I bought several sacks and checked out a book on egg tempera. Cracking that first egg into water and mixing it with luminous powdered earth began what is now my twenty-year fascination with the medium of egg tempera.

The man who was to become my husband introduced me to the hunt. We stalked deer. Gradually, we entered their world as he taught me first to look for sign: fresh beds, scat, tender brush leaves nipped. So as not to alert the deer with our scent, we would feel the direction of the breeze on our faces or observe where the dust blew as we tossed it. Into the shadows of branches we would peer, searching for the arc of an antler, the curve of a haunch, movement. Long minutes would pass as we listened, simply listened, for the sound of a hoof cracking a brittle branch in its path. As we slowly and quietly followed the impressions the heart-shaped hooves had made on the trail, our muscles grew taut and strained.

In this way he reintroduced me to my youth, but there was a difference. The intent was to take a life, and this added a seriousness that was new, a depth of engagement that was primal.

With this difference, a deep conflict and paradox surfaced. While the pursuit of game activated my bodily senses to a degree of acuteness previously unknown to me, the ingredient necessary was the intent to kill. I could not have the pleasure of a heightened sense of aliveness without being a harbinger of death.

Were these conflicting feelings, I wondered, a result of our technological way of life, which removes us from natural processes? Or had these questions been with us from the beginning? Henry David Thoreau read Virgil's *Georgics* and was reminded of the identity of all ages. The natural world Virgil described was the same world as Thoreau's, and the same men inhabited it. Thus, Thoreau concluded, neither nature nor human nature had changed, in essence, from Virgil's time to his.

When I hunted, I realized that I re-entered not only my childhood but the elemental relationship of prey and predator, and in a tangible way the history of art and the family of man. Our origins and almost all of our history lie in the pursuit of game. Man's first images were born from the life-giving and death-bearing intensity of the hunt. For millennia, the necessity of the hunt profoundly shaped our bodies, minds—also our art.

Through the medium of the hunt, I touched the Cro-Magnon who brought down the stag and painted the image of the stag onto the cave wall. Over time, the cave wall became an Etruscan tomb enlivened with representations of plentiful game, and the tomb wall later was rounded into the ceramic surfaces of Attic pots with images of fleeing stags and gods and goddesses in pursuit. Woven into medieval tapestries were forms of the hunted, and upon the weave of canvas, Thomas Eakins captured the lucid geometry of pushing for rail.

After a time, I began to hunt on my own in the mountains near Yellowstone, and I began to notice that hunting in some ways paralleled the process of painting. In painting, one strives to fashion an aesthetic structure. With each painting, this structure is initially only vaguely sensed, and it is the work of the painter to find its contours.

In hunting, it is the work of the hunter to uncover and take the game. In so doing, the contours of the hunt are drawn, but never as initially imagined.

In painting, one wants an image, a vital image, to materialize. To bring this about, the painter works within the limitations and potentialities of the pictorial elements, elements that have been developed and employed over the centuries and that have their roots in the natural world: color, line, shape, texture, form, value, space.

The painter cultivates a sensitivity to these elements and with long practice brings into view the fleeting image that is our essence, the contours of a human consciousness—the aesthetic structure.

In hunting, one wants the animal to appear. But the animal is always wary and, when not feeding, is in hiding, invisible.

To raise the game, the hunter, too, must carefully sense elements—ancient elements of landscape. She moves through the landscape as through a canvas in search of her quarry. Alert. She follows the line of repeating trails drawn by slender legs and delicate hooves. These trails are defined by the limitations and profound capacities of instinct. They lead to feeding areas—color fields of luminous grass, highly textured shrubs and brilliantly hued berries; trails diminish into pools of darkness, places of sleep and repose, out of summer's heat or hidden from the probing eyes of mountain lions. These trails rhythmically repeat and transect over a mountainside, creating shapes. As they are walked, one is imbued with the harmony of their proportions and feels an organizing principle in the wild.

Both the painter and hunter are pulled along their courses by an interplay of intuition and analysis. Thoreau writes of this intuitive pull in his essay "Walking": "I believe that there is a subtle magnetism in Nature, which if we unconsciously yield to it will direct us aright. It is not indifferent to us which way we walk. There is a right way."

The hunter must remain open in a bodily sense to the pull of the surroundings. Does she move toward the quaking light of the aspen grove or up the draw dense with Douglas fir? But she also relies on his knowledge of daily feeding patterns and thermal winds, and assesses them in relation to the time of day.

The painter tests a color against an interior feeling but also observes whether it occupies the right plane of space. If not, then through analysis, the proper amount of tint or tone is mixed with hue, and the color then settles in proper relation to surrounding colors.

The natural landscape is not static; it is evolving, but at a pace slower than our awareness can perceive. At times I have come to an area in the forest that feels different. The light quickens: Leaves are smaller, and the shadows, too, with swatches of intense light between. Wild rose hips cling to the bushes, and not far off, I suspect, is the rapid heartbeat of a grouse, its plumage a replication of this habitat.

Similarly, as the pressures of a life lived shape the painter's being, colors are selected that conform to his evolving way of seeing. As she steps back from her canvas, she asks, Is it true?

When the animal does finally appear (or *if* it does, for like painting, one is never assured of success), it is always disarming, as if the appearance occurs entirely independent of her actions. The animal simply materializes before her eyes, and she is enchanted.

This moment arrives, too, for the painter, when after long hours an image emerges on the canvas that is alive, that surprises and is immediately recognized. Because the painter isn't sure of the sequence that brought this unique living image into view, it is as if the image had appeared of its own volition, and so she simply experiences the moment with gratitude.

Whatever our technologically generated illusions might be, we *are* a part and will always be a part of the natural world, and yet, from within our technological cocoon, we think this is not so. The archaic pursuit of the hunt can, in late twentieth-century America, bring us closer to an understanding of that of which we are made and restore to our minds and fading memories the power, magnificence and horror of the natural world and our place in it. And the medium of paint, derived from plants, animals and minerals, possesses by its very nature an intimacy with landscape. Perhaps the pulse of living things and our complex relationship to them can best be expressed by it.

When in Siena, looking into the eye of Duccio's Madonna, I realized that what distinguished his work from the work of his contemporaries was that the eye I was looking into was the eye of the Divine. I had seen that eye before, I thought, that intensity, that remoteness, that otherness— the exquisitely shaped eye of a wild elk.

PAGE LAMBERT

Deerstalking: Contemplating an Old Tradition

(1991)

FOUR STRANDS OF WIRE, BARBED, RAN IN TIGHT HORIZONTAL LINES NEXT to the highway. Four hoofed legs hung limply, earthbound, the struggle gone from them now as the last breath was gone from the buck. He lay draped over the top wire, suspended between his world and ours.

The deer have grown fat and courageous, browsing in the meadow, sleeping in the thickets of oak brush, wandering across the roads. This deer had seen several hunting seasons already, bounded across many highways, vaulted easily over many fences. But this time he misjudged the distance, confused perhaps by the unnatural speed of an oncoming car. Such a waste, a loss. I cursed the highway silently, the ribbon of death, this by-product of progress.

We've watched the deer all summer, seen the fawns grow taller as they stood next to their mothers in the meadow, counted the muddy hoof-prints left behind them at the spring. The young bucks band together and cruise the countryside, sensing change. I find the deer paths and walk in single file through the woods with our small children, our eyes searching the ground and trees around us. With each sign, droppings on the path or a patch on the limb of an aspen rubbed antler-smooth, we feel one step closer to their world. We get one quick magic glimpse of forest life.

With November came our first hunting season on the ranch. The Bear Lodge Mountains in which we live are part of the Black Hills of northeast-ern Wyoming. Our small town, Sundance, is known as the whitetail deer capital of the world and hunters come here eagerly each fall. Many are responsible, hard-working men who look forward to being in the hills and outdoors. They marvel at the quickness of the whitetail and give thanks if they are skilled and lucky enough to take meat home to their families. But there are a few who bring no honor with them and leave no honor behind when they are gone. Ungutted deer ride their tailgates, heads slumped with the weight of heavy, useless antlers. Later, these men boast to their peers of their prowess, the imposing trophies looking down upon them from above the mantelpieces. Their friends may not know that the flesh of deer rots by the roadside, but the hunter knows. He has become less than a hunter, he has betrayed an age-old trust and the link which joins him to life's cycle is broken.

Matt, our son, is keenly aware of the ambiguity of the situation, his questions to the point. All summer we have shared the land with the deer, felt privileged to see them. Then hunting season approaches and he knows his father will hunt. Matt looks forward to the chance to hike the woods and walk the deer paths, but he feels an inner conflict even at his young age. He anxiously awaits this grown-up privilege, this chance to be alone with his dad. But at night, when I am tucking him into be and we are alone, he speaks with questions.

"Remember the fawn we saw this summer, Mom, the one out in the horse pasture where Dad was fixing fence?" And then I remember, too, the newborn fawn hidden in the deep grass. It was the first hot day of summer and he was panting from dehydration when we found him. He was much smaller than normal, a twin perhaps. By the time the kids and Mark got back with a baby bottle filled with milk it was too late.

"Remember him, Mom? He was so cute. He had those little spots all over him and he was so tiny. How come his mom just left him there? Do you think we scared her away?" We could have, I knew. But I wondered why had she chosen a spot so close to the barn to have her baby? Were we less of a threat than the coyotes on the hill?

"I wouldn't want to shoot a doe, Mom, 'cause what if she had a baby? Do you think someone shot the momma deer?" No, I explained, it wasn't hunting season yet, not for a long time, not until the fawns were much older and could run as fast as their mothers across the meadow.

"I want to go with Dad to shoot a buck when I get older. How old will I have to be, Mom?" Then I remember a story my father told me, not about the first time he ever hunted, but about the last time. He and my mother were spending their honeymoon by Lake Tahoe near Yosemite. As they walked arm in arm through the forest, my father spotted a nice buck through a clearing in the trees. He knelt, lifting his rifle to take aim. My mother stepped quietly away, watching him. Their eyes met and he saw a sad, gentle expression on her face. Across the clearing, the buck stood motionless, alert and wary, nostrils flared. That is when my father saw the doe. She was standing a few yards away from the buck, and she was staring straight at my dad. He looked from her dark eyes to my mother's, and then slowly he lowered the rifle and rising, took her arm and walked away.

When you are grown, Matt, will you remember the fawn that died in the grass? Will you say a prayer for him, as well as for the deer that graces our dinner table?

"Mom, can I ask you something?" Of course, but I may not have the answer. I wait patiently for the question, and it seems to take a long time.

"Mom, how come I want to hunt so much but I get sad inside at the same time?" I see the beginning of a tiny tear in his eye and wonder if he has noticed the one in mine.

Ah, the double-edged sword. I should have all the answers, yet I have none. His father respects life, he understands why I anguish over the buck draped across the barbed wire. What inner drive is it, then, that causes him to hoist the rifle onto his shoulders and traipse quietly across the draw and into the thickets of oak brush in the cold pre-dawn? Filling the freezer is part of it but it is not the entire answer, not in this age of super-market convenience. It goes deeper than that.

It is partly the challenge of the tracking, meeting the whitetail, so alert and cautious, in his own territory, knowing that all the while he sees more, is deaf to nothing—an intuitive creature. But that still is only part of the explanation.

It is also the sensuous and gratifying sound as one foot after another touches the earth, causing the dry leaves to mate with the dirt. It is step-ping outside our door and breathing the same air that the deer breathe, seeing them graze on our meadow. This is no more our land, though, than is the sky above us our sky. Our ownership is fleeting, superficial, man-made.

Part of the answer is looking up into the sky when the sentinel hawk takes flight and circles, knowing that somewhere nearby a buck watches the same hawk, hears the dry leaf. It is the memory deep within of a great-grandfather walking a similar path, seeing a similar hawk.

That is only the first, conscious layer of memory, however. If I peel back the layers, go centuries deep, draw the bowstring taut and chant a song of praise to the Great Provider, then I begin to sense the natural order of things. I begin to put the pieces together. My father's story was romantic and he did the right thing, for him, at that moment in the woods. But I know now that the antlers which adorn our log walls are not a trophy, but a key to an ancient past.

How do I put all this into words that a seven year old will under-stand? I talk to him about God, I read to myself from Deuteronomy, and I try to teach him about honor—esteem for all that lives, respect for all that dies. When Mark brings venison home for our table, I want Matt to appre-ciate the hard winters that were endured, the fawns that were fathered. The double-edged sword cuts deep, right to the quick of the matter.

On opening day of hunting season Mark did, indeed, bring venison home. It was snowing lightly, the timid winter sun hung close to the earth. He headed out past the barn and across the draw, the dry snow crunching beneath his feet. He tracked the deer for two hours in the early morning, and then shot him clean—dropping him fast. He had to drag him a mile, up a steep-sided gulch, through the tall brush and then out of the woods and across the hay field. The buck was well developed and almost out-weighed him. When I first saw the deer, stripped of his tawny coat and hanging by the antlers in the granary, he stood taller than either of us. His muscles lay exposed, covered by transparent membranes. I touched a front hoof and it moved loosely in response, not yet stiff with death. That night,

I fried the tenderloins cut from his back for supper and saw his glassy eyes in the hot grease.

Eating game was not new to me: We often had elk in the freezer. But this was my first time to experience it from beginning to end, from deer grazing in the meadow to meat frying in the pan. When Mark brought the heart and liver into the house and Matt and Sarah asked to see them, I was confronted by a moment of truth. To understand this thing, I needed to face it full on. So I reached inside the plastic bag and withdrew the heart. Matt and Sarah stood on each side of me, their expressions full of curious amazement.

"That's his heart," they said, needing no answer. It was warm in my hands, the pulsating memory still strong. I had never seen blood so red, not even my own. It clung to my hands and to the spaces between my fingers. For a moment I felt the civilized memory peel away once again. Genetic impressions surfaced, revealing the beginnings of a nervous system no longer guided solely by instinct, but embracing tradition as well. The blood on my skin became, for a split second, familiar.

Then I slowly placed the heart back in the bag while Matt and Sarah "oohed" and "aahed." It was with reluctance that I washed the stubborn blood from my fingers, for I was glad that I had held this deer's heart in my hands, giving to him a proper farewell.

The questions that my children ask force me to look inward, to examine my beliefs and actions. And sometimes this probing makes me uncomfortable, for it strips me of my cloak of rationalization. Hunting is not a tradition to be taken lightly. Traditions, like legacies, are passed on from one generation to the next and should have meaning and value. When Matt is grown and has a family of his own, he may also choose to hunt and fill his winter freezer. And if his children question him, as he questions me, I hope his answers do not come too easily. I hope that he will still shed that solitary tear.

GENEEN HAUGEN

The Illusory Distance Between Pacifist and Warrior

(2000)

There are many different levels of violence and non-violence. . . . If the motivation is negative, even though the external appearance may be very smooth and gentle, in a deeper sense the action is very violent. On the contrary, harsh actions and words done with a sincere, positive motivation are essentially non-violent.

—His Holiness the Dalai Lama

Like the skeleton of a shameful relation, the rifle had been hidden in the basement for ten years. I was contemptuous of guns, even more contemptuous of the barbarians who owned them. But this gun, *my* partner's weapon, was stored in my house. It was a bolt action hunting rifle, to be sure, not a black market Uzi or a semi-automatic substitute for self-esteem. Still, like the multiple contradictions concealed within any life, the presence of the gun was one I couldn't rationalize or accept.

So instead, I ignored it.

As a coping strategy, disregarding the rifle's presence had worked brilliantly. Until another incongruity began worming the subterra of my awareness, a maggot born in the dark: I found myself contemplating the hunt, and my own unaccountable leaning toward it.

The possibility of hunting arose like an unwanted visitor from a verboten country. Like any truly distasteful guest, this one was disinclined to leave until it had cornered my attention completely. I was afraid it would rub off on me, contaminate me with social unacceptability.

Just as I feared, the idea of the hunt began to win me over.

What lured me to such an appalling thicket, a thorny wood that pricked and ripped and shredded a fancy quiver of beliefs? It was a clamor of feelings, ideas, experiences. The beat underneath them all—a jarring rhythm I couldn't tune out—sounded something like this: Why does someone who cherishes wildness no less than the human heart endure a facsimile of wild existence? I wanted to engage with the wild world in the oldest, most intimate manner of all.

I knew very little about the physicality of hunting.

339

I knew less than nothing about weapons. In truth, handling a gun was a barrier I doubted I was capable of crossing.

But my partner David knew how to shoot, and he owned the rifle I'd been zealously ignoring for a decade.

We exhumed the weapon from the basement, carried it upstairs and unzipped the brown imitation-leather case. A vague impression of hunting sharpened into an alarming reality as I examined the rifle, whose walnut stock and crosshatched handgrips were both beautiful and menacing. The barrel was oiled and black, imprinted with the name, Ruger M77, and the caliber, 30.06.

David confidently drew back the bolt and displayed the empty bullet chamber. My heart pounded anyway when I picked up the gun. But the consequence of holding an unloaded weapon is hardly equivalent to firing a loaded one. Even the sight of my hands on the Ruger did little to convince me that I could fill the chamber with cartridges, aim and pull the trigger.

I shouldered the gun, feeling its dead weight, how hard it was to balance with my left arm upraised and partially outstretched. David—who'd owned the rifle for twenty years but never used it—advised me to lie down and aim. He had learned to shoot courtesy of the U.S. Army but had never hunted, and I was suspicious about his advice to lie down. How could I drop to my belly in the wild without alerting any creature I stalked? Flattening myself against the rug, I supported the Ruger on meditation pillows on the living room floor and peered down the scope. Cushioned, the gun's crosshairs were steady.

The Buddhist monks who had sewn the meditation cushions had never, I was sure, envisioned their zafus stabilizing a gun. Designed to assist a practitioner in cultivating peaceful awareness, my maroon zafu was a place to center, a portable sanctuary, an object whose purpose was distinct—not ordinary furniture, certainly not a gun stand.

The rifle juxtaposed against the cushions summoned a faint, disturbing image of the Chinese army's devastation of Tibetan monasteries. The weapon against the cushions gave rise to impressions of the destruction of temples and sacred sites throughout history, throughout the world. Thought to have evolved so far from savages, human beings still did not cultivate balance in the sacred-and-profane spectrum: The holiest leanings often gave rise to the bloodiest conflicts.

In the physical world, winners usually control the most deadly weapons. In the metaphysical world, winners and losers are less easy to define.

The Ruger was not meant for hunting humans, but hairier kin born of the same stardust. The gun was unloaded. Other than the written or spoken word, it was the most deadly instrument with which I'd ever had contact. The pen, it's been said, is mightier than the sword—such lofty words, issued from a writer, not a warrior. But if the pen can alter troublesome ideas, who can deny that the sword is a more efficient tool for quashing troublesome individuals?

Weapons ask no questions, and of themselves, require no accountability.

The gun conveyed a kind of power to me, but it hardly conveyed consciousness. How had I, a person who had long fancied myself on a "spiritual path," arrived at this strange juncture: practicing meditation with the intent of deepening my awareness of life, now entering a practice whose intent was taking a life?

I had begun meditating some twenty years earlier, when I got my mantra and quickly forgot it. Sitting still wasn't my style. I meditated anyway, haphazardly, giving attention to my footfalls as I ran, to wind, to the sound of water.

Yoga worked better for a kinesthetic person like me, especially the flowing postures. But I was an erratic practitioner, a beginner for more than two decades. I never mastered full lotus, though I did learn to focus on breathing.

From chanting, I'd discovered the power of sound to induce ecstatic, near-visionary states of consciousness. I loved those highs, psychedelia without side effects, but overall, I figured life is less painful for those who aren't trying to escape it. So through *vipassana,* I was learning about presence. The be-here-now thing. In reality this meant I was learning about the billions of ways I'm not here, there, or anywhere in particular.

Vipassana—or insight meditation—comes from the Theravada ("school of the elders") line of Buddhism, and thus said to be older than Zen, Tibetan and Soto, but its practice had only been brought to the West in the nineteen seventies. It's thought to be the technique practiced by the Buddha. The simplicity of *vipassana* pleases me: Begin with the breath. When attention wanders like a willful toddler to memories, feelings or fantasies, simply note where it's traveled and return to the breath. The purpose: to erode the layers of inattention, and eventually, to discover the nature of consciousness and thus, the nature of reality.

So far, I had primarily discovered the chaos of my own mind.

One does not have to "be Buddhist" to practice *vipassana,* but during formal meditation instruction, I had taken the Buddhist vows of refuge. Taking the "triple-gem" of refuge in the Buddha (or possibility of enlightened mind), in the *Dharma* (teaching or truth), in the *Sangha* (community of practitioners) is generally all that's required for one to be considered Buddhist. But unlike Catholicism, Mormonism or Methodism, Buddhism— at least at the layperson level—is a pretty loose affair, and taking the vows of refuge did not necessarily make me a Buddhist. Neither did vowing to observe—as I had—the most basic moral obligations of Buddhism, the Five Precepts.

The First Precept: not to destroy life.

Many Westerners imagine that all Buddhists are vegetarian, and certainly many practitioners choose the veggie path. But on the high, dry Tibetan plateau, for example, vegetarianism is a luxury few can afford. Monks and others dedicated to the *dharma* get around the first precept by accepting meat, as the Buddha advised, as long as it was not killed by them or for them—thus removing themselves from karmic consequence for taking the life.

The Jungian analyst, Jean Shinoda Bolen, once told me a story about the Dalai Lama wherein he was asked about eating meat. The Dalai Lama—who complies with his doctor's instructions to eat meat—said that, in the course of a lifetime, a human being might eat one cow (obviously, he was not talking about Americans). Then, with his customary chortle and smile, the Dalai Lama asked, "But what about a bowl full of shrimp?"

In the Buddhist tradition, the smaller creatures do not possess a lesser soul than the largest beings. When I relayed Jean Bolen's story of the Dalai Lama to a woman who would willingly eat fish—low on the food chain—but not mammals, I asked if considering the number of souls added another dimension to the issue. She paused, then said, "It changes everything."

But the Buddha's teaching does not appear ambiguous about the matter of taking a life, which begs a question: What karmic retribution befalls those who willingly stop the heartbeat of another creature? What of, say, the karma for the butcher who provides meat for His Holiness the Dalai Lama? Of the hunter who provides for less exalted family and friends?

It's particularly American to reinterpret Buddhist philosophy for the western hemisphere. I have lived in that mythic and peculiar subset of the western world—the American West—all my life. In terms of intact natural systems, my homeland is among the wildest left in the lower forty-eight states, perhaps even the world. Any vows of the spirit are meaningless if they can't be filtered honestly through the visible web of animal and plant lives I share.

Perhaps more than the other Precepts—not to steal, not to lie, to avoid sexual misconduct, and not to take intoxicants—taking the vow not to kill is easy to say, and virtually impossible to act out. Practitioners of Jainism—a religious system emphasizing asceticism and concern for all life—wear masks over their mouths to avoid accidentally doing away with flies. Some Buddhist monks do not dig in the garden out of respect for worms.

But I am not a Jain or monk. I'm hardly in line for Buddhahood. I do my best to live with care, but I'm not able to pretend there's no blood on my hands. Perhaps the toughest reckoning for those who attempt to hold all life in equal regard is this: The existence of every individual is fueled entirely by other lives.

It may be foolish and hopelessly unenlightened, but I'm willing to risk karma that consuming what's been killed by others does not guarantee a happier next-round than taking the life with intention.

And so I reinterpret the First Precept: to do least harm. It's an admittedly odd notion to ally with hunting.

Least harm may be more challenging than no harm at all, but it seems more honest. And perhaps what the Buddha intended.

The shop that sells ammunition also carries nice clothing, shoes, beautiful pottery patterned with bears, trumpeter swans, elk and moose. The hunting department is on the top floor, in the back, and although I'd been in this shop dozens of times, I had never investigated the section devoted to weapons and camouflage. David strode ahead to request rifle cartridges and targets while I lurked on the edge, between the tents and binoculars, feeling furtive, rather illicit, as if I hovered in the shadowed entry of a porn shop. There was a wall of rifles, a case of handguns, stacks of videos with provocative titles: *Bushwackin' Bulls. Playing in Predator Country. Fatal Calling* (Learn to master the ABC's of doe talk! How buck body language will help you score!). There were displays of packaged cow elk urine. Packets of bull-rage, guaranteed to infuriate bull elk during rutting season. Scent-killers in pine and sage. Bear calls, moose calls, "Terminator" elk calls.

Exploiting the sexual behavior of animals is a popular hunters' tactic, particularly for trophy hunters. By imitating a bugling bull elk or scenting an area with bull urine, a hunter tries to lure another rutting bull—intent on protecting his harem—into the open. Hunters also scent with cow elk urine to seduce the normally-wary bull, now hormone-drugged like a teenaged boy in a girl's locker room. Although it's an ancient practice, the association of sexual behavior with hunting stirs deep resentment in me, brings to mind date-rape and other predatory human sexual behavior. If the bulls aren't bugling with the fever of the rut, the hunter's difficulty escalates, but is preying upon instinctual, reproductive behavior in the spirit of fair chase? It seems to bring out the worst in some people: A friend once suffered through an AA meeting where a hunter bragged that he'd killed a bull elk while the bull was mounting the cow.

The association of sex and violence, the eroticization of acts of violence (and violation of erotic acts) is endemic to Western culture, so widespread that we seem nearly immune to it. A hunter friend—someone I would call extremely sensitive to the ethics of hunting and killing—described to me the process of field dressing an elk in great detail. The purpose of this elaboration was to make sure I would know exactly what to do if I killed an animal without an experienced hunter along. My friend's instructions were mostly lost on me, though, when he described how, before making the gutting incision, I would need to roll the creature on its back and "spread its legs, just like a woman having sex."

But the link between sexuality and violence—or sexuality and death—is not just a freak of human culture. In *The Time Falling Bodies Take to Light,* William Irwin Thompson writes, "Sexual reproduction introduces death, for it produces new individuals that, by virtue of being limited and highly specific beings, must die. . . . Reproduction is the climax of life; in some species, the postcoital male immediately dies or is consumed by the female." In the insect world, the Black Widow spider is famous for her tendency to devour her mate. The Carolina Mantid might eat her partner while still copulating. Anadromous salmon, both female and male, die after returning to their freshwater birth-river to spawn.

Bull elk spar to establish possession of the harem of cows, although, as David Peterson writes in *Among the Elk:*

> [S]ince it runs counter to the survival and successful evolution of the species for prime males to kill and mutilate one another, conflicts between rutting bulls have evolved to be more symbolic than physical, including profiling, bugling, antler shaking, bluff charges, minimal-contact sparring, and the like. Still, on the rare occasions when serious physical violence does erupt, it can prove fatal to one or both contestants.

There is little indication that bull elk direct violence toward the harem, although a bull may vigorously attempt to keep a wayward cow in line. Experienced cows will usurp young, unaware cows in the breeding line-up, shoving to be first. The harem hierarchy is perhaps less a matter of horniness than of survival for future generations: The earliest bred cows will also calve earliest, and their offspring will have the longest season to fatten before winter.

In elk, as in many animal species, male and female come together only during rutting season, when reproductive instinct overrides normally secretive habits. The animals' cyclic hormonal ritual causes a companion migration among hunters, who congregate in hunting shops to purchase bullets, orange hats, packaged urine and manufactured elk calls.

Next to the rack of hunting videos, a boy stared with longing at the wall of rifles, then knelt in front of the handgun display and said, "Wow, Dad, come look at these." His father hurried over to kneel beside him. I broke into cold sweat, but summoned courage to ask the polite, young salesman if rifles come in different weights. I wouldn't have asked if he had seemed like a guy who drove around with weapons displayed in his truck window all fall—there's something about men with guns that can make normally conversant women unwilling to expose vulnerability. The salesman's polite manner did not change. Yes, he informed me, there is a range of weights, now that the stocks are made in synthetic materials as well as wood. I asked him how he keeps his aim steady; does he lie down? No, he said, he braces in different positions for practice shooting. In the field, he said, adrenaline gives him his aim. He laughed, squinted and slid a private, sidelong glance at the other salesman.

David asked me if I'd like to look at the rifles. I said no and we hurried toward the exit, carrying the paper targets in a bag and large boxes of 30.06 (thirty-aught-six, I could say that out loud like I knew something) cartridges in our bare hands.

When someone I knew nodded at me from the counter in the tent section, I flushed with embarrassment. What if she thought I was a gun enthusiast? Or a hunter?

On the public land bordering our home, chokecherries bowed with blossoms. Newly leafed aspen rippled under the wind's light hand. A hawk screeched warning from a high bare limb, then arced against the blue, its auburn tail fanned and backlit. Mosquitoes were just coming to life. On the damp trail in front of my running shoes, silvery blue butterflies fluttered up like winged prayers. Masses of balsamroot bloomed, the first extravagant yellow of the season. The trail mud was impressed with deer tracks. Coyote musk stung my nostrils near a tree that marked territory. The ranchers who leased this land had just resurrected the barbed-wire fence from the ground where it lay all winter; the fence goes up in summer to contain cows, down in autumn to allow migration of deer, moose and elk.

Even though the trail was more a footpath than a road, four-by-four trucks and ATVs prowled it every autumn. In a meadow, near a spring that would be mostly dry by September, two enormous piles of automotive parts, broken beer bottles, crushed Budweiser cans and boards prickly with rusted nails were heaped and partially burnt. New since the end of last summer, the piles marked the dregs of a hunting camp.

Unease filled me like sudden sickness. In the brief early summer, after the snowmelt but before the reappearance of cows—well before hunting season—hardly anyone ventured here. For me, the land had been a nearby refuge. Now, like sanctuaries everywhere, it had been trashed.

Though surely no one watched from the shadows, my legs felt lead heavy and I wanted to get away, wary of others who had traveled this trail. From the meadow every escape was uphill; I moved as if in a dream, loggy, slow, breathless.

I am afraid of hunters.

I am afraid to walk the National Forest in autumn, even while wearing a fluorescent orange vest.

I am afraid of encampments of men who might be high on blood and weapons and alcohol.

I am afraid that someone might take aim on my blonde hair, or on the reddish fur of my dogs, and squeeze the trigger before certain what's centered in the crosshairs.

It happens.

A few years ago a mule was shot in the leg by a hunter who apparently mistook the mule for a moose, then left it to die. On the National Elk Refuge, a man blew an elk call and when he heard a responding bugle from the trees, he aimed and shot his friend in the head. In Utah, it has been said that if you want to get rid of relatives, take them to the woods in deer season.

Even though I had never shot a gun, and in fact considered myself a peacemaker, I'd had a recurring daydream in which I hoisted a rifle with confidence and fired a few well-aimed rounds. The daydream had begun as a reaction to my first solo encounter with an armed man. One long ago spring in the Santa Cruz mountains, I walked the old logging roads until a nearby gunshot made me scramble into the brush. I waited, my heart thudding, until a man moved out of the shadows, his rifle raised to firing position, sighted on me. "Hey," I said, my voice barely a squeak, "What are you shooting at?" He put down the gun and talked me out of trembling cover to find out why I walked alone in the redwoods.

When I ventured solo in the woods again, a sharpshooting fantasy began to accompany me, though it was unspoken and hardly acknowledged. I was, after all, a gun control advocate and pacifist, at least in mind if not in gut reaction.

But if I cared to examine the shadow that accompanied me everywhere, I knew I was capable of violence. As a very young woman I had once flattened a drunk who'd hit me in the head and knocked me down a staircase. I pummeled him with my fists and feet until he was helpless. Though I seldom admitted it aloud, in my darkest heart I knew I could do it again.

In fact I was afraid I would do it again, punch out some child-slapping parent in the grocery store, or kick some tough in the balls if I saw him grab an unwilling woman. Even though such monumental stupidity could get me killed, I was afraid I'd act without thinking. Who wouldn't want to be a kickboxing master in these situations?

But to take possession of a weapon was another matter entirely, an elaborate new construction in the psyche. What happens to a woman's self-confidence if her proficiency with a gun diminishes a man's strength advantage?

The South Dakota rancher and writer, Linda Hasselstrom, has an essay, "Why One Peaceful Woman Carries a Pistol," that pissed me off enormously the first and second and third times I read it. She writes of confronting four men who were urinating and dropping beer cans on her property. The men responded:

> "'I don't see no beer cans. Why don't you get out here and show them to me, honey,' said the belligerent one, reaching for the handle inside my [car] door.
> "'Right over there,' I said, still being polite, 'there and over there.' I pointed with the pistol, which had been under my thigh. Within one minute the cans and the men were back in the car, and headed down the road."

This wasn't the only time Hasselstrom pointed her pistol at a per-ceived threat—an action that struck me as aggressive, not "peaceful" or even plainly defensive—and I had dismissed her as self-delusional and ridiculously naive to rely on a gun rather than wits. But I still clung to a younger, stronger and faster self-image, residual from years of traveling—even hitchhiking—alone. Outwitting predatory people (truth be told, I haven't ever encountered a woman that required outwitting) had been a routine hazard. But I never scared or threatened anyone, just managed my own escape.

Perhaps I was the one more naive.

None of my women friends owned guns, to my knowledge, so I was star-tled when I found that some had been to the practice range. Connie, who claimed good hand-eye coordination. Susan, who said that, except for the noise, she had enjoyed target practice almost as if it were a shooting gallery at a carnival. My vegetarian sister, Lori, who had gone with her husband to fire both shotguns and handguns on more than one occasion.

Anyone who'd grown up with guns might not appreciate the weight that firing one bore on me. Weapons had been a lifelong taboo, imposed first by my father, and later by my own affinity for anti-war pacifism and left-leaning politics. As with many taboos, once the decision had been made to break it, I felt a rush of liberation as well as fear. Like a virginity no longer cherished but still held intact, I was glad to postpone the first shot a while yet, though I was anxious to cross that boundary.

In my childhood home, there had been no hunters or weapons of any kind. My father had joined the Navy as a teenager; an early photograph of him in uniform shows a soft-eyed, soft-faced young man. The youth who volunteered to fight the war was not the icy-eyed man who emerged. Whatever his experience during World War II had been, he never spoke of it. All we knew is what my mother said: "Your father had enough of that in the war. He won't have any weapons in the house."

But in my mother's family there had been hunters. In an out-of-focus honeymoon photograph of my grandparents, my grandmother carries a rifle. Her mouth lifts in a faint smile. She could not have known what her future held: eight children and the Great Depression. My grandmother shot crows from the pantry window to keep them off the garden, and at least once, she shot a deer from the same location. The garden was well-tended and productive, but it was deer hunting that sustained the family of ten through the bad years. "We ate venison in season and out of season," my mother said.

If my grandfather knew of the boundary that my father had circumscribed on our weaponless home, he believed in hunting enough to violate it. When he sent my thirteen-year-old brother a .22 rifle—an initiation into manhood—the weapon disappeared quickly, as if there were something shameful about it, shameful about the man who had sent it.

But in 1968, when my brother turned eighteen and reported for his draft physical, my father was outraged when my brother, a professional musician, successfully faked the hearing test to be exempted from military service. Weapons at home were not acceptable, but my father, like many WWII veterans, considered fighting unknown Viet Cong as patriotic and honorable. In an era of contradictions, it was a war that divided families.

Summer solstice dawned mostly clear, with overnight dew evaporating like wild perfume off meadow grass and wildflowers. The longest day, for me, always signals the shortening of the light, just as solstice night in winter heralds not darkness, but returning sun. On June solstice, while others rushed outdoors to celebrate, I turned inward to prepare for the coming darkness. I gathered the meditation cushions and sat cross-legged, eyes closed, focused on breathing. In. Out. In.

Random, unruly thoughts skidded around the breath, bounced off, shuddered their way back in. It's almost always that way. To steady my attention, I practiced a *metta*, or "loving-kindness" meditation: *May all beings be happy. May all beings be peaceful. May all beings be kind. May all beings be safe.* The phrases strung together like rosary beads. *May all beings be happy.* In the eye of my mind, an elk herd broke free of a camouflaging forest. *May all beings be peaceful.* I imagined I prayed for them. *May all beings be kind.* Behind the meditative refrain, I had an unsought image of myself raising a rifle, pulling the trigger, an elk buckling to the leafy ground. *May all beings be safe.* I squirmed on the cushion, wanting to get up, to move about, shake the image away.

But this, I knew, was the contradiction I struggled to embrace.

One June solstice years ago, I attended the Sitka Symposium on Human Values and the Written Word. It was held indoors, but I kept finding myself outside. Bald eagles rained from the sky, following fishing boats toward harbor. A pulp mill spewed waste into Sitka Sound. Whales breached and spyhopped in sight of shore. Glaciers careened between mountains, inching to the sea. At low tide, I walked the water's edge, picking kelp and eating it. I plucked ripe salmonberries too, and rugosa rose petals for tea.

Sitka's inhabitants included loggers and environmental activists, fishers, writers, people who played croquet after midnight, and others who drove ten miles to the end-of-the-road campground to see who'd just disembarked from the Alaska ferry.

It's a community and environment of contradictions, like most places, but I—who dwell in arid mountains—was lulled by Sitka's watery beauty. When I finally emerged from reverie I was stunned by how retro some of the symposium conversations seemed, as if I'd been transplanted to a smoke-filled midwestern coffee shop at dawn during deer season.

I came to and found the anthropologist and writer Richard Nelson— a resident of Sitka—extolling the hunter's life. The anthropologist, writer and filmmaker Hugh Brody claimed that, in his view, the hunter-gatherer era was the high point in human development. The anthropologists spoke of the Inuit and Koyukon belief that animals give themselves to the hunt. When James Nageak, an Inupiaq Eskimo from Barrow, Alaska, told stories of whale hunting, the symposium seemed to tilt alarmingly toward a glorification of animal-killing, distressing several of the vegetarian-inclined, a few women like myself in particular.

Among ourselves, over cappuccino at the bookshop, we agreed that the men cleaved to an ancient male ritual; that hunting was no longer necessary for most people, especially those who live in temperate climates where plant food is abundant and varied. But weighted by the hunters' enthusiasm, we felt the weakness of our voices and bloodless arguments. We were defeated, until Linda Hogan stood up and offered a giant paw of a poem that swiped the hunters' assurance aside:

Bear

The bear is a dark continent
that walks upright
like a man.

It lives across the thawing river.
I have seen it
beyond the water,
beyond comfort. Last night
it left a mark at my door
that said winter
was a long and hungry night of sleep.

But I am not afraid; I have collected
other nights of fear
knowing what things walked
the edges of my sleep,

and I remember
the man who shot
a bear,
how it cried as he did
and in his own voice,
how he tracked that red song
into the forest's lean arms
to where the bear lay weeping
on fired earth,
its black hands
covering its face from sky
where humans believe god lives
larger than death.

That man,
a madness remembers him.
It is a song in starved shadows
in nights of sleep.
It follows him.
Even the old rocks sing it.
It makes him want
to get down on his knees
and lay his own hands
across his face and turn away
from sky where god lives
larger than life.

Madness is its own country
desperate and ruined.
It is a collector of lives.
It's a man
afraid of what he's done
and what he lives by. Safe,
we are safe
from the bear
and we have each other,
we have each other
to fear.

                              —Linda Hogan

The image of the bear bleeding, crying, covering its eyes in pain or fear matched no one's fantasy of a wild creature who had given itself to the hunt, nor did the madness of the hunter summon any illusion of a tender and mutual wounding.

It has been said by the mythologist Joseph Campbell that animals—unlike humans—have no knowledge of death. I do not believe this.

The Sitka Symposium stirred me up enough that I was prompted to return a couple of years later. Some of the same hunters and anthropologists attended as well. In the interim, I had developed a new theory about hunting.

Blood rituals pulse through women's lives, via menstruation and birth. Such regular engagement with blood gives women, I theorized, a deep and ongoing intimacy with the life force. Men cannot bring forth life from their bodies; therefore they are drawn to other blood rituals, perhaps maiming and killing as a way of engaging with the greatest mystery, life itself.

I had not tried to fit women hunters into my theory.

Some called her a contemporary shaman. Janet Bishop practiced the Chinese healing art, jin shin jyutsu, and taught classes on contacting your angels. She made—and played—hoop drums. Such credentials might bring to mind hippie-granola heads, but Janet was also a hunter with over twenty years of experience.

"I don't hunt," she told me, "unless I have the dream." She paused, brushing her long hair back from her shoulders, then tipped forward from the waist, leaned closer. "I've never missed and I've never caused suffering." Janet did not blink. "I always get the license, but I don't always get an elk. Sometimes I've hunted with people who've asked why didn't I take the shot, but I hadn't had the dream. One year I hadn't had the dream and the season was nearly over. Then I dreamed the elk and in the morning my husband Benj was surprised to hear me say, 'We're hunting today.'"

"We went out and walked a long way—you have to be willing to walk a long, long way—and I could hear elk and smell them. I crept along on my belly and raised my head and there she was, a cow elk looking at me. Presenting herself, like in the dream. I took the shot. She trotted off about a hundred yards and went down. I got up and walked toward her, singing. I sang and her soul went"—Janet raised her hands to the sky—"and she died."

Janet rocked forward and nodded, slightly. Her eyes never left mine, and in them I recognized something old as fire. "Yes, that's how it was," she said. "That's how it is."

To ease my preparing-to-kill conscience, I would have liked to believe that animals present themselves willingly to the human hunter, but I doubted it, just as I couldn't imagine relinquishing my own body without a struggle to grizzlies, wolves or maggots. But I wondered how my beliefs would transform if elk dreams came to me in the expanding darkness of autumn.

David and I drove south on Highway 89 to the gun club and followed the posted instructions to check with the range tender before removing the rifle from the car. We paid three dollars each and carried the Ruger in, unloaded, chamber open. The only other shooters were at the edge of the range, aiming at the sky.

The range tender set us up at shooting stations, gave us sandbags to brace the rifle barrel on. He called, "Cease fire," through a bullhorn, and the man and woman shooting clay pigeons unloaded and laid down their weapons while David and I walked onto the range and placed our paper targets on stands at the twenty-five yard line. Tucked between the splayed flanks of the higher slope, the firing range was V-shaped, with the farthest targets in the crease of the mountain. I couldn't imagine shooting a target 200 yards away or more, but this, I'd been told, was what I would eventually aim for, the average distance between hunter and kill. The range tender drew on a pipe. I found the tobacco smoke strangely reassuring, a smell that I've—stereotypically, of course—associated with philosophers, surprising in an atmosphere where I'd expected another stereotype, gunslingers spitting tobacco juice. He told us to take a few shots at twenty-five yards, then a hundred. Then, he said, we could sight the gun.

David slid a brass cartridge into the chamber. We covered our ears. Janet had suggested that he shoot first, with me holding his shoulder and biceps lightly, to sense the rifle's kick. I stood behind him and placed my hands on his body. He aimed. With a crack, David's arm and shoulder jerked back and the dirt exploded about 150 yards away. There was no delay between events; they occupied the same loud, crowded moment. Thinking he'd missed the target—thinking: If *he* has missed, how will I hit it—I asked, "Where did it go?"

"Just about dead on," the range tender said.

David shot again, an inch to the right of center. The boom reverberated like thunder trapped in my ears. He handed me the rifle.

I sat on the small bench at my station and fumbled a cartridge into the chamber, drew the bolt closed. My heart thudded as I adjusted position, squinted down the scope, tried to keep my elbow on the table. I reached around the heavy sandbag that padded my shoulder to crook my index finger over the trigger. Crosshairs lined up center target and I breathed. In. Out. In. I shook with fear, made myself breathe steady. In. Out. In.

I held my breath and squeezed slightly—I didn't feel the trigger move before the bullet exploded, the butt slammed my shoulder, the distant dirt whirled up. "What happened?" I asked David.

"I think you missed the target," he said. "Try again."

Re-loading, my eyes watered up. Blinking, breathing, holding my breath, I fired again. When the rifle kicked, the scope slammed my forehead. "Where did it go?" I asked.

David studied the target. "Let me look through the scope," he said. "I think you hit the bull's eye."

"Cease fire," the range tender shouted through the bullhorn, even though the clay pigeon shooters had left and no one else had arrived. David opened the chamber, left the rifle on the stand, and we walked out to relocate the targets. On mine, dead center: two overlapping, blackened bullet holes, a sideways figure-eight, an infinity sign.

"I guess I didn't miss," I said to David. My eyes filled up again.

I could kill somebody, I thought, unprepared for the sensation of horror colliding with pride, annihilating the distance between pacifist and warrior, uniting Gandhi and Rambo like overlapped bullet holes, closing in on the fierce range of the creator/destroyer, Artemis.

Nothing had prevented me from firing the gun. No anatomical barrier, no crisis of conscience, no staying hand of the peaceful goddess. Afraid but willing, I had loaded the rifle and pulled the trigger. And I would do it again.

David and I re-positioned our targets at one hundred yards and returned to the shooting stands. The bull's eyes gave me a bizarre courage to throw off anonymity, and I introduced myself to the range tender. Puffing smoke with inscrutable calm, he told me his name was Blake.

"Ever fired a gun before?" he asked.

"No," I replied.

"Gonna get an elk this year?" he wanted to know.

"I hope so," I said without flinching, as if "getting an elk" was not a dramatic departure for me. I couldn't believe I said it so calmly. After nearly twenty years of eating no red meat at all, no mammals, I'd tasted elk for the first time only a year and a half before—wild elk from Janet's freezer. I had been prepared to hate it, to be revolted by it; instead, I found the elk nourished some estranged and desiccated place inside me. I had chewed slowly, imagining the elk's muscle, her tongue and teeth, so like mine yet missing the sharp canines of a carnivore. I took plenty of time to contemplate the elk's life. Through her, I ate the sun and rain and plants my own body could not digest.

She tasted faintly red, of iron and flowers.

At one hundred yards, I stared down the scope at the concentric circles of the paper target. My peripheral vision registered motion: a herd of animals running onto the firing range? But when I turned toward the movement, the long grass rolled under the wind like a silver-and-dun pelt undulating across the hillside. I gave my attention to the crosshairs again, aimed and shot slightly high, slightly left of target center, three bullet holes within one inch of each other: a lethal triangle. My shoulder burned. Even after removing my ear protection, I could hardly hear David and Blake. Laying his pipe on the table, Blake adjusted the rifle sights.

When I asked David if everyone with a good scope shot close to center, he said probably, but he thought it unusual for multiple bullets from a first-time shooter to hit so near one another. Blake handed me the rifle to fire again. The bullet pierced the right side of the target. The next time I took aim, I winced, unconsciously anticipating the kick, and found myself about to squeeze the trigger with my eyes closed, ready to flinch, guarding shoulder and forehead. I forced my eyes open, concentrated on breathing.

"I'm scared," I said, "I'm starting to cringe before I pull the trigger."

"It's scary," David replied.

I aimed, squeezed and the bullet blasted instantly, no perceivable delay for the sequence of ignitions—the firing pin sparking the primer which ignites the gun powder whose expanding gas launches the bullet like a miniature rocket. The bullet tracked slightly right again, and Blake stared through the spotting scope and said he believed he mis-sighted the gun.

"The 30.06 might be too big for me," I said.

"If you're not gonna be shooting this gun, you should quit before you learn bad habits," Blake said. "Let me know a few days ahead when you're coming again, and I'll get something smaller for you to try."

Relieved, I stood the rifle in the rack to let the barrel cool.

Near the shoulder joint, my upper arm swelled and turned blue-black, a self-inflicted, temporary tattoo, a mark of violent passage. Inexplicably proud, I soothed it with arnica liniment that evening and displayed it to Janet Bishop the next day.

But such hollow pride was riddled with shame, and loss. Crossing the boundary from sharpshooting fantasy into a real gun experience extracted a toll in innocence. I couldn't deny that I'd just opened the gate to harm or kill. To stalk and kill, in particular, a beautiful, wild creature who embodied an instinct to live, just as I did.

I took up a firearm on a journey to do least harm.

The contradiction was so immense—like my father who wouldn't allow weapons but wanted a soldier son—that I could hardly carry it whole. It nearly sunk of its own weight into unconsciousness. The mind could only exhume one end at a time, running back and forth to extricate fragments. When the bones were laid out, stained but bare, I identified the warrior skeleton as mine. Pacifist and warrior inhabit the same body, like opposite ends of spinal vertebrae, each with unique purpose, each necessary to the functioning of the whole. When one overpowers the other, it's a trip to the chiropractor.

Yogis infuse each small bone, organ, muscle of the body with awareness. Buddhas turn from nothing, stay present for the terrible and sublime. Artemis brings forth life and takes it without regret.

Balance requires nothing less.

I didn't know if learning to shoot would tilt my behavior toward the violent end of the spectrum.

I did know that meditation had not, of itself, rendered me more peaceful. Seated on my zafu, focused on the breath, observing the rising chaos of my own feelings and ideas had only begun to illuminate how much is numbed, buried, suppressed, ignored.

Perhaps the greatest harm we do ourselves and others is not recognizing that we each encompass the full catastrophe, the total spectrum of behavior. How would we ever know compassion if all possibility is not contained within each human heart?

"Everybody's scandalous flaw," Rumi wrote, "is mine."

I was one of the barbarians.

PAUL [PAULINA] BRANDRETH

The Spirit of the Primitive

from Trails of Enchantment *(1930)*

THE SPIRIT OF THE PRIMITIVE IS IN MOST OF US, STILL STRONG. IF THIS were not true, why, then, do so many turn to life in the open in preference to more complex forms of relaxation and enjoyment? Why do we take a holiday with our camping kit instead of going to some comfortable and well appointed resort where we can be served and waited on instead of doing for ourselves? Why do we like to sleep on boughs or in tents, and cook our meals over campfires, and tramp, and fish, and hunt rather than imbibe the saccharine cup of civilized pleasures? If there was not a deep-rooted desire in our beings to get back to the best and most enlivening methods of our primitive forebears, we would rest content and experience no particular urge outside of our self-imposed conventional channels. But, although this may be the case with some to whom the idea of "roughing it" is distasteful and even repugnant, it is not the case with a vast majority. The man of wealth takes his family on a vacation out West, or to the wilds of Canada; the poor man packs his outfit on a Ford and camps nearer home. Both are prompted to do the same thing by the same primitive call. Both wish to enjoy themselves by conforming once again to a simple and expansive mode of life; by tasting the old freedom amid natural beauties and quietude, and by stripping themselves, for the time being, at any rate, of cast-iron responsibilities and needless restraints.

It is essentially a primitive passion which draws men to the mountains, the sea, the desert, and all the wild and lonely places of the earth. It is the spirit of the primitive which makes us willing to undergo actual discomfort and sometimes real hardship, in order to gratify our ancestral longing for an open-air existence. In spite of civilization, in spite of luxury and money and modern conveniences and mechanical progress, we are products of nature, and to nature we turn for the realization of things that are often infinitely more satisfying and stimulating than the creations of our brains and hands. No—the cave man is not extinct. He is smoothed off and polished and spiritualized, and he no longer is a savage; but he is not dead, and may it be hoped that he will never die utterly.

Shams and artificialities crowd the highroads constructed by human effort, but nature is always real. She is salutary, she is health-giving, she is profound. Augmented by mental progress, cultural development, and scientific enlightenment, we find in her the well springs that are perennial. While the untutored brain of the savage fails to grasp that which the civilized mind absorbs and is nourished by, the influence of nature on all races of mankind has along certain lines invariably reacted to something higher. Worship and reverence are primitive, and they are both golden inheritances.

I do not wish to be misunderstood in trying to interpret what I mean by the spirit of the primitive. I have no sympathy with "back to Nature cults" and fanatical extremists and people who seek to avoid certain social obligations that are necessary to human advancement. We do not have to be uncouth or crude or weirdly eccentric in order to establish a fundamental and stimulating relationship with the source of all things. What I do wish to make clear is the belief that a complete submerging of the spirit of the primitive, in an over-civilized state, would not be a gain, but a loss. Just as soon as we begin to depend too much on others and become helpless with regard to looking after ourselves then individual self-reliance, purpose, and physical vitality suffer. It has been written in history that nations become effete and perish because of super-civilized conditions and too great prosperity. And this is undoubtedly caused by the weakening of the individual unit. That contact with the rugged forces of nature keeps at bay the decline of those elements which are productive of health, independence, and resourcefulness is an indisputable fact.

A love of outdoor life is the greatest antidote in the world for the strain of modern living. When we are out in camp we have perforce to look after our own bodily needs. If we want fuel, we have to chop it; if we want a fire, we have to make it; if we wish to eat, we very often have to secure, as well as cook, our food. Should we find ourselves in a tight place, or in actual physical danger, we must use our wits and muscles to get clear of the predicament. We cannot go to the telephone and call for help. We must learn to depend on ourselves. It is splendid. The beautiful moods and aspects of nature broaden our vision and feed our souls, but her raw relentless side teaches us lessons of incalculable value.

Contrary to much popular belief and the idea that man's innate tendency to the savage is encouraged and fostered by living in a so-called uncivilized environment, there are men who, having lived their lives in such places, are yet more humane and possess a deeper philosophy of life than many who have known only the influence of bustling communities. Nature molds according to character and intelligence. The wilderness is accused of making brutes out of some individuals, but undoubtedly they would have reverted to the brute under any unfettered condition. Quiet manners, a refinement that is not artificial, a kindness that seeks no reward, are more often the fruits of solitude. And what Conrad says of the men of the sea "who understand each other very well in their view of earthly things, for simplicity is a good counsellor, and isolation not a bad educator" applies also to the men of wild and remote habitation.

May it be hoped, indeed, that our ears shall never grow deaf to the call of the Red Gods. Reassuring, moreover, is the thought that on our own continent alone, there are still thousands of square miles of rugged territory where the thirst of the primitive spirit within us can be assuaged.

I am speaking primarily of the mountains and the forest, for it is these I know best. Majestic and inspiring manifestations of the universe, the sea and the desert are at times vain sanctuaries and show no mercy to the human atoms who invade their dominions. The jungle, too, is often treacherous. But the forest and mountains retain a more beneficent attitude towards man. Food, shelter and water they offer us, and within their boundaries, howsoever desperate the situation, there is always a fighting chance. To know them intimately is to love them. They yield us a sense of security, support and friendliness which in the lure of salt water and desert wastes and jungle mystery can never be realized.

Men like to hunt because of a primitive instinct. Nor does this necessarily mean that they are prompted solely by a desire to kill. Rather it is the fascination of the chase, the pitting of skill and energy and intelligence against the wild creature's power of self-preservation and ingenuity to escape which stirs the blood and lends excitement and interest which the sportsman is seeking. After the shot is fired, and this is especially true with regard to big-game hunting, the best part of the adventure is nearly always finished. Up to that moment we must work and often work hard to attain the end desired. We must use strategy and cultivate ability if we are going to win out. Blundering into an animal and shooting it down is never the same as the trophy brought to bag in a painstaking and thoroughly clean sportsmanlike fashion.

If, as some people believe, the enjoyment we take out of hunting is merely a gratification of the savage instinct to possess and destroy, there would then be no need for us to go into the wilderness. A rifle in the barnyard would furnish us with ample sport according to the above idea. We would be satisfied with knocking over sheep and cattle if our chief desire was to kill something. Such, of course, is not the case. As a matter of fact, I have found good sportsmen to be invariably more gentle and understanding in their treatment of animals than many individuals who have no interest or predilection for the pastime of hunting. When we commence to analyze the cruelty attached to sport and decry it on that count, we must in all sincerity become vegetarians or the argument can have no weight.

The most fundamental part of the spirit of the primitive, as we are trying to understand it, certainly does not lie in pleasure derived from the taking of life. Among a rough type of hunters and uncivilized races the lust to kill is undoubtedly a very potent factor. But this is not so with regard to the sporting instinct of men and women whose mentalities are refined. People of the latter class are prompted to hunt by the lure of the chase, by a love of nature, by a desire to study the habits of wild creatures, and by the charm and freedom of life in wilderness places.

Yet a word remains to be said of the esthetic value of the spirit of the primitive. Within the magic circle of forested and mountainous solitudes we find inspirations that cannot be found elsewhere. There is much more attached to hunting than the mere pursuit of a game animal. First of all we learn to be patient and observant. Through experiences we become self-reliant and attuned to influences that are strengthening and beneficial. Communication with nature makes it possible to commune with ourselves. In the present age of high tension and hurried endeavors, we are constantly under the pressure of the nerve-racking forces which surround us. But of this atmosphere, the mountains and forests and unreclaimed places of the earth know nothing. Here is peace, here is beauty, here is time.

We cannot live in close touch with beautiful scenes and stimulating environments without being enriched by them. Is it likely that we will forget the way the wilderness appeared on a certain autumn morning when every brilliantly hued leaf was encased in glittering snow-crystals and kindled into prismatic fires by the beams of the rising sun? Do we cease to remember the advent of the Hunter's Moon—a blood-red and fabulous lantern as it peered at us across the lonely mazes of a black spruce swamp? Do we fail to recollect the spell-bound mystery of a secluded lake, girdled by virgin timber, and sleeping like a liquid tourmaline in the shadowland of twilight? These are things permanent and priceless—poems of loveliness and beauty impressed

Into the forest, elk hunting, November 2001. © Anne Pearse Hocker.

upon the mind by nature in her wild state. These are things that time cannot take from us as long as memory lasts. The deerskin on our study floor, the buck's head over the fireplace, what are these after all but the keys which have unlocked enchanted doors, and granted us not only health and vigor, but a fresh and fairer vision of existence?

Notes

INTRODUCTION

1. Isabel Savory, *A Sportswoman in India* (London: Hutchinson & Co., 1900), 404. See her "Tiger-Shooting" below.
2. Geneen Haugen, from "Stalking Fear," below.
3. See Gerda Lerner, *The Creation of Patriarchy* (New York: Oxford University Press, 1986), 12–13.
4. Desmond Morris, *The Naked Ape* (New York: McGraw-Hill, 1967), 53.
5. George Reiger, "Instinct and Reality," *Field and Stream* (September 1991), 12–15.
6. Robert M. Jackson, "The Characteristic and Formative Experiences of Female Deer Hunters," *Women in Natural Resources* 9:3 (1987), 17–21.
7. Lynn Woods, "First Estate," *Adirondack Life* 33:6 (September/October 2002), 36–45.
8. Quoted in Kenneth P. Czech, *With Rifle and Petticoat: Women as Big Game Hunters, 1880–1940* (Lanham and New York: The Derrydale Press, 2003), 99–103. Borden's *Adventures in a Man's World* was subtitled *Adventures of a Sportsman's Wife.*
9. Lest the reader suspect a typographical error here: Ernest Thompson Seton was born Ernest Seton Thompson, and changed his name, apparently, to satisfy the expectations of one of his grandparents. Grace, when she married, used his given name—which she retained, in her writing life, after they divorced.
10. Agnes Herbert, *Two Dianas in Alaska* (London and New York: John Lane, 1909), 1.
11. Quoted in Czech, 129.
12. In a related context, and by way of comparison, such female "disciples" of Louis Leakey as Jane Goodall and Dianne Fossey come to mind here, as does Mary Leakey herself.
13. An exception here is Delia Akeley, Carl's first wife, who after their divorce and his marriage to Mary mounted a photo safari, recounted in her *Jungle Portraits* (New York: Macmillan, 1930), on which she was not only the only woman, but the only Caucasian.

14. Dust jacket copy on Osa Johnson's *I Married Adventure* (Philadelphia: J. B. Lippincott, 1940).
15. Ernest Hemingway, in a letter to Maxwell Perkins; quoted on the back cover of the North Point Press reissue of Markham's *West with the Night* (San Francisco: North Point Press, 1983). I am aware that some biographers and critics have suggested that Markham's book was ghost-authored. But I conclude that while she may have had some editorial help, the work is substantially her own—a conclusion with which Hemingway, who knew her and the other hunters and writers of her circle, certainly seems to have concurred. Interestingly enough, and perhaps for not unrelated reasons, Agnes Herbert's authorship of her three big-game hunting books was also called into question. The grounds, in her case: The writing was too good to have been by a woman. And, according to her accuser, not only did Herbert not write her own books, she never went on the hunting trips she claimed to have. One supposes Markham never flew an airplane, either.
16. "A Woman Who Wants to Hunt," *Outdoor Life: A Magazine of the West* (July 1915), 65.
17. J. M., "Woman's Column: A Michigan Sportswoman," *Forest and Stream* (February 1880), 17.
18. "Women in Arcadia," *Forest and Stream* (8 May 1879), 270.
19. "A Hobby," *Forest and Stream* (22 June 1912), 792.
20. Quoted in R. L. Wilson with Greg Martin, "Little Miss Sure Shot," *American Rifleman* (October 1998), 59.
22. "Woman in the Field," *Forest and Stream* (6 March 1880), 126. It is possible that this "N. B." was Nellie Bennett, who in 1904 was employed by *Outdoor Life* as the magazine's "lady representative," and whose "A Colorado Outing" appears in this volume.
23. "Women in Arcadia," *Forest and Stream* (8 May 1879), 270.
24. "The Modern Sportswoman," *Forest and Stream* (22 April 1911), 605.
25. William Rae, "Long Live Outdoor Life," *Outdoor Life* (June 1968), 6.
26. Margaret G. Nichols, "The Proper Perspective," *Field & Stream* (March 1973), 179.
27. Nichols's; column ran sporadically in the 1970s; in the early 1990s, *Outdoor Life* ran a "Women Outdoors" department in a few issues, before deciding it was not cost-effective. Among national outdoor publications, only *Bugle*, the publication of the Rocky Mountain Elk Foundation, has committed to publishing a women's feature in each bimonthly issue since the mid-nineties.
28. An editor at one of the "Big Three" hunting magazines, in a private communication to Douglas Stange, early 1970s. It would not be until 1998 that a woman would again appear on the cover of a major hunting magazine, *Sports Afield*.
29. See Donna Haraway, *Primate Visions: Gender, Race and Nature in the*

World of Modern Science (New York: Routledge, 1989); and Susan Faludi, *Stiffed: The Betrayal of the American Man* (New York: Harper Perennial, 1999).

30. In 1993, the National Shooting Sport Foundation (NSSF) estimated that the number of women hunters had increased by a quarter, to approximately 2.5 million, between 1988 and 1993. While, owing to a variety of factors, it is difficult to determine the precise number of female hunters in any given year, sources as ideologically different as the U.S. Fish and Wildlife Service and the anti-hunting Fund for Animals have tended to agree that women constitute about ten percent of the hunting population—which essentially supports the NSSF estimate.

31. See Mary Zeiss Stange, *Woman the Hunter* (Boston: Beacon Press, 1997); and Mary Zeiss Stange and Carol Oyster, *Gun Women: Firearms and Feminism in Contemporary America* (New York: New York University Press, 2000), Chapter 4.

32. Mary Zeiss Stange, "Women Afield: The Invisible Hunters," *Sports Afield* (January 1994), 98–99; "Women in the Woods," *Sports Afield* (June 1995), 100–103; and "Look Who's Stalking," *Outdoor Life* (May 1998), 62–67.

33. Gretchen Cron, *The Roaring Veldt* (New York: G. P. Putnam's Sons, 1930), 15.

PART FOUR: TROPHIES
1. This was in the days before there was a motor-road.

PART FIVE: PREDATORS AND PREY
1. Marjorie Kinnan Rawlings, *The Yearling* (New York: Charles Scribner's Sons, 1938), 232.
2. Mary Stange, *Woman the Hunter* (Boston: Beacon Press, 1997), 139.

PART SIX: FOOD
1. Gary Snyder, "Survival and Sacrament," *The Practice of the Wild* (New York: North Point Press/Farrar, Strauss, Giroux, 1990), 184.

PART NINE: DEATH
1. Aldo Leopold, *A Sand County Almanac, With Other Essays on Conservation from Round River* (New York: Oxford University Press, 1966), 130.

PART TEN: BODY, SOUL, AND THE HUNT'S AFTERLIFE
1. Paul Shepard, "A Theory of the Value of Hunting," *Transactions of the Twenty-fourth North American Wildlife Conference* (Washington, D.C.: American Wildlife Institute, 1959), 510–511.

Selected Bibliography

PRIMARY SOURCES

Akeley, Delia. *Jungle Portraits*. New York: Macmillan, 1930.

Akeley, Mary Jobe. *Carl Akeley's Africa*. New York: Blue Ribbon Books, 1929.

———. *Congo Eden*. New York: Dodd, Mead and Company, 1950.

———. *Rumble of a Distant Drum: The True Story of the African Hinterland*. New York: Dodd, Mead and Company, 1946.

Baillie, Mrs. W. W. *Days and Nights of Shikar*. London: John Lane the Bodley Head, 1921.

Borden, Mrs. John (Courtney). *Adventures in a Man's World*. New York: Macmillan, 1933.

———. *The Cruise of the Northern Light*. New York: Macmillan, 1928.

Boyd, Joyce. *My Farm in Lion Country*. New York: Frederick A. Stokes Company, 1933.

Bradley, Mary Hastings. *Alice in Elephantland*, drawings by Alice Hastings Bradley. New York: D. Appleton, 1929.

———. *Alice in Jungleland*, drawings by Alice Hastings Bradley. New York and London: D. Appleton & Company, 1927.

———. *Caravans and Cannibals*. New York and London: D. Appleton and Company, 1926.

———. *On the Gorilla Trail*. New York and London: Appleton, 1922.

———. *Trailing the Tiger*. New York and London: D. Appleton and Company, 1929.

Brandreth, Paul. *Trails of Enchantment*. New York: Watt, 1930.

Chasseresse, Diane. *Sporting Sketches*. London: Macmillan, 1890.

Cron, Gretchen. *The Roaring Veldt*. New York: G. P. Putnam's Sons, 1930.

de Watteville, Vivienne. *Out in the Blue*. London: Methuen and Company, 1937.

Diamond, Rickey Gard. *Second Sight*. Corvallis, OR: Calyx Books, 1997.

Dinesen, Isak (Karen Blixen). *Out of Africa*. New York: Random House, 1938.

Douglas, Gertrude M. *Rifle Shooting for Ladies.* London: Arthur Pearson, 1910.

Eden, Frances (Fanny). *Tigers, Durbars and Kings: Fanny Eden's Indian Journals, 1837–1838,* Ed. Janet Dunbar. London: John Murray, 1988.

Fischer, Helen. *Peril Is My Companion.* London: Robert Hale, 1957.

Gardner, Mrs. Alan. *Rifle and Spear with the Rajpoots: Being the Narrative of a Winter's Travel and Sport in Northern India.* London: Chatto & Windus, 1895.

Greville, The Lady, Ed. *The Gentlewoman's Book of Sports.* London: Henry and Company, no date.

———. *Ladies in the Field: Sketches of Sport.* London: Ward & Downy Ltd., 1894.

Hamerstrom, Frances. *Is She Coming Too? Memoirs of a Lady Hunter.* Ames, IA: University of Iowa Press, 1989.

———. *My Double Life: Memoirs of a Naturalist.* Madison, WI: University of Wisconsin Press, 1994.

Handley, Mrs. M. A. *Roughing It in Southern India.* London: Edward Arnold, 1911.

Hasselstrom, Linda, Gaydell Collier, and Nancy Curtis, Eds. *Leaning into the Wind: Women Write from the Heart of the West.* Boston & New York: Houghton Mifflin, 1997.

Herbert, Agnes. *Casuals in the Caucasus: The Diary of a Sporting Holiday.* London: John Lane, 1912.

———. *Two Dianas in Somaliland.* London: John Lane, 1907.

Herbert, Agnes, and A Shikari. *Two Dianas in Alaska.* London and New York: John Lane, 1909.

Houston, Pam, Ed. *Women on Hunting.* Hopewell, NJ: The Ecco Press, 1995.

Jenkins, Lady. *Sport & Travel in Both Tibets.* London: Blades, East & Blades, 1910.

Johnson, Osa. *Four Years in Paradise: The Lives and Adventures of Martin and Osa Johnson.* Garden City, NY: Garden City Publishing Company, 1944.

———. *I Married Adventure.* Philadelphia: J. B. Lippincott Company, 1940.

Legler, Gretchen. *All the Powerful Invisible Things: A Sportswoman's Notebook.* Seattle: Seal Press, 1995.

MacDonald, Sheila. *Tanganyikan Safari.* Sydney: Angus and Robertson, 1948.

Mallett, Marguerite. *A White Woman Among the Masai.* New York: E. P. Dutton, 1923.

Markham, Beryl. *West With the Night.* San Francisco: North Point Press, 1983.

Martineau, Alice. *Reminiscences of Hunting and Horses.* London: Ernest Benn Ltd., 1930.

Menzies, Mrs. Stuart. *Women in the Hunting Field*. London: Vinton & Company, Ltd., 1913.

Murray, Hilda of Elibank. *Echoes of Sport*. London & Edinburgh: T. N. Foulis, 1910.

Ness, Mrs. Patrick. *Ten Thousand Miles in Two Continents*. London: Methuen, 1929.

Rawlings, Marjorie Kinnan. *Cross Creek*. New York: Charles Scribner's Sons, 1942.

Savory, Isabel. *A Sportswoman in India*. London: Hutchinson & Co., 1900.

Seton, Grace Gallatin. *Nimrod's Wife*. New York: Doubleday, Page and Company, 1907.

———. *"Yes, Lady Saheb": A Woman's Adventurings with Mysterious India*. New York: Harper and Brothers, 1925.

Seton-Thompson, Grace Gallatin. *A Woman Tenderfoot*. New York: Doubleday, Page and Company, 1900.

Sheddon, Lady Diana and Lady Apsly. *To Whom the Goddess: Hunting and Riding for Women*. London: Hutchinson & Company, circa 1932.

Slaughter, Frances, Ed. *Sportswoman's Library*. London: Archibald Constable, 1898.

Smythies, Olive. *Tiger Lady: Adventures in the Indian Jungle*. London: William Heinemann, 1953.

St. Maur, Mrs. Algernon. *Impressions of a Tenderfoot, During a Journey in Search of Sport in the Far West*. London: John Murray, 1890.

Stewart, Elinore Pruitt. *Letters on an Elk Hunt by a Woman Homesteader*. Lincoln: University of Nebraska Press, 1979 (reprint; originally published 1915).

Strickland, Mrs. Diana. *Through the Belgian Congo*. London: Hurst & Blackett, 1924.

Sucksdorff, Astrid. *Tiger in Sight*. New York: Delacorte Press, 1970.

Tyacke, Mrs. R. H. *How I Shot My Bears; or, Two Years' Tent Life in Kullu and Lahoul*. London: Sampson Low, Marston & Company, 1893.

Vassal, Gabrielle M. *Life in French Congo*. London: T. Fisher Unwin, Ltd., 1925.

———. *On & Off Duty in Annam*. London: William Heinemann, 1910.

SECONDARY SOURCES

Buxton, Meriel. *Ladies of the Chase*. North Pomfret, U.K.: Trafalgar Square, 1989.

Czech, Kenneth P. *With Rifle and Petticoat: Women as Big Game Hunters, 1880–1940*. Lanham, MD: The Derrydale Press, 2003.

Dizard, Jan E. *Mortal Stakes: Hunters and Hunting in Contemporary America*. Amherst & Boston: University of Massachusetts Press, 2003.

Herman, Daniel Justin. *Hunting and the American Imagination*. Washington D.C.: Smithsonian Institution Press, 2001.

Imperato, Pascal J., and Eleanor M. *They Married Adventure: The Wandering Lives of Martin and Osa Johnson.* New Brunswick, NJ: Rutgers University Press, 1992.

Lovell, Mary S. *Straight On Till Morning: The Biography of Beryl Markham.* New York: St. Martins, 1987.

MacKenzie, John M. *The Empire of Nature: Hunting, Conservation and British Imperialism.* Manchester: Manchester University Press, 1988.

Olds, Elizabeth Fagg. *Women of the Four Winds.* Boston: Houghton Mifflin, 1985.

Pakenham, Valerie. *Out in the Noonday Sun: Edwardians in the Tropics.* New York: Random House, 1985.

Petersen, David. *Heartsblood: Hunting, Spirituality, and Wildness in America.* Washington, D.C.: Island Press, 2000.

Reiger, John F. *American Sportsmen and the Origins of Conservation.* Corvallis, OR: Oregon State University Press, 2000.

Riley, Glenda. *The Life and Legacy of Annie Oakley.* Norman: University of Oklahoma Press, 2000.

Stange, Mary Zeiss. *Woman the Hunter.* Boston: Beacon Press, 1997.

Stange, Mary Zeiss, and Carol K. Oyster. *Gun Women: Firearms and Feminism in Contemporary America.* New York: New York University Press, 2000.

Swan, James A. *The Sacred Art of Hunting: Myths, Legends, and the Modern Mythos.* Minoqua, WI: Willow Creek Press, 1999.

Wilson, R.L. *Women at Arms: Women and the World of Firearms.* New York: Random House, 2003.

Contributors

Mary Jobe Akeley (1886–1966) was an explorer, author, and educator. A graduate of Bryn Mawr College, she traveled to the Canadian Northwest, where she studied the native tribes of British Columbia (1913); discovered, mapped, and named Big Ice Mountain (1914); and mapped the headwaters of the Fraser River (1915). In recognition of her work as a geographer and mountaineer, the Canadian government in 1925 named a peak in the Canadian Rockies Mount Jobe. She met the noted conservationist and taxidermist Carl Akeley in 1918, and the two married in 1924, after his divorce from Delia Akeley. Carl persuaded Mary to give up her independent career (she had founded and directed an outdoor camp for affluent "city girls" in Mystic, Connecticut), to accompany him to Africa in January 1926 to collect specimens for the dioramas in New York's Museum of Natural History's African Hall. The Akeleys hunted and collected trophies in the Congo, Kenya, and Tanzania. In November 1926, Carl Akeley died after a persistent illness. Mary completed the work of the expedition, a story which she recounts in *Carl Akeley's Africa* (1929). She subsequently wrote, lectured, and raised funds for the Museum's African Hall, which in 1936 was renamed Akeley Hall in Carl's honor. The author of numerous works, including *Restless Jungle* (1936) and *Rumble of a Distant Drum: A True Story of the Africa Hunterland* (1946), Mary Jobe Akeley was awarded the Cross of the Knight, Order of the Crown by King Albert of Belgium, and was inducted into the Connecticut Women's Hall of Fame. The land that formerly housed her Camp Mystic remains open to the public as a Peace Sanctuary.

Kim Barnes (1958–) grew up in Idaho in the 1970s. Rebelling against her Pentecostal Christian upbringing, Barnes left home shortly after graduating from high school and went to college. She married and eventually resettled in rural Idaho, where she writes and teaches. A contributor to numerous periodicals and anthologies, Barnes's books include her autobiographical works *In the Wilderness: Coming of Age in an Unknown Country* (1996) and *Hungry for the World: A Memoir* (2001), and *Circle of Women: An*

Anthology of Contemporary Western Women Writers (1994), edited with Mary Clearman Blew. Her work has garnered many awards, including a PEN Jerard Fund Award for *In the Wilderness*, which was also a Pulitzer Prize finalist.

Nellie Bennett (dates unknown) was employed by *Outdoor Life* magazine in 1904 to be its "lady representative," writing articles geared toward women readers and generating female subscribers. It is unclear how long she held this position.

Durga Bernhard (1961–) is an illustrator, artist, musician, hunter, and the mother of three children: Jonah (14), Eve (11), and Sage Ursa (1). She is the illustrator and/or author of numerous children's books, including *A Ride on Mother's Back* (written by Emery Bernhard, 1996) and *To & Fro, Fast & Slow* (2001). To view more of her artwork, please visit www.durgabern-hard.com. Durga Bernhard lives in the Catskill Mountains of New York with her children and her partner, Eric Wood.

Courtney Louise (Letts) Borden (dates unknown) was the wife of natural-ist/explorer John Borden, heir to the Borden Condensed Milk fortune. Having taken up hunting shortly after their marriage, in 1927 she accom-panied Captain Borden on his voyage to explore the Alaskan coast and collect specimens of walrus and polar bear for Chicago's Field Museum. Along with her friend Frances Ames and a band of Sea Scouts, Captain and Mrs. Borden sailed his specially built two-masted schooner "The Northern Light" along the northwestern coast of North America, with a side trip to Siberia; the party bagged a total of seven walrus and seven polar bears. Upon their return, Courtney (writing under the name Mrs. John Borden) transformed the journal she had kept during the expedition into *The Cruise of the Northern Light*, published in 1928. When the Great Depression hit, the Bordens retired to a country home in Mississippi, when Courtney wrote her second hunting book, *Adventures in a Man's World* (1933). The Bordens were divorced in 1933, and shortly thereafter Courtney married the Argentine ambassador to the United States, Felipe Espil. She later recounted her adventures as a diplomat's consort, between 1933 and 1943, in *The Wife of the Ambassador*.

Jennifer Bové (1973–) obtained her B.S. in biological science from the University of Missouri in 1996 and has traveled cross-country to pursue work in fisheries and wildlife biology. A native of the Midwest, she now feels most at home in elk country west of the Continental Divide. Cur-rently, she devotes her time to raising two daughters with her husband, Chris, and she writes when she gets the chance. She has been published in *Women in Natural Resources*, the *Missouri Conservationist*, and *Wild Outdoor*

World. "A Place Among Elk" was first published in *Bugle: Journal of Elk Country and the Hunt* in July 2002.

Mary Hastings Bradley (c. 1880–1977), educated at Smith College, lived in her birthplace, Chicago, her entire life. She was, in a career spanning five decades, a prolific travel writer, novelist, and lecturer. Her novels include *The Palace of Darkened Windows* (1915), *The Road of Desperation* (1932), and *Murder in the Family* (1952). Bradley twice won the O. Henry Award, in 1931 and 1938. When she was not working at home in Chicago, she was hunting and exploring Africa (sometimes with Carl Akeley as her guide) and Asia. Her works recounting these explorations include *On the Gorilla Trail* (1922) and *Trailing the Tiger* (1929). Her daughter Alice, who at the age of five accompanied Bradley on her first African safari, went on to write highly regarded science fiction under the pseudonym James Tiptree, Jr.

Paul [Paulina] Brandreth (1885–1946). As a poet, naturalist, and conservationist, Brandreth was a woman way ahead of her time. By the age of nine, she had already published articles in Charles Hallock's *Forest and Stream*. She is best known for her deer-hunting book *Trails of Enchantment* (1930). Editor Hallock listed her material as coming from Camp Good Enough, Brandreth Lake, and considered her to be "one of the most skillful of the *Forest and Stream* family of hunter/naturalists." She spent her entire life pursuing the enchanting trails of the Adirondacks in the company of famed Adirondack guide Reuben Cary. Her writings exhibit a visionary quality that one seldom sees in the field of outdoor literature and natural history. Roy Chapman Andrews ranked *Trails of Enchantment* as a standard contribution to the natural history of the white-tailed deer.

Deb Carpenter (1959–) is a teacher by trade and finds it a natural progression to use the art forms of poetry, song, and story to instruct as well as to entertain. In partnership with the poet Lyn Messersmith, Carpenter performs an educational program about women who traveled and settled the Great Plains. Messersmith and Carpenter have recently developed a second program, about leaders and legends who helped shape the American West. Carpenter lives in northwestern Nebraska with her husband, Don, and their daughters, Jamie and Jessica.

Jill Carroll (1963–) is a Lecturer in Humanities and Religious Studies at Rice University in Houston, Texas. She is the author of *The Savage Side: Reclaiming Violent Models of God* (2002) and *How to Survive as an Adjunct Lecturer: An Entrepreneurial Strategy Manual* (2001). She writes a monthly column called "The Adjunct Track" for *The Chronicle of Higher Education*. Most importantly, however, she hunts ducks and geese on the coastal prairie outside Houston as well as dove and quail on her two-hundred-acre ranchette in west Texas. "My Mother's Shotgun" is her first hunting story.

Eileen Clarke was born in 1947 to, she says, the wrong family. They wanted to live in New York City; she wanted grass between her toes and to be on the right end of the crosshairs. At eighteen she made her escape from her home city and never looked back. Her family still clings to civilization. Today, Clarke lives in Montana. She is the author of seven wild game cookbooks and the novel *Queen of the Legal Tender Saloon* (1997), and her hunting and fishing stories have appeared in many outdoor magazines, including *Gray's Sporting Journal, Field & Stream, Wyoming Wildlife,* and *Rifle's Hunting Annual.* When she is not writing, she and her husband John Barsness are out hunting, fishing, and keeping their bird dog, Gideon, tired and happy. Clarke lives and writes thirty miles from the headwaters of the Missouri River.

Judy Clayton Cornell (1955–) lives with her husband and son in Montana's Flathead Valley and spends several months each year along the Rocky Mountain front. She began hunting at the age of thirty-five and subsequently began writing about it. She has written for *Big Sky Journal* and *Sporting Classics* and is currently working on a book. She has been a correspondent for *Big Sky Journal* since 1994 and has written for other publications, including *The Los Angeles Times, The Great Falls Tribune,* and *Sporting Classics.*

Gretchen Cron (dates unknown), the daughter of a New York shipping executive, was schooled in Switzerland and traveled widely, serving as the secretary for her father's company during World War I. Her marriage to Herman Cron, a German landowner of hunting estates along the Rhine and in the Black Forest, introduced her to the world of hunting. During the 1920s, she and her husband undertook four African safaris, on which Gretchen hunted with a camera as well as with a double-barreled rifle. Her sole literary work, *The Roaring Veldt* (1930), recounts her hunting adventures.

Sandra Dal Poggetto was born in Sonoma, California, in 1951. She is a painter and since 1989 has lived in Helena, Montana.

Vivienne de Watteville (c. 1900–1957) was the daughter of Swiss naturalist Bernard de Watteville. She accompanied her father on his second African excursion, the purpose of which was to collect elephants for the Berne Natural History Museum. Vivienne was never entirely comfortable with the killing involved in their work. She let her father do all the shooting (sometimes hoping his aim would be off), and she preferred to concentrate on skinning and preserving the hides of the animals he took. Her role changed, however, when Bernard de Watteville was mauled to death by a lion he had been stalking. Forced to supply her native porters with meat, and compelled to complete the project her father had started, Vivienne shouldered his .416 Rigby and went to work. She recounted the story of that safari in *Out in the Blue* (1927). Subsequently she returned to Africa, "hunting with a camera" now, and produced her second book, *Speak to the Earth: Wanderings and Reflections among Elephants and Mountains* (1935). When her publisher scheduled a second edition of *Out in the Blue* in 1937, de Watteville considered expunging the hunting scenes. Fortunately for the book and its readers, her editor persuaded her that this would be a disservice to her father's memory.

Rickey Gard Diamond is best known, both as a journalist and fiction writer, for her work concerning women and issues of poverty. She has her MFA in Writing from Vermont College, where she is now a professor of liberal studies, teaching American literature, women's history, and writing. Her fiction has appeared in *The Sewanee Review, The Louisville Review, Other Voices, Kalliope, Plainswoman,* and other journals. Founding editor of *Vermont Woman* in 1985, she has widely published articles and book reviews and is among recognized writers in *Vermont Odysseys: Essays on the New Vermont.* Her work as a persuasive social critic has won her the YWCA's Susan B. Anthony award, the Business and Professional Women's Woman of the Year award, and a grant from the American Association of University Women. *Second Sight,* from which the passages in this volume are excerpted, is her first novel.

Susan Ewing (1954–) lives in Montana. She is the author of several regional nature guides, most recently *The Great Rocky Mountain Nature Factbook* (1999). She is also the author of *Lucky Hares and Itchy Bears,* an illustrated children's book of animal poems, and co-editor of *Shadow Cat: Encountering the American Mountain Lion* (1999). Ewing's nonfiction essays have appeared in *Gray's Sporting Journal, Sports Afield, Bugle, Big Sky Journal, Fly Rod & Reel,* and other publications, as well as in numerous anthologies. She is currently working on a series of short stories, and has recently discovered the pleasures of shooting a compound bow.

Helen Fischer (dates unknown), originally from Switzerland, relocated to the United States in the early part of the twentieth century, where she took up hunting. A noted photographer in her time, she hunted with both rifle and camera and is best known for her photo safaris in Kenya, Tanganyika, and the Congo.

Erica Fresquez, a flight attendant and avid hunter, lives in Colorado.

Frances Hamerstrom (1907–1998), well known for her work on wildlife conservation, throughout her life used her writing to urge better relationships between humans and the nonhuman world. One of very few women in the first generation of American wildlife biologists, Hamerstrom left Smith College to study with her husband Frederick at the University of Iowa. They subsequently worked under the tutelage of Aldo Leopold, the originator of the science of wildlife management and the ecological concept of a "land ethic." Frances Hamerstrom specialized in the study of the prairie chicken, as well as birds of prey. Hamerstrom wrote two memoirs of her life as a hunter-naturalist: *Is She Coming Too? Memoirs of a Lady Hunter* (1989) and *My Double Life: Memoirs of a Naturalist* (1994). Hamerstrom also wrote nature-oriented children's books. She continued hunting, and writing about it, into her eighties.

Linda Hasselstrom (1943–) is a writer, rancher, and educator. Her prose and poetry are dedicated to celebrating the life of the Great Plains—which constitute for her a "personal, emotional, and political landscape as well as the physical one." Hasselstrom is author of numerous books, including *Next Year Country: One Woman's View* (1978), *Windbreak: A Woman Rancher on the Northern Plains* (1987), *Going Over East: Reflections of a Woman Rancher* (1993), *Feels Like Far: A Rancher's Life on the Great Plains* (1999), and *Between Grass and Sky: Where I Live and Work* (2002). Her poetry collections include *Roadkill* (1991) and *Dakota Bones* (1996). Hasselstrom has also edited or co-edited a number of collections, including *Leaning into the Wind: Women Write from the Heart of the West* (1997) and *Woven on the Wind: Women Write about Friendship in the Sagebrush West* (2001). Her many awards include fellowships from the National Endowment for the Arts and the South Dakota Arts Council, the 1979 South Dakota Press Woman of Achievement Award, and in 1989 the South Dakota Hall of Fame's Author of the Year Award. Hasselstrom was the first female recipient of the Center for Western Studies' Western American Writer Award, and her essay "Buffalo Winter" was included in *Best American Essays 1995*. Devoted to nurturing women authors, Hasselstrom directs writers' retreats at Windbreak House, her South Dakota homestead.

Geneen Marie Haugen (1952–) lives amidst elk, bison, moose, and other inscrutable wild souls in northwestern Wyoming. Her narrative essays have appeared in *American Nature Writing 2000; Another Wilderness: New Outdoor Writing by Women; Solo: On Her Own Adventure; High Country News; Northern Lights;* and in other anthologies and journals.

Agnes Herbert (1880–1960) was born Agnes Elsie Diana Thorpe, in England. As a young women she married and took her husband's surname, under which she did all of her writing. While the date and circumstances of this first marriage are unclear, it appears she only began writing after her husband's death. Widowhood apparently gave her the freedom and means to travel as extensively as she did. In the first decade of the twentieth century, Agnes and her cousin Cecily undertook hunting excursions on three continents. These adventures yielded three books: *Two Dianas in Somaliland* (1907), *Two Dianas in Alaska* (1909), and *Casuals in the Caucasus* (1912). Upon her second marriage in 1913 to Commander Archibald Thomas Stewart, Herbert discontinued hunting but continued to travel extensively, writing books and working as a journalist.

Osa Johnson (1894–1953) was, with her husband Martin, a pioneer in the field of wildlife filmmaking. From the time they married in 1910 until Martin's death in a plane crash in 1937, the Johnsons made numerous trips to the South Seas (on one of which they were kidnapped by cannibals and only narrowly escaped becoming themselves the main course), and a total of twelve expeditions to Africa. They discovered Lake Paradise in Uganda, where they established a camp that became their home away from home. The couple's modus operandi was for Martin to do the camera work, while Osa wielded her gun, both to provide thrilling action shots—including one in which she downed a charging rhino—and to feed the camp. The Johnsons financed their film projects by lecturing stateside in between safaris. Together they produced more than fifty films, ranging from single-reel silent films to feature-length sound films. Osa recorded their life and work in *I Married Adventure* (1940) and *Four Years in Paradise* (1944). After Martin's death, Osa continued to lecture and to write on behalf of wildlife conservation; altogether she authored three adult and ten children's books, and over forty magazine articles. She also lent her name to a line of women's and children's sportswear, featuring African motifs and made from a fabric trademarked "Osafari" cloth. The Martins's adventures are today memorialized, and their mission of conservation education carried out, in the Martin and Osa Johnson Safari Museum in Osa's hometown of Chanute, Kansas.

Jean Keezer-Clayton (1949–) is a Nebraska native whose roots go deep in the land. She earned a master's degree in English from the University of Nebraska at Kearney and is currently serving as chaplain at a nursing home. She is an avid reader and landscape gardener.

Page Dunton Lambert (1952–) is author of the best-selling Rocky Mountain memoir *In Search of Kinship* and the novel *Shifting Stars* (a Mountains and Plains Book Award finalist). Lambert has presented over 100 writing events from Arkansas to British Columbia. One of fifteen writers selected from around the nation to contribute to *Writing Down the River: Into the Heart of Grand Canyon,* she now facilitates river writing journeys (to find out more about upcoming events, e-mail *plambert@rangeweb.net*). Currently at work on three new books, she was recently awarded a residency by the Jentel Artist Residency Program, where she will be completing *The Water Carrier,* a contemporary novel set in Denver. Widely anthologized, her work appears in numerous publications, including *Ranching West of the 100th Meridian,* the *Chicken Soup for the Soul* books, and forthcoming *Deep West: A Literary Tour of Wyoming.* Still in love with her native Colorado, Lambert has lived for the last seventeen years on a small ranch in the Black Hills of Wyoming, where she shares the land with mule deer, white-tails, and wild turkeys.

Gretchen Legler (1960–) was born in Salt Lake City. Her interests include earth spirituality, hunting, fishing, feminist and gay/lesbian issues, women's art, and gardening. She worked as a journalist in North Dakota and Minnesota before joining, in 1987, the faculty of the University of Alaska at Anchorage where she has taught creative writing, literary arts, and women's studies. Her autobiographical *All the Powerful Invisible Things* (1995) contains two Pushcart Prize–winning essays: "Border Water" and "Gooseberry Marsh." Legler won a National Science Foundation Artists and Writers Program Fellowship to Antarctica in 1997.

Sheila Link was the first contributing editor of *Women & Guns* magazine, for which she regularly writes feature articles as well as the "Gear and Gadgets" column. The first woman president of the Outdoor Writers Association of America, she is an avid hunter, active competition shooter, and certified firearms safety instructor. She is the author of the *Women's Guide to Outdoor Sports* (Tulsa, OK: Winchester Press, 1982).

Beryl Markham (1902–1986) was born Beryl Clutterbuck in Leicestershire, England. At the age of four she accompanied her father to British East Africa, where she received little formal education but became well-trained in hunting and fluent in several African dialects. When her father lost his fortune and emigrated to Peru, a teenaged Beryl determined to stay in Kenya. At eighteen she became the first woman in Africa to be licensed as a horse-trainer. In her late twenties, she learned to fly and made her living as a freelance pilot and sometime hunting guide. In 1936, she made history as the first solo pilot to fly east to west across the Atlantic, reversing Lindbergh's route. In addition to this accomplishment, Markham is known for her 1942 book, *West with the Night.* While the book garnered scant attention when it was originally published, in the late twentieth century (partly as a result of the popularity of the film *Out of Africa*), *West with the Night*— depicting life in colonial Africa and chronicling the complex interrelationships among Isak Dinesen, her husband Bror Blixen, and Markham herself—enjoyed considerable and favorable critical notice.

Barney (Barbara) Nelson (1947–) was born in Bellevue, Iowa, the daughter and granddaughter of commercial hunter/fishermen. She began hunting at age six. An associate professor of English at Sul Ross State University in Alpine, Texas, she specializes in teaching courses connected to rural culture, including one on "Predators in Literature." She has published several books, including most recently *God's Country or Devil's Playground: The Best Nature Writing from the Big Bend of Texas* (2002) and *The Wild and the Domestic: Animal Representation, Ecocriticism, and Western American Literature* (2000), and numerous scholarly essays focusing on western life and culture. Nelson also writes popular essays and cowboy poetry. Her photographs are in the permanent collections at The Gene Autry Museum in California, the Buckaroo Hall of Fame and Museum in Nevada, the American Quarter Horse Association Museum in Texas, and the Texas and Southwestern Cattle Raisers Museum. Nelson has been inducted into both the Range Animal Science and Rodeo Ex-Student Hall of Fame at Sul Ross State, and the Big Bend Hall of Fame in West Texas.

Annie Oakley [Phoebe Ann Mosey] (1860–1926) was, arguably, America's first female "superstar." A natural shot, she began hunting at roughly the age of seven, to help support her mother and sisters after her father's death; by the time she was in her teens, she was not only supporting the family through market hunting game for sale to local restaurants, she was able to pay off the mortgage on the family farm in Darke County, Ohio. Sometime between 1875 and 1881, she bested traveling sharpshooter Frank Butler in a shooting challenge. Shortly thereafter, they married and began touring the circus and vaudeville circuit as "Butler and Oakley" (the derivation of her stage name remains uncertain). In 1885, the couple signed with Buffalo Bill's Wild West show, and Annie became an instant headliner as the "Maid of the Western Plains," even though she had never been farther west than her Ohio birthplace. From this point forward, Frank was her business manager. While touring with Buffalo Bill's show, Annie befriended the Lakota chief and holy man Sitting Bull, who nicknamed her *Watanya Cicilia*, "Little Sure Shot." An extraordinary sharpshooter, Annie toured North America and Europe, earning over $100,000 in prizes during her lifetime—an unprecedented sum for a female entertainer. Although she did not call herself a feminist or a suffragist, Oakley was an early champion of women's right to work (for pay equal to men's) and to defend themselves with firearms. She also advocated Native American rights. Oakley volunteered during the Spanish-American War, and later during World War I, to train female sharpshooters for action on the front lines; Presidents McKinley and Wilson declined her offers. She and Butler performed for the troops during the First World War, and while she later said that service had made her "the happiest woman in the world," she would have preferred serving in combat herself. In historical fact far more complex and intriguing than the caricatures of her that subsequently appeared on Broadway and in films, Annie Oakley was a woman literally generations ahead of her time.

Nellie O'Brien (1913–) was born in a log cabin in Wyoming, the middle child of nine born to her homesteading parents. She graduated from the University of Wyoming at the age of eighteen, taught school in Wyoming, and subsequently moved with her husband to Missouri, where for twenty-five years she worked for state government. Forced to retire when her husband was stricken with Alzheimer's disease, she used the next twenty years of being homebound to cultivate a writing career and published, in addition to poems, short stories, and newspaper articles, two books: *We Made the West Wild* (Salt Lake City: Northwest Publishing, 1994) and *On the Bosom of the Green* (Philadelphia: Xlibris, 2002). She is a member of the National League of American Pen Women, Wyoming Writers and Poets, and Missouri State Poets.

Marjorie Kinnan Rawlings (1896–1953), a native of Washington, D.C., lived most of her adult life in Cross Creek in the Florida Everglades, where she settled in 1928. She rose to regional prominence as a nature writer during the 1930s and, although she published essays and stories in such national magazines as *Scribner's* and *Cosmopolitan*, was regarded by critics primarily as a "local colorist," who wrote about the lives of Florida "Crackers" (a term evidently derived from the "crack" of the cattle-herder's whip). That changed in 1938, with the publication of her novel, *The Yearling*, which shot to the top of the best-seller lists, garnered a Pulitzer Prize for fiction, and catapulted Rawlings to national notoriety. Pressed by her editor to write more about her own life in rural Florida, she produced her memoir *Cross Creek*, which was published in 1942. She subsequently published *Cross Creek Cookery*, a collection of her favorite recipes, some of which originally appeared in the chapter from *Cross Creek* excerpted in this volume. The 1946 film version of *The Yearling* was nominated for Academy Awards in all major categories. In 1983, *Cross Creek* was made into a feature film, starring Mary Steenburgen as Rawlings.

Diana Rupp (1969–) grew up hunting and fishing in the forest of northern Pennsylvania and began writing about her adventures while still in college. After receiving a journalism degree from Susquehanna University, she became associate editor of *Sports Afield* magazine and later served that publication as a field editor. In 1999, she took over as editorial director of *Pennsylvania Sportsman, New York Sportsman,* and *Michigan Hunting and Fishing*. In 2002, Rupp was named editor of *Gun Dog* and *Wildfowl* magazines. She is the author of *Pennsylvania: A Guide to Backcountry Travel and Adventure*. She currently lives in Los Angeles with her husband, Scott.

Isabel Savory (1869–?) was born in Weybridge, Surrey, England. From childhood, she relished outdoor sports, particularly golf and fox-hunting. As an adult, she yearned for more far-flung adventure and organized an expedition to India for the purpose of exploration and, more particularly, hunting. While she was unsuccessful in her quest after bears and tahr (wild goats), she proved an adept tiger-hunter. In 1900 she published *A Sportswoman in India,* which blends travelogue with hunting narrative. She went on to write two further books, about her travels in northern Africa (*In the Tail of the Peacock,* 1903) and the French Pyrenees (*The Romantic Rousillon,* 1919); however, she is chiefly remembered for her book about India, and more especially for the tiger-hunting narrative excerpted here.

Grace Gallatin Seton-Thompson (1872–1959) was born in Sacramento, California; at sixteen, she began a journalistic career, writing for the *San Francisco Call & Examiner* and for several magazines, under the pseudonym Dorothy Dodge. She largely suspended her own writing career when she married Ernest Thompson Seton, who employed his wife as his literary assistant and editor. Introduced by Ernest to hunting, however, she managed to craft two books of her own during the early years of their marriage: *A Woman Tenderfoot* (1900) and *Nimrod's Wife* (1907). Seton-Thompson was especially interested in drawing other women into hunting and provided detailed descriptions of how to outfit oneself for the field, how to pack for hunting camp, and what kinds of guns and calibers were best suited to women's needs. With Ernest, she co-founded the Girl Pioneers, which later became Camp Fire Girls. During World War I, she raised money for the French and British war efforts, and then sold U.S. Liberty Bonds. From roughly that time forward she was a globetrotting free spirit (she eventually divorced Ernest in 1933, though their marriage was effectively over in 1918). During the 1920s she participated in Field Museum archeological and specimen-collecting trips to various parts of South America. Seton-Thompson was also fiercely devoted to women's suffrage and to social reform on the national and international levels. She traveled widely and wrote about women's and human rights issues on four continents. Her works arguing for social reform include *Woman Tenderfoot in Egypt* (1923) and *Chinese Lanterns* (1924). Whether traveling for scientific research or social activism, she apparently always brought along her guns and factored hunting into her itinerary. From 1933 through 1939 she served as chair of letters of the National Council of Women in the United States.

Florence Krall Shepard (1926–) was born and now lives most of her days on the sagebrush/bunch grass steppe of western Wyoming. She is an essayist, author of *Ecotone: Wayfaring on the Margins* (1994), and editor of three posthumous books by her late husband, Paul Shepard: *Coming Home* *to the Pleistocene* (1998), *Encounters with Nature* (1999), and *Where We Belong* (2003). She is Professor Emerita at the University of Utah, where she taught educational and environmental studies. She serves as a board member of The Murie Center in Teton National Park in Moose, Wyoming, and the Norwegian Outdoor Exploration Center in Park City, Utah.

Mary Zeiss Stange (1950–) is the author of *Woman the Hunter* (1997) and coauthor, with Carol Oyster, of *Gun Women: Firearms and Feminism in Contemporary America* (2000). She has written widely about women's and environmental issues, guns and hunting, for publications such as *USA Today, Bugle, Outdoor Life, Sports Afield, Big Sky Journal, High Country News, American Hunter, Women in the Outdoors,* and *American Rifleman*. She is an associate professor of women's studies and religion at Skidmore College in Saratoga Springs, New York, where for eight years she directed the women's studies program. Stange divides her time between upstate New York and southeastern Montana, where she and her husband Doug operate the Crazy Woman Bison Ranch.

Elinore Pruitt Stewart (1878–1933) is the author, most prominently, of *Letters of a Woman Homesteader* (1914), which inspired the 1981 feature film *Heartland*. Born in Arkansas and raised in the Indian Territory (Oklahoma), she ventured in 1909 to Wyoming with her young daughter, after the death of her first husband, to work as a housekeeper for the man she eventually married. A copious note-taker and native literary talent, Stewart commenced an epistolary writing career documenting homesteading life on the Wyoming prairie. Her letters were first published by *Atlantic Monthly* and subsequently in book form. In 1915, she published *Letters on an Elk Hunt,* from which the selection in this volume is taken.

Marilyn Stone (1954–) has been hunting for over twenty years with a recurve bow, rifle, shotgun, and muzzleloader. Now in her second career, she is an outdoor writer, specializing in women's issues, the social issues of hunting, and business. Her work has been published in *American Hunter, North American Hunter, Women in the Outdoors,* the NRA's *Woman's Outlook, SHOT Business,* and *Sporting Goods Business,* among other publications. Stone's initial career was as a vocational counselor for people with disabilities. This background and a degree in psychology give her a unique perspective on the subjects she addresses.

Astrid Bergman Sucksdorff (1927–), a filmmaker and expert markswoman, went to India in the 1960s to make a movie, but found herself unexpectedly called into service to help eliminate jungle tigers that were ravaging the farms and villages in the area where she was working. The result was her 1965 book, *Tiger in Sight* (translated from the Swedish in 1970 by Joan Bulman), in which Sucksdorff writes with depth and compassion about the dilemma of feeling compelled to kill the "most beautiful of all living creatures." Sucksdorff writes with equal compassion about the lives of rural villagers.

Gretchen Dawn Yost (1977–) is a 1998 graduate in philosophy from the University of Oregon. For three years she lived in a remote cabin near Bondurant, Wyoming. Currently she resides in Pinedale, Wyoming, where she works and hunts in the surrounding Bridger-Teton National Forest.

Alberta Claire, **Dorothy Doolittle**, and "**Marjorie**" are, alas, lost to history.

Credits